The HEART of the HEARTLAND

950

The HEART of the HEARTLAND

Norwegian American Community in the Twin Cities

DAVID C. MAUK

MINNESOTA HISTORICAL SOCIETY PRESS
NORWEGIAN-AMERICAN HISTORICAL ASSOCIATION

FRONTISPIECE: In St. Paul, Norwegian community activity developed around stores such as Larsen's grocery on Jackson Street in the Mount Airy section of town. ***Courtesy of Luci J. Baker Johnson***

The publication of this book is supported by an anonymous endowment for Norwegian American history in Minnesota.

mnhspress.org

The Minnesota Historical Society Press is a member of the Association of University Presses.

Published in cooperation with the Norwegian-American Historical Association, naha.stolaf.edu.

Manufactured in the United States of America.

10 9 8 7 6 5 4 3 2 1

♾ The paper used in this publication meets the minimum requirements of the American National Standard for Information Sciences—Permanence for Printed Library Materials, ANSI Z39.48-1984.

International Standard Book Number
ISBN: 978-1-68134-236-8 (paper)
ISBN: 978-1-68134-237-5 (e-book)

Library of Congress Cataloging-in-Publication Data
Names: Mauk, David, 1945– author. | Norwegian-American Historical Association.
Title: The heart of the heartland : Norwegian American community in the Twin Cities / David C. Mauk.
Other titles: Norwegian American community in the Twin Cities
Identifiers: LCCN 2022011551 | ISBN 9781681342368 (paper) | ISBN 9781681342375 (e-book)
Subjects: LCSH: Norwegian Americans—Minnesota—Minneapolis Metropolitan Area—History. | Norwegian Americans—Minnesota—Saint Paul Metropolitan Area—History. | Immigrants—Minnesota—Minneapolis Metropolitan Area—History. | Immigrants—Minnesota—Saint Paul Metropolitan Area—History. | Minneapolis Metropolitan Area (Minn.)—Ethnic relations—History. | Saint Paul Metropolitan Area (Minn.)—Ethnic relations—History.
Classification: LCC F614.M6 M25 2022 | DDC 977.6/5790043982—dc23/eng/20220323
LC record available at https://lccn.loc.gov/2022011551

This and other Minnesota Historical Society Press books are available from popular e-book vendors.

CONTENTS

ACKNOWLEDGMENTS

This book is titled *The Heart of the Heartland* because on-site research demonstrated that the critical factor in the history of Norwegian community in the metropolitan area has been the magnetic attraction of St. Paul and Minneapolis for people in Norwegian settlements across Minnesota and the Upper Midwest. Relations between city and country have remained vital for over 170 years, waxing and waning with shifting economic, familial, and political conditions, but becoming ever more important with the urban ethnic community's rise as the throbbing life center for the group across the region, state, nation, and finally, in two great centennial celebrations, between the United States and Norway.

The leaders and staffs of the Norwegian-American Historical Association (NAHA) and the Minnesota Historical Society (MNHS), the joint sponsors of this study, have been essential supports for bringing the project to fruition. NAHA's editor in 1995, Odd S. Lovoll, asked me to take on the work of researching and writing a history of Norwegian Americans in Minneapolis–St. Paul. Over the next years, he negotiated with NAHA's board and the MNHS to set the terms of my residence and primary research with two full-time research assistants in the Twin Cities. Drawing on his experience as the author of *A Century of Urban Life,* about Norwegians in Chicago, Lovoll offered wise advice over the course of the project. Debbie Miller, then the MNHS librarian in charge of its resident research group, was a source of ideas, encouragement, and knowledge on a daily basis during the research team's year at the Minnesota History Center in St. Paul. We discussed our research strategies and findings with the MNHS research group on a regular basis and received invaluable suggestions from its members.

During his time as NAHA's editor, Todd Nichol advised the work's progress. NAHA's current editor, Anna Peterson, and its publications committee chair, Daron Olson, reviewed the study and made suggestions for further alterations. As managing editor at MNHS Press, Shannon Pennefeather guided the processes of transforming the text into a published volume, examining it closely and motivating me with her insight and cheerful enthusiasm.

Robert Mikkelsen and Mette Løvås, then doctoral students in Norway, worked full-time with me in Minneapolis–St. Paul for a year as the research team for the Twin Cities History Project (TCHP). With the part-time assistance of Lee Rokke, we registered information about Norwegians who gave their destination as Minneapolis–St. Paul in Norway's emigration protocols between 1880 and 1924 and linked those details with data about Norwegian-born residents in the Twin Cities in the federal censuses of 1880, 1900, and 1920. Dr. William Block and the staff of the North American Population Project at the History Department of the University of Minnesota helped the TCHP digitize and analyze this large mass of data. The team also studied the archives and anniversary booklets of local Norwegian American organizations, as well as many local, state, and regional histories.

The TCHP conducted scores of in-depth interviews with a wide spectrum of people of Norwegian background in both cities. Moreover, the team's oral histories included members of other population groups as part of the study's investigation of intergroup relations. We consulted with the Minnesota Historical Society's oral history officer and used its procedures and forms for gaining permission to use the information and opinions from interviews in the history produced by the TCHP.

Residents of the Cities and members of the Norwegian American community who shared their local knowledge and family's history transformed this book. We are grateful for their generosity and willingness to point our research in fruitful directions. Perhaps most important, their stories brought flesh-and-blood reality to the public records documenting the power of urbanization for the growth and evolution of Norwegian community in Minneapolis–St. Paul. A list of those who contributed through interviews and the dates on which they spoke with the TCHP appears in the appendix.

Barb Sommer transcribed hundreds of hours of TCHP interviews in a thoroughly professional fashion. These transcriptions allowed me to quote verbatim some of these people's most striking statements and vivid memories. As best I could, I supplemented these transcripts with ones supplied by the archives of the Evangelical Lutheran Church in America, the Sons of Norway, and graduate students in Norway. Making transcriptions is expensive and very time consuming, however; unless more funding becomes available, many interviews will remain untranscribed.

Indispensable help to find and use sources has come from the highly competent staff and rich libraries of the University of Minnesota, Augsburg University, and St. Olaf College and archives ranging from the ELCA offices in Chicago to collections at NAHA, MNHS, and the Center for Western Studies at Augustana College.

Expenses for the TCHP research team were supported through full-time paid leave for me from the Norwegian University of Technology and Science (NTNU) in Trondheim and the University of Oslo and a leave of absence from Østfold University College in Halden, Norway, for Robert Mikkelsen. NAHA's fundraising efforts for the TCHP, as well as grants from MNHS and the Minnesota Humanities Center, paid many bills, providing a foundation of support and making this research possible.

Many friends have lived with this work and me through the years—Robin and David Beatty, Stanley Dorn, Winston and Carole Kulok and family, Karin and Eric Mandeville and godchildren E. J. and Elizabeth, who made wife Marit and me great-godparents. I have also received academic support from many fellow workers in the field of immigration and ethnicity studies over the years: David Reimers, Odd Lovoll, Elliott Barkan, Betty Bergland, Lori Lahlum, Orm Øverland, Dag Blanck, and Jørn Brøndal, to name a few. They encouraged, taught, and believed, all of which helped me bring this project to a worthy conclusion. However, the person most affected and most willing to support me over the longest time has been my best in-house assistant, reader, and critic—my wife, Marit. I dedicate this book to her.

CHAPTER ONE

An Introductory Overview

Norwegian Immigration, Urbanization, and Community in the Twin Cities

[1849–2020]

"HOW CAN YOU TELL THE DIFFERENCE BETWEEN AN INTROVERTED AND AN extroverted Norwegian by looking at him?" A few days after arriving in the Twin Cities from Norway, I faced that riddle from the barber who had just heard that I had come to write about Norwegians' history in the Cities. The other men waiting for a haircut seemed to know the answer, and the barber said I needed to know it to write the history. Everyone chuckled as he exclaimed, "The extroverted Norwegian looks at *your* shoes when he talks to you."

Apparently, "Norwegian jokes" were public property, something everyone in Minneapolis–St. Paul knew. The stereotype of the very shy or reserved Norwegian seemed out of date after my years of living in contemporary Norway, but it impressed me that a riddle about any Norwegian "type" was common parlance in 1998 Minneapolis. The research ahead revealed a series of public reputations and responses Norwegian Americans experienced over more than a century and a half in the Twin Cities and their hinterlands.

Studies of Norwegian Community in American Big Cities

This book builds on the efforts of other historians who have closely examined the life of Norwegian immigrants and their descendants in American big cities. The paragraphs that follow give an overview of important book-length studies that have been published about Norwegians in Chicago, New York, and the Twin Cities. In 1988, Odd S. Lovoll commented on the flyleaf of *A Century of Urban Life: The Norwegians in Chicago before 1930* that he designed that work "to correct a strong rural bias in the historiography of the Norwegian American population." The project's completion, he notes, represented the fulfillment of one first proposed by the Norwegian-American Historical Association sixty years earlier. Researched in close cooperation with community leaders, the book relies on a multitude of private as well as public sources and historical views to create a fine-grained documentation of the origins, growth, and multifaceted development of community among Norwegians in the city.

Lovoll marshals evidence to portray the group's gathering in employment areas and the resulting creation of ethnic residential and business districts that also housed churches and a wide assortment of social clubs and leisure-time activities. The book's chapters highlight Norwegians' migration to newer areas of Chicago where housing was often built by compatriot craftsmen. Community institutions followed. He then traces the appearance of educational, professional, and economic elites and their residential and social locations. Exploring internal group archives and the public records of the city, Lovoll contributes to knowledge of Norwegians' participation in political activity and religious institutions as well as in the union and business organization of economic life in Chicago.

April R. Schultz's *Ethnicity on Parade: Inventing the Norwegian American through Celebration*, the next major study of urbanized Norwegian Americans, reached the public six years later, in 1994. The chronological focus here is the celebration of the centennial of Norwegian immigration to the United States in the Twin Cities in 1925. The title reflects the currents then prominent in historical research: the interpretation of public displays of ethnicity as a means of revealing how the leadership of ethnic groups "invented" (negotiated) a positive self-portrait for acknowledgment by American society at large. While Schultz provides a selective overview of earlier Norwegian American history, the locus of her work is the anti-immigrant mood of the First World War. She portrays that context as part of the motivation for the group leadership in the Twin Cities to portray Norwegian Americans as a loyally patriotic population without inner conflict or dissatisfaction with life in America. In her view, this book would correct the traditional view of Norwegian American historical work that the 1925 celebrations were a last hurrah of the group's ethnicity, which faded after that. Schultz emphasized that ethnicity would continue to evolve rather than disappear through assimilation. The 1925 celebration, Schultz wrote, was a "conservative, accommodative" form of ethnicity, derivative of its period context.[1]

In 1997, my book *The Colony that Rose from the Sea* explored several little-studied aspects of Norwegian American urban life. Unlike most work in the field at the time, the book focuses on the experiences of Norwegians in another region, the East Coast port of New York, and examines a later period than Lovoll's, the second half of the nineteenth and the early twentieth centuries. Equally important, *Colony* closely analyses the international forces that motivated seamen, especially from maritime nations such as Norway, to use seafaring as a concealed form of emigration. As steamships replaced sailing vessels, the bottom fell out of the country's shipping industry and sent thousands of unemployed men and their families to coastal cities around the world. In these cities seamen were usually transient residents between voyages. In late nineteenth-century Brooklyn and New York maritime transients greatly outnumbered settled Norwegian residents. As a result, settled families developed ways of earning extra income and protecting the stability of their families through living patterns such as upstairs rooms for "hallboys" and "table-board" kitchens to feed transients. By the early 1900s, the maritime "colony" increasingly became a more settled Little Norway whose residents included many sailors who had gone ashore to find other work.

In 2019, *Scandinavians in Chicago: The Origins of White Privilege in Modern America* by Erika K. Jackson took the historiography of urban Norwegian Americans in its most recent new directions. The author concisely states her purpose as exploring "ideological, gendered concepts of Nordic whiteness and Scandinavian ethnicity employed by native-born Americans in Chicago during the late nineteenth and early twentieth centuries to construct societal hegemony." Jackson frames the evolving status of Scandinavian Americans in terms of their rising position in the racial-ethnic hierarchy of the city's peoples, as the mainstream and Nordic language press popularized it. Between the 1840s and 1880s, asserts Jackson, the common view of Scandinavian Americans in Chicago changed from swarthy or "dumb blond" immigrants from the river slums to the fairest of whites living in better parts of town. By the 1880s, Scandinavian immigration, now mostly young and single, included many women, who became the most sought-after domestic help in Chicago because of their whiteness and "natural, bucolic femininity." Scandinavians' rise in prestige occurred through the media's popularization of the pseudoscientific race theories of the period and the exploitation of these by Scandinavian elites to enhance their opportunity and status. Instead of portraying the struggles of European ethnic groups such as the Irish or Italians to be accepted as white, Jackson explores the experience of immigrants endowed with whiteness on their arrival.[2]

The Twin Cities Context and Design of this Book

This study of Norwegian migration and community in the Twin Cities of Minneapolis and St. Paul, Minnesota, builds beyond its predecessors in several ways. The chief differences are summarized here. First, it discusses a much longer period of time, scrutinizing developments over more than a century and a half, from 1849 to 2020. Second, the book examines the history of place to an unprecedented degree, analyzing events and processes in distinctive though neighboring cities. Third, the study examines closely the relations of local Norwegians with other population groups, not just other European American communities but also Native Americans, African Americans, and Asian Americans. Fourth, the book depicts the series of forms Norwegian community evolved through as a result of immigration and urbanization over so long a period and relations with other groups.

The place—the context—that Norwegian newcomers adjusted to changed enormously over this long stretch of time, both in its physical development due to rapid technological change and in the shifting groups of people who lived there. Recent in-depth academic studies of the Cities, moreover, were lacking in the late nineties, thus demanding basic research to generate new historical knowledge about the physical and demographic context of this study.

Focusing on both of the Twin Cities gives this work a comparative dimension in several important ways. St. Paul developed first, largely because it stands at the point on the Mississippi River where steamboat and other large-boat navigation stopped for much of the period. Minneapolis began to grow nearly a decade later through efforts to industrialize by using the waterpower of the only falls on the river. Different cities evolved from these divergent economic foundations. Distinctive American elites, mostly from New England, and a generation of assorted immigrant groups built up the rapidly expanding—and competing—river towns.

Always a transportation hub because of its location, St. Paul supported regional commerce that rapidly switched from oxcarts to railroads thanks to the efforts of James J. Hill. Irish, Swedish, and smaller numbers of Norwegian newcomers provided many of the construction crews for Hill's railways. German immigrants initially composed a large population in St. Paul, and during the 1870s Jews joined their mixed Protestant and Catholic community. German immigrants also constituted a large and influential population group in the towns by the falls. With adjacent waterpower, Minneapolis and St. Anthony entrepreneurs soon developed those towns into a milling powerhouse, with lumber and flour milling and related craft shops as their first industrial base.

Initially, Norwegians were the largest Scandinavian immigrant group in the falls area, but from the late 1870s many more Swedes settled in what became the consolidated city of Minneapolis in 1874. Together these two Nordic immigrant populations made up 46 percent of the city's residents by 1890. This was about twice the size of the Scandinavian presence in St. Paul, even though it too experienced a large wave of Scandinavian immigration in the 1880s. By the end of that decade, in popular discourse the two cities had developed demographic identities. In simplified terms, people thought of St. Paul as dominated by Irish Catholics and of Minneapolis as overwhelmingly Scandinavian. These monolithic self-images persisted into the 1950s and beyond, despite the

KNUTE NELSON

OPPOSITE: Knute Nelson and Leif Erikson statues near the state capitol, St. Paul. *NAHA.* | TOP: Henrik Ibsen statue in Como Park, St. Paul. *MNHS.* | ABOVE: Ole Bull statue in Loring Park, Minneapolis. *MNHS.* | RIGHT: Norwegian Lutheran Memorial Church (Mindekirken), Minneapolis. *Courtesy of the author*

ABOVE: Ingebretsen's Scandinavian Gifts, Minneapolis. **BELOW:** "Of C'Horse We're Norsk": author David Mauk at the entrance to Norsk Hostfest at the North Dakota state fairgrounds, 1998. *Both courtesy of the author*

presence of a large, long-resident German American population and the arrival and integration of smaller groups of Mexican and eastern European immigrants from the late 1880s into the 1920s.

Against the backdrop of the Twin Cities' physical, economic, and population growth, this study documents three additional themes that frame local Norwegian American history. The second theme is that Norwegians' movement to Minneapolis–St. Paul has consisted of a shifting combination of international migration—*immigration*—and movement from the surrounding countryside to the Cities—*urbanization*. At different points one or the other of the two kinds of movement dominated, but to an unexpectedly large degree urbanization revealed itself as the most important migratory process in the growth of the local Norwegian community's size and significance over time. Put simply, the importance of urbanization resulted from the combination of the historical timing of developments in Norway and the United States, as well as of the Twin Cities' long status as the sole urban magnet in the US region most heavily settled by Norwegian farmers.[3]

Between 1890 and 1925, the country's Norwegian Americans increasingly acknowledged Minneapolis–St. Paul as the "capital," the most important communications and organizational center, of the nationality group in the United States as a whole. The Cities' strategic location and demographic magnetism eventually made them the preeminent urban location for the group, a reality recognized by both American politicians and Norway's political leaders. A pervasive thread in this study is the analysis of the causes and effects of immigration and urbanization on the experiences of local Norwegians, the forms of community they created, and the international prominence these reached. After World War II, another migratory process, *suburbanization*, dominates changes in the Norwegian American community in the Twin Cities.[4]

A third central theme in the book arises from an investigation of local Norwegian Americans' adjustments to other population groups in and around the Cities. This relational, interethnic history explores their integration into the human diversity of American life. These interactions with and responses to other groups reveal Norwegian Americans' changing position in the local status hierarchy, as well as their evolving attitudes and behavior as a result. For example, in periods a century apart—in the 1860s and 1870s and in the 1960s and 1970s—Norwegian and Native Americans and Norwegian and African Americans in the Cities experienced conflict and cooperation after, in the latter period, the two non-white groups moved into traditional Norwegian neighborhoods. By the early 1860s, some Norwegian immigrants homesteaded on Dakota land and experienced the Native Americans' uprising. Around a century later, Native Americans from reservations settled in Scandinavian immigrant districts in the Twin Cities. African Americans migrated into northern Minneapolis and western St. Paul near Norwegian first settlement areas around a century after Norwegian immigrants fought in the Union Army in the Civil War. The book analyzes what these interactions reveal about both Norwegian Americans and their new neighbors.

The fourth theme of this history is the evolving forms of Norwegian American community that developed from the influences of migration, the urban context of the Twin Cities, and intergroup relations. The chapters that follow explore how these influences interacted in successive periods of time and, in one case (chapter five), how they affected local Norwegians' involvement in social issues in the Progressive Era.

Shifting Forms of Norwegian American Community: An Overview of Chapter Topics

The fourth theme, the changing forms of Norwegian American community, organizes the book into a series of chapters that discuss the growing size and complexity of their group life and activities in the Cities in a largely chronological order. A variety of factors ushered in new forms of community. The migratory processes already described and changes in technology affected their urban and demographic contexts. For instance, a series of transportation revolutions made it easier for Norwegian immigrants to leave original settlement areas like the east side of downtown St. Paul and Cedar-Riverside in Minneapolis. The Cities developed into a large metropolitan area during successive eras of technological change, and Norwegian American work and residence spread across both cities as their number and socioeconomic status grew.

Events in the nation and world had local impacts that led to different phases of community. For example, the arrival of steamboat travel to St. Paul in the 1840s brought the first explorer who evaluated the sites of the future Twin Cities for Norwegian settlement. In 1849, the Reverend Claus Lauritz Clausen, a Lutheran minister, decided neither the village of St. Paul nor the future site of Minneapolis was suitable for a Norwegian colony. Nonetheless, by the early 1850s the first Norwegian newcomers made their presence in the territorial capital known. The immigrant group's history in St. Anthony and Minneapolis began around a decade and a half later but becomes the most important focus of community developments in this study.

By the 1880s, the exploitation of waterpower on the Mississippi had drawn many more Norwegians to the falls area, and from then on, the balance of this history is increasingly weighted toward Minneapolis, whose Norwegian population, activities, and leadership elites grew much larger and more prominent than those in St. Paul. On the one hand, revealing the history of Norwegians in St. Paul required lifting people, events, and institutions there from the shadow of the greater attention the source materials give to Minneapolis's Norwegians. On the other hand, the greater size and influence of the larger community at the falls deserves proportionately more space in the resulting book.

Another factor that influenced the series of community forms is the length of time included in the study. In the more than 150 years considered here, Norwegian American group life in the Twin Cities changed quite significantly. These immigrants were a little-noticed collection of foreign-born river-town pioneers from 1849 to 1865, the situation discussed in chapter two. Four great waves of arrivals from Norway became part of the Twin Cities' shifting body of foreign-born, foreign-language-speaking immigrants. Most of these people for the rest of their lives remained recognizably different from the old-stock, general population of whites. This status was true even for many of the Norwegians who had first lived in the rural Midwest and then moved into the Cities. Between 1849 and 1930, such immigrants put their stamp on and provided the leadership for the local Norwegian American community. For this reason, four chapters focus on the immigrant phase of community.

Chapter two, "Foundations of Urban Life: The Frontier-Pioneer Context in the River Towns and Their Rural Hinterlands," attends to two main themes. One examines the development of the Cities and their population in these years with emphasis on the early settlement of Norwegians and other Scandinavians that provides background for understanding later Norwegian urban settlement. The other makes the initial argument that many of these urban settlers strongly felt the Americanizing impact of their participation in the western movement of white homesteaders, as well as in the Civil and Indian Wars.

As the title of chapter three, "In the Aftermath: An Immigrant Subculture Takes Root in River Boomtowns after the Civil and Dakota Wars, 1865–1880," suggests, the analysis here demonstrates how early Norwegian immigrants established community centers and that these illustrated aftereffects of the wars on the local immigrant population. With the end of hostilities, immigration to the United States soared. The river towns turned into rapidly expanding cities, and their immigrant quarters (Mount Airy in St. Paul and Cedar-Riverside in Minneapolis, among others) bustled with many more Norwegians than ever before. Among these were both refugees from the Dakota War and transients on their way to farmland farther west. Soldiers came to town looking to make civilian lives for themselves. War veterans and their families played prominent roles, and Norwegian American leaders, such as Judge Andreas Ueland, rose from humble beginnings to elected positions of high status. In St. Paul, as in Minneapolis at the time, the Norwegian immigrant community's leadership consisted of a few, often unmarried, small-businessmen and professionals who served a large and rapidly growing group of young, single people, the women mostly working in domestic service and the men in city construction jobs. Norwegians met in these businesses, in the first pan-Scandinavian churches, and in lodging houses.

The fourth chapter, "Expansion's Golden Age: The Flowering of Norwegian Immigrant Culture in the Twin Cities, 1880–1905," shows how Norwegian immigrants made up one of the Cities' largest and most influential foreign-language immigrant communities by the early years of the twentieth century. In the decade of the 1880s, a mounting crest of Norwegian newcomers from the surrounding region and Norway took up residence in Minneapolis–St. Paul. At the same time, the Cities' population as a whole increased enormously. The flour mill and timber economy offered a wealth of opportunity. They became "big cities" on a national basis. Swedes and Norwegians came in such large numbers that by 1890 they and their children accounted for nearly half of the population of Minneapolis (46.2 percent) and over a quarter of the people in St. Paul (27 percent).[5]

The second part of the fourth chapter marks the turn to a focus on events, people, and processes in the twentieth century. The next four chapters analyze evolving forms of Norwegian American community through 2000, establishing a rough balance of attention in the book between the 1800s and 1900s. Due to a second surge of urbanization from the region and immigration from Norway after 1900, foreign-born Norwegians remained a large group in the local Norwegian American community and the population of the Cities as a whole at the start of the First World War. They and a growing second generation developed a new phase of community—not a colony of foreigners, but an integrated part of the local establishment, with an elaborate array of community institutions, including churches, seminaries and a college, hospitals, and old-age homes. Leaders of these institutions admonished Carl G. O. Hansen, editor of *Minneapolis Tidende*, the largest local Norwegian-language newspaper, to remember this phase of community and not to refer to the Norwegian "colony" in print. By then it was so much more.

Understandably, then, the Twin Cities became the site of the primary celebrations of the centennial of the group's immigration to America in 1914, by which time the multifaceted Norwegian American community had become a well-known feature of both cities. Its members included elected municipal officials and appointed city engineers. While the most successful foreign-born immigrants dominated its leadership elites, children and grandchildren of residents from Norway were becoming noticeable in its activities and relations with the public at large. In St. Paul as well as Minneapolis, multiple Norwegian American centers had developed, and members of the group resided in nearly all parts of town.

Chapter five, "Social Issues in Expansion's Golden Age, 1880s–1920s," documents the social and political involvement of the immigrant community's mature stage. At this point, its members reached out beyond internal concerns to work with other parts of the public to solve problems affecting the whole population of the Twin Cities, the nation, and Norway. A stream of visitors from among the most prominent authors and opinion-makers in Norway kept leaders of the local community updated about debates in the homeland and over time came to recognize the achievements of "migrated Norway" and of the Minneapolis–St. Paul center as its preeminent hub. Local responses to this acknowledgment became evident in strong support for Norwegian independence from Sweden and cooperation with homeland organizations in planning and carrying out elaborate celebrations of the centennials of the Norwegian constitution in 1914 and of Norwegian immigration to the United States in 1925. These cooperative responses demonstrated that the center of Norwegian American life in the Twin Cities had become the capital of a "transnational greater Norway," a leading site of discourses concerning issues of general concern to the entire nationality group.

The chapter examines the immigrant community's engagement with a series of social issues that caused debate and reform in cities across America: temperance campaigns to control alcohol abuse, women's fight for the vote, and efforts to reduce urban poverty, especially among immigrants. Norwegian immigrants needed public support, despite the mutual benefit orders they founded in times of crisis, such as the 1890s, when members of the group in the working-class district of north Minneapolis organized the Sons and Daughters of Norway.

Chapter six, "Community Transformations: Boom, Bust, and War, 1925–1945," traces the completion of the transition from an immigrant to an ethnic community among Norwegian Americans in the Twin Cities. Partly because of strong antiforeign feeling during the First World War and the 1920s, as well as immigration restriction, the community changed into a largely English-speaking American-born ethnic group in the 1920s. That transformation also resulted from the growing preponderance of the second and third generations in the Norwegian American population. The large majority of the group were no longer distinguishable from other white Americans in language, education, occupation, or place of residence. World Wars I and II brought many people, including Norwegian Americans, from rural parts of the region to military and related industrial work in the metropolitan area. The large numbers of relocated people from the countryside kept the Twin Cities in touch with rural relatives, values, and perspectives on life. During the 1930s and World War II, ethnic community life weakened because of financial hardships, but also strengthened through the efforts of mutual support and mobilization to celebrate ethnic heritage and to send aid to occupied Norway.

By the end of the 1920s, the generational transition from an immigrant to an ethnic community was complete. The peak percentage of foreign-born Norwegians in the population of both Minneapolis and St. Paul (7.7 and 2.6 percent, respectively) appeared in 1890. Due to an influx of foreign-born people arriving after 1900, their highest *absolute number* resided in the Cities in 1910 (16,401 in Minneapolis and 4,063 in St. Paul). The total population of each city grew rapidly decade by decade, however, so that by 1920 the *percentage* of Norwegian foreign-born dropped to 4.3 percent in Minneapolis and 1.6 percent in St. Paul. On the other hand, in those twenty years the American-born second generation increasingly surpassed the size of the foreign-born generation in each city. By 1920, the children of immigrants outnumbered their parents in Minneapolis 24,901 to 16,389. In St. Paul the difference appeared even more pronounced. There the second generation numbered 6,732, and the city contained only 3,818 first-generation Norwegians. By 1930, the second generation was roughly three times the size of the first in both cities. See Table 1.1.[6]

No one knows how many of these later-generation Norwegian Americans migrated to the Cities from rural locations in the region after World War I. The family histories reported in interviews suggest strongly, however, that such postwar urbanization was common. Family members living in the metropolitan area during the war years encouraged veterans to join them as spouses, to share lodgings or employment, or to take advantage of educational opportunities. Despite the last massive wave of immigration from Norway between 1900 and 1914, the later generations of Americanized people in the group so outnumbered the newcomers that the change from a largely Norwegian-language community to the dominance of English progressed rapidly. Observing the pace of linguistic change, leaders such as Carl G. O. Hansen successfully campaigned to have courses in Norwegian made available as electives at local public high schools. Young people arriving from the surrounding countryside, however, usually adopted English as their first language for school, work, and free time activities.[7]

Chapter seven, “One of the Twin Cities’ Later-Generation Ethnic

TABLE 1.1

Norwegian and Swedish Immigrants and Their Children in Minneapolis–St. Paul, 1880–2000

	1880	**1890**	**1900**	**1910**	**1920**	**1930**
MINNEAPOLIS	46,887	164,738	202,718	301,408	380,582	464,356
		38th	18th	19th	18th	15th
Norwegian-born	2,651	12,624	11,532	16,401	16,389	15,492
Percentage of city	(5.7%)	(7.7%)	(5.7%)	(5.4%)	(4.3%)	(3.3%)
Norwegian parentage	1,273	17,839	22,182	17,870	24,901	33,917
(= 2nd generation in %)	(2.7%)	(10.8%)	(10.9%)	(5.9%)	(6.5%)	(7.3%)
Total Percentage of City	**8.7%**	**18.5%**	**16.6%**	**11.3%**	**10.8%**	**10.6%**
Swedish-born	3,188	19,398	20,035	26,477	26,515	24,866
Percentage of city	(6.8%)	(11.8%)	(9.9%)	(8.8%)	(8.1%)	(5.4%)
Swedish parentage		26,122	35,740	26,768	34,805	45,597
(= 2nd generation in %)		(15.9%)	(17.6%)	(9.0%)	(9.2%)	(9.8%)
Total Percentage of City		**27.7%**	**27.5%**	**17.8%**	**17.3%**	**15.2%**
TOTAL NORWEGIAN/ SWEDISH PRESENCE		**46.2%**	**44.1%**	**29.1%**	**28.1%**	**25.8%**

	1940	**1950**	**1960**	**1970**	**1980**	**1990**	**2000**
MINNEAPOLIS	492,370	519,645	761,835×	1,7904,197×	370,951	368,383	382,452
	16th	17th					
Norwegian-born	11,777	8,568	8,043×	4,036×	18,260√	22,624√	41,917√ =ancestry
Percentage of city	(2.4%)	(1.7%)	(1.1%)×	(.2%)×	(4.9%)√	(6.1%)√	(11.0)√
Norwegian parentage			44,602×	34,973×			
(= 2nd generation in %)			(5.9%)×	(2.0%)×			
Total Percentage of City			**7.0%×**	**2.2%×**			
Swedish-born	19,244	13,442	13,114×	6,656×			
Percentage of city	(3.9%)	(2.6%)	(1.7%)×	(.03%)×			
Swedish parentage			62,833×	46,905×			
(= 2nd generation in %)			(8.2%)×	(2.6%)×			
Total Percentage of City			**9.9%×**	**2.9%×**			
TOTAL NORWEGIAN/ SWEDISH PRESENCE			**16.9%×**	**5.1%×**			

* only the foreign-born first generation in 1880
× = metropolitan area (SMSA) Minneapolis–St. Paul
√ = ancestry, not birth, 1980–2000

	1880	1890	1900	1910	1920	1930
ST. PAUL	41,473	133,156	163,065	214,744	234,698	271,606
	45th	23rd	23rd	26th	30th	31st
Norwegian-born	664	3,521	2,900	4,063	3,818	3,414
Percentage of city	(1.6%)	(2.6%)	(1.8%)	(1.9%)	(1.6%)	(1.3%)
Norwegian parentage	238	5,014	6,144	5,321	6,732	9,023
(= 2nd generation in %)	(.6%)	(3.8%)	(3.8%)	(2.5%)	(2.9%)	(3.3%)
Total Percentage of City	**2.2%**	**6.4%**	**5.6%**	**4.4%**	**4.5%**	**4.6%**
Swedish-born	1,897	11,787	9,852	11,335	9,912	8,404
Percentage of city	(4.6%)	(8.9%)	(6.0%)	(5.3%)	(4.2%)	(3.1%)
Swedish parentage	*	15,542	18,695	13,305	14,246	17,026
(2nd generation in %)	*	(11.7%)	(11.5%)	(6.2%)	(6.1%)	(6.3%)
Total Percentage of City		**20.6%**	**17.5%**	**11.5%**	**10.3%**	**9.4%**
TOTAL NORWEGIAN/ SWEDISH PRESENCE	**6.2%**	**27 %**	**23.1%**	**15.9%**	**14.8%**	**14.0%**

	1940	1950	1960	1970	1980	1990	2000
ST. PAUL	287,736	310,220	761,835×	1,704,197×	270,230	272,235	287,151
	33rd	35th					
Norwegian-born	2,548	1,692	See ×.	See ×.	22,112√	24,893√	24,035√ =ancestry
Percentage of city	(.9%)	(.6%)			(8.2%)√	(.9%)√	(8.4%)√
Norwegian parentage							
(= 2nd generation in %)							
Total Percentage of City							
Swedish-born	6,100	3,923	See ×.	See ×.			
Percentage of city	(2.1%)	(1.3%)					
Swedish parentage							
(2nd generation in %)							
Total Percentage of City							
TOTAL NORWEGIAN/ SWEDISH PRESENCE			**See ×.**	**See ×.**			

SOURCE: US Census, Population, 1880–2000. In 1970 the census included “mother tongue” data, which suggested that Minneapolis was home to 10,481 second- and 5,967 third-generation Norwegian Americans. In St. Paul the second and third generations comprised 2,814 and 1,969 residents, respectively. See Carlton Qualey and Jon Gjerde, “Norwegians,” in Holmquist, *They Chose Minnesota*, 231.

Groups during the Postwar Decades, 1945–1975," discusses yet another phase of the group's changing forms of community. A part of third or later generations, members of the community in this period voluntarily chose to identify as people of Norwegian lineage in selected dimensions of their lives. For the great majority of these people, Norwegian American ethnicity became, as sociologist Herbert Gans has asserted, largely symbolic, centering on family traditions and memories, combined with a few public holidays, such as *Syttende mai* (Seventeenth of May) and Norway Day at Minnehaha Park. The ethnic population developed into an ancestry group whose collective activities depended on a small core of devoted ethnic activists.[8]

In these years, Norwegian Americans raised their children in suburbs to a much larger degree, and if still residing in St. Paul or Minneapolis, they often lived near city borders. After 1945, unprecedented suburbanization took place as returning veterans reestablished themselves and started families. When they found spouses, these servicemen and -women, carrying experiences of distant places among a wider variety of races and nationalities, migrated to the greener, less congested suburbs of the Twin Cities. In the 1950s, a small wave of immigration from Norway and other Norwegian American centers refreshed the memberships of established Norwegian American institutions and led to the founding of clubs and societies by the newcomers.

In the first decade and a half after the war, significant numbers of African Americans and Native Americans arrived in search of economic opportunity and settled largely in quarters that had once held many Scandinavian immigrants. In the 1960s superhighways crisscrossed those inner-city neighborhoods near the city centers. In the next decade and later, immigrants from Asia, Africa, and Latin America joined African Americans and urban Indians in replacing the departing populations by taking up residence in housing made inexpensive by suburbanization and highway building. Norwegian Americans, like most other longer-settled groups, found that jobs and much of their institutional network from earlier decades drew them downtown to attend church or ethnic affairs.

The Twin Cities' Native American and African American communities grew considerably in the 1950s and following years, even though both groups remained relatively small compared to their size in other industrial metropolitan areas of the North and on the West Coast. In both cities, these recent arrivals frequently found inexpensive housing in the central sections of town that held the historic institutions of Scandinavian immigrants who no longer lived there. Between 1945 and 1975, the established, largely Scandinavian American postwar leadership in Minneapolis and the state government in St. Paul faced the difficulties of negotiating with these groups over their grievances in these particular parts of town.

Chapter eight, "The Norwegian American Ancestry Group in the Minneapolis–St. Paul Metropolitan Area, 1975–2000," deals with the final form of Norwegian American community that this book examines. By carrying the research to the end of the twentieth century, the analysis traces community characteristics through life among fourth- and fifth-generation Norwegian Americans. These people were no longer immigrants or even their "ethnic" grandchildren, but Americans who chose to identify themselves as later-generation members of an "ancestry group," in the terminology the census bureau began to use in 1980. Officially viewed as part of the general American public, they saw themselves as having another significant level of identity, and the census bureau's use of "ancestry group" stemmed from pressure from groups like these. The story here traces family and community in the last twenty-five years of the century, when the ethnic group increasingly became an ancestry group widely dispersed across the metropolitan area. A core of active members nourished connections to the Norwegian and Norwegian American past through private, symbolic activities and conscious efforts to pass on the ethnic legacy to later generations through public celebrations and historical publications.

By 2000, most remaining residents of Norwegian American ancestry inside the city limits in Minneapolis lived in its outskirts—the better housing of the upper north side, the modest developments of the lower southeast toward the airport, or the fine single-family homes of the far west. Many lived in the city's suburbs, towns such as Bloomington, Richfield, Edina, St. Louis Park, Golden Valley, Fridley, Robbinsdale, Plymouth, Brooklyn Center, and Brooklyn Park. In the state capital, the outward movement was parallel—to the outskirts of St. Paul's northeast, northwest, or south and the adjacent suburbs of Maplewood, White Bear Lake, Roseville, Arden Hills, and Eagan. Considerable numbers of Norwegian Americans lived even farther out in the thirteen-county metropolitan area at the end of the twentieth century.

From 1975 onward, long-established ancestry groups like the Norwegian Americans adjusted to the difficulties of their dispersion across an increasingly extensive metropolitan area. The censuses of 1980, 1990, and 2000 document the growing percentages of people who do not live in the Twin Cities or even in their inner rings of suburbs but instead in the counties surrounding those built-up areas. By the end of the century, neither Minneapolis nor St. Paul contained as high a percentage of people claiming Norwegian ancestry as did Dakota, Scott, Carver, Wright, Sherburne, Isanti, and Anoka Counties. Taking part in ethnic occasions, services, and anniversary celebrations frequently involved long commutes from outlying areas to the downtowns.

To mark the sesquicentennial of Norwegian immigration in 1975, Norwegian National Archives, the Norseman's Federation, historical organizations in the homeland, as well as the country's consulate in the Twin Cities marshaled resources and arranged activities. A wide range of Norwegian American organizations, including the Norwegian-American Historical Association, Sons of Norway, and Lutheran Brotherhood, mobilized in cooperation with the efforts in Norway. The result was the preservation of many irreplaceable records of the ancestry group's past, a very effective information and public relations campaign, a royal visit to the Cities, and a remarkable if relatively short-lived revival of local Norwegian American community life. At the same time the settling of new groups—of Latin Americans, Africans, and Asians—in the downtown districts that once were largely Scandinavian American presented new challenges of historical memory and cultural outreach.[9]

From 1975 to 2000, meeting these challenges continued to occupy much of the energy of the ancestry group's activist core. Family maintenance of naming traditions, foodways, and holiday traditions bolstered a perceived sense of ethnic identity. While living in the Twin Cities and their suburbs, individuals and groups inspired by traditional Norwegian handicrafts, music, and dance cooperated with Vesterheim (the National Norwegian-American Museum in Decorah, Iowa) and like-minded Norwegians in the homeland to create a transnational exchange of knowledge and skills. A continuing renaissance of this heritage produced great authenticity and innovation in binational forms. Some ethnic businesspeople and business organizations, such as the Scandinavian-American Chamber of Commerce, enhanced the possibilities for establishing or strengthening bonds with the ancestral homeland. In these years, for example, Kjell Bergh's Volvo dealership helped purchasers of new Swedish automobiles arrange to pick up the car in Sweden, tour Scandinavia, and then return with it to the Twin Cities and vicinity. Parents and grandparents with the interest and means added a Norwegian dimension to their descendants' lives by arranging trips to Norway, attendance at the Norwegian American language camp Skogfjorden, or tours to events such as the Norsk Hostfest ("Norwegian Autumn Festival") in Minot, North Dakota, or the Nordic Fest in Decorah, Iowa. Some ethnic institutions assisted in making these activities available. A few young people won acceptance at the University of Oslo International Summer School and developed long-term relationships with people and places in Norway, although that program became much less oriented toward American students than it was in its early years.

Significant Loss but Innovative Revival in the 2000s

The final chapter highlights developments in the early twenty-first century and interprets these in terms of long lines of community creation since the middle of the nineteenth century. Most institutions and traditions that helped maintain ancestral legacies of the Norwegian American group remained vital in these years, but their character changed. The effects of very little immigration from Norway for over a century became increasingly evident. The average age of the membership in historically Norwegian American churches and in the Cities' founding Sons of Norway lodges, like that in many other ancestral organizations, continued to rise, and the size of the active membership in many cases continued to decline. Many members of the "Contact Youth Club," founded in the 1950s for newcomers, were now in retirement. The Norwegian-American Technical Society had become an organization dominated by retirees, because their bylaws prohibited any but the foreign-born and -educated from joining, even though it successfully recruited a few younger members from among the very small number of recent immigrants from Norway. In the aging of the active core and the difficulty of attracting the allegiance of the later-generation young, the situation for the group in the Twin Cities resembled that of Norwegian Americans across the nation.

Some signs marked the decline of Minneapolis–St. Paul as the preeminent hub of Norwegian America. Latter-day Norwegian American newspapers in New York and Seattle competed (in place of the Twin Cities) to produce a national voice in print for the nationality group. For a generation, Norwegian Americans had had no newspaper, in Norwegian or English, written for and addressed to them as its primary audience. An iconic business for the group, Lutheran Brotherhood, thrived and broadened its originally Scandinavian American base, but in 2002 it became submerged in the larger fraternal insurance firm Thrivent Financial, and its ancestral background was no longer evident, even though its skyscraper headquarters remained in downtown Minneapolis.[10]

Norway's Ministry of Foreign Affairs, after several earlier debates over the issue, closed its full, professionally staffed consulate in Minneapolis. No longer would the country send a diplomat to the Upper Midwest. From 2008, Norway sent royal consuls general to New York, San Francisco, and Houston but not to Minneapolis, where an honorary consul general replaced the professional emissary from the homeland. Until 2010, former vice president Walter Mondale served in the honorary position, after which Eivind Heiberg, chief executive officer of Sons of Norway and Sons of Norway Foundation, succeeded him. Both men's selection and service testify to the continuing prestige of the consulate among Norwegian American leaders in the region.

Other developments demonstrated a combination of attitudinal, economic, and demographic changes. For example, leading Norwegian American women in business and the professions in the metropolitan area founded Lakselaget, a women-only group parallel to the men's clubs, Torske klubben and Norske Torske klubben. In the politics of the metropolitan area, Norwegian American representative to Congress Martin Sabo, who repeatedly won reelection between 1979 and 2007, retired, and Keith Ellison, the first Muslim to serve in the House of Representatives and the first person of color to represent Minnesota in that chamber, took the seat. On the municipal level in the Cities, the children of current immigrants from Africa or Asia also stepped in to elected office following later-generation members of long-resident ancestry groups. These developments reflected larger shifts in the character of the population of Minneapolis–St. Paul by this period and the great historic change in status for Norwegian Americans, who, even though they continued to move into the suburbs from the countryside, were now one of the metropolitan area's longest resident populations.

Through greater substance in the chapters that follow, this study sheds light on 170 years of the life of Norwegian Americans and their descendants in two major American cities at the center of a large metropolitan area in the Upper Midwest. A central part of the story is how different elements of the group came to the Cities from Norway or the surrounding countryside. Another part of the story involves their stages of migration away from the city centers and suburbanization from there or adjacent counties. Further, the book explores a series of evolving community forms in the nationality group, as well as its relations with the shifting groups around it. This work attempts to interpret Norwegian Americans' responses to these contexts, finding that, in fact, if one refers to the riddle that introduces this chapter, Norwegians' historical experiences in Minneapolis–St. Paul witnessed few Norwegian introverts and many extroverts, who looked far beyond their neighbors' shoes as they adjusted to their adopted urban American home.

CHAPTER TWO

Foundations of Urban Life

The Frontier-Pioneer Context in the River Towns and Their Rural Hinterlands

[1830s–1870s]

THIS CHAPTER FOCUSES PRIMARILY ON TWO TOPICS. THE FIRST EXAMINES the origins and early development of the Twin Cities in terms of the mixture of populations, cultural attitudes, and economic opportunities that met the first Norwegian and other Scandinavian settlers. The point here is to give background for a better understanding of later Norwegian urban settlement. The chapter's second topic explores the ways that rural Norwegian emigration, combined with settlement in the rural Upper Midwest, created a double rural heritage, one that preserved traditions of country life in Norway and, simultaneously, one that involved the immigrants in deeply Americanizing historical processes—the westward movement of European American settlement and the Civil and Dakota Wars. Both of these processes also trace another theme of this history: Norwegian immigrants' initial relationships with Native Americans, other immigrant groups, and old-stock Americans.

For most members of the group, the characteristics of Norwegian American community in the river towns during these years were enormously different from life in the twenty-first century. The few Norwegians in town were transient residents who lived in boardinghouses with members of unfamiliar nationality groups. They witnessed a shifting gender imbalance from a single, male-dominated bachelor society in civic life to female leadership and inspiration in the first pan-Scandinavian churches. Until their numbers grew large enough to support separate institutions, Norwegians joined Swedes and Danes in Nordic enterprises. Even the first local Seventeenth of May celebration was a shared Scandinavian affair. Not least, early Norwegians in the river towns had to adjust to the larger context of life on the edge of white settlement, where seeing Native Americans, French fur traders, and mixed-race families was a daily occurrence.

Meanwhile, during the same decades much larger numbers of Norwegian immigrants homesteaded. They joined thousands of other white settlers who took up former Native American homelands to establish farming districts and small towns across western Wisconsin and northern Iowa and along a diagonal from southeastern to northwestern Minnesota. They and their children found themselves involved in the life-and-death struggles of the midcentury wars, which both Americanized the attitudes of many and led growing numbers to join the rush into the river boomtowns of St. Paul and Minneapolis.

The Land-Taking Pioneer Generation: A Norwegian American Hinterland Developed First

Between the 1830s and 1880s, close to 80 percent of the pioneer generation of Norwegian immigrants in the United States settled in a rural area stretching from northern Illinois and Iowa and on a northwesterly diagonal through much of Wisconsin and Minnesota into the Dakotas. The appearance of this vast arc of settlement resulted from conditions in Norway that brought on a large-scale exodus of the country's rural population. After 1815 and the end of the Napoleonic War, the population of Europe grew rapidly and "more in Norway than in almost any other country," according to Norwegian historian of emigration Ingrid Semmingsen. Over nine of ten of Norway's people lived in the countryside at the start of the 1800s and were overwhelmingly engaged in farming. This was still the case for four-fifths of the population in 1810 and two-thirds in 1865.[1]

Therefore, the large population increase appeared in Norway's rural areas, where mounting adjustment problems developed as the century went on. The traditions of family and community life depended on land ownership. By law, the oldest son inherited the family farm, but even he frequently found that longer-lived parents remained unwilling to give him the land so that he could marry and start a family. Even if parents did turn over the farm to the oldest son, the rest of the children were left without livelihoods. Too often, dividing up the farm for the next generation produced unsustainably small plots. Usually, therefore, while they waited, sons became landless farmworkers and daughters took jobs tending animals on neighboring farms or worked as servants in nearby towns. Observing the evolving fate of the younger generation, between the 1830s and 1850s some parents helped sons clear new land. Others liquidated their property and cleared land in far north Norway. Sons and daughters made lives for themselves in coastal towns or went to sea. In the same decades, at first a few and then, with the spread of information, many chose instead to emigrate to the American Midwest. There, it was said, was an enormous amount of good land with which they could pass on their traditional farm culture to future generations.[2]

Thus, most Norwegians arrived with a rural heritage until after 1870, when a growing majority of people leaving the country departed from residences in urban areas. The number of rural arrivals continued to be large, however, and records show that many of the newcomers who left from Norway's towns had first moved there from the countryside. They migrated to the United States in stages, leaving home districts for coastal towns and sometime later making the transatlantic journey. In America, this study demonstrates, many of them or their descendants urbanized again, this time from the rural Upper Midwest to Minneapolis–St. Paul.

In Minnesota, the first Norwegian immigrant settlers appeared at the start of the 1850s. By the state's 1875 census, the main course of their settlement as a major component of the rural population traversed the state from its southeastern corner to its northwestern Red River Valley. Adjacent to a contiguous area of older settlements in northeastern Iowa, their largest and most established farming communities lay in southeastern Houston, Fillmore, and Goodhue Counties. Through the newer Lake Park Region, their farms stretched through compact settlements in Kandiyohi, Pope, and Douglas Counties. The newest wheat-growing Norwegian farmers clustered in northwestern Otter Tail, Clay, Norman, and Polk Counties, where their stepping-stone path of communities crossed into the Dakota Territory with little concern for the state line.

Many Norwegian immigrants passed through or sojourned in St. Paul, and later Minneapolis, until after the Civil War. According to the federal census in 1860, the counties that would become the Twin Cities area together contained but fifty-three Norwegian-born and seventeen second-generation Norwegian American residents, the large majority of both these groups living in Ramsey County, where St. Paul lies. How many of these were more or less temporary residents included in this official enumeration is impossible to know. By 1875, by contrast, the state census found that Norwegian immigrants and their children numbered 11,345 or 40 percent of the population of Fillmore County and 4,104 or 45 percent of Otter Tail County. At the same time, they comprised 517 people or 1.5 percent of Ramsey County and 2,553 or just over 5 percent of Hennepin County, the home of rapidly growing Minneapolis. The dramatically reversed position of the two cities shows Minneapolis early assuming its preeminent position as the urban center for Norwegians in Minnesota. The Norwegian American proportion of Hennepin County's population rose to nearly 10 percent in 1880 but then dropped to around 5 percent by 1900 and remained at almost the same point in 1960. The relative stability of the group's size in relation to the whole of Hennepin County's population, of course, hides the enormous growth in the urban population of the area and the much larger absolute numbers that 5 percent of that population represented as the twentieth century progressed.[3]

The original inhabitants of the overwhelmingly rural New Norway in the Upper Midwest were "striking rather than attractive" but "built for pioneering," claimed historian Laurence M. Larson in 1937. An insider, the product of a Norwegian American frontier community himself, Larson formulates a personality and cultural profile for the immigrant generation that coincides remarkably well with the self-image of many Norwegian Americans in Minneapolis–St. Paul interviewed for this book at the end of the twentieth century. This close correspondence suggests the enduring force of the starting point provided by the culture of the homeland and simultaneously illustrates the power of the enshrined early experiences of the first generation of Norwegians in the Upper Midwest.[4]

Larson felt that these rural people brought from their homeland traits trenchantly summarized by the Norwegian novelist Arne Garborg: "A strong, stubborn folk who dig their way through a life of brooding and care, they putter with the soil and search the scriptures, force a little corn from the earth and hopes from their dreams, and put their faith in the penny and their trust in God." Elaborating on his cultural profile, Larson gives first priority to the centrality of owning land. In the nineteenth century, the need for land was fundamental, for few families could establish themselves or care for coming generations properly in rural Norway without legal title to farmland that they owned as a freehold. The emigration from Norway to the American Midwest, as many historians have emphasized, primarily represented a way of preventing the next generation from falling into landlessness and the lower social status and material poverty it would bring in a rural peasant society.[5]

Without ownership of land on the American frontier, the first-generation immigrants had no new home, no place to resume the family lineage and history after breaking with the ancestral plot of land in Norway. Such attitudes inevitably colored their sense that Native Americans—with their land and resources held in common—represented a culture alien to the Norwegians' and made them support removal of the Natives or the loss of their title to the land.

Bicultural Influences in Norwegian American Rural Settlement

The risky and intricate process of understanding the law of the land in America when their own culture and language were foreign can only have reinforced Norwegians' concern with the legalities of land ownership. In a catalog of generic qualities in the pioneering generation of Norwegian Americans, Larson explains the dense settlement patterns of these homesteaders in part as clannishness justified by the need for "economic protection." Compatriots could warn them of the exploitation perpetrated by "the [American] banker, the lawyer, the wheat buyer, and other 'smart' businessmen." The Norwegian immigrant in the Upper Midwest "felt that he was safer among his own countrymen, and in this he was usually correct."[6]

Larson attributes values to rural Norwegian immigrants that should have made integration into American culture easier. The stubborn individualism that often had put them at odds with authorities in their homeland, he asserts, included the faith that Norway's farmers had in an ancient tradition of democratic freedom dating from Viking times. Foreign-born residents asserting independence from constituted authority in the United States were seldom looked upon favorably by old-stock Americans. This was especially true when overcompensation for a "troublesome suspicion of inferiority," as Larson calls it, led Norwegians to speak "freely and sometimes boastfully of [the] fatherland and its glorious past." Somewhat contradictorily, these Norwegians had a reticent, unemotional way about them; yet, regarding their practice of religion, as in most matters, they were strenuous in their defense of the specifically Norwegian forms and traditions they had carried from northern Europe. They took land in compact if not always contiguous areas, says Larson, for the common reasons that immigrants usually congregate: because it was so much easier to settle among *landsmenn* who shared those dear traditions, cultural expectations, and a native tongue. Larson states the case with unusual strength, asserting that "no active spiritual life is possible among 'strangers' one does not understand."[7]

All the immigrant groups in Minnesota clustered in the emerging farming areas when they could, often to the near exclusion of even closely related nationality groups. Censuses show that in one of Minnesota's earliest heavy areas of Norwegian land claims, Houston County, Irish and Germans settled the eastern half and Norwegians the western, and the two sections retain their distinctive character still. In Goodhue County, census counts between the 1850s and 1870 show that what seemed perhaps the "sister cultures" of Swedish and Norwegian settlers remained largely segregated. Swedes populated the northeastern area of the county, while Norwegians initially gathered elsewhere in the countryside and in Red Wing, with intermarriage between the groups remaining low well into the twentieth century.[8]

In fact, localism and regionalism, so strong in Norway during the period of emigration to the Upper Midwest, made the country's distinct regional subcultures the natural self-identification for most Norwegian immigrants. They saw themselves, to name just a few examples, as *Trønder,* from "flat land" areas of the counties in mid-Norway; *Valdrisser,* from a small mountainous section of the country's central highlands; or *Gudbrandsdøler,* who, though natives from a valley near Valdres as the crow flies, exhibited significant cultural differences—at least to *Valdrisser* and in their own eyes. People who lived on neighboring farms in Norway later lived on neighboring farms in Wisconsin, Iowa, or Minnesota. The early arrivals spread the word about their new homes in America to neighbors and relatives in the local community at home. They thus stimulated more movement, a chain migration, to the transplanted offshoot of the *bygd* (the distinct local Norwegian subculture) in America. A minority even traveled back to Norway to arrange personally for this to happen. The first such New World bygd thus became a "mother" colony for strings of similar rural communities that eventually stretched from Illinois and Wisconsin across Minnesota into the Dakotas.[9]

Grouping of Norwegians appeared in the Twin Cities, too. As we have seen, people from Trøndelag, in particular from Selbu, clustered in north Minneapolis. Interviews revealed that similar, though smaller, groupings from local and regional areas of Norway appeared in other parts of the Cities. As with other immigrant groups from countries where a national culture developed only late in the nineteenth century, they became "Norwegians" through the processes of adjustment to American conditions and in the eyes of old-stock Americans, who often failed to distinguish even among northern European nationalities.

Neighborhoods moved together and reassembled in the Upper Midwest. It is common in studies of rural land ownership patterns among Norwegian Americans to find whole communities and sections of communities where a single local or regional group long predominated. There were exceptions to this pattern, of course. Historian H. R. Holand prominently notes communities that formed with a mixed batch of first settlers and from the start showed no particular dominant origin in Norway, such as the western part of Houston County and the eastern half of Fillmore County, which received settlers from many different parties of Norwegians. These groups moved into the area with no knowledge of each other and came at the same time as many old-stock Americans. Still, in the 1860s and 1870s later groups of emigrants from one place strove to stay together in the new country. Neighbors in the mother communities tried to be neighbors again if they moved westward, occasionally developing a limited secondary, Americanized version of the old bygd culture. It and the secondary Norwegian migration within the United States in general was colored, perhaps even transformed, by the American frontier idea—and often the repeated experience—of seizing opportunities for moving to greener pastures to the west. Historian Carlton Qualey drew attention to this concept in the 1930s, stating that "having established a first place of residence, the immigrant ceases to be an immigrant. . . . If he makes further moves he must be termed a migrant." Consequently, Qualey concludes that Norwegian settlement should be less viewed as emigration from Norway and more understood as an American phenomenon, as part of the frontier movement.[10]

Qualey notes that, much like the rest of the land-hungry westering European American population, some Norwegian Americans squatted illegally beyond the edge of settlement. In the classic pattern of white settlement that stretched back to the seventeenth century, traditional legal scruples were overwhelmed by impatience for territory to be ceded by Native Americans and fears that others might stake claims, however dubious, to the best farmland first. Many Norwegians waited until land was ceded but claimed and occupied prime sites before officially mandated land surveys or the opening of land sales by American governments. Subsequent events often justified—or tacitly accepted—their independent occupation when those same governments granted preemption rights to most or all categories of squatters. In *The Promise of America,* Odd Lovoll places in a larger context the story of settlers from the Sogn region of Norway who formed a kind of vigilante society in Goodhue County to protect their retention of larger parcels of land than the 160 acres permitted by law. Common among squatters and first settlers on the frontier before the Homestead Act, these grassroots organizations or clubs attempted to enforce their own "club law." In Goodhue County, such settlers gave up extralegal claims only when other Norwegians, people from the Telemark district of the homeland led by "Big Svein," a man of indomitable physical strength and determination, arrived and overcame the club.

This story—like Guri Rosseland's experience, related below—forcefully illustrates that Norwegian settlers in frontier Minnesota partook in fundamentally American processes during the creation of the rural hinterland from which some of these people and many of their descendants would migrate to the Twin Cities of Minneapolis and St. Paul. This form of ethnic mobilization for the acquisition of land bowed only to superior force. As Orm Øverland remarks of Kristofer Janson's views after a lecture tour of the Norwegian Midwest, by the end of the 1870s some educated visitors from Norway were convinced that the pioneers' experiences had worked a "radical transformation of the docile and subservient Norwegian peasant into the independent and self-reliant American farmer."[11]

The Beginnings of Urban Life in Neighboring River Towns

An early visitor evaluated Minnesota's neighboring Mississippi River towns as potential sites for Norwegian settlements. The Reverend Claus Lauritz Clausen, one of the first Scandinavians to pass through early St. Paul, was for generations esteemed as the original pioneer pastor in Muskego, Wisconsin. Clausen was a religious leader frontier settlers could genuinely appreciate, and for more than the usual qualities expected in a minister. He was a Dane but so devoted to the spiritual and material well-being of the early Norwegian immigrants there and in neighboring states that they complimented him by popularly considering him Norwegian. By the latter 1840s, members of his congregation at Rock Prairie, Wisconsin, like many another frontier community formed by the expectation of better opportunities farther west, were eager to move on. On one of his longer journeys to find a suitable site for a "larger Norwegian settlement," Clausen arrived in St. Paul on the first steamboat that reached the river town in the spring of 1849.

The Mississippi was then the key channel of the town's commercial livelihood. One vital piece of information in St. Paul's early records as the head of navigation on the Mississippi (the most northerly point that craft much larger than canoes could reach) was when and how many days the river was open to steamboat traffic each year. In 1849 the channel was open for 242 days, ninety-five steamers arrived, and the first boat to dock after the ice had left its course, the *Dr. Franklin, No. 2*, arrived at night on April 9 amid lightning bolts, thunder, and pouring rain. As Hjalmar Holand relates Clausen's story, the pastor arrived on that very boat and saw the "entire inhabitants of the town rush down the hills to meet the boat. The rain fell in sheets and the lightning lit the sky, but everyone who could walk or crawl swarmed over the decks like a host of bees, starved for news and newspapers." Soon the word was out: "A howl of joy of long duration rose up, was repeated on the shore and echoed from the rolling hills, announcing that Minnesota was a territory and St. Paul was its capital!"[12]

As Holand has it, Clausen looked around the town once the nocturnal jubilation subsided and saw that fledgling St. Paul had but thirty houses and was inhabited for the most part by "French 'half-breeds' who hoped to strike it rich" by selling lots in the new capital. The town and its vicinity—the whole territory—had barely four thousand inhabitants, and these "were nearly all 'trappers' and 'township squatters' with hardly a single genuine 'farmer' among them." It was clearly not a hospitable place for a Norwegian settlement. Nothing there appealed to a "countryman with good judgment." Clausen moved on to inspect the future site of Minneapolis, which was as yet without European American settlement. Its chain of lakes surrounded with woods and areas of prairie between them attracted him. The open areas were too small for the considerable contingent of Norwegian parishioners he knew wanted to move again, however, and the soil was quite sandy. So, says Holand, Clausen did not become the founder of one of the world's great cities. Instead, he listened to the advice from a Native American in St. Paul and, traveling east again, founded large Norwegian settlements in Wisconsin's Pierce and St. Croix Counties before returning to Rock Prairie.[13]

Like many an early visitor to the nascent cities on the northern reaches of the Mississippi, Clausen became famous for his deeds elsewhere. The largest number of rural Norwegian settlers entering Minnesota in the early 1850s found the land they wanted without going up the river as far as St. Paul. Many migrated farther west from the Norwegian settlements in neighboring states, as Clausen's congregation had planned to do. Numerous other groups took boats up the Hudson River to the Erie Canal, which carried them to the Great Lakes, where they sailed to Milwaukee and traveled by wagon from there. Yet another host of Norwegian newcomers came by way of Canada, down the St. Lawrence to Quebec and then across the lakes to Chicago or Milwaukee.

For various reasons, however, some Norwegians and other Scandinavians, along with German and Irish immigrants and Americans from farther east, did take the paddle wheelers to their end stop. Some of the earliest, like Clausen, came because they quite literally did not know the lay of the land. Others took the river farther north because until 1866 it seemed a convenient route. Some came for temporary work and, as the next chapter documents, stayed.

The Panic of 1857 had disastrous effects on the plans of Minnesota's earliest railroad visionaries, and the Civil War redirected or drained resources from such projects. The first trains ran in the state in 1862 and then only from St. Paul to St. Anthony, located across the Mississippi's falls from the future site of Minneapolis. That line, the St. Paul and Pacific, did not reach St. Cloud, Minnesota, until 1866. Other lines, which circumvented the river cities or outpaced water travel by running south along the river, were not completed until 1869 or the early 1870s. Thus, until the late 1860s, river steamers to St. Paul, rather than railroads, often served for the first leg of the journey to farmland in central or northern Minnesota for people coming from the south and east.[14]

St. Paul's founding and conversion from a bankside still and whiskey den called Pig's Eye to Minnesota's territorial capital and chief trading center occurred before Norwegian immigrants settled there. The young hamlet had developed a great diversity of population and near total dependence on the Indian trade before mass immigration from Europe transformed its demography. Social and economic realities of the place, including fundamental attitudes and assumptions about intergroup relations and the status of Native Americans and people of mixed ancestry, formed an important part of the "found" environment in early St. Paul. In making their way in this new place, immigrants had to learn and negotiate not only its socioeconomic opportunities and limits but also the mentality that had developed there and the local residents' resulting expectations for newcomers.

St. Paul took shape between the late 1830s, when the US Army ordered squatters off the military reservation connected to nearby Fort Snelling, and the late 1850s, by which time the town's first Scandinavian institutions provided the rudiments of community for Norwegian settlers. The miliary reservation, a land cession negotiated in an unauthorized fashion with the Dakota by Zebulon Pike in 1805 for building the fort, ran nine miles wide on both sides of the river from above the falls at St. Anthony to below the confluence of the Mississippi and Minnesota Rivers. As historians have noted, the federal government's management of the reservation at Fort Snelling "helped scatter the seeds of settlement from the fort and Mendota to the sites of the future cities of St. Paul, St. Anthony, and Minneapolis."[15]

The scattered village of relocated European Americans that became St. Paul sprouted up just outside the military reserve on a bluff opposite and a little north of Kaposia, a primary site of the Dakota. Both towns, though on different heights and sides of the Mississippi, spread along a U-shaped curve of the river a few miles below the falls, St. Paul in the center of the curve and Kaposia a little farther along its downstream leg. The Dakota called the community on the bluff White Rock, after the color of the stone on which it stood. As the settlement above them grew, the Dakota became accustomed to crossing the river and mounting the bluff to visit European Americans' homes and stores. In 1837 Little Crow's Mdewakanton Dakota band and the Ojibwe sold the territory between the St. Croix River and the Mississippi to the United States but continued their centuries-old warfare through territory now officially in European American hands. Kaposia lay on the west bank river flats, which marked the verge of Dakota territory. To the north and northeast was Ojibwe land. In the 1840s and early 1850s, the line of the river, including occasionally St. Paul's streets, witnessed the continuing conflicts between the two Native peoples.

Only the small triangle of land between the rivers, a wedge along the Wisconsin state line, was US property when the Reverend Clausen observed the ecstasy in St. Paul at the announcement of Minnesota's territorial status in 1849. The rest of Minnesota was Indian territory, that is, land that belonged to Native Americans. A necessary legal prelude, territorial status was in practice a confining skin territorial governor Alexander Ramsey and other American leaders wanted to shed as quickly as possible. Statehood, however, depended on recruiting a tide of easterners and European immigrants to the territory. They would come, and passing through or settling in St. Paul, would transform its scattered shanties into a wealthy city deserving the title of capital on one condition: the rapid removal of both Dakota and Ojibwe people that would open the territory's lands to European American settlement. As the Minnesota historian Rhoda R. Gilman remarked a hundred years later, "facing St. Paul across and just down the river lay . . . Kaposia, a daily reminder of the fundamental barrier that stood in the way of new immigration."[16]

In his inaugural speech to the territorial legislature, Governor Ramsey proclaimed that the immediate and most pressing goal facing the body consisted in convincing the Dakota to sell southern Minnesota to the United States. Ramsey knew his audience—in that chamber in St. Paul and in the rest of the so-called white wedge. He and the territory's other influential men lobbied Congress to begin negotiations with the Dakota and to sweeten the talks with promises of large sums in payment and annuities. Naturally, as the territorial capital, St. Paul was the center of agitation for the Native Americans' removal.[17]

Yet, from its beginnings, St. Paul depended on the "Indian trade" for its economic survival. First, Pierre "Pig's Eye" Parrant sold whiskey to soldiers and Native Americans alike just outside the reserve on the edge of today's city. When the fort's commander, Major Joseph Plympton, expelled settlers from the reserve in 1838, some of them moved close to Parrant's place, and it became even more attractive to the various elements in its clientele. Most of the frontier liquor outlet's new neighbors had not squatted at the fort reserve. Swiss-born refugees from a failed Canadian Red River settlement of the Hudson's Bay fur company had received permission to settle in the reserve along the west bank of the Mississippi from Colonel Josiah Snelling, the fort's first commander, in 1827. Their numbers eventually grew to an estimated five hundred, but many of the refugees moved on after a time, and although squatters, including former soldiers at the fort, joined the refugee group during the 1830s, when the eviction orders were posted, 157 people not connected to the military lived on the reserve.[18]

Thinking himself shrewd, Plympton redrew the reserve lines in 1840 to include Parrant's whiskey dispensary and give destruction of the place a veil of legality. The ejected Parrant and his neighbors, however, merely moved a bit farther down the river to the site of the present-day city's downtown. Called Pig's Eye originally, the new location attracted additional population, such as French rivermen, trappers, and fur traders—often with Native American wives—and as the wedge of land open to European Americans began to "settle up," the town attracted people who were refused land on the reserve. In 1840 this group, which was largely Catholic, drew the attention of the bishop of Dubuque on a visit to Fort Snelling. A year later his emissary, the Reverend Lucien Galtier, convinced two of the settlement's French residents to donate land and labor and thus erected the Chapel of St. Paul, which soon gave the hamlet a new name. Initially it was called St. Paul Landing, indicating that from the start its position at the head of navigation on the river spurred its growth. In 1842, one year after the chapel was dedicated, the landing was already developing the infamous character for which it was known for a decade or more. In that year, Henry Jackson opened his trading house and bar. His immediate employment of a clerk-bartender who spoke Dakota reveals the importance of that group for his business.[19]

By 1846, more than five such establishments made the town of some thirty families a magnet for Natives and European Americans. The attraction had more to do with the hamlet's growing role as a regional trading center in furs and other Native goods from the middle of the 1840s. With the advent of the Red River cart caravans, which could number more than one hundred ox-driven vehicles, St. Paul's influence in the vast Native American hinterland began to be felt as it exploited the commercial potential latent in its position at the head of steamboat transportation on the Mississippi and tributary rivers.[20]

Natives from throughout that huge expanse came to depend on St. Paul's stores—not only for alcoholic beverages but also for the full range of goods that European traders made available. To purchase these things the Native Americans revolutionized their subsistence economy, developing a commercial engine that threatened to exhaust the stock of wild game in the area as they proffered furs and meat for sale. Native Americans also sought employment in ways entirely new to them. At the stores, some Native American men made agreements to act as scouts, hired hunters, or hunter-guides for European Americans exploring the area.

Fredrika Bremer, the famous Swedish visitor who toured America in 1850, entered several Native homes in Kaposia during her stay in Minnesota. In each, she found the Dakota men occupied with the manufacture of red stone pipes for sale to European Americans. Native Americans in the region had already adjusted traditional crafts to provide cash

In the early 1850s, Kaposia, a large Dakota town, lay on the Mississippi river flats directly visible from St. Paul. Little Crow's Village on the Mississippi, ***by Seth Eastman, 1846–48, MNHS***

or a basis for barter in the region's developing commercial economy. To make the most of their new economic situation, they used ancient trade networks across a vast hinterland as yet little known to Europeans. Bremer's guides, who included Governor Ramsey and his wife, told her that the red stone came from quarries at the far northwesterly reaches of the Missouri River. Ojibwe and other Native peoples also met and married European Americans in St. Paul. It was a community where, according to J. Fletcher Williams's 1876 history of the city, so many of the French were intermarried with the Natives that "not more than half the families in the place were white, if that many." Native American tongues and French were the languages spoken by all but "three or four families," claims Williams.[21]

By 1849 about half the population in the white wedge, 4,535, lived in Stillwater on the St. Croix River boundary to Wisconsin, in the village of St. Anthony, or in St. Paul, whose population was far more diverse than the other two. The Indian territory that surrounded the wedge on three sides held perhaps twenty-five thousand Native Americans. In the years after the removal of the Natives in 1851, the demographic character of St. Paul, according to Williams, "and its easy acceptance of *métis*—people of mixed heritage unions and their descendants—would rapidly change." A remembered tradition of tolerance, it can be argued, would remain and help to differentiate St. Paul from the nearest Mississippi River towns, St. Anthony and Minneapolis, in later years.[22]

The Conditions that Met the Norwegian Urban Pioneers

Norwegian immigrants arrived in St. Paul at this stage in its development. The community they found, according to a local editor, was a boomtown "but yesterday unknown" and changing so fast that a month-old description of it seemed out of date. Its streets laid out in 1847, it was incorporated as a town two years later and officially became a city in 1854. Between acquiring that net of streets and 1855, its population exploded from 840 to 4,716. The pace of expansion, moreover, driven by immigration from the eastern states and Europe, continued to accelerate. Just one year later St. Paul held twice as many people. Constantly promoting St. Paul and Minnesota as the most promising of destinations for the migrating masses, the local press exhausted hyperbole in celebrating the parallel rising arc of the local building boom. The speculative mania infected everyone, they said, even those who could only afford to squat and count on rises in lot prices. Immigration was so rapid that workmen could not turn out buildings fast enough, so that many families threw together shacks in a day and then lived in them much longer than intended.

The streets and open spaces were littered with piles of "lumber and building materials . . . scattered everywhere in admirable confusion," boasted one journalist. As far back as the spring of 1849, the first issue of a newspaper printed in Minnesota warned the immigrants "swarming" into the town to bring tents because their numbers overwhelmed local builders. So it continued from 1849 to later in 1857—until the speculative bubble inflated on the potential future value of St. Paul's and Minnesota's real estate burst in the financial panic. St. Paul was especially hard-hit by the crash. Neither its nor Minnesota's economy fully recovered until the Civil War, when the Union Army's demands for food, firewood, and soldiers lifted commodity prices.[23]

Before the panic and the wartime recovery there were eight golden, hectic years during which the first Scandinavian settlers came to St. Paul. Nils Nilsen, a nineteen-year-old agricultural worker from Modum, Norway, arrived on foot in St. Paul in late summer of 1849. H. R. Holand, who interviewed him many years later, tells how Nils remembered working briefly in the lead mines of Galena, Illinois, before leaving to work for an American farmer near Decorah, Iowa, and then moving on again when a Norwegian American offered him a job as a teamster helping to drive wagons filled with pigs to Prescott in southwestern Wisconsin. As soon as the pigs were safely transported, Nils left and walked the roughly twenty miles northwest along the river to St. Paul. The districts he visited before coming to Minnesota, well-known settlement areas for Norwegian immigrants, indicate that he very likely found support and advice from compatriots with more experience in America. We can only suppose that they, the Norwegian American farmer for whom he drove, or another acquaintance suggested that he might find opportunities aplenty in the boomtown near the fort. In St. Paul he worked for about a year in the stable at Moffett's Castle, a hotel for new settlers in the middle of town, and then left for Stillwater, where he found work in one of its sawmills. As will soon be clear, his youth, footloose wanderings, and willingness to take whatever jobs presented themselves were qualities typical of many in the region's floating male-dominated population at the time.[24]

A young brother and sister, Amund and Ingeborg Langeberg, found themselves in St. Paul by another characteristic route and filled typical labor needs there from 1850. Leaving Hallingdal, one of the districts of heavy early emigration in Norway, they traveled to Rock Prairie, Wisconsin, the Norwegian "mother settlement" where the perceived need to move on to Minnesota had sent the Reverend Clausen north only a year earlier. Perhaps he or others in Rock Prairie informed the sibling pair about potential jobs for them in St. Paul. Like Clausen, Amund Langeberg found life in a rural farm community much more to his liking. He left town after only three months' work at odd jobs and followed the course typical among rural Norwegian immigrants at the time. One of the first pioneers to homestead in a Worth County, Iowa, settlement near the Minnesota border, he lived among fellow Norwegians from Hallingdal, close to other communities planted from Wisconsin by the good Reverend Clausen.[25]

Ingeborg Levorsdatter Langeberg remained longer in the city. St. Paul's runaway growth made her chances of finding work as a single woman much better in town. Domestic workers were in high demand in a frontier town where women in general were scarce. Her exceptional luck consisted in finding a position that was prestigious for any single woman of her class in St. Paul—working as a cook in Territorial Governor Ramsey's home, which introduced her to the manners and language of the highest level of American society the town had to offer. Such a position, of course, also enhanced her desirability as a marriage partner in a place where many men of considerable prospects were searching for a wife. It cannot have been easy for such as the governor's wife to keep good female household help under the circumstances. In any event, domestic service was then already well known as a premarital phase or a stepping-stone to an advantageous marriage for immigrant girls, which was certainly true in Langeberg's case.[26]

In 1850, the federal census found but seven Norwegian-born persons in the territory of Minnesota, which was then limited to the small wedge of land previously described. We have now accounted for three of these, who at the time were living in St. Paul. Norwegians and other European immigrants who stayed in the city for a while in the mid-1800s had to accommodate themselves to a diverse resident population composed largely of the groups earlier named. New Englanders, the immigrants soon found, composed a sizeable portion of this population and controlled most of the territory's emerging economy. After listing all the town's adult male residents in 1850, J. Fletcher Williams concludes that most of St. Paul's pioneers were Yankees or French, rather than the Germans or Scandinavians who were so numerous by 1875. Census records include tabulations for country of birth for only whole states or territories until 1860, but at that point St. Paul stands out on census maps as an island of concentrated New England settlement in a state where the largest foreign-born groups in order of size were German, Irish, Norwegian, and Swedish.

As Bremer's *Sketches of Minnesota: The New England of the West* emphasizes, however, newcomers at midcentury also found a city near the "dividing line of civilized and savage life," where they could look across the river and see "Indians on their own soil" or observe them crossing that line in canoes gliding across the Mississippi. In 1850, Bremer called the town "one of the youngest infants of the Great West" and noted with disbelief that tastelessly painted Native Americans with uncovered weapons visited Governor Ramsey's drawing room, which also served as his office, and "thronged" the streets.[27]

From Bremer's visit through the summer of 1857, St. Paul enjoyed the attraction of being the fastest-growing, liveliest point on the Mississippi. The town dozed in frozen isolation in the coldest quarter of the year, and then burst into life when, as the decade passed, the thaw brought increasing numbers of steamboats to its docks on the first day the river opened. Suddenly in excess of a thousand passengers disgorged from three to seven boats lined up at the levee; filled the streets, lodgings, and stores to overflowing; and led to scenes of unrestrained "jollification" by evening.[28]

In the early boomtown years, those who remained in town were disproportionately young, single, and male. In 1847, there were 540 males to 300 females, and in 1850 the city contained 1,337 men to its 860 women. The imbalance, however, only lasted until sometime past mid-decade. By 1860, when St. Paul's 10,331 inhabitants were almost evenly divided between men and women, the typical male-dominated, frontier-town character of the population had all but disappeared. But until then, the wildness of the spring spree resulted in part from the large number of footloose young white men whose bright prospects had suddenly returned. The largest part of these men took whatever work they could get as common laborers, construction workers, road graders, and stablemen, but many of the town's leaders—its professional men, traders, store owners or managers, real-estate speculators, politicians, and journalists—also belonged to the same group of men who had yet to settle down.[29]

At the beginning of the 1850s, in commentary after her visit, Bremer chose to emphasize the comparison of European American and Native American women's conditions in Kaposia and St. Paul. While she finds "cultivated" European American women often confined to a "hard grey domestic life" and "hedged in by conventional opinion," she condemns Dakota culture for reducing its women to beasts of burden and prizes to be bartered in arranged marriages. Bremer shows no appreciation for gender roles in the division of work in Dakota society. She notes and evaluates the quality of the men's work in carving red stone pipes for the European American tourist market but provides no larger context for understanding or commentary on what a revolutionary and traumatic cultural change this represents from the men's traditional role in providing food, furs, and bone tools through hunting. Immigrants also often found the traditional gender roles of their homelands misunderstood and criticized in America.[30]

In the customary division of labor among men and women in the Norwegian countryside, for instance, women cared for goats, pigs, and cattle and assisted in fieldwork such as haying, but in the United States Norwegian men found themselves termed hard masters who exploited their wives and daughters if they clung to these traditions. As a result, men took over all outside duties on the farm, and many of their single female relatives found there was little left for them to do—and consequently migrated to male-dominated boomtowns like St. Paul, where they could get work as laundresses, maids, housekeepers, and cooks. Thus it was that Fredrika Bremer made Ingeborg Levorsdatter Langeberg famous as the first Norwegian-born woman to reside in Minnesota by documenting her presence in Governor Ramsey's home as the cook in 1850. In the course of the 1850s, a number of Norwegian women joined Langeberg in the vanguard of Scandinavian, German, Irish, and other immigrant women who found domestic work in St. Paul and its river-city neighbors.[31]

Pan-Scandinavian Cooperation in St. Paul during the 1850s

Norwegian immigrants in St. Paul next appear in the persons of Anne Hovey and Ingeborg Gilberts, whose religious zeal, "right out, of Holy Peter's revivals, became flaming torches" of inspiration at the first Protestant congregation in the city, the Episcopal Methodist Church. "Holy Peter" in this case referred to Ole Peter Petersen, the Norwegian immigrant minister whose revival meetings in Winneshiek County, Iowa, had brought many of his compatriots into the Methodist fold. Petersen's earlier missionary work had resulted in the first of the denomination's congregations in Norway. The two young women converted to

Quakerism before leaving Norway and then became Methodists in the United States. They came to the territorial capital in 1852 to find work as domestic servants.[32]

Like a number of the early immigrants from Norway, Hovey and Gilberts were among the small but fervent minority of low-church dissenters who had experienced religious repression before they left for the United States. Hovey worked her way across the Atlantic as a servant for a departing Swedish family. In America, it seems, the great demand for domestic workers allowed her to use the occupation as a way to move as a single woman through a series of Norwegian settlements. Her conversion to Methodism took place in 1849–50 while she was working for a family in Prairie du Chien, Wisconsin. In 1851, she moved with other pioneering Norwegians to the Washington Prairie settlement in northern Iowa, where she remained in the same line of employment and enthusiastically worked to convert other Norwegians to her new faith. In Prairie du Chien or northern Iowa, she met and became close friends with Gilberts, sixteen, another servant girl whose religious conversions and means of migration were identical with hers. Together they set off for St. Paul on a steamer in the fall of 1852. On board they met a married American woman of some means who was well established in the city and generously promised to assist them there. Before she could, however, they took rooms at Moffett's Castle, the same temperance hotel for newcomers where Nils Nilsen had stayed. They found positions as housekeepers for two prominent bachelors among the city's many single men, Hovey with David Day, a medical doctor from Virginia, and Gilberts with James M. Goodhue, the owner-editor of the *Minnesota Pioneer*, the first newspaper published in Minnesota.[33]

These two spiritually restless women were also geographically restless, like most of the people around them at the time. The ferment of the frontier was religious, economic, and psychological for old-stock Americans and immigrants alike as they moved west, and Hovey and Gilberts shared in the Americanizing common experience of it all as much as anybody. The two women earned a reputation for a religious enthusiasm that was particularly effective in moving groups of young women. Hovey so elevated her audiences that she early along was christened "Anne on the Mountain." For the purpose of understanding the growth of a pan-Scandinavian and then a Norwegian community in St. Paul, the important point here is the route these religious activists took to the city. That path exemplifies, as did the earlier visit of Lutheran minister Clausen, the critical importance to Norwegian settlement patterns of religious associations, friendships, and obligations. The two young women moved from pious family to pious family—and from congregation to congregation—to the city. They brought new members from the community to each church they joined.[34]

In St. Paul their religious testimonials "infused new life into the American members" of the existing Methodist congregation. At the same time, their proselytizing among immigrants from the Nordic countries directly led to the formation of the first Scandinavian congregation of any denomination in Minnesota. The American pastor of the Episcopal Methodist Church wrote that Hovey and Gilberts "brought their people to our class and prayer meetings" and led Scandinavians in the city to "pray and testify in their own language" and hold meetings in their own homes. In his journal, he recorded that they caused such a revival that he asked the Methodist clergy to organize a Scandinavian congregation in St. Paul.[35]

American Methodist networks responded to a Scandinavian presence in St. Paul in the early 1850s. They encouraged further movement of these nationalities to the city by making that presence more widely known. They cooperated with the immigrants in institutionalizing a Scandinavian religious subculture that, among other things, provided a safe haven for the groups' single young women in the male-dominated frontier boomtown. In 1853, those people that Hovey and Gilberts had brought to Methodism conducted meetings and officially gathered as charter members of the Scandinavian Episcopal Church, establishing a formally constituted congregation the next year. In a town that was overwhelmingly male at the time, a large majority of the congregation's members were young women, many of them recorded in the first pages of the church book as having arrived from northern Iowa in 1853 and 1854. It is probable that others among these early women settlers, like Hovey and Gilberts, found work as domestics.[36]

Forming the congregation and building a church home for it were a thoroughly Scandinavian affair, judging from information culled from church records and Arlow Andersen's work on Dano-Norwegian

Methodists in America. The initial membership, leadership, and sponsors of the congregation included Danes, Norwegians, and Swedes. Norwegian members came from both newly settled Carver County southwest of the city and, as mentioned, from northern Iowa. Samuel Andersen, formerly the first Norwegian Methodist minister in Chicago, proved to be the most effective advocate for its building fund among Americans in the East and was "mainly responsible" for the completion of the congregation's first building in 1855. The Danish immigrant Charles W. Borup donated lots on the east side of the old town center at the corner of Tenth and Temperance Streets. One of the early settlers in St. Paul, Borup was its first banker and consul for his homeland. The city's Scandinavians could hardly have found a better man to vouch for them financially.[37]

Carl Peter Agrelius, a Swede, and Samuel Andersen, a Norwegian, together served as circuit preachers who traveled from group to group in the emerging circle of Scandinavian Methodist congregations in the adjacent rural areas of Iowa, Wisconsin, and Minnesota that included the urban church in St. Paul. During the first several years of the church's existence, the conference officially called the congregation the city's Scandinavian Mission, offering a secure meeting ground for young people who shared religious and ethnic proclivities. Scandinavians were three small nationality groups of recent newcomers who needed to pool their resources in the St. Paul of the early 1850s, even before the economic bust times came in 1857.[38]

The influx of Scandinavian immigrants to St. Paul led to the founding of the city's first Lutheran congregation by these nationalities remarkably close to the same time. Following visits by pioneer preachers who conducted services and meetings in Danish, Norwegian, or Swedish in the early 1850s, immigrants of all three nationalities joined in officially organizing the city's Scandinavian Lutheran Church in May 1854. A Lutheran church is what one would expect first among Scandinavian immigrants. Other Protestant faiths, such as Methodism, were just then sending converts made among these immigrants to Lutheran Scandinavia as their first missionaries to those countries. The surprise is that in St. Paul a Methodist institution had appeared a few months earlier than the Lutheran one. That occurrence, as earlier suggested, may have resulted in part from the religious ferment and restlessness among a minority of the earlier Norwegian immigrants. More important, however, are a number of other factors related mainly to the town's fluid frontier character and the fact that Norwegian settlement was just beginning there. In a strange, in-flux environment, the small number of newcomers from Norway first took comfort and assistance where they could find it. American Methodists reached out to them and helped them come together with the nationalities most like them in the city. Even together, they needed American assistance, which the local Methodists were willing to give.[39]

The similarities between the two congregations went beyond a pan-Scandinavian character typical of the earliest stage of settlement and a near simultaneous founding date. The Scandinavian Lutheran group also depended at first on American help. The liberal Evangelical Lutheran Synod of Northern Illinois, which then, in addition, contained most Swedish immigrant congregations and pastors, was its original sponsor. This was an uncomfortable fit for the pietistic and theologically orthodox in the congregation, who were mostly Norwegians. No other Lutheran organization in the western United States at the time accepted mixed Scandinavian groups. This awkward synodical alignment was a signal difference that accounts for the disparity in how quickly the Scandinavian collaboration in the two congregations ended.[40]

The city's Scandinavian Methodist church survived for twenty years. An important reason for its longevity was its members' common experience of conversion to an American denomination. After only three years, on the other hand, a faction in which Norwegians in the Scandinavian Lutheran congregation predominated split off to form its own congregation. "The liberal element," consisting mostly of Swedes, had "won control" in the Lutheran congregation and accused them of behavior both un-Christian and "contrary to the freedom of this country."

The controversy became enmeshed with issues of church polity and charges of Norwegian immigrants' unwillingness to accommodate their ideals to those of their adopted country. The Norwegians in particular seem to have been troubled over having fallen away from strict adherence to theological orthodoxy as it was then defined in their homeland. As regards nationalistic issues, at the time both the ideal of pan-Scandinavian cooperation and romantic nationalism inspired passionate allegiance in Norway and among the country's immigrants in

America. In any case, the departure resulted in a new, largely Norwegian congregation that began its life in the spring of 1858, just when the financial panic had made itself felt locally. It was hardly an auspicious time to start a new congregation, and as a result, for more than two years the departing faction met in homes, the city's old courthouse, and a German Lutheran church.

With some right, the new congregation called itself the "Scandinavian Lutheran Church of St. Paul." Its membership did include Danish and Swedish minorities, but at its founding it applied for acceptance in the Norwegian Synod. In response, those remaining in the original church rechristened it in the city directory as "First Scandinavian Evangelical Lutheran Church." St. Paul thus found itself with two Lutheran congregations that were Scandinavian—at least in name—before the decade's end, although in fact one was largely Swedish American and the other Norwegian American. The *St. Paul City Directory* for 1875 lists one Swedish and one Norwegian Lutheran church, and the addresses given leave no doubt that these are the formerly, at least nominally, Scandinavian congregations that emerged at the end of the 1850s.[41]

Scandinavians in St. Paul on the Eve of the Civil War

Coming just two years before the outbreak of the Civil War and at the very time the city's first Norwegian-dominated church appeared, the *St. Paul City Directory* for 1858–59 provides useful glimpses of the cultural and demographic context of this early congregation and the larger Scandinavian population from which it drew members. A close look at the directory, however, reveals that among these glimpses are authorial perceptions and information gaps that suggest the directory may have undercounted Scandinavians. At the end of the 1850s, these immigrants clearly were not yet as expected or visible—and therefore not likely significant participants in the directory's compilation—as other population groups. Initial evidence comes near the end of the historical sketch introducing the directory, where the city's diverse population is characterized as follows: "Like all cities in the North-West, [St. Paul] is inhabited by men of different nationalities. The sanguine temperament of the French, the steady industry of the Germans, the brilliant though somewhat fickle disposition of the Irish, united with the stern and unflinching faith of the New Englander and Middle States man, have blended harmoniously together in building up a city which will be no mean rival to any other on the Mississippi River, and which within a few years may claim a population of one hundred thousand."[42]

Scandinavian immigrants have no place in this ranking of ethnic stereotypes conflated with an early suggestion of an American melting pot and local boosterism. Their absence in this picture also plays out in the incomplete and erroneous information about Scandinavian institutions in the directory's enumeration of churches. It lists five Methodist churches in the city, two American, two German, and one Scandinavian, which the directory mistakenly labels "Norwegian." The next-largest denominations in number of congregations are three Presbyterian churches, all American, and two Catholic places of worship, one a German church and the other the cathedral with its bishop and offer of weekly mass in English and French. A Congregational and a Baptist congregation complete a listing that, with one exception, well reflects the city's demographic configuration at the time. The largest element consists of the American-born, most visible in the number of English-language Protestant institutions. Some old-stock Americans may have taken mass at the cathedral, but Catholicism's strength was among the local Irish and German immigrants and the old settler French. The exception to the list's accurate reflection of the religious situation is the absence of any Lutheran churches.[43]

The catalog of political and civic officers and institutions also sheds light on community life at the time. Every name in the list of city officials is old-stock American. Its aldermen, on the other hand, include C. H. Schurmeier from the First Ward and Patrick O'Gorman, William McGrorty, and A. L. Larpenteur from the Second, suggesting that ethnic representation at that level of local government was already established. In similar fashion, the seventeen-man police force, led by two Anglo-Americans, includes German, Irish, and old American names, but none of Scandinavian origin. The small four-company fire department consists almost entirely of Americans. The only city institution more dominated by old-stock American names is the educational system, with its three gender-segregated boys' and girls' schools. The size and organization of the Catholic population is evident in the detailed description of the city's only hospital, St. Joseph's, which the sisters of that order ran. St. Paul's civic-minded American men associated in four Masonic and four Odd Fellows lodges, but the only immigrant society listed is the German *turnverein*. The one labor organization that finds a place in the directory, the local printers' union, was in many American cities among the first associations of craftsmen. The officers' names listed suggest a mixed membership of the native-born and German and Irish immigrants.[44]

The 1858–59 *St. Paul City Directory* does not include the young Scandinavian women who served as housekeepers, cooks, and maids for men living on their own or families that are evident in the records of the Methodist church. A few male waiters and laborers with Scandinavian names are listed, but no servants of either gender. Judging by their names, some Scandinavians are also likely among the artisans, skilled craftsmen, and entrepreneurs who were able to make their services and products known through the directory—in both its general listing and its separate catalog of businesses and professionals. The male workers consist of several laborers, a shoemaker, a harness maker, two bakers, two tailors, a lithographer, a stonemason, a painter, a carpenter, two gunsmiths, and two undertakers. The small-businessmen whose shops typically served as informal meeting places in immigrant communities include a barber, three grocers, a barkeeper, a saloonkeeper, and the proprietor of a livery stable. C. W. Borup, the previously mentioned Danish American banker, in business as one partner in Borup and Oakes Bankers, which bought the entire front page of the directory for its advertisement, likely represented the pinnacle of success for a Scandinavian immigrant in St. Paul then. A physician, a wholesaler, an "architect-builder," and an insurance agent connected with Borup made up the small circle of Scandinavian men with somewhat more prestigious occupations. In a category of his own was Ole Nelson, the Norwegian editor-publisher of *Folkets Røst* (*The Voice of the People*; misspelled as "Folkets Roost" in the directory), a Norwegian-language newspaper printed as a Democratic Party campaign organ in the same building as Goodhue's *Minnesota Pioneer*. The presence of this journal since 1857 demonstrates the political importance the large number of Scandinavian, especially Norwegian, settlers in Minnesota were acquiring before the Civil War. As the period's premier urban center, St. Paul had already become the natural hub from which information and political views were disseminated across an expanding Norwegian hinterland, even though the city's Scandinavian population was evidently still insufficiently explored by some local publications.[45]

Some sense of the location of St. Paul's early Scandinavian settlement is available by collating information in the 1858–59 directory, newspaper ads, and congregational history. Perhaps the most striking aspect of the directory's general listing is that so many of the men of all backgrounds and occupational classes lived in hotels, boardinghouses, or rooms above shops and saloons. Approximately 60 percent of the forty-some men with Scandinavian names in the directory live as roomers in such housing. The men's frontier town was vanishing quickly at the end of the 1850s, but it is still salient in the residential patterns marked by bachelor living, which is especially evident in a directory that lists few women. Other sources, such as Fredrika Bremer's mention of the Norwegian cook at Governor Ramsey's home in 1850 and the Methodist records that tell of Anne Hovey and Ingeborg Gilberts's coming to work as domestics, suggest that young Scandinavian women in town may also have lived dispersed around its streets—as residents of boardinghouses or as live-in servants.

One result of these living arrangements was the probable delay of community formation. Family residences among Scandinavians were still in the minority. The majority in the Nordic nationality groups consisted of unattached men and women who lived scattered across much of the central commercial district—wherever rooms were available—or as help in the non-Scandinavian residences of families sufficiently prosperous to employ servants. The more successful Scandinavian men resided in hotels. A sliding scale in the quality of rooms literally followed the slopes down to the riverside loading areas: the few professionals and highly skilled craftsmen lived higher up, and the unskilled laborers farther down, with the majority of shopkeepers in the middle. Saloonkeeper Anton Ness lived above his bar on Third Street between Washington and Franklin, but most of the shopkeepers boarded at another address. These shops, the two churches, the clerics' homes, and a few skilled workers' homes, however, all cluster on the east side of town around Jackson and Temperance and Tenth Streets. This east-side concentration was the initial locus and would remain the main center of Scandinavian settlement in St. Paul. At the same time, however, the congregational histories mention a higher number of Swedish residents to the east as far up as Tenth Street and a clustering of Norwegians a few blocks farther north around Canada and Thirteenth Streets and into the Mount Airy section of town.[46]

The Rise and Fall of St. Anthony and Great Prospects of Minneapolis by 1861

Focused on agricultural potential, the Reverend Claus Lauritz Clausen and his Norwegian immigrant constituency had little or no interest in the industrial potential of the waterfalls. Because of the era's technology, the falls represented the critical asset that distinguished the development of St. Anthony and Minneapolis. The two towns at the falls emerged when the industrial strength of the United States rested chiefly on power generated by transferring the force of falling water to machinery through waterwheels. Between them, the river fell a greater distance—and so held more potential for economic exploitation—than the waterfalls that powered the nation's most modern and profitable Massachusetts mill towns. Years before Clausen saw the falls, there were eyes that had seen what he could not and minds that had planned futures he did not choose.[47]

From the time of the seventeenth-century French explorers, the potential of the falls for power had attracted visitors from Europe, where waterwheels had been in use for centuries. When Zebulon Pike negotiated the purchase of the military reserve from the Dakota in 1805 to assert American control in the area, he was careful to place the falls inside its boundary. To change logs into lumber for building a fort there in 1820, Commander Josiah Snelling had soldiers build the first structure erected by European Americans within the boundaries of present-day Minneapolis, a rude sawmill on the east side of the river some feet below the falls. Three years later, he initiated another of the uses typically made of waterpower by ordering troops to build a gristmill to make flour for bread—which on that first occasion was so inedible that its issue to the soldiers nearly led to mutiny. The critical era for the birth and growth of towns at the falls, however, came in the later 1830s, when a few ambitious white men saw the tide of American settlement approach Minnesota. With it they assumed would soon come the end of military control over the banks of the falls, the removal of Native titles to the land, and a rush to develop mill towns on both sides of the river. While the Falls of St. Anthony became North America's "best-known tourist attractions," these men laid their strategies.[48]

In the meantime, the falls' fame spread information about the military reservation and the Dakota lands near it, helping to strengthen the trickle of European American settlers to sites on both sides of the river that were nearer the falls than to St. Paul. To begin with, this population was much like that at the older settlement downstream, a mixture of Dakota and Ojibwe visiting ancient homelands, French Canadian and American trappers and traders, people who had intermarried with Natives or were the offspring of those unions, former soldiers and refugees at the fort, and missionaries to the Dakota. As at St. Paul, Dakota villages were just slightly farther west, in this case on the shores of the chain of lakes inside today's Minneapolis. The growth of this European American population led the fort's commander, Joseph Plympton, in 1838 to eject squatters and people earlier permitted to settle on the military reservation. Plympton's unspoken motives were to free the east bank of the falls from military control just prior to its release from Native ownership. He hoped to lay claim to the vital plot by the falls before anyone knew how he had managed it. Unfortunately for him, Franklin Steele, a young shopkeeper at Fort Snelling with political connections, became apprised of ratification when the news came on July 15, 1838, and got ahead of the commander. Having met the requirements for improving the claim in the night, he sat eating breakfast and unwilling to budge when Plympton's men arrived.[49]

These events became one more instructive tale for settlers and developers alike. Rushing in to secure claims at the birth of frontier towns and cities was also an essential part of what newcomers, immigrant or native-born, learned about how to make their way and do well in America. Steele, Plympton, and all the others who staked out claims on the east bank of the Mississippi "and in the whole wedge of ceded land that was Minnesota in 1838" were squatters. They relied on the American tradition that squatters had preemptive possession by first occupancy and that the government would let them purchase their claims at minimal prices when the land was put up for public sale. The same diverse mix of peoples who had squatted on the military reserve also squatted on the ceded east bank land. The "flood of immigration in 1847" in anticipation of the land sale, however, consisted largely of New Englanders and transplanted New Englanders who had lived for a time in states from Ohio to Wisconsin. People from specific parts of northern New England were particularly notable. Relatives followed relatives. School classmates from Vermont went west together. The family and local community migration that characterized movement from Norway and other European nations was just as typical of the westering of old-stock Americans.[50]

The outlines of settled life soon appeared. The first settlers bought and sold land as if they held legal deeds. Pioneer real-estate barons arose. No one tried to usurp the old settlers' rights when the time to buy came. The next year, the pioneer real-estate developers subdivided their acres at the falls and registered town plats showing streets and building lots, and the boomtown years began. The population skyrocketed from three hundred in 1848 to nearly three thousand when Minneapolis was incorporated as a city in 1856. Boardinghouses, homes, stores, and mills were thrown up with great speed, much as they were in St. Paul during those hectic years. St. Anthony produced twelve million board feet of lumber a year by the latter date and boasted that a flour mill with growing capacity on the river's Hennepin Island was a harbinger of things to come. In the 1850s, St. Anthony's widely spaced buildings were scattered up the slope from the river, its empty lots and even its streets often strewn with pigs and piles of lumber. Above the roar of the falls, one could hear the incessant whine of the saws.

Yet in 1857, St. Paul hotel owner James M. Winslow opened a two-hundred-room luxury hotel overlooking this scene. Winslow House, he boasted, commanded a "full view of the falls" and the "finest views of the cities of St. Anthony and Minneapolis." Thousands of well-to-do southerners came upriver with their household slaves to escape the summer heat and see the famous falls of the Mississippi by the "New England of the West" until the Civil War broke out in 1861.[51]

The peaceful meeting of American sectional cultures by the Minnesota river towns had actually ended the year before. Recalling the Dred Scott decision involving an enslaved man kept at Fort Snelling in 1836, Eliza Winston, an enslaved woman brought to Winslow House as a babysitter and personal maid, alerted free Blacks and white abolitionists in Minneapolis that she wished to win her liberty by virtue of being in a free state. Primarily because abolitionists secretly spirited her to Canada shortly after a local judge confirmed her freedom, the violence that broke out between local pro- and antislavery demonstrators ended. The collapse brought to St. Anthony by the Panic of 1857 inspired some residents to view the Winston affair as the loss of the city's last economic support, as fewer slave owners came to town for their holidays. From a peak of 4,689 in 1857, the city's population dwindled to 3,499 by the end of the Civil War, and its economy recovered only after it became a part of its sister city across the falls in 1872.

Minneapolis developed later because its site remained within the Fort Snelling reserve when Joseph Plympton placed the east side of the falls outside the military precinct. The west side became the object of mounting pressure from squatters. In 1849 the great prize they sought, control over the military's west bank mills and with them the all-important western water rights, went instead to an outsider whose political connections were apparently better than theirs. The War Department granted Congressman Robert Smith of Illinois a lease on the mills. The year after the Dakota signed land-cession treaties, 1852, witnessed the takeoff of the west-side boom. "Sooners," settlers who rushed to stake out claims while waiting for the treaties to be ratified, grabbed up every remaining available bit of the military reserve.[52]

It took two years' lobbying for the squatters to secure preemption rights from the government. Finally, they could buy their property in 1855, when Minneapolis was incorporated as a city. The heavily New England and Middle States settlers grew from a few hundred to more than fifteen hundred and established stores, social and business clubs, churches, and political groups by 1857. As Lucile Kane keenly notes about the causes of the later but also much greater success of Minneapolis, the west-side waterpower owners did little to foster a settlement, but, on the other hand, their business acumen, trust in each other, and long-term view of their investment bequeathed the area a tardy but sure future. Mary Wingerd concisely summarizes the situation of the three river towns in the later part of the decade, commenting that the "panic was a blow from which the [St. Anthony] company never recovered, [and while] St. Paul was devastated by the 1857 crash, the setback was not nearly so severe for Minneapolis. Incorporated for less than a year, it did not have as far to fall. In fact the panic cleared the board of fly-by-night speculators and investors, leaving the development of the new city in the hands of a small group of New Englanders who had the resources not only to survive but to profit from the crash."[53]

The Falls Communities on the Eve of the Civil War

The *St. Anthony and Minneapolis Directory, 1859–1860,* like its nearest chronological counterpart in St. Paul, reveals the reigning attitudes of the time and place and also provides some information about the beginnings of Scandinavian settlement. The historical sketch that opens this directory is remarkable by comparison with its downriver companion for the complete absence of references to foreign-born immigrants or people with non-American ancestry. Thus, of course, it makes a silent comment, especially when one notes that the sketch does list by name the first settlers and prominent people in the "dual city" by the falls. A single one, Pierre Bottineau, among the dozens of people given prominence here, has other than an Anglo-American name. Repeated phrases emphasize progress quickly made "far out on the Frontier, in an Indian country" by the tirelessly energetic pioneers. In descending order, the first entrepreneurial developers and builders; the first doctor, minister, and schoolteacher; and one or two skilled craftsmen receive credit. All of these are male save one, the Yankee "school marm."[54]

After an introduction that credits the rapid achievement locally entirely to the efforts of old-stock Americans, it strikes the reader with particular force when the only explicit reference to foreign-born immigrants comes unexpectedly in the alphabetical listing of people with their occupations and approximate residences. After "Sprewgrocer, S, wagon maker, h[ome] 2nd bt Wood and St. Paul," one suddenly reads the following joke, an ethnic slur on German immigrants: "Sphikenshpokenblunggerfungger, Hans Von, Main Street, nr sidewalk." It is an open question how much one should infer from the inclusion of this attempt at editorial humor, but the obvious points lie in the implication that German is a comically incomprehensible language, that Germans supposedly love titles, and, it is suggested, that Germans are homeless people or lack the industry to provide themselves with housing. This is very different from the stereotyped but generally positive characterization of Germans in the contemporaneous St. Paul directory, where they are said to exhibit steady industry. Since Germans bear the brunt of the only mention of foreigners in a listing where old-settler Bottineau is the single other non-Anglo worth mentioning, moreover, the attitude shown suggests at best an environment unaccustomed to the immigrants from northwestern Europe who were arriving in the United States at the time. More likely, the "joke" is a relatively minor example of the nativism, the dislike of the foreign that included these immigrants, which rose to a climax in America just before the Civil War.[55]

It appears that the towns at the falls had a nearly equal number of American churches at the time. The directory catalogs seven congregations in St. Anthony and eight in Minneapolis. The Minneapolis congregations include no Catholic institutions, but two Presbyterian and two Baptist groups as well as Congregational, Methodist, and Episcopal churches and an evangelical sect. Across the falls one could affiliate with an identical range of mainline Protestant groups or the Universalist church. The directory includes no Lutheran congregations and names no institutions having parishioners belonging to a particular national background. All the clergy have Anglo-American names except for the priest at the Catholic church in St. Anthony, the Reverend F. Fayolle. The same Yankee dominance appears in the political and civic leaders outlined here. No foreign-sounding names suggest immigrant group representation among aldermen, the police, or firefighters, such as those found in St. Paul. In similar fashion, four Freemason, one Order of Foresters, and two temperance lodges are found in the falls communities, but the two or three likely Irish names among the dozens of lodge officers noted stand out because of their rarity. Fraternal activity organized by nationality group, like the German turnverein in St. Paul, is completely absent here. The staffs of schools in all three cities were apparently entirely old-stock American. On the other hand, the directory for the boomtowns at the falls is distinguishable from the catalog of economic activity downriver at St. Paul in boasting a much lengthier and detailed list of business enterprises, especially those developing the waterpower, but mentions no unions among the workers at the falls.[56]

The available sources do not suggest that the St. Anthony–Minneapolis directory misnamed or left out Scandinavian or Norwegian immigrant institutions, as did the St. Paul catalog. There were none near the falls to be included. The weight of the evidence is rather that the origins and development of these two communities prior to the Civil War may have owed less than St. Paul to the large immigrant groups arriving from Europe in the 1830s, '40s, and '50s. Published census reports that covered these communities in the territorial enumeration of 1857 and the 1860 federal count of the state tallied only whites, without reference to birthplace. The manuscript schedules of the 1857 census lend credence to this view, at least with regard to the Norwegian-born and their children. At that point, the enumerators found but two single Norwegian-born individuals in all of Hennepin County, where the dual cities then lay. In 1860, the federal census manuscripts include one more Norwegian. The local ethnic historian, Carl G. O. Hansen, identifies one of the three—Andrew Matteson, a blacksmith working in St. Anthony. He also claims that "only four Scandinavians are known to have located in Minneapolis or St. Anthony during the fifties" and gives a few facts about the two Swedes and one Dane in question.[57]

The actual listings from the dual cities' directory cast doubt on Hansen's and the census enumerators' information. Conversely, it is evident that the mixed European Natives and French or French Canadians of the falls' pioneer period receive little attention. In the dual cities' directory, Native Americans seem no more than an initial impediment overcome. The St. Paul writer describes their former presence as an element of departed romance. These attitudes help explain the surprise with which so many white Minnesotans witnessed the Dakota War of 1862. A later section of this chapter discusses the effects of that conflict on Norwegian Americans in the river cities and their rural hinterland.[58]

The introductory sketch in the St. Anthony and Minneapolis directory states that the combined population of the dual cities in 1860 was 12,000, but the US decennial tabulations put the total at 5,809, with 3,254 of those in St. Anthony and 2,555 in Minneapolis. Like the St. Paul directory, this one exaggerates community numbers, but here the inflation is more than a doubling of the falls cities' actual size.[59]

No fewer than forty people with commonly Scandinavian names appear in the 1859–60 directory, nearly equally distributed between the two communities at the falls. Twenty-four of the names consist of Andersons, Johnsons, and Thompsons—surnames that are not unusual among people of British ancestry in the United States. While it is perhaps probable that a large majority of these men (no women appear) were not Scandinavians, it is unlikely that none of them were. If one supposes that the immigrants were fairly new arrivals, they might be among the relatively unskilled transients that the directory caught when its tabulations occurred. Thus, the eight single men living as boarders with no occupations might include Scandinavian men trying their luck in town. While it is doubtful that a merchant and a physician-druggist named Anderson are anything but old-stock Americans, it is more difficult to consider the two "lumber dealers" named Hanson and the grocer and provisioner called "R. Olsen" anything but Scandinavian Americans. In addition, there are laborers and teamsters named Bull, Hanson, and Nelson, a stonecutter called Matson, and a handful of carpenters and other skilled craftsmen with equally Scandinavian-sounding names. And then, of course, one can only wonder if at least a few young, single—and uncounted—women of Norwegian, Swedish, Irish, or German birth may have worked as domestics for visiting tourists at the Winslow House or as live-in domestics in the rapidly growing dual cities. But while they were a tiny presence among the Mississippi river towns, Norwegian and Swedish homesteaders were settling the vast rural areas of territorial Minnesota in much greater numbers.[60]

The Civil War and Dakota War Heritage for the Postwar Decades

As the historian of Norwegian America Odd S. Lovoll has expressed it, the Civil War era is a "heroic and dramatic period in the history of the Norwegians, as well as of other immigrant groups, idealized by later generations and given great symbolic value." Estimates of the number of Norwegians from the Upper Midwest who fought, Lovoll notes, reflect the relative newness of settlement in these states: three thousand men from Wisconsin, at least eight hundred from Minnesota, and more than four hundred from Iowa. Given the geographic patterns of Norwegian settlement and later internal migration among these states, it is likely that many of these men's descendants lived or still reside in the regional hinterland or municipal limits of today's Twin Cities.

The Fifteenth Wisconsin Regiment, commanded by the most famous Norwegian hero of the war, Colonel Hans Christian Heg, has deservedly received much attention. It was the only regiment composed almost exclusively of Norwegians, and Heg recruited his countrymen in the above-named states as well as in Illinois, including an entire company of men from Chicago. In 1916 Waldemar Ager, a well-known Norwegian American writer whose works were much read and whose views much respected, memorialized the Fifteenth Regiment in *Oberst Heg og hans Gutter* (Colonel Heg and His Boys). His choice of topic and the wide popularity of the volume among his compatriots testifies to the central importance of the war for the group's evolving sense of itself and its place in American history and society. This was an armed struggle for the elimination of slavery and the preservation of the Union that occurred when the greatest part of the Norwegians in this country were foreign-born and could testify to their patriotic loyalty to America by risking their lives.[61]

Ager's account includes a detailed register of the men who fought in the Fifteenth Regiment that, along with other information, indicates the residence of each at the time he was mustered into service. Although there is some uncertainty concerning place names, about forty of the men in the register came from Minnesota. Despite the attractions of serving in an all-Norwegian regiment, a host of factors led Norwegians in Minnesota to enlist in their home state. Not least of these were the recruiting activities of fellow Scandinavian Minnesotans. Ole Paulson, who later served as the first pastor of Trinity Lutheran Church near downtown Minneapolis and as a major figure in the development of the city's Norwegian community after the war, became one of these recruiters in 1861. Paulson was a young man considering ministry while farming among Swedes and Norwegians in Carver County, just southwest of the city, when hostilities began. Americans who knew of his ability to communicate well with both Swedes and Norwegians in the area pressed him to become a recruiter. He eventually agreed to serve in this fashion, telling himself and comforting his wife with the promise that he would, of course, not enlist because he was soon entering a theological seminary. Hesitant at first, Paulson tells in his memoirs how he grew to be an effective recruiter and assembled twenty or so Swedes and Norwegians so committed to enlistment that together they set off for St. Paul, where the men had to report to muster into a regiment. Once there, as the men lined up to enlist, Paulson moved to the rear, wished them well, and prepared to leave. But they vehemently protested: this was not at all what they expected, and if he was not with them, then none of them would enlist. So it was that Paulson served in the Union Army, despite his promise to his aggrieved wife and before beginning his theological studies.[62]

The Minnesota adjutant general's report of 1866, a book of more than nine hundred pages, contains careful summary tables of brief but moving service records, by regiment and company, of all those from the state who fought for the Union cause. Large numbers of Minnesota Norwegians and some of their American-born children were among the people of many nationalities, the report documents, who enlisted, served, were wounded, and died in the war. As one would expect, the largest part of the Norwegian enlistees came from the southeastern counties of the state, where the immigrant group was already very concentrated by the end of the 1850s. Fillmore, Goodhue, Houston, Rice, and Scott Counties are among those from which came the majority of Norwegian soldiers. But among the men who served in the First and Second Minnesota Regiments, who came mostly from St. Paul, St. Anthony, and Minneapolis, are a dozen or so Norwegians—mostly listed as living in the state capital, but also including men like Paulson from the counties nearest the Cities.[63]

The Third Minnesota Volunteer Infantry Regiment occupied a very special place in the state's Scandinavian contribution to the war effort, one that has gone generally unheralded in studies of the ethnic group. Recruiting for this regiment did not begin until the fall of 1861, when the North's fortunes were dimmed by early Confederate successes and the state's first regiments had already left. Therefore, as its official "Narrative" explains by way of introduction, the Third was drawn

> from all parts of the state, and the work was rather slow in the more sparsely settled counties. Even in such counties there were a few who were eager to go to the war, but it was often too great a pang for their parents to consent. . . . Instances occurred where, after a full talk and consideration of the matter, a young husband agreed to enlist, but the wife, on hearing his decision, burst into tears, and seemed unable to consent to spare him. . . . If one had dreamed that in the course of a year our peaceful frontier would have been swept by Indian war, success in recruiting would probably have been much less than it was.[64]

Sentimental ties and fears of losing loved ones forever through battlefield fatalities no doubt played a strong part in wives' and parents' reluctance to consent, in Minnesota as everywhere, but just as clearly, this was the frontier of European American settlement, and homesteaders needed their men to carve farms from the pristine prairie sod. Farming there, just making subsistence farming work, let alone raising cash crops like wheat, required all the men the pioneers could get—especially as they adapted perforce to limiting women's work to the house and chickens. Among the outpost farmers in Minnesota were Scandinavians as well as Germans, French, and other nationalities.

Some of the young Norwegians and Swedes on frontier farms enlisted despite family ties and economic needs because Hans Mattson and others, such as Ole Paulson, recruited them for Company D of the Third Regiment, which consisted entirely of Norwegian- and Swedish-born immigrants. Compatriots from more populous agricultural areas with large numbers of Scandinavian settlers joined them. Of the 154 men registered in the adjutant's report listing for Company D, 69 percent are Swedes and 31 percent Norwegians. The company officers are more evenly divided, and while the commanding officer, Captain Mattson, was Swedish, his first lieutenant was Norwegian, which suggests that there was some attempt to attract both nationalities and give them a kind of parity. However, the company is called "mostly Swedes" by the regimental historian, who otherwise remembers only that the Scandinavian soldiers introduced neighboring companies to the practice of singing the Lutheran doxology after evening roll call, carrying on that tradition from the army in Sweden.[65]

The story of the Third Regiment's wartime experience is a series of tragedies that heaped disgrace and high casualties on all its companies. Company D's forces, for example, originally totaling seventy-three men, had to be replenished with sixty-nine recruits and two substitutes before the end of the war. That was in some ways not the worst of it, because during the regiment's first engagement at Murfreesboro, Tennessee, its old-stock commander Henry C. Lester of St. Paul, fooled by the bluff and arrogant bravado of Confederate general Nathan Bedford Forrest, asked his officers to vote with him for surrender. When the proposal failed to win a majority, he called a second vote after crucial opponents to the idea had left and got his majority. The Third's officers were imprisoned by the Confederates, and those who voted for surrender were dismissed in disgrace by Minnesota's government. The regiment's rank and file soldiers had to sign a pledge not to fight for the North again until they were exchanged with Confederate troops in the same situation, which meant they spent listless months in St. Louis with plenty of time to weigh how events beyond their control had made them look like cowards. Luckily for Company D, Captain Mattson was in Minnesota when the surrender took place, and his substitute was absent from the votes on the regiment's fate. Thus the company's men were at least absolved of having leaders who "contributed to their disgrace, and when they were exchanged, it was untarnished Mattson who led them."[66]

The ultimate irony was that the whole regiment, publicly still a symbol of the state's dishonor, was shunted off to fight the Dakota when that war broke out, rather than put into a central theater of the Civil War. Thus the men from the frontier found themselves defending their own homesteads or ones very much like theirs despite their earlier decision to enlist in the Civil War. A conservative tally of Scandinavian names among the 531 European Americans killed in the Dakota War indicates that sixty-seven of the dead or 12.7 percent were Swedes or Norwegians. That figure is more than twice the percentage of the state's population that was born in those two countries at the 1860 census. Even allowing for continuing immigration in the following two years, there can be little doubt that the two groups were overrepresented among outpost homesteaders and, consequently, among the slain. There was a strange justice for the Scandinavians in Company D to restore their honor by defending their own.[67]

For several years before fighting broke out between Dakota and Anglo-Americans, bitter resentment grew among the Dakota living nearest to white settlement. The Native Americans gave up their land in what became Minnesota and agreed to settle on a twenty-mile-wide reservation that extended 140 miles along the Minnesota River, according to treaties signed in 1837 and 1851. These agreements with the federal government promised the Dakota annual payments for food and shelter in return for the land that had traditionally supported them through hunting and gathering. As early as the 1820s, however, these resources showed signs of depletion due to the Dakota's growing dependence on the fur trade with Anglo-Americans and appearance of the colonists' forts and farming homesteads, which undermined the Dakota's economic and cultural independence. By 1862, although around a quarter of Dakota families were taking up Anglo-American farm methods, the majority attempted somewhat futilely to continue their traditional hunting life. Meanwhile a métis population of Franco- and Anglo-Dakota grew up through family formation between Native and European Americans. Many of these people as well as a small minority of Dakota became Christians in the same years.

This context created conflict. Dakota complained of failing at farming and finding too little wild game to sustain them. Settlers complained of Dakota hunting on land they had ceded. Métis, Native American, and Anglo-American households found themselves working at cross-purposes. Dakota and reservation agents interpreted treaty texts differently, especially in regard to the debt of individual Dakota to traders or reservation agency stores. Métis Dakota often found themselves in the middle of conflicts as they acted as translators and tried to explain one side to the other. When hunters and settlers turned on each other, life was lost. The federal government's preoccupation with the Civil War was the spark that ignited an explosive situation. During the critical months before the US–Dakota War broke out, Congress failed to pass legislation to appropriate funds for food and shelter for the Dakota, who faced starvation. The attacks on the reservation station and homesteaders were initiated mostly by young Dakota men with families to feed. These men overwhelmed their leaders' opposition to war and attacked.[68]

What happened to the Rosseland family is representative of important effects of the Dakota War on the Norwegian immigrant generation and European–Native relations in the state, including the Twin Cities. When Dakota men attacked the Rosseland homestead during the war, they killed the father and oldest son in the family, wounded the younger son, and carried away the oldest of four daughters. The mother, Guri Endreson Rosseland, hid in the root cellar with her youngest daughters until the Dakota left. In accounts of these events, Rosseland's heroic responses became the main lesson of the story. Celebration of her as a frontier ideal developed a popular version of her narrative that appeared in newspapers and later in local and regional histories. Putting her to the fore, it made helpless wounded men of those she said assisted her and her surviving family to safety. In the public domain, she gained larger-than-life qualities—retaining the calm, clarity of mind, and physical strength and endurance needed to dress the party's wounds, help them into an oxcart, and lead them safely to a town farther east.[69]

Four years passed before Rosseland could put words on paper about what happened at the family homestead. Even then, she wrote about it only in a private letter to her closest relatives in Hardanger in western Norway. She apologized for not sharing the details of her fate earlier because she had been incapable of thinking of "anything except being murdered, with my whole family." The story she tells rings with the unpretentious truth of one talking to her most intimate circle. A wider public did not know the letter's contents until her descendants allowed the historian Theodore Blegen to translate and publish it in 1929.

Rosseland's letter shows no wish to be a hero. She fervently thanks God for what mattered most: her own and her family members' survival, keeping her sanity, and receiving vital help from other people. She makes no attempt to understand the Native Americans who did this to her family. They are "wild men," savage pagans, and she concludes later in the letter, "God permitted this to happen thus, and I must accept my heavy fate and thank him." Native Americans constituted part of the alien strangeness, the unforeseeable nature of the new land she had come to and could explain only in the terms of her home culture's traditional faith.[70]

The State of Minnesota established a homestead historical site and monument at its centennial in 1958 to commemorate the heroism of frontier settlers during the Dakota War, choosing the Rosselands' farm, which had been on the edge of European American settlement. The popular image of Rosseland and the heroic version of her narrative held sway for over half a century and remains a well-known pioneer story today. Such highly dramatic experiences of the pioneer generation have evidently played a part in the group's evolving ethnic identity. In the celebration of Guri Rosseland as a frontier ideal, for example, we see both the entire ethnic group gaining legitimacy and an American national identity in formation.

Rosseland retained the title to her family's land and returned to that neighborhood four years later. Though she could not bear to live in the farm's original home, she rejected the often proffered advice to sell the

After the Dakota War in 1862, the stories of attacks on homesteads became legend in county histories, where the bravery of women like Guri Rosseland, a Norwegian immigrant, were the stuff of frontier heroism. Her family's cabin, shown here, was restored by the state as a historic site for the Minnesota centenary in 1958. *MNHS*

land. Eager to see her own family members get ahead in America, she disliked losing the practical advantage she had gained by settling early on the Minnesota borderland.[71]

This story also contradicts the view that Norwegians often arrived in the Upper Midwest with westering Americans, Germans, other Scandinavians, and Irish immigrants in a second wave of newcomers. According to this conventional narrative, the initial wave, the first whites the Native Americans had seen, was generally composed of explorers, military men, and trappers, who had little interest in owning land. Land speculators from states farther east followed them and were the harbingers of the American and immigrant pioneer farmers of the second wave, those who were often the first European Americans to cultivate the land and erect homes on it. However, the Rosselands and other Norwegian immigrant families, according to family history passed on to later generations, were the first settlers on the land that they later bought from American authorities.

Conclusion

The Norwegian communities in the Twin Cities have always exhibited a special form of the common mix of greenhorns newly arrived and a large, more acclimated Norwegian American population because of in-migration from the Cities' vast hinterland. Inspecting any map of the United States makes obvious the unusually long distances in all directions between the Twin Cities and another large urban center. In the entire Upper Midwest no town or city—not even Duluth—came near to approaching the magnetic attraction of Minneapolis–St. Paul. Moreover, no other urban area in the nation, not Chicago or New York or Seattle, was surrounded by anything like the density and geographic extent of rural Norwegian American communities as the Twin Cities. If members of the ethnic group in this unexampled hinterland migrated to urban work, chances were good that eventually they would find themselves in the Cities.

Prominent among the causal processes of urbanization in the Upper Midwest, as in other highly agricultural regions, however, were technological revolutions in farming methods and machinery, transportation and marketing crises, and periods of low farm commodity prices.

These trends and circumstances have repeatedly reduced the need for agricultural workers and so made it necessary for many children in traditionally large rural families to find their own farm or leave for work in towns or cities. From the end of the 1870s onward, moving to the city usually looked both less expensive and more promising. With the passage of time, moreover, Norwegian Americans had increased personal connections that could help them make realities of the opportunities and exciting social life that beckoned from afar in Minneapolis–St. Paul. The urbanization of Norwegian Americans with these cities as their primary destination has been a constant of their history in the Upper Midwest. The essential point is that a very large number of late twentieth-century Norwegian Americans in the Cities have a double heritage of rural culture—of rural traditions in Norway and of rural American pioneer traditions—that they have brought with them decade by decade in the ongoing movement to the Cities.

Rural Norwegian immigrants to the Upper Midwest brought transformed habits of mind with them when they arrived in Minneapolis–St. Paul. Through their experience of homesteading on Native American land they became aware of the racial and ethnic hierarchy on the frontier of white settlement and formed attitudes about their status relative to that of other groups. They had learned how to compete with other settlers to find and keep the best farmland before it was made available by the American authorities. Some of them had personally experienced—or knew people directly affected by—the Dakota War. On the question of slavery, they chose overwhelmingly to support the Union, in uniform or at home. They had in these ways completed the first chapter of their relational history with other groups in America.

The growing mass of the multigenerational, increasingly well-established Norwegian American communities in the Twin Cities naturally also enhanced the urban area's attractiveness for emigrants arriving directly from Norway. In the waves of Norwegian immigration between 1880 and 1893, 1900 and 1914, 1920 and 1929, and 1946 and 1960 were large numbers of people who knew of the region's unparalleled Norwegian American population base and who not infrequently also had relatives or friends and acquaintances in the Cities or their hinterland. Thus, the Cities' magnetism retained its force for Norwegians and Norwegian Americans over time.

CHAPTER THREE

In the Aftermath

An Immigrant Subculture Takes Root in the River Boomtowns after the Civil and Dakota Wars

[1865–1880]

ENORMOUS CHANGES TOOK PLACE IN MINNEAPOLIS–ST. PAUL AND THE CITIES' Norwegian communities in the first decade and a half after the Civil and Dakota Wars. The aftereffects of the wars and the influence of their veterans strongly molded the following decades. With the coming of peace, the energies of the nation and the state redirected themselves toward economic development, immigration from Europe, and westward expansion. Departures from Norway to the United States mounted to a peak in the years immediately after 1865. The Norwegian American community in the expanding river towns evolved into new forms as the number of local Norwegian-born residents increased rapidly thanks to immigration directly from Norway and secondary migration from the surrounding countryside. Members of the growing nationality group increasingly left shared Scandinavian institutions to form their own separate clubs, associations, and congregations. Making up a significant part of the total urban population in both cities by 1880, Norwegians or Scandinavians developed well-known districts, with religious and educational institutions as well as a variety of leisure-time organizations and commercial enterprises. Socioeconomic distinctions among Norwegians grew. The group's small number of professional and educational elites played an important part in leading their community and earning it recognition in the greater urban area. The large and quickly growing Norwegian American laboring class performed a major portion of the Cities' domestic service and construction work. Even as they adjusted to contact with other immigrants and Americans—especially the large Swedish, German, and Irish communities—many foreign-born Norwegians lived a full life while speaking their native tongue as they worked and associated with compatriots.

Massive Immigration Fuels the Postwar Boom

Immigration from Europe to the Upper Midwest continued during the Civil War, although at a lower rate. Appealing especially to Scandinavians, the immigration route down the St. Lawrence River to Quebec and across the Great Lakes to Minnesota seemed relatively safe because it was distant from the battlefields. In addition, the Homestead Act of 1862 encouraged land-starved Scandinavian immigrants to follow that route to nearby "free" homesteads in Minnesota and the Dakota Territory. With the war's end, an unprecedented wave of immigration from Norway began. The number of departures from the country tripled in one year, jumping from under 5,000 in 1865 to more than 15,000 the year after. The wave crested at a peak of some 17,000 in 1868 before dropping back to Civil War levels in 1875. This was the beginning of mass emigration from Norway, and the timing of the first large wave from the country could hardly have been more auspicious for concentrated Norwegian settlement in western Minnesota, the Red River Valley, and the eastern Dakotas—vital parts of the Norwegian American hinterland to the Twin Cities in the future.[1]

Extensive recruitment efforts spurred emigration from Norway to the United States. Steamship companies and the State of Minnesota sent agents throughout the length and breadth of Norway and Norwegian America to promote migration. The federal and state governments encouraged railroads to recruit settlers to Minnesota by granting the companies acreage in the state that amounted to an area twice the size of Massachusetts. The state first officially promoted immigration by distributing literature extolling Minnesota's advantages in Norwegian and several other northern European languages in 1858, but its campaign became more systematic after the Civil War, when competition among the western states intensified.[2]

In 1867, Minnesota established a Board of Immigration composed of the governor and secretary of state as ex officio members and a prominent Swedish American, Colonel Hans Mattson—who had risen to commanding officer of the Third Minnesota Regiment—as secretary and chief actor for the board. For a time, the board also included the Reverend John Ireland, later the Catholic archbishop of St. Paul. This group aimed to influence immigrants' choice of destination with publicity in several languages as well as agents and interpreters who met the immigrants at their port of entry and shepherded them on their journey to Minnesota. The state also provided temporary housing, offered employment services, and assisted immigrants in finding land.

Minnesota's legislature expanded the state board's activities between 1868 and 1872, placing agents in Germany and Scandinavia. Mattson twice traveled there and set off with parties of Swedes and Norwegians to Minnesota. Two individuals who influenced Minnesota's immigration policy in the direction of recruiting more Scandinavians were Norwegian American state senator Lars K. Aaker from Goodhue County in southeastern Minnesota, an early center of heavy Norwegian settlement, and F. Sneedorff Christensen, a Danish-born editor of early Dano-Norwegian newspapers in that part of the state and Minneapolis–St. Paul. Their recommendations seem to have convinced Governor William R. Marshall to name the Norwegian journalist Paul Hjelm-Hansen as a special agent of the state Board of Immigration in 1869.[3]

Hjelm-Hansen's report about conditions in Minnesota was the more persuasive because in Norway he was known as a capable journalist with critical views of the United States. He journeyed to America in 1867 as the emissary of the Norwegian Society for the Advancement of Public Information (*Selskabet for folkeoplysningens fremme*). Knowing his previous reputation in Norway, Christensen and Aaker realized how powerful positive reports from Hjelm-Hansen about conditions in Minnesota's Red River Valley could be, and indeed, he published an enthusiastic account in Norwegian American newspapers and several newspapers in Norway. Though he extolled the rural life, Hjelm-Hansen's message came from journals in Norway's or America's cities, making urban settlements in the United States better known in the homeland. The recruiting campaign also attracted Norwegian immigrants to cities for a variety of reasons. In the 1860s, emigration from Norway's cities first became significant, and these urban people often envisioned a future in an American city. Other newcomers worked in town for a while to buy land, tools, and equipment. Yet others had personal contacts who drew them to town. Letters from relatives or friends in America came from reliable firsthand knowledge and frequently enclosed the prepaid tickets that made a new life possible for the poorer classes of Norwegian society.

Rural Trials and Rising Urbanization

In the course of the 1870s, immigrants to the state and Minnesotans generally learned additional lessons about private responsibility for the common good and public support for portions of the larger community in crisis. The longer-settled agricultural counties in the southeast and south-central parts of the state enjoyed buoyant boom years from 1858 until 1870. These conditions encouraged the farmers in those areas, among them large contingents of German, Swedish, and Norwegian immigrants, to buy heavily into the new farm machinery—McCormick reapers and other devices—in order to expand production. The immigrant farmers wrote detailed letters home including statistics documenting the astounding harvests and material progress they experienced. Their eyewitness correspondence brought the rising crest of newcomers that washed over the state's western counties and into the Dakota Territory, following the investment advice of those who had arrived before them.[4]

Then the postwar recession took effect, and the bottom fell out of the agricultural commodity market in the early 1870s. Like an Old Testament plague, in 1873 clouds of grasshoppers descended on the western counties and stripped the fields bare. Not until 1878 did the insects disappear. In an age when self-reliance was a prized American ideal, especially on the frontier, people did not ask for public aid easily. Nor were governments accustomed to considering that public handouts were appropriate. Many families had relatives in the Cities and sought their assistance. Husbands, sons, and daughters took jobs in the Twin Cities, lived frugally, and sent home all the earnings they could spare in an effort to save the family homestead. Others left the countryside more permanently and took up nonagricultural occupations in the Cities. Migration to the city during periods of agricultural depression would become a long thread in the state's and the region's history.

These crises and disasters occurred precisely when considerable numbers of Norwegians were beginning to assume influence in township, city, county, and state governments. Immigrant farmers and workers found starkly revealed the fragility of the dreams on which they had founded their decision to leave their homelands. The events of the decade laid bare the mutual economic foundations and interdependence, the financial as well as personal relationships of city and country.

Between 1860 and 1870, the number of foreign-born and second-generation Norwegian Americans in Ramsey County including St. Paul grew by more than 420 percent. Expanding from sixty-seven people divided between twelve families and twenty-four individuals, Ramsey County's Norwegian community in 1870 included 282 people: thirty-nine families and 119 individuals. In Hennepin County, where the two communities by the falls lay, the rate of increase was much higher, in part because the 1860 census noted so few Norwegians there, just three individuals. Ten years later, after a staggering 295-fold increase, the county contained a Norwegian American population of 146 families and 312 individuals, 886 Norwegians in all. In one decade, primarily during the five years following the Civil War, Minneapolis had become the premier urban center for Norwegian settlement in the Upper Midwest.[5]

While the *rates* of increase are most impressive between 1860 and 1870, the actual numbers of Norwegian Americans residing in the three communities become more considerable by the end of the following decade, when the federal census bureau published figures on the number of foreign-born in towns and cities but not on the size of the second generation. By 1880 St. Paul's Norwegian-born population alone, 664 people, approached 2 percent of the city's 41,000 people, and the immigrant generation in Minneapolis, more than 2,600 residents, accounted for a little less than 5 percent of that city's nearly 47,000 people. (See Table 3.1 below.)[6]

TABLE 3.1

	1860	1870	1880	PERCENT OF CITY
Minneapolis	2,555	13,066	46,887	
Norwegian-born	?	?	2,651	(4.7%)
St. Paul	10,331	20,030	41,473	
Norwegian-born	?	?	664	(1.6%)

SOURCE: US Census for Minneapolis–St. Paul, 1860, 1870, 1880

Norwegian American War Veterans and Dakota War Survivors

Norwegian, Swedish, and Danish Americans who had served in the Civil War made up a small but much honored minority during the period of Scandinavian cooperation in the Twin Cities that lasted into the late 1880s. As Minnesota's Civil War regiments ceremoniously mustered out one after another in St. Paul during the spring and summer of 1865, along with the city's other communities, St. Paul's Norwegian Americans welcomed home their veterans, including a dozen or so men born in Norway with the surnames Bensen, Christensen, Johnson, Oleson, Peterson, and Skog. The Minnesota adjutant general's report for 1866 records that other Norwegian-born men from St. Paul did not return because they had either deserted or died during the war.[7]

Various companies and the Ninth Regiment composed mostly of men from Minneapolis or Hennepin County basked in a public fete some days after their return when they marched through the streets of town. According to the adjutant general's report, Minneapolis, whose Norwegian American community developed largely after the war, greeted only one native of Norway among its returning veterans. In nearby Carver, Washington, Dakota, Scott, Rice, and other counties, as well as in rural Hennepin County, however, were veterans who joined the migration into the city. Among the Norwegian veterans arriving in Minneapolis after the war was Albert E. Rice, who represented a district of Minneapolis in the state legislature in 1870 before returning to his hometown of Willmar, Minnesota, from which he was later elected lieutenant governor of the state. George H. Johnson was a veteran who

Civil War veterans parade with their battle flags on Cedar Avenue, Minneapolis, to the admiration of local crowds. ***MNHS***

became the first policeman of Scandinavian birth in Minneapolis in 1869 and began several terms as Hennepin County sheriff the year after. The Reverend Ole Paulson, the Civil War recruiter and member of the Ninth, played a leading role in the development of the city's Norwegian center in the Cedar-Riverside section in this era and preached two sermons annually on the wartime actions of the Dakota. During the war years he witnessed the deaths of comrades, neighbors, and friends at the hands of Dakota warriors. At its end, he was present at the execution of dozens of defeated Natives at Mankato.[8]

Not all veterans became prominent community leaders or politicians. In the postwar decades, however, a significant number of the Scandinavian Americans who rose to leadership positions in the Cities and state had seen military service in the Civil and/or Dakota War and found their business, political, and civic careers promoted as a result. Risking their lives for great national causes gained universal respect for veterans from all groups, and that public acknowledgment held particular importance for immigrant soldiers, many of whom also won American citizenship through military service. Until their deaths near the end of the century and beyond, such veterans often functioned as featured speakers and honored guests for Norwegian immigrant organizations. The group's war heroes and veterans provided political leaders who had won the respect of local society in general and so accorded respect and acceptance to the Norwegian immigrant subculture as a whole. Through these men's and women's experiences, the body of Norwegian immigrants partook in the major events and processes of American history and became Norwegian Americans.

Greenhorns from Norway and Norwegian American Pioneers from the Countryside

The Twin Cities' Norwegian American communities in the later 1860s and 1870s included a variety of groups, both newcomers coming directly from rural Norway in the first massive immigration wave and a mixture of people with prior experience in America. The latter included veterans and refugees of the Civil and Dakota Wars and agricultural crisis as well as the seekers of better fortune from among the Norwegian pioneers and their children. Reliable evidence does not exist for determining the relative proportions of greenhorn immigrants and longer-resident Norwegian Americans in this period. Contemporary newspaper accounts of the migration into the region from abroad, however, are unanimous in describing the 1866–73 wave as the movement of a mostly rural population from northern Europe traveling to the least-settled areas of the Upper Midwest to take up farming. Local histories and collections of biographies from the time, moreover, are replete with stories of men and women who moved to the Cities from longer-settled agricultural districts in northern Iowa, western Wisconsin, and southeastern and south-central Minnesota.[9]

The weight of historical memory and historians' accounts thus strongly suggest that the largest number of Norwegians in the Cities at this time were making their initial adjustments to city life but had already learned a considerable amount about American conditions and at least some English in the upper midwestern countryside. The newcomers directly from Norway very likely composed far less than a plurality in the emerging Norwegian American centers in St. Paul or by the Falls of St. Anthony. In their number were a few highly educated individuals, both clerics and other professionals trained in Norway and on the Continent, as well as people with connections to the highest levels of Norwegian society. More numerous among the newly arrived Norwegians were skilled craftsmen and women brought up with traditions of domestic work that would serve them well in affluent Twin Cities homes. The critical point, however, is that, despite their vital contributions, these Norwegians did not set the tone of Norwegian American life or the status of the Norwegian American communities in the Cities.

It was instead those with a *double rural experience*, first a life in rural Norway, and then a history as frontier farmers and war veterans of the Upper Midwest, who set the foundation for their compatriots' rapid advance in St. Paul and Minneapolis. For these people—the Dakota and Civil War veterans, the re-settled civilian refugees from the Indian war, and the flood of other new initiates to urban life—the first accommodation to the United States was for the most part to rural and agricultural midwestern ways. Accommodation to life in St. Paul or Minneapolis was a second adjustment, this time to urban America, by people who had already picked up some English, acquired some sense of the customs of their adopted country, and, in many cases, won respect or acceptance for their participation in war and frontier pioneering. In the course of the 1870s, new contingents from the countryside would join them. The spread of customs limiting women's outdoor work and the introduction of farm machinery during men's wartime absence reduced the need for farmhands of both genders. The depressed agricultural economy of the 1870s and five years of grasshopper infestations in western Minnesota sent ruined farmers to town looking for other means of livelihood.[10]

On the other side of the coin were the powerful attractions of St. Paul or Minneapolis for both new immigrants and people relocating from the countryside. The decade of the 1870s witnessed the rise of Minneapolis to international fame as an industrial center. The city's sawmills produced such a prodigious amount of lumber that they quickly exceeded competitors' output, and the ripple effect of their success included the rise of vast lumberyards and sill, sash, window, and door firms. The start of the decade witnessed the wheat boom, when the record harvests of prairie "bonanza farms" deluged the city's gristmills. The extension of railroads in the state carried this ocean of grain into the industrial core by the falls with unprecedented speed and in unheard-of quantities. The multiplying jobs in St. Paul and Minneapolis became a powerful magnet for immigrant as well as native-born workers.[11]

Movements and Ties between the Cities and the Countryside

The rapidly developing economies of St. Paul and Minneapolis depended on seasonal labor migrations. Teamsters, draymen, and boatmen ferried goods out to the countryside from St. Paul's wholesale merchants. The city's railroad entrepreneurs, led by James J. Hill, assembled armies of men—among them many Scandinavian immigrants—into railroad gangs, and city outfitters followed their progress with shipments of supplies. Both cities, but especially the communities by the falls, lived by the cycles of saw and flour milling. For most of the 1870s, the seasonal timetables of timber and grain work set the dominant labor movements. In the fall, merchants and their clerks scurried to equip the many hundreds of men who left town in logging crews. Then the crack of axe against trunk sounded in the pine forests to the north, while relative silence settled over the Cities until the Mississippi thawed and logs jammed its springtime tumult from bank to bank. Whining saws shrilled through the air in later spring and summer after logging crews returned, ready for city entertainments and work in the sawmills after a winter of isolation. Simultaneously, the expanding flour industry went through another seasonal labor movement. As loggers arrived in town, other crowds of workers left to work on the vast acreages of the region's enormous bonanza farms, which covered huge tracts of prairie and yielded harvests of unprecedentedly large size. Approaching harvests saw the peak of agricultural laborers' outward migration, after which these wearied workers came back to town and slaked their thirst for relaxation and release.[12]

In human and economic terms, city and country were intimately bound together. Norway had long had a timber industry based on floating logs downriver to mills near the coast and traditions of agriculture

Using skills learned in the homeland, many young Norwegian men worked in Minnesota logging camps in the winter and floated timber down the Mississippi River to sawmills in north Minneapolis, where they worked in lumberyards in the summer.

founded on the seasonal movement of farmhands and servants for haying and harvest. Many a Norwegian immigrant therefore brought both skills and an acceptance of such work cycles, even though they kept him away from home and family for long periods. This strategy was how many families managed and how young single men tried to accumulate a nest egg in their homeland. There was, however, an unheard-of scale to these labor migrations in Minnesota. In Minneapolis and St. Paul, which quickly became bigger cities than any in Norway, large districts arose near the mills to meet the needs of seasonal workers. Here the city landscape consisted mostly of saloons, outfitting stores, and inexpensive lodging houses, where men were crammed in two or more to a bed and several beds to a room. The hugeness of it all transformed life for the immigrant, carrying him beyond what he had known at home. Groups of Norwegian immigrants in the nearby countryside found niches in tributary economies that flowed to the large economic sectors of the Cities. Some who lived along the Minnesota River, for example, felled trees and chopped them into firewood that barges carried upriver to St. Paul wholesalers. At the city levee, however, these entrepreneurs occasionally found themselves in pitched battles with Irish immigrants at the river dock who had found their niche by taking pay for unloading and stowing cargoes. Other Norwegian immigrant communities—in Carver County near the Cities—raised flax and produced household linens for sale in town.[13]

Just to the north of Minneapolis in Fridley and neighboring Brooklyn Township, the only Norwegian settlement of considerable size on the borders of the Twin Cities, a community of immigrants from Selbu in middle Norway, began to take shape during the Civil War. In the late 1860s and early 1870s, large numbers of these immigrants, called *Selbygg* in their native tongue, made their living as seasonal workers employed in Minnesota's pine forests in the winter and in Minneapolis sawmills, lumberyards, or building industries during the rest of the year. Ingeborg Levorsdatter Langeberg, the Norwegian woman who cooked for Territorial Governor Ramsey, played a central role in the origins of the Selbygg enclave, although she did not come from Selbu herself. She inherited her first husband's farm and fortune when he died. It was the news about Selbygg Mikkel Johnson's good fortune in marrying this affluent widow that brought a tide of people from that district of Norway to the Minneapolis area. Rumors of his marriage spread among Selbygg in Meeker County and then, through their letters home, in Selbu itself. Thus began a significant chain of migrations from Selbu to Brooklyn Township and Fridley.

Local historian Carl G. O. Hansen, who interviewed Mikkel and Ingeborg Johnson's daughter in the early 1900s, reports that on one occasion in 1866 a party of more than sixty immigrants arrived from Selbu. Because Mikkel could not find work for them all on nearby farms, some began rafting logs on the Mississippi while others took jobs on a nearby railroad project. During the course of the 1870s, increasing numbers moved to the northern reaches of the city as their main occupation became logging on the river and work in the sawmills that were locating in or near north Minneapolis. By the end of the decade, clusters of houses built or occupied by Selbygg appeared along stretches of streets from the rural districts near the edge of the city to the streets just north of its central commercial district. Some lived around Shingle Creek and Camden in the far north of the urbanizing area. Others gathered in the center of the "colony" near Twentieth Avenue North, Second Street, and Washington Avenue in an area that then amounted to little more than handfuls of recently built houses surrounded by prairie land. Finally, numbers of young, single Selbygg took up residence close to downtown in boardinghouses or in Selbygg family homes just north of the more densely built-up central milling district. According to Hansen's and other interviews with descendants of immigrants from Selbu in Minneapolis, the large majority of male wage earners in this community composed part of the seasonally mobile logging and sawmill labor force in the early years. Later, as family men who wanted to avoid long absences from home strove to get steady work in the lumberyards and construction trades in the city, the north Minneapolis Norwegian American community became more typical of the city's settled family neighborhoods.[14]

The early career of Andreas Ueland, later a prominent Minneapolis lawyer, judge, and civic leader, well illustrates a number of common features in the experience of Norwegian immigrants who moved in and out of the Twin Cities in the 1870s during their first years in Minnesota. One of thousands of younger sons who left Norway mostly because traditional inheritance laws gave the family farm undivided to the oldest son, Ueland briefly considered taking up teaching or a craft but felt disinclined to those kinds of work. The sole exceptional aspect of his situation was that his father, Ole Gabriel Ueland, was nationally famous for his long career as a member of Norway's parliament who championed the rights and interests of the country's small farmers. In his *Recollections of an Immigrant,* Andreas says that he caught an incurable case of America fever at eighteen when a visiting farmer from Houston County, Minnesota, told of the plentiful flat, fertile, stoneless soil there. Andreas left that same year in a party of thirty inspired by this farmer from southeastern Minnesota, but when they got to Houston County, he alone did not head for the farmer's homestead. Instead, he took the train to the next stop—Rushford, Minnesota—in his determination not to "crowd myself on somebody's hospitality."[15]

As a young immigrant, Andreas Ueland engaged in seasonal labor in town and country. He worked on outlying farms in the summer and studied law at night while working for the Minneapolis street department in the winter. *MNHS*

Less than an hour after walking into Rushford's village tavern and speaking only his native tongue to communicate, Andreas managed to find a Norwegian American farmer who hired him as a field hand. The family treated him well and he felt at home in the heavily Norwegian settlement, but Ueland stayed only ten days. After the other hired hand on the farm told him about "Minneapolis, the biggest city in the state and how it was booming," he felt that it must offer better prospects than grubbing in fields for fifty cents a day. Looking back late in his life, Ueland realized that if he had stayed on that Rushford farm he might have eventually had his own farm, and in such a heavily Norwegian area, he might have won election as a member of the state legislature. In short, if he had been more patient and stayed put, he might have had in Minnesota something like the career his father had had at home in Norway.

Instead, along with a minority that nonetheless counted in the thousands, Ueland tried his luck in the boardinghouse and mills district on the south side of Minneapolis. In short order, he discovered that he needed more brawn to do the rough work that required little communication—or more English to secure other types of jobs. Before his twenty dollars in savings ran out, Andreas bought *100 Lessons in English,* bolted to the countryside, and took work with a series of non-Norwegian farmers. From his book and his employers, he learned some English while salting away his earnings for another try at making it in the city when winter came. His clothes wore out before then, so he walked the thirty miles to town to save his hundred dollars in capital, took his second set of clothes from his immigrant chest, which was stored at the boardinghouse, and tried for success in the city again. This time he found two single Norwegian men near his age who were willing to split the rent for a room with one bed, and so, by cooking for himself in the same room, he reduced his living expenses to $1.50 a week.

He helped dig some of the city's first sewers on Washington Avenue South and waited for winter, when he hoped to study and live on his savings for several months before returning to the countryside at planting time in the spring. This plan was hardly uniquely his. As he remarked, "I found a chance to [improve my education] in an ungraded school, kept by the city in the basement of a schoolhouse. . . . The teacher was an elderly ex-Baptist minister and the pupils nearly all Scandinavians like myself." For the next five years he kept to his migratory pattern, "out at hard work, sometimes on farms, sometimes in the city sewers . . . then to a school; then out on farms again; then to school again, etc, etc." Such was the pattern of life for many an immigrant and nearly as many native-born youths in and around the Cities at the time. Ueland was, however, highly ambitious and highly disciplined. He practiced the "strictest economy" and availed himself of a chance to learn law while clerking at a local legal firm.

The Emerging Scandinavian Immigrant Subculture in St. Paul

Indulging in barely restrained boosterism, Rice and Company's 1871 city directory for St. Paul asserts that "St. Paul has beyond doubt, *now commenced on the period of its most rapid growth* . . . and may eventually exceed all our expectations." The directory estimates that the city's population will reach 51,482 by the end of the decade, overshooting the reality documented by the 1880 census by almost precisely ten thousand. The author is more perspicacious, however, when he devotes separate sections of his introduction to phenomenal population expansion locally and regionally and notes that the "growth of the city must receive an impetus from the growth of the state." Describing immigration to Minnesota as a flash flood rushing into the state along its rail lines and rivers, he emphasizes repeatedly the essential attraction of "free homesteads of the choicest lands." The point comes home to the reader: the city's growth will swell in unprecedented fashion because of this tidal wave spreading across the surrounding countryside.[16]

Reading through the 1871 directory produces a very different impression, as far as the presence of Scandinavians in the city is concerned, than does an examination of the directory for 1858–59. Unlike the first directory, the later volume's general introduction makes no mention of immigrant groups, and its list of public institutions and societies ignores Scandinavians entirely while itemizing old-stock American, French, Irish, and German organizations. The alphabetical catalog of individuals in the directory confirms the city's much larger Scandinavian population in the later year, however. Even a rapid paging through the book reveals lists of typically Scandinavian surnames: 25 Andersons, 9 Ericksons, 11 Hansons, 55 Johnsons, 9 Larsons, 17 Nelsons, 6 Olesons, 17 Olsons, and 21 Petersons.

One essential fact is clear from the 1871 city directory: by then there were considerably larger numbers of Danish, Norwegian, and Swedish immigrants in St. Paul than at the end of the 1850s. Instead of some forty men, the later directory lists some 245 likely Scandinavians. Well over four-fifths of these were working people who advertised in the directory to attract customers or employers for their crafts and services. Judging from the family names listed at the same private address, children or female relatives working for their families at home make up most of the people with no occupation listed. Skilled craftsmen, a good number of them likely operating their own shops, make up somewhat under half (44 percent) of the 216 Scandinavian men listed. The greatest number of skilled workers found jobs in the construction trades, nearly one in five as carpenters, but also considerable numbers as stonecutters and masons. For them, as for the forty-one businessmen and nine professional men and officials listed, a place in the city's catalog had obvious advantages. The dozen or so bookkeepers, clerks, agents, and salesmen documented in the directory give evidence of an emerging white-collar class among the Scandinavian immigrants. "Laborer," the second-largest occupational category among the men, probably included many workers who helped build the Cities' transportation and drainage systems and large numbers of the seasonally mobile workers so typical of the river towns at the time.

By 1871, the capital city's pioneer boomtown days were over. A more settled family life with near equal numbers of men and women had replaced the bachelor-dominated society of the 1850s. Many women, not only wives but also their daughters, apparently chose not to have their names recorded in the city directory unless they held a wage-paying occupation. Thus a much smaller group of women than men appears in its pages. Among the fifty-seven women with Scandinavian names who listed their skills and services were a cook, a washerwoman, two widows who took in boarders, a dressmaker, two milliners (one of whom offered both hats and dresses in her shop), and fifty household servants. The tradition of Scandinavian women leaving farms and small towns for domestic work in St. Paul, begun by Ingeborg Langeberg, Anne Hovey, Ingeborg Gilberts, and others in the early 1850s, provided a livelihood in the city for nearly nine in ten (88 percent) of the Scandinavian women who listed an occupation in St. Paul's directory twenty years later.

Only two noncommercial Scandinavian community institutions can be found in the 1871 city directory for St. Paul. The Scandinavian Methodist congregation, the mostly Swedish Scandinavian Lutheran church, and their ministers, although absent from the directory's catalog of public institutions and societies, appear in its alphabetical listing of names. However, the predominantly Norwegian Lutheran church, which lacked ministerial leadership through much of the 1860s and emerged as a reorganized congregation in the early 1870s, was recorded nowhere in the directory. A new interest in and awareness of St. Paul's Scandinavian residents is evident in the officials listed. The city's First Ward justice of the peace was B. A. Froiseth, who lived as a boarder on Mount Airy Street. His address placed him within walking distance of the two churches mentioned above, which themselves were located in the center of the neighborhood that held the most Norwegian immigrants as early as the 1850s. A vice president of the city's fire department, F. Janson, also bears a Norwegian surname, and the city's first Scandinavian policeman may have been P. Wahlstrom, who was very likely Swedish, judging by his last name. Although local historian Carl G. O. Hansen claims Norwegian-born Hagbart Sahlgaard "became in time one of the city's and state's leading citizens," he is unlisted in the 1871 directory, even though he came to St. Paul in 1869 and a year later became the Swedish Norwegian vice-consul there, a position he held until his death in 1892.[17]

The Scandinavian commercial presence was extensive in 1871, when St. Paul contained some seventy-one skilled tradespeople, thirty-six small businesses, and five manufacturers with Scandinavian names. The manufacturing companies consisted of two planing mills, one specializing in construction elements, such as sashes and doors, and the other in chairs and furniture, and three factories, producing leather goods, shirts, or furniture. The small businesses range from seven saloons and three hotels to a long list of individual shops. The planing mills are among a handful of larger Scandinavian-run businesses that may have offered work for immigrant countrymen as well as other laborers. M. A. Hakonson and Adam Scott's Planing Mill and St. Paul Door and Sash Factory were located on Seventh Street by the St. Paul and Pacific Railroad tracks. Hansen Brothers' Planing Mill, Chair Factory, and Furniture Manufacture and Dealership, which occupied the corner of Franklin and Eagle, also must have employed a number of men. Finally, it seems likely that E. P. Johnson and C. C. Mason's shoe, boot, and leather fittings fabrication business and wholesale outlet on the near east side provided some Nordic craftsmen with work. The 1871 directory lists five Scandinavian shoemakers and two harness makers, some of whom may have earned a living at Johnson and Mason's.

The most Scandinavian commercial district of St. Paul lay in the near east side of the city, housed in a rough rectangle of blocks with north-south boundaries around Thirteenth Street to the north and Third Street near the river and an east-west span from Jackson Street on the west to Rosabel (now Wall) Street on the east. Here were most of the small stores and businesses—many of them skilled craftsmen's shops—that composed the bulk of the community's commercial activity. The streets most crowded with Scandinavian businesses and employees were the short stretches of Third, Seventh, and Jackson Streets in the district, which together were lined with a total of twenty-seven of the community's thirty-three businesses and sixty-eight of its Nordic employees. Here customers could find shoe stores, clothing shops, fur and cloth dealers; a confectionary, a grocery, a photographic gallery; and carpet and variety stores—as well as a wide range of tradesmen and clerks—and all of them could serve customers in at least one of the Scandinavian languages.

Scandinavian saloons spread across a wider area. Most operated where they could expect to find the largest number of Scandinavian customers, on Mount Airy streets or the near east side, but some served the public along the lower levee riverbank and in the town center, where men in these immigrant groups may have worked. One of the hotels, the St. Thomas, was in the Mount Airy section, but the other, whose two proprietors were A. Hanson and A. McFarland, lay in a more affluent area (according to the directory) at the corner of Summit Avenue and St. Peter Street. Hanson, like M. A. Hakonson and Hans Mattson, allied himself with a partner whose name indicates an Anglo-American background. Mattson is listed separately with several titles, as a land agent for the Lake Superior and Mississippi Railroad Company with his residence in Sweden, as the principal member of H. Mattson and Company downtown, and as an emigration agent at another central commercial district address. John Johnson, with no business address, is listed as an agent of the "Scandinavian Emigrant Society."

With two exceptions, the residential patterns of the Scandinavian Americans in the 1871 city directory show a clustering in and around the near-east-side commercial district. A considerable number lived above or in back of stores, shops, and saloons in the district, but more have addresses on nearby residential streets. The most clearly Norwegian names have home addresses close to the Norwegian Methodist or Lutheran churches north of the commercial district in the Mount Airy section, a fact confirmed by early histories of those congregations. While laborers and widows are often found in the district's less attractive sites near the river levee, the railroad yards, or the gasworks, skilled workers lived in more pleasant surroundings farther away from its commercial-industrial development. The directory includes no addresses in "Swede Hollow," the ravine in which Phalen Creek runs southwest diagonally through the near east side from Phalen Lake to the Mississippi River, but among the Swedish immigrants who settled in shanties there from 1850 to 1870 and worked in nearby mills and breweries lived other Scandinavian newcomers, including Norwegians.[18]

The exceptions to these general residential patterns are the living arrangements of the thirty-one boarders and fifty servants. None of the domestic workers were men, and only one of these women, who resided in a boardinghouse, lived outside her employer's home. Along with a uniform and meals, domestic work often offered the advantage of life in the city's best residential areas. Eight residences on St. Paul's prestigious Summit Avenue employed Scandinavian house help, and many of the other domestics listed lived in homes on nearby streets. In 1871, roughly 60 percent of Scandinavian domestics lived in affluent neighborhoods apart from the Scandinavian community. Two of them worked in a hotel downtown, and the rest were spread across the near east side. Although it is impossible to know how many Scandinavian boarders were among the short-term guests at the two hotels run by their compatriots, the directory shows that Nordic residents of the city's hotels and boardinghouses did not prefer living with Scandinavian hotel proprietors in the near-east-side or Mount Airy districts. Perhaps to live near their work or to take advantage of lower rents, the 13 percent of the city's Nordics recorded in the directory as living in such housing spread themselves evenly in groups of two or three people at fourteen different establishments across St. Paul.

The Demise of Pan-Scandinavian Religious Cooperation in St. Paul

"Scandinavianism in church affairs is a three-headed monstrosity and cannot continue," exclaimed the editor of the Swedish Methodist weekly *Sændebudet* (The Messenger) in early 1875. Methodist missions to the

Scandinavian immigrants in the Midwest grew during the early 1860s, so much so that American Methodists supported steps to establish a Scandinavian Methodist seminary in Chicago. The discussions quickly ended because the Swedes and Norwegians could only resolve that each nationality group ought to freely pursue possibilities for founding separate theological colleges. The proposal for a joint undertaking revealed the American Methodists' inadequate sense of the felt differences between Swedish and Norwegian immigrants, whose acceptance of a Scandinavian identity rapidly lost strength when circumstances permitted separate institutions for each group. In 1872, factions based on national origin in the Minnesota Scandinavian mission committee disagreed so adamantly that they were unable to present a joint report. The bishop of the Minnesota Conference cut the Gordian knot by dividing the mission into separate Norwegian and Swedish districts. The announcement drew spontaneous calls of "Amen!" and "Hallelujah!" from the Norwegians every time their new district was named during the meeting. Their main spokesman, Andrew Haagensen, summarized their views: "No wonder. The Norwegians were at last winning some rights after working under the constraints of another language [Swedish] and having their efforts labelled 'Scandinavian' for twelve whole years."[19]

By the fall of 1873, St. Paul's Norwegian Methodists formed their own congregation, even though they by then numbered only six people. Near the end of the 1870s they moved their recently purchased parsonage and church to the neighborhood of Thirteenth Street and Broadway, where many members of the growing group lived, and their affairs assumed a settled state. The Lutherans among St. Paul's Scandinavians had split before the war, leaving a rapidly expanding Swedish-dominated congregation and forming a small and impoverished Norwegian-dominated group. After 1859, the latter was unable to muster funds for buildings or a regular minister and lapsed into the remnants of a congregation that gathered only sporadically when itinerant preachers from the countryside visited. As newcomers from Norway and the region joined them between 1868 and 1875, they incorporated as the Norwegian Evangelical Lutheran Congregation of St. Paul, raised funds, bought a lot, and built a modest church among the hills and swamps that then characterized the Mount Airy section just to the east of today's state capitol. The inauspicious site was so sandy, as the oft-told congregational story goes, that the minister had to join the wheelbarrow brigade carrying sand from the upper to the lower end of the building to keep it from slipping down the hill.[20]

In the 1866–73 surge of immigration, the city received considerably more Swedes than Norwegians, which encouraged local residents to call all the city's Scandinavian inhabitants "Swedes." The Norwegian presence grew during these years, but it was Swede Hollow and the Swedish east side that became established in the public mind by the 1880s, while the growing size and number of Norwegian immigrant institutions attracted less attention.[21]

The organization of the city's second Norwegian immigrant church, Trinity Lutheran of St. Paul, provides another vivid example of the difficulties of maintaining Scandinavian American religious cooperation. The original group of Norwegian immigrants separated from St. Paul's First Scandinavian Lutheran Church in 1858, joined the Norwegian Synod, and established its principal congregation in the city. After the Civil War, a second contingent of Norwegians assembled in the Scandinavian Lutheran congregation. They were comfortable with its lower church, lay orientation but restive in a predominately Swedish congregation. In 1870, they left First Scandinavian Lutheran and joined the Conference for the Norwegian-Danish Evangelical Lutheran Church in America. The Reverend Ole Paulson led a similar breakaway group in Minneapolis and guided the St. Paul contingent in the same direction. He ministered to both groups, which organized as Trinity Norwegian-Danish Lutheran Church of Minneapolis and Trinity Norwegian Congregation of St. Paul.

The Growing Scandinavian American Community by the Falls of the Mississippi

By the 1870s, the Scandinavian settlement in St. Anthony and Minneapolis was large enough to make for revealing comparisons with its sister settlement in St. Paul. The number of Norwegian-born in Hennepin County exploded in ten years from under a handful to nearly nine hundred. Considerable numbers of these individuals must have been among the residents recorded in the falls cities directory at the start of the decade. The several secular and religious organizations and the variety of personal situations documented stand in sharp contrast to the situation a decade earlier. Now, moreover, there were about twice as many Scandinavians by the falls as in St. Paul. Scandinavian settlement by the falls had caught up with its neighboring community downstream in complexity and far outstripped it in size.[22]

At the start of the 1870s, Scandinavian-name women in St. Anthony–Minneapolis made their living in much the same way as their female compatriots in St. Paul. Only slightly fewer of the ninety-eight women listed in the St. Anthony–Minneapolis directory worked as domestic servants, and in both cities the needle trades employed the large majority of the remaining working women. One significant difference in the larger Nordic community at the falls was the presence of two midwives, one teacher, and a single saleswoman. There and in the state capital, a handful of Scandinavian women operated their own small business. In St. Anthony–Minneapolis the women entrepreneurs consisted of the midwives, two dressmakers, and one "hairworker," who operated their businesses out of their homes, as did their sister businesswomen in St. Paul. In both communities the small number of women listed in the directories excluded those who helped their husbands in family shops and lodging houses as well as nearly all of the large number of the "unemployed" married women who worked at home as housewives and mothers. If the woolen and cotton mills by the Falls of St. Anthony employed Scandinavian-name women, none of these appeared in the city directory.[23]

The occupational profile of Scandinavian-name men in St. Paul diverged in revealing ways from that of their compatriots in the cities by the falls. Some of the important differences seem to result from the greater age of the capital's Scandinavian community or the much greater number of unskilled industrial jobs available by the falls. The professional and official elite in St. Paul made up three times as large a part of the city's employed Scandinavian men as it did in St. Anthony–Minneapolis. Both elites were tiny, but an additional ten to fifteen years had given Scandinavian American professional men in St. Paul and the institutions supporting them more time to establish themselves. As the state capital, St. Paul attracted another level of officials, such as emigration agents, and during its early dominance as a transportation center it also held more opportunities for civil engineers. On the other hand, the communities by the falls already contained three Scandinavian attorneys, and in Minneapolis lived Hennepin County's Norwegian-born sheriff, George H. Johnson, the first of many elected officials who owed a critical part of their support to the already much larger Scandinavian American population in Minneapolis than resided in any other Mississippi river town. A medical doctor and one minister, the Reverend Ole Paulson, complete the Nordic professionals recorded in the enclaves by the falls.

Far more impressive for St. Paul's Scandinavian community at the beginning of the 1870s, however, was the evidence from the city directories that the proportion of businessmen and industrial entrepreneurs in the capital city's enclave was twice as large as that in the Nordic settlements of St. Anthony and Minneapolis. Part of this difference resulted from the larger public in St. Paul, which was still the state's most populous city by a clear margin at the start of the decade. According to the editor of the falls cities directory, Minneapolis alone held nearly 17,500 residents in 1871, but a year earlier the federal census found only some 13,100 there and a population of more than 20,000 in St. Paul. The earlier start of Scandinavian settlement in St. Paul likely provided the time needed for a greater part of its men to enter business or manufacturing. The cities by the falls held no mills or factories owned or operated by Scandinavian-name men in 1871, while the St. Paul directory listed five such concerns.[24]

The commercial district of the immigrant settlements at the falls and in St. Paul included a predictable range of shops—a baker, a barber, a builder, a news dealer, a tailor, and so on. Yet, to a degree, the activity of St. Paul's Scandinavian businessmen reflected the city's traditional mercantile economy. Prominent among the immigrant community were the outfitters that typified a wholesale center oriented toward supplying retail distributors across a region. Its two planing mills specializing in furniture and building elements may also have been aimed somewhat at supplying the needs of construction projects outside the city, given the much more rapidly expanding cities upriver at the falls.

The Scandinavian commercial enterprises that characterized the immigrant community in St. Anthony and Minneapolis further documented the contrasting development of these urban centers. Here retailers were more numerous than in St. Paul's Scandinavian community.

Near the falls, the opportunity most often seized by Nordic small-businessmen was not the saloon, as in St. Paul, but the boardinghouse. The capital city enclave contained no boardinghouse keepers but three hotels with Scandinavian proprietors. In Minneapolis, no fewer than eight boardinghouses and two hotels run by men with typical Scandinavian names dotted the streets adjacent to the mill district. The importance of the mills for Scandinavian men working near the falls is explicit in the Nordic names of five "mill workers," seven coopers (flour barrel makers), and the cooperage firm that provided work for some of these craftsmen. Since it has been commonly assumed that the mills offered the largest employment opportunity in the city, the surprise is that the directory for the falls communities lists so few Scandinavian-name men as employed in the mills.

St. Paul and the falls communities held a small, nearly equal portion of low-level white-collar workers. Since only 6 to 7 percent of the men in both places worked as clerks, bookkeepers, salesmen, or agents, no significant upward mobility into nonmanual work apparently occurred during the longer history of the capital's older immigrant community. Skilled workers, on the other hand, did make up a noticeably bigger part of the workingmen contingent in St. Paul, and that difference may have been achieved through longer experience with American working conditions. In St. Anthony and Minneapolis, as in St. Paul, the construction trades employed easily the largest group of skilled workers, and the range of other skilled occupations in the two Scandinavian communities consisted mostly of similar trades in roughly the same proportions.

The important contrast between the cities' Scandinavian working classes consisted in the bottom-heavy workforce near the falls, where unskilled workers made up over 36 percent of the employed men listed in the directory. In St. Paul, the unskilled composed barely 16 percent of the Scandinavian working people listed. The title of "laborer," the work classification in the St. Anthony–Minneapolis directory for these men, does not specifically identify them as mill workers. A considerable number of them may have found work in the mills because the saw and flour mills were by far the largest source of unskilled jobs at the falls. But only if "laborer" was a general category of work that included many mill workers can one conclude that the mills themselves were a major employer for Scandinavian immigrants, and there is still the problem that some men in the directory have the more specific title of "mill worker."

The First Immigrant Neighborhoods in the Towns by the Falls of St. Anthony

The 1871 falls cities directory reveals a mere two dozen or so Scandinavian-name residents in St. Anthony on the east bank of the Mississippi. Nonetheless, local church histories report that traveling ministers of the Norwegian Synod from southeastern Minnesota preached to an organized group of Norwegians there as early as 1869. Still, this group did not grow strong enough to organize formally as Immanuel Norwegian Lutheran Church until 1874, when St. Anthony and its sister city fused, and the neighborhood soon became known as the near northeast section of Minneapolis. Swedes constituted by far the largest immigrant group in the "northeast" by the end of the decade, but the settlements of both groups there remained small compared to the size of the older Scandinavian centers on the river's west bank.[25]

The North Side

During the decade and a half following the Civil War, increasing numbers of the Selbygg community settled into seasonal and then more permanent residence in the northern stretches of the city. Here was a unique pattern: This was the only Norwegian settlement close to the Twin Cities in which one regional Norwegian subculture predominated, and the only rural Norwegian immigrant community that gradually made a second migration into the city from just beyond the edge of the urban area. In the late 1860s a number of Selbygg built homes around Twentieth Avenue North and Second Street, and from that beginning inside the built-up area grew a sizeable community that stretched from the edge of downtown to the northern city limit by the end of the 1870s. The Minneapolis city directory for 1871 documents the presence of a dozen or so laborers with common Scandinavian names in boardinghouses a block or two to the north of the city center. At the time the distinctive north-side Norwegian community was small and little organized compared to the Scandinavian enclave on the southern edge of downtown Minneapolis. This later district is remembered as the city's first immigrant neighborhood.[26]

The Edge of the Commercial Core and New Residential Streets at Seven Corners

The residential patterns among Scandinavian immigrants in Minneapolis in the early 1870s resembled those among their compatriots in St. Paul in two ways. In both urban areas, nearly all women in domestic work resided with their employers and so lived in the better parts of town. In Minneapolis that placed them farther west than the center of Scandinavian settlement. And, like the state capital, Minneapolis also contained a Scandinavian residential district made up mostly of families with children that was located near the immigrant churches but somewhat farther from the city center and commercial arteries such as Washington Avenue. Most of those recorded as living in boardinghouses in Minneapolis, however, were distributed differently than in St. Paul. Instead of living outside the enclave in establishments spread across the city, here a large part of the Scandinavian lodging house residents lived in the midst of the initial Scandinavian settlement area—in or very near its main commercial street and population center. The core of this enclave, the city's largest, and the commercial core lay beside each other or overlapped. The Nordic lodgers downtown consisted of men living on their own and a few single women who were employed at manual labor in the adjacent mills or in workshops dependent on the mills. In all, nearly half the Scandinavian-name residents in the 1871 Minneapolis city directory lived in city center lodgings. A large majority of the community's small-businessmen and professionals lived above shops and offices in the district or in neighboring downtown lodging houses.

At the start of the decade, however, the Scandinavian district was already spreading south of downtown to "Seven Corners," at the intersection of Washington and Cedar Avenues. A few Scandinavian businesses were located as far south as Eighth and Ninth Avenues in 1871. The location of these, such as Johannes Berg's Norwegian grocery on Fourteenth Avenue South, represented small-businessmen's response to the movement of Scandinavian families away from the blocks nearer Bridge Square, as it and the section of town closest to it became increasingly commercial or industrial. During the rest of the decade, the primary Scandinavian business district became concentrated near the square. In 1878, for example, Paul Hjelm-Hansen's *Business Directory of Scandinavians in Minnesota* found nearly fifty Nordic business enterprises near Bridge Square, including all three of its liquor stores. The addresses of eight of the ten retail grocers Hjelm-Hansen lists, on the other hand, are close to their chosen customers in the more residential Cedar-Riverside district.[27]

In the later 1860s and 1870s, the civil and commercial life of Minneapolis converged in the vicinity of Bridge Square, where Hennepin and Nicollet Avenues—then dirt thoroughfares lined by three-story brick and stone buildings and boardwalks—met on their way to the suspension bridge over the Mississippi. By 1873 the last triangular block between the two streets held the new blue limestone city hall, and the Gateway District—the buildings in a radius of a few blocks from the square—housed the large majority of the town's finest shops, restaurants, hotels, public halls, and entertainments, including the Pence Opera House. The Gateway attracted people of all classes and was a lively place day and night. A largely male public that patronized the drinking houses and brothels in or near Bridge Square made it the scene of sometimes boisterous activity into the late hours. In short, unlike later, more compartmentalized cities, the core of post–Civil War Minneapolis hummed with nearly the entire range of its activities.[28]

In these same years, the first south-side Scandinavian enclave developed in the Gateway District. A couple of its businesses operated in buildings on the square, but most opened their doors in the smaller wooden storefronts on Washington Avenue from the square southeast along the line of the river just west of the milling district and the Milwaukee Station railway lines. Except for the alternative of making a living north of downtown through logging on the river and truck farming, as the Norwegian Selbygg settlers did, for the working and lower-middle classes the most practical choice was to live downtown. Minneapolis was a "walking city," where only the better-off had the means to move about in carriages on a daily basis. From the mid-1870s, working-class people could ride the horsecars or horse-drawn omnibuses to their jobs. However, this transportation, like the electric streetcars that appeared a decade later, at first made living outside the city center affordable and convenient mostly for the middle and upper classes. Most industries, civic and business institutions, and the residences of many foreign-born immigrants, a large part of the working people of Minneapolis, remained at the city's core.

By 1873 on Bridge Square itself visitors could find the office of the Norwegian-language newspaper *Budstikken* (The Messenger), a Norwegian tailoring shop, and three Nordic liquor stores. Around two-thirds of Scandinavian stores and workshops lay along Washington Avenue within five or six blocks of the square or in the first blocks of side streets running to the west. On the avenue, which was unpaved, like the rest of the city's thoroughfares, citizens promenaded along raised wooden sidewalks under store and business signs on beams that connected to supporting poles at the street's edge. A few minutes' walk from the square near the corner of Helen Street (now Second Avenue), one found the most important business blocks in the Norwegian community. Here pedestrians saw signs for John Ofstie's gentlemen's furnishings and clothing store, Mark's (Mørk's) Pharmacy, the Norwegian dentist Dr. Tischendorf, the tailor shop of Olaf Throbeck, and the bookstore, press, and offices for the community's second newspaper, *Nordisk Folkeblad* (Nordic People's Paper). Directly across from the Milwaukee station, a block farther down the avenue, customers could do business in a shoe repair shop, a shoe store, a second pharmacy, a furniture and casket store, and a dry goods shop—all of them owned and run by Norwegian immigrants. On the side streets nearby, people wanting to patronize Scandinavian immigrant businesses found products and services to satisfy most daily needs.[29]

On or within one block of Washington Avenue were also the lodging houses run by Scandinavians that attracted the largest number of Nordic residents. Most prominent among these in the anecdotes that have survived from the 1870s are Lars Erikson's Scandia House, which in 1866 opened as the city's first residential hotel owned by a Norwegian, and Albion House, where the colorful John "Lutefisk" Johnson offered house residents and diners all they could eat of the Scandinavian delicacy. Many Scandinavians also roomed at Normann House, Eriksen Hotel, Laurvig House, and the residences run by John Chilstrom or

The Norwegian community's earliest commercial district in Minneapolis—wooden storefronts and boardwalks along an unpaved roadway—was on Washington Avenue southeast from Hennepin Avenue. *MNHS*

Petter Ness. In short, the Scandinavian community and the west bank boardinghouse district near the falls were located in the same place.

Making the Community Visible: A Pan-Scandinavian Seventeenth of May in Minneapolis

Given the small size and instability of the city's Scandinavian population in 1869, it is remarkable that a few local immigrant men successfully arranged to celebrate Norway's Constitution Day in the city. The preponderance of single men living as lodgers or renters seemed to some contemporary observers one of the most striking features of the

Norwegian population of Minneapolis at the time. In his *Memoirs*, Reverend Ole Paulson recalled by name only two Norwegians who owned living quarters. One of these, the shoemaker Ebenhart M. Titterud, temporarily housed the new pastor in the family's apartment above his shop on Washington Avenue. Housing filled by unmarried men living as roomers or boarding residents was then the rule rather than the exception. The raw frontier mill city was as dominated by men living without wives or children as St. Paul had been in the 1850s.[30]

Most of the male population of Minneapolis in the early 1870s consisted of seasonal workers at harvesttime or in logging camps who came to town as construction labor. Most were young and single, and, if immigrants, were in the first phase of their adjustment to American life. Such a population was an unlikely basis for the origin of civic celebrations organized in town. In the Minneapolis of the 1870s, men with skilled crafts, an entrepreneurial bent, or more education were few and only somewhat more stable residents. The significant fact in connection with the city's first Syttende mai, however, is that the largest part of the nascent community's occupational and educational elite in the first fifteen years after the Civil War also consisted of young, unattached men living on their own as lodgers in downtown Minneapolis.

These conditions gave birth to the kind of informal Scandinavian bachelor society that arranged the first Norwegian Constitution Day celebrations in Minneapolis. Carl G. O. Hansen comments that many of the men in this small elite were young and ambitious bachelors who enjoyed each other's society. Andreas Ueland, a veteran of the group who started his career in the city by digging ditches, later told Hansen that their "aristocracy" in the 1870s was the small coterie of clerks who had already risen above manual labor. But even then the elite of downtown bachelors also included the community's first Norwegian-born lawyer, Johan Arctander, as well as its doctor and dentist, and the older experienced journalist with good connections to the press in Norway, Paul Hjelm-Hansen. The newspapermen and entrepreneurs W. T. Rambusch and Hjalmar Eger, who owned *Nordisk Folkeblad* in 1871, were cordial associates of these men and of several among the young bachelors who later won local or state office. At the time, Rambusch was also the first Swedish Norwegian vice-consul in what was then the northwestern frontier region of the United States. Among the future Norwegian

American politicians who associated with Rambusch and Eger were George H. Johnson, who served as Hennepin County sheriff from 1871 to 1877; A. H. Edsten, who won election as the city's first Norwegian-born alderman in 1874; Andreas Ueland, who served as county court commissioner and probate judge in the 1880s; and Albert E. Rice, who served as Minnesota's lieutenant governor from 1887 to 1891.

A few married men, like Titterud, were a part of this budding commercial-professional "fraternity." It was freedom from family obligations and leisure time spent in the close proximity of the single elite's lodging, work, eating, and drinking places, however, that encouraged frequent communication and companionship. After work during these early years, for example, the clerks, hotel- and shopkeepers, and craftsmen of the Scandinavian business district on Washington Avenue met regularly to discuss politics and business in "Edsten's back yard," the open space behind the furniture store of A. H. Edsten.[31]

The needed spark for more formal organization flashed when the group heard that the Norwegian violinist and nationalist Ole Bull planned to perform at Pence Opera House in early May 1869. Determined to receive Bull in a fashion appropriate to his fame and to draw the general public's attention to the Scandinavian presence in the city, some of these promising young entrepreneurs and journalists founded the Scandinavian Society, the enclave's first secular association. Having entertained Bull to his and their satisfaction, the society's next undertaking was the city's first observance of Norway's Constitution Day, the Seventeenth of May, just two weeks later. The inaugural celebration consisted of a private gala banquet for members and their guests at the new society's rooms in Harmonia Hall, one block north of Bridge Square.[32]

In the 1860s, Constitution Day festivities were not common in the Norwegian countryside. In the cities they were viewed as the province of liberals or radicals, as political agitation against the union with Sweden. They were a form of rebelliousness of which conservative elements did not approve. A half century earlier, in May 1814, Norway won a limited degree of independence when a representative body of its leaders met and adopted an American-style constitution on the seventeenth of the month. They acted swiftly, because control over Norway was soon to be decided through treaties following Napoleon's defeat.

The constitution writers in Norway—and Ole Bull at the end of the 1860s—had advanced views, perceptions well beyond the national consciousness of many of their contemporaries. Most Norwegians felt their strongest loyalties for regional or district cultures well beyond the century's midpoint. Like many who came to the United States from parts of what later became Germany and Italy, immigrants from Norway arrived as proud identifiers with these local cultures—as *Gudbrandsdøler, Telemarkinger, Østlendinger,* and *Trønder*. Seventeenth of May celebrations became one of the customs that—in both America and Norway during roughly the same time period—assisted in the formation of a Norwegian (or Norwegian American) *national* identity on a broad popular basis.

Perhaps the weak national identity of the early Norwegian immigrants in Minneapolis made it easier for its elite members to frame the first Seventeenth of May event there as a *Scandinavian* event. Not only was the organizing group an elite that kept the celebration an exclusive private affair, but the organizers and participants were explicitly pan-Scandinavian. The first toast raised to Norwegian liberty on the Seventeenth of May in Minneapolis was proposed by the Danish vice-consul. The evening's program included a speech to the glory of each of the Nordic nations by one of its natives as well as one in praise of Nordic unity by a Norwegian. All this fitted the genuinely pan-Scandinavian character of the society, whose officers included representatives of Denmark, Norway, and Sweden. But Ole Bull would not have been pleased. One of the pronouncements for which he is remembered occurred at a Seventeenth of May banquet in Wisconsin, where he declared how glad he was to see that only two Danes and one "invisible Swede" were present.[33]

The Beginnings of Norwegian Religious Life at the Falls in the 1870s

In the second half of the 1860s, when newcomers from Scandinavia initially sought to establish a church near the falls, Swedish immigrants made up the largest part of the group and, as in St. Paul, dominated the organizing process. Swedish immigrant Lutheran ministers' visits from the countryside inspired the formation of the first Scandinavian congregation by the falls, the Evangelical Lutheran Augustana Congregation in Minneapolis. These men alternated performing services with a Norwegian immigrant pastor who also came in from a rural settlement. Since a significant number of the church's founding members had migrated into the city from these largely Swedish or Norwegian Scandinavian communities in the nearby countryside, both the pastors and the congregants found their continued cooperation natural. The same pattern of itinerant rural clerics providing ministerial services to urbanized coreligionists from the surrounding region had occurred earlier in St. Paul, when visiting ministers followed parishioners from southwestern Wisconsin and northeastern Iowa into that city.[34]

The large proportion of single Scandinavian men in Minneapolis after the Civil War also influenced the development of religious community among Scandinavians by the falls, although not in the same way as these men's informal association in downtown Minneapolis decisively influenced the organization of their first secular society and patriotic celebration there. Single men are prominent in the lists of founding members of the Augustana Lutheran congregation. Four families and four bachelors established the congregation, giving unmarried men an equal number of votes in the ecclesiastical arrangements agreed on, since women were denied the franchise in church affairs at the time. Nonetheless, at first the group met in rented quarters on Seventh Avenue South—nearer the Scandinavian residential section where the family men lived than to downtown, which made church attendance easier for married couples and children. Furthermore, when the congregation grew rapidly due to the wave of immigration and so decided that same year to erect a church building, it picked a site at Thirteenth and Washington Avenues—nearly twice as far from the Nordic business district and its lodging houses occupied largely by the single male population.

When the congregation dissolved into a Swedish and a Norwegian church just two years after its founding, single men again played visible roles, but as before, their action emphasized the importance of family and children in the group's religious life. The Norwegians did not want their children taught the catechism in a foreign tongue. The language objected to was Swedish, not English. The Sunday school divided into two sections along national lines before the formal schism in the congregation took place. As soon as one of the downtown bachelors,

A. H. Edsten, made known his Sunday school teaching experience at a Norwegian-language church in Chicago, his countrymen supported his objection to the use of Swedish, and classes were separated by language.

The last straw, the conclusive proof that Scandinavian cooperation in the church was impossible, came when the Norwegian members of Augustana Lutheran discovered that their national identity was to be concealed in the legal name of the new church building. Edsten, who was the Norwegians' representative on the building committee, informed them that the committee's Swedish leader had incorporated the congregation under Minnesota law as the "Swedish Lutheran Augustana Assembly." Shortly after, in the fall of 1867, the Norwegian members (and a few Danes) held a mass meeting at which more single men—including Edsten, future sheriff George Johnson, and Lars Erikson of Scandia House—than married fathers, such as Ebenhart Titterud, signed the resolution to form the city's first Norwegian Lutheran church, the Norwegian-Danish Evangelical Lutheran Trinity Church, or "Trinity," as it was later generally known.

As its first pastor, Ole Paulson, noted, Trinity was the congregation whose founding membership contained a majority of young bachelors. After the break from their Swedish coreligionists, these men and the families in the new church could more easily preserve Norwegian language and culture in a religious setting. The congregation also offered its single men a feeling of belonging to a group that honored a traditional sense of family and leadership. These qualities were acutely important in the immigrant group's early community life, particularly in a booming frontier city where the physical environment altered rapidly and they lived close together with Americans and other immigrant nationalities.[35]

The members of Trinity were part of an immigrant group in the process of assembling during the large post–Civil War wave of migration. These newcomers assiduously transplanted elements of their religious heritage that reminded them of home—even when the Reverend Paulson would have preferred to leave some of these traditions behind. Equally important, especially during their first year or so in the new country, they based their perceptions of people's position and status on norms learned in Norway. In his *Memoirs*, for example, Paulson explains how he at first did not conduct church services in the long black robe and stiff white renaissance ruff collar then customary for Lutheran ministers in Norway. He hoped to avoid its use because he considered it "inhumanly old fashioned, unbecoming and homely" and had learned to dislike Norwegian congregational customs during his pastoral training among the Swedish Americans of the Augustana Scandinavian Synod in Illinois. Finding the whole congregation opposed to this departure from Norwegian tradition at church meetings, he explained that the most esteemed Lutheran authority in America expected each congregation to keep a gown for its preacher. If Trinity wished to buy the gown, he would wear it despite his opposition. On hearing the price the congregation voted unanimously not to buy one, and the matter was apparently dropped for over a year.

The problem was that when he appeared without the ruff, Norwegian immigrants in town doubted that he was a minister and told new arrivals that they thought he might be a *klokker* (sexton). As a result, both he and Trinity Church seemed inadequately Norwegian to precisely the people they hoped to attract. Giving in to the general expectations of his compatriots, Paulson discreetly ordered a gown and collected contributions for it—only to be surprised when parishioners purchased it on their own. After a congregant sewed him a passable imitation of a ruff, Paulson wryly comments, people said that Trinity had an "old state's [state church] preacher who had a preacher's gown and who even chanted before the altar." Under those circumstances, the congregation grew rapidly in the 1870s as the wave of immigration and the urbanization of Norwegian settlers from the surrounding countryside continued. By the end of the decade the congregation had moved to a bigger building and then enlarged it to relieve crowding at services.[36]

Religious Accommodation and Transplantation in American Conditions

Conservative liturgical practices at Trinity revealed both a yearning for the familiar religious sights and sounds of the homeland and the practical adjustments of an immigrant institution in an American city. The way the congregation organized itself internally and the characteristics of the larger church bodies it joined—its choices regarding church polity—showed a similar mixture of transplantation and accommodation.

Several factors made the organizational process a new and exhilarating grassroots affair, among these the separation of church and state in the United States, the near-frontier stage of the city's development, and the lack of any Lutheran precedent in Minneapolis except the pan-Scandinavian Augustana congregation the founders of Trinity had just left. Accustomed to a state church whose central clerical authorities prepared and determined the order of religious services, hymnal, and prayer book, Trinity's founders held congregational meetings at which they democratically structured their church service in great detail, choosing locally what had previously been provided for them centrally. The minutes of these congregational meetings, where the number, kind, and length of the minister's prayers and sermons were set by voting laymen, demonstrate a strong sense of the powerful local democracy these immigrants found themselves exercising. Some members may have participated in the growing church reform movement of the time in Norway before emigrating. One of the movement's chief demands called for giving individual congregations the right to have a voice in selecting their pastor. In America that right was commonplace, and Trinity congregation chose the Reverend Paulson. But the order of service, hymnal, prayer book, and ministerial practices they specified for their congregation were all traditional for churches in Norway. American freedom was thus employed to preserve Norwegian state church liturgical forms.[37]

Despite the dominance of Swedish American congregations in the Scandinavian Lutheran Augustana Synod, the Norwegians who founded Trinity at first resolved to remain in that church body when they left the Augustana congregation in Minneapolis. After all, concern for balancing Scandinavian religious forms and traditions with measured adjustments to American circumstances marked the synod as much as it marked the first Scandinavian Lutheran church in Minneapolis. All these institutions showed the combinations of convenience that were accepted because of the rapidly shifting circumstances of the western movement and immigration in America. When many of the early Scandinavian Lutheran settlers reached the Midwest, they joined American and German immigrant Lutheran organizations at first. Some Norwegian immigrants allied themselves with the German American Missouri Synod and remained closely associated with it even after they formed the independent Norwegian Synod.

In 1870, not only did the Swedes and Norwegians part company at the synodical level, but the Norwegian Augustanans divided into two separate bodies. Trinity's membership allied itself with the Conference for the Norwegian-Danish Lutheran Church in America, the new organization that favored high-church forms from Norway, such as the clerical gown and ruff that had become so symbolically important for the Minneapolis congregation, but a "low-church, free congregational type of polity." This combination suited the negotiated balance they had found between their new circumstances and the religious conventions dear to them from their homeland.[38]

Augsburg Seminary Comes to Minneapolis

Trinity's Pastor Paulson, a founder and prime mover in the conference, was instrumental in bringing Augsburg Seminary to Minneapolis. Shortly after his arrival, the pastor became friendly with Charles Edwin Vanderburgh, a state district judge who was something of a local patriot. Vanderburgh told Paulson about his vision of Minneapolis as a metropolitan hub and the "headquarters for Scandinavians in the Northwest." Paulson remembered Vanderburgh's conclusion that such a city ought to have a Scandinavian institution of higher learning. During the schism among the Norwegian Augustanans, the conference considered new locations for the school. Its leaders were undecided between Minneapolis and Madison, Wisconsin. At that point, Paulson reminded Vanderburgh of their earlier discussion, and the judge convened a meeting of leading men which resulted in promises of land, building materials, and money to erect a new seminary building. When the conference held its second annual convocation in Minneapolis at Trinity Church in 1871, the agenda included choosing a site for Augsburg and reviewing the inducements the city offered. The convocation delegates promenaded the few blocks from the church to the prairie on the edge of town, surveyed the property in question, and on their return voted unanimously to make Minneapolis the permanent home of Augsburg.[39]

It is remarkable that city fathers showed such interest in attracting a Norwegian immigrant institution to Minneapolis. Not merely Judge Vanderburgh but also the city's mayor and leading flour milling businessmen contributed building lots or cash pledges. The men the judge called together to secure the school's presence included ambitious members of the emerging Norwegian business elite—men who were already playing roles in the larger community. In general, the cooperation of immigrant and old-stock American businessmen-promoters made Reverend Paulson's efforts a success. Once the conference had decided on Minneapolis for the site of the seminary, however, the project evidently lost its urgency, and Paulson later recorded in his memoirs that only a loan of sixty dollars from a young single female member of Trinity made it possible to start construction on time.[40]

The lavish but tempered acceptance showered on the immigrant community at the dedication of the new building in the fall of 1872 reveals the ambivalent feelings Minneapolis's large Scandinavian population inspired in some municipal leaders at the time. The *Minneapolis Daily Tribune* printed a lengthy article describing the meeting of "Scandinavian delegations . . . from all quarters of the state" and their procession to ceremonies at Augsburg Seminary and services at Trinity. The article includes the full text of Mayor E. M. Wilson's speech at

Augsburg Seminary and College, the core institutions of Norwegian free church Lutheranism. ***NAHA***

the dedication, which, like the news article, focused pragmatically on the socioeconomic impact. The emphasis was not individual national origins but the bright prospects for the city because, as Wilson put it, "You of the Scandinavian race are making this the grand center of your large emigration to America." Moreover, he betrayed the concern of the native-born for the immigrants' assimilation, remarking first on the large portion of the city's population that was already Scandinavian and then concluding that "any class of emigrants can be better trusted who are accompanied by their ministers." The training of Lutheran ministers at Augsburg would help prevent what was termed the "abuse of free suffrage," which is the "cankerous disease our nation has most to fear."[41]

Augsburg Seminary's early leaders also felt a deep concern for developing responsible citizenship among immigrants. In 1874, the conference approved Augsburg's plan to expand its campus, faculty, and teaching programs, and August Weenaas, the institution's first president, was joined by three young professors from Norway. Sven Oftedal, Georg Sverdrup, and Sven Rud Gunnersen were all disciples of low-church piety and movements for a more democratically oriented clergy. The four men designed educational programs founded on the conviction that immigrant groups could best enrich US society by training their young to participate fully in American democracy.[42]

Through its annual convocations, the conference had determined the accommodation to American conditions that defined the immigrant church body's middle position in Norwegian American Lutheranism. Augsburg's most explicit responsibility would be to prepare ministers who could translate into local church practices the devotion of the conference to the Augsburg Confession of faith, liturgical forms from Norway, and a high degree of independence and layman leadership in its congregations. The designers of the new curricula at Augsburg initiated a thorough application of liberal religious principles in Norway. They rejected the state-church definition of the clergy as learned members of an official class. The Augsburg leaders so valued the independence of local congregations that they became the founders of the Norwegian American Lutheran "free church" tradition in the United States.[43]

The professors aimed to remove the potential of a clerical elite's "religious tyranny." They dreamed of a bicultural population equipped to offer Norway's history, literature, and democratic heritage to an

English-speaking American audience. Therefore, in all of the school's preparatory curricula students had to master these subjects: both Norwegian and English language, literature in written English, and the geography and history of the United States. Augsburg was fortunate in these farsighted young academics, who realized that they were privileged to train a more ambitious, serious segment of Norwegian Americans, a student body mainly composed of those their home communities viewed as most promising, the very people who would likely occupy leading positions later in life and bridge the distance between an immigrant subculture and mainstream American society.[44]

From their positions at Augsburg Seminary, their stands on the religious and political issues that then stirred Norwegian Americans made them famous and controversial partisans in the immigrant subculture. Georg Sverdrup and Sven Oftedal became known as the defenders of the conference's and Augsburg's views in the turbulent controversies among Norwegian American Lutherans during the next several decades. The seminary and Trinity congregation, moreover, remained very closely affiliated and rightly perceived as a unified center of the views forwarded by Augsburg. Students as well as faculty so commonly made the congregation their church while they were in Minneapolis that in 1877 it was decided that Augsburg would not found its own congregation. Thus it developed that, in the minds of students coming in from the surrounding region and later returning to it as ministers or lay leaders, Augsburg and Trinity represented a single tradition and a single loyalty—one that in the course of later events would make up a distinct and separate part of the network that bound Norwegian Americans throughout the region to Minneapolis.[45]

The Norwegian Synod in Minneapolis

While these institutions defined their particular accommodation of elements in the Lutheran heritage, the growing number of Norwegians settling in Minneapolis after 1865 supported the formation of several other congregations. The first of these, Our Saviour's Lutheran Church, marked the entrance into the city of the Norwegian Synod, the largest Norwegian American religious body at the time and the sharpest critic of the conference and Augsburg. The early histories of Our Saviour's gratefully thank a local German American church for the temporary use of a building as the new congregation organized but make no mention of nearby "Norwegian" Trinity in the core of the south-side Scandinavian quarter. The situation illustrates the view of church historian Todd Nichol, who concludes that in controversies among Lutheran groups, national background mattered much less than differences over theology and church polity.[46]

In the 1850s, the Norwegian Synod had turned to the German-American Missouri Synod for aid in educating ministers, and the local German immigrant congregation was "Missourian." Our Saviour's called Hans G. Stub, a Norwegian American who followed the customary path to become a minister in the Norwegian Synod, graduating first from Luther College and then from Concordia Seminary, the Missouri Synod's theological school. Stub would leave Our Saviour's to become president of Luther College in 1878. The Stub family, producing several leading clerics, would have later connections with Our Saviour's in Minneapolis and become an increasingly illustrious part of the Norwegian Synod tradition. Thus, the leadership of the congregation became as central to the synod as Trinity's became to the conference.[47]

The early leaders of both these immigrant church bodies saw in their American circumstances a grand opportunity for religious renewal. Both applauded and quickly adapted to the separation of church and state in the United States. Both set up democratic organizations that gave individual congregations considerable power. But the first cadre of synod leaders left Norway twenty or so years earlier than the new professors at Augsburg. Norwegian church historian Vidar Haanes remarks that the synod was typical of an "emigrated or isolated group that clings to its identity more strongly than [does] the milieu it left" and concludes that its leaders were judged at the time to have gone too far even for Norway's conservative circles. In general, as Nichol notes, synod leaders favored "the preservation of Norwegian culture and language, [but] their most fundamental commitment to this cause was the propagation of pure Lutheran doctrine among the children of their church." Many leaders of the conference, however, arriving after the Civil War and devoted to a reform of Norwegian Lutheranism and politics that embraced rather than rejected recent developments in Norway, disagreed strongly with the synod stance on contemporary issues.

The commitment of the two groups of Norwegian-born church leaders to contrasting visions of developments in Norway and America's promise, it can be argued, drove them further apart than they would have been had they remained in Norway.[48]

Religious controversy reinforced the evolution of two largely segregated networks of Norwegian American religious and educational institutions in the Upper Midwest, both of them with vital centers in Minneapolis–St. Paul. For Norwegian Americans these developments functioned as a natural feature in the relationships between the region and its preeminent urban hub. As they resettled in the Cities from the group's older centers in Wisconsin, Iowa, and southeastern Minnesota—areas of Norwegian Synod strength—Norwegian Americans added to the urban constituency in St. Paul and Minneapolis that was loyal to the synod view of denominational controversy and public affairs. In the same way, as west-central and northwestern Minnesota attracted large numbers of immigrants in the post–Civil War wave from Norway and developed bastions of conference strength, those congregations received aid from Trinity and Augsburg in Minneapolis. The synod's schools—Luther College in Decorah, Iowa, and Luther Seminary in Madison, Wisconsin—like Augsburg, nurtured secular leaders and pastors who recommended their alma maters. It is true that the majority of Norwegian Americans, in the countryside and to an even larger degree in the cities, did not become church members or concern themselves greatly about religious controversies. But the churches were the best organized segment of Norwegian American life, were respected by many immigrants who did not become members, and provided a disproportionate part of the immigrant culture's leaders. For those reasons, these religious networks exercised an influence far beyond their numbers in the history of Norwegian Americans in Minneapolis–St. Paul and the surrounding region.[49]

The Foundation for Many-Sided Norwegian American Communities

Of the Twin Cities, Minneapolis was the stronger urban magnet during the 1870s, outstripping its sister city downriver in size during the decade. The Norwegian-born population of Minneapolis numbered roughly a thousand in 1870 and more than doubled by 1875. The rapid rate of increase in both cities laid the foundations of a varied and visible immigrant subculture by 1880. The Twin Cities at this stage represented a pioneer mission field for Norwegian American immigrant churches, and both Trinity and Our Saviour's congregations devoted themselves to setting up chapels or missions in the Cities' expanding Norwegian neighborhoods. In 1870, Trinity in Minneapolis organized the first of these daughter churches, Trinity of St. Paul. Meanwhile, in 1874 in Minneapolis, the immigrant group's mother churches organized a second synod congregation, Immanuel, in the city's near northeast and another conference church, St. Olaf, in its near north. The diversity of Norwegian American Lutheranism in the Cities increased when the Hauge Synod established a church in south Minneapolis in 1872 and another near downtown St. Paul between 1871 and 1880. At the same time, the interest of local American Protestant groups resulted in the appearance of Norwegian-language Methodist and Baptist churches in Minneapolis. In both cities, Scandinavian and then Norwegian-origin congregations appeared before other immigrant community institutions. The "church party" among the immigrants and their descendants, moreover, showed a more steadfast devotion to maintaining churches than Norwegian Americans in general did to the secular organizations they founded, and thus these and later congregations were much more long lived than secular associations.[50]

The first flowering of secular organizations among Norwegian immigrants also took place in the 1870s and was pronouncedly Scandinavian in character. Although their cooperative efforts survived only if negotiation among the competing nationalities succeeded, Scandinavian immigrants joined forces because they were too few as separate nationality groups to mount the activities that attracted them. Inspired by shared leisure interests, they associated with the immigrants most like themselves and were happy for the opportunity to perform for an audience that could understand their closely related native tongues. The centuries of union between Denmark and Norway and a heavily Danish administrative class in the latter country created a common cultural legacy for those two nationalities, and the dual kingdom of Sweden and Norway from 1814 produced a sense of shared loyalty that survived the transition to life in America. Moreover, some old-stock

Americans lumped them together as "Swedes" or taunted them as "Yon Yonson."[51]

Nonreligious activity began in 1869 with the Scandinavian Society that had hosted Norwegian violinist Ole Bull and arranged the first local Syttende mai. After five years the society expired, Alfred Söderström suggests, because Norwegians were the dominant component in the membership. Hansen, on the other hand, indicates that its demise resulted more from the formation of the rival and more broadly representative Scandinavian Dramatic Society (later called Norden). But first Danes and then Norwegians departed Norden, complaining of domination by one of the other nationalities. As an exclusively Swedish American group with a Scandinavian name, however, Norden thrived for decades. These developments are typical of the difficulties in maintaining a durable balance in pan-Scandinavian cultural associations, especially when language use plays a central part of their activities. The small-scale enterprises that were founded along national lines, such as Norwegian immigrant literary societies, lecture series, and male quartets, had better chances of enduring. Still, the repeated founding of larger—and thus necessarily pan-Scandinavian—groups in the pioneer period testifies to the strength and similarity of the choral music and dramatic traditions that these immigrants brought to the Twin Cities.[52]

In retrospect, the 1870s appear to have witnessed the golden age of Scandinavian American cooperation. In Minneapolis the "early Scandinavians wished to make an impression on their fellow citizens of other nationalities." Scandinavian Twin Citians wanted to be visible in ways that would make their combined strength evident to the larger public. Public performances of plays at the Pence Opera House drew attention to the Scandinavian element's cultural sophistication. No Scandinavian organization put on a show in the 1870s to match the one provided by the uniformed members of the Scandia Lodge of the Knights of Pythias or the seventy-five men of Scandinavian Sharp Shooters Company of the Minnesota National Guard when they marched down city streets. Marking the Seventeenth of May during the decade functioned primarily as another opportunity to publicize the growing Scandinavian presence in the Cities. From 1870 on, Constitution Day festivities always included a public arrangement, usually at a big downtown hall. By the end of the decade Syttende mai had become a large event that included a massed chorus of Scandinavians and public addresses by immigrants elected to the city council or other local offices.[53]

The pooling of group resources on a regional basis proved necessary for several reasons in the post–Civil War period. Getting a hearing in the marketplace of ideas within the Norwegian American subculture or in American society provided one motivation for cooperation. Negotiating group priorities and the distribution of resources for further community development played equally central roles in these early indications of the Cities' growing importance as regional centers. One marshaling of resources in this period, publicizing the religious views and securing the financial foundations of Augsburg Seminary, involved one of the two religious networks among Norwegian American Lutherans in the Upper Midwest. The other efforts at combining strength were largely Scandinavian American in scope and focused on political representation, at either the municipal or the state level.

In the two years after its opening Augsburg Seminary grew with extraordinary rapidity. It maintained all but its practical studies program, increased its faculty to six, expanded its buildings, and yet suffered from overcrowding as its student body nearly doubled to 102 by 1876. In that year seminary president Weenaas left for Norway and Sverdrup was elected president of the seminary at the conference's annual meeting. From that point, he and Oftedal became the main focus of controversies with the synod. Religious mobilization and division, however, took a back seat because of a financial collapse that threatened the institution. The conference's annual meeting in 1877 mobilized to fund the school.[54]

Augsburg Seminary had always depended on contributions from the conference's rural congregations to pay its bills, but local pastors could block contributions because they, rather than lay leaders, were responsible for guaranteeing congregational payments. In 1875, however, the congregations themselves were made financially responsible, and the conference not only elected Sverdrup treasurer of the school but also gave him power to contact congregations directly to secure their contributions. The 1877 meeting approved financial measures that saved both the school and the conference. The delegates put Oftedal in charge of a campaign to raise the funds needed to eliminate Augsburg's debts. Sverdrup and Oftedal inspired an impressively quick and large groundswell of support. Oftedal founded a newspaper, *Folkebladet* (The People's Paper), and sent out ten thousand copies of an issue explaining the crisis and his plan to turn to lay committees in each congregation to solve it. In only three months, the lay committees raised more than enough funds to pay all the seminary's debts. Augsburg historian Carl Chrislock memorably sums up the result: "from now on Augsburg Seminary was not the concern of some ministers or of a clique, but [became]—as of right it ought to be—the school of the churches, of the people. The farmers got into the habit of calling it 'Our School.'"[55]

This important precedent was the first instance of a grassroots effort among Norwegian Americans to preserve an institution located in the Cities because they seemed the natural hub for the immigrant group's regional population. This more than any other single factor, it can be argued, helped Augsburg grow into the spiritual gathering point for Norwegian Americans that they hoped it would become. Inspired by belief in the laity, for the first time a large segment of the rank-and-file Norwegian Americans in the Upper Midwest—one of the two largest Lutheran bodies in the immigrant group—waged a coordinated campaign to collect resources on behalf of an institution that made the Cities the center of an important dimension of their lives.[56]

Early Political Mobilizations

Immigrants from the Nordic countries in the Twin Cities during these years mobilized to secure fair treatment from and representation at all levels of government. Among the first actions of the Scandinavian Society of Minneapolis in 1869 was lobbying the city government for the appointment of policemen from their national backgrounds. The *Minneapolis Tribune* reported the organization's appreciation later that year when the mayor satisfied the request with the hiring of George H. Johnson, a Norwegian immigrant, as the city's first Scandinavian-born patrolman. Before the end of the 1860s, eleven Scandinavians—a Dane, five Swedes, and five Norwegians—joined the city's police force. St. Paul's smaller numbers of Scandinavian immigrants also won positions in the police and fire departments during the 1860s, as municipal leaders recognized more recent population concentrations in the distribution of public work. In May 1869 the president of the Scandinavian

Society was reported in the *Tribune* as asserting that the "day was not far distant when it [Minneapolis] would be the Scandinavian metropolis" of the region. In August of that year, his boosterism seemed to have some substance when the Scandinavian Republicans of Minnesota held their first state convention in the city.[57]

At that date, the city's significance for the convention was as the urban center where the state's rural Scandinavian population could send its political representatives. The Nordic immigrant groups were then more numerous, longer established, and consequently most politically significant in the rural southeastern corner of the state, in such counties as Goodhue and Houston, where Norwegian settlers especially had been among the first to take up land in the 1850s. At the end of the 1860s, they were also assuming local political prominence in central and west-central Minnesota counties, where they represented in places a large proportion of the population in newly homesteaded areas. Their political clout in the Cities was small by comparison because their numbers then composed but a small portion of an urban public that included larger groups of old-stock Americans, Germans, and Irish. But in political attitudes, Scandinavian Americans from the countryside and their urban brethren had much in common at the time. As we have seen, many of the Cities' Scandinavian Americans had arrived in town after spending some years in the countryside and had family and friends who remained in rural areas. In many cases, they had formed their political views in the same historical and geographical environment as had their rural cousins.

Whatever their place of residence, most Scandinavian immigrants in 1869 were Republicans. They were mostly typical of the first of the three political generations of Scandinavian Americans defined by historian Lowell J. Soike. They had joined the Republican Party in defense of free-soil agriculture in the 1850s, had their antislavery sentiments confirmed during the Civil War, and continued to feel more comfortable with the largely Protestant Republicans than among the Irish and German Catholic immigrants who gave their allegiance to the Democratic Party. The developing crisis in agriculture that affected the growing Norwegian settlements in west-central and northwestern parts of the state in the late 1860s and 1870s, however, had just begun to make inroads in the Republican Party's popularity among rural Norwegian American voters in those areas.[58]

The presence of the Scandinavian Republican Convention in the city probably owed more to the efforts of F. Sneedorff Christensen, the Danish-born editor of the first Dano-Norwegian-language newspaper in Minnesota, *Nordisk Folkeblad* (Nordic People's Paper), than to the involvement of any other individual. In nineteenth-century political affairs, as in the religious activity of the period, newspapers played central—and explicitly partisan—roles in public persuasion and the dissemination of information. Christensen began to edit the paper in 1868 for its American owners in southeastern Minnesota and moved it and his residence to Minneapolis the year after purchasing the paper. Like a number of Scandinavian American journalists, Christensen thought the time had come for Nordic immigrants to win political representation in the areas of their heaviest settlement. He used *Nordisk Folkeblad* to advocate for the election of a Scandinavian to state office, settled on proposing qualified Scandinavian American candidates for Minnesota secretary of state as the best opportunity for success in the upcoming elections, and promoted the idea of holding a convention of the state's Scandinavian Republicans in Minneapolis to endorse one of those candidates.[59]

As president of the Minneapolis Scandinavian Society, Christensen called the convention to order. He was also soon elected to chair its committee on resolutions and serve as its secretary. A preconvention caucus of Norwegian Americans, some claimed, had argued for choosing Captain Mons Grinager, a candidate of their background, because Norwegians composed much the largest of the state's Nordic nationality groups. Early in the day, however, the convention passed a resolution to resist all attempts to weaken Scandinavian American unity, and after lengthy debate, the delegates decided not to admit to the convention the chief supporter of a candidate other than Hans Mattson, a Swede. After an informal vote, which showed only minimal support for other candidates, the assembly resolved to ask the Republican Party to place Mattson's name on the ballot for secretary of state. In return, the Scandinavian delegates in Minneapolis promised to "heartily support" the nominees and platform adopted by the party convention a month later in St. Paul. After three cheers for the city, the convention, and Mattson, the meeting was adjourned. The Scandinavian Society then showed delegates sights of the city, parading them through it in a procession of carriages, before hosting a banquet at a downtown hall.

The convention of Scandinavian American Republicans dramatically raised the curtain on the political ambitions of the Cities' Nordic populations in the pioneer period. In the following years Norwegians won places in both county and city governments. Because Minneapolis patrolman George H. Johnson was the earliest and longest serving of the local Norwegian American politicians, his career was a phenomenon that attracted comment from community observers. Hennepin County voters elected him sheriff in 1871 and kept him in that office until the end of 1877, when they sent him to the state house of representatives. In his position of eminence as probate judge in the 1880s, Andreas Ueland characterized Johnson as exceptionally electable because he seemed American rather than foreign-born and suited to the personal style of politics in the United States. He spoke Norwegian only poorly but had an unaccented American English as well as height and good looks. Both Carl G. O. Hansen and Johannes B. Wist repeat these features of Ueland's explanation, the latter stressing in addition that Johnson had arrived in America at a very young age and grown up in the Midwest. All accounts agree on the decisive role played by Johnson's Civil War service, which, in combination with these qualities, explained how a Norwegian could succeed so well politically when the immigrant group was still small and recently settled in the county.[60]

In municipal politics, Scandinavian Americans also made successful efforts to combine politically in the 1870s. Republican A. H. Edsten, a pillar of the Trinity Norwegian congregation and in whose commercial backyard many shopkeepers in the Scandinavian American business district met, became the first Nordic immigrant to win a city council seat. In 1874, local voters elected him to represent Ward 10, which coincided with the city's first Scandinavian American district. By the later 1870s, the burgeoning Scandinavian immigrant population resided in the Sixth Ward, redistricted to include the old Tenth Ward and stretch southeast toward the Cedar-Riverside section. After the 1878 elections, two Norwegian immigrants, Democrat Dr. Karl Bendeke and Republican A. C. Haugan, won seats on the council from Ward 6 and a Swedish American Republican represented the adjoining Ward 3. Although Bendeke, the ward's most prominent Norwegian American physician, left office after one term, Haugan brought his constituency's concerns to the city fathers for a decade and simultaneously functioned as one of the immigrant community's most important bankers. Political mobilization among Scandinavian Americans in Minneapolis brought results within a decade of the groups' large-scale migration to the city. This rapid success shows the benefits of exercising electoral solidarity, but it also illustrates the political advantage of Scandinavians' compact settlement southeast of the downtown district. A third essential factor in achieving political representation so early is likely that, as Carl G. O. Hansen emphasizes, most of the early Scandinavians in the city came through secondary migration from older Nordic communities in the Midwest. Most were not greenhorns fresh from Scandinavia but people who had prior experience with American society and politics.[61]

Similar Scandinavian American representation in St. Paul's municipal government would not come until the early 1890s. One explanation for this delayed development may be that Scandinavian Americans made up only half as large a part of St. Paul's population even at that later date. In the capital city, however, Nordic immigrants found a voice through state offices. Hans Mattson served as secretary of state in 1870–72, when he lived in St. Paul, and Norwegian American Carl Frederick Solberg of Minneapolis held office as assistant secretary of state for the following two years. Norwegian Americans from the southeastern and west-central parts of the state—such as state senators Lars K. Aaker and Albert E. Rice (then a resident of Willmar, Minnesota) and secretary of state Johan S. Irgens—augmented the immigrant group's contingent working at the capitol in the later 1870s. During the decade, moreover, three Scandinavian immigrants served as members of the state house of representatives from Minneapolis: Rice in 1870, George H. Johnson in 1878, and Andrew Tharaldsen in 1879. The last named two were Republicans like most Scandinavian Americans, but Rice took office as a Populist. His and Dr. Bendeke's election may suggest an early tendency among the Cities' Scandinavian Americans to support a range of political alternatives but might also arguably illustrate political sympathies influenced by the candidates' and immigrant groups' ties to agricultural communities in the region.[62]

A few characteristics stand out regarding urban Scandinavian Americans' involvement in politics during the 1870s. The first was the previously noted heavy preponderance of Republicans among the Nordic immigrants. The second was that regardless of national background, the majority of successful first-generation Nordic candidates shared the experience of having demonstrated their commitment to the United States by serving in the Civil War, the defining political event of the epoch. The third consisted in the large number of immigrant politicians with occupational experience as journalists for or owners of Scandinavian American newspapers. F. Sneedorff Christensen's use of *Nordisk Folkeblad* to recruit and sponsor Republican political candidates was typical rather than exceptional. The newspaper, never a profitable business, changed hands twice in two years before Hennepin County Sheriff George H. Johnson bought it in 1872 and maintained it as a Republican paper until he won a seat in the state legislature. In similar fashion, Carl Frederick Solberg and Hjalmar Eger launched *Minnesota* in the same year and quickly switched it from a Republican to a Democratic newspaper to compete with *Nordisk Folkeblad* for Scandinavian Americans' political allegiance. Eger owned and operated the paper alone after it had helped Solberg win political office in 1873. *Minnesota* closed up shop when its campaign to see a Norwegian American Democrat elected Minnesota secretary of state failed later that year. When local political organs ceased publication, their subscription lists were either sold to established ethnic newspapers like *Skandinaven* in Chicago or bought by local pressmen who were more interested in a career in journalism than one in politics. In 1873 three experienced compositors for *Nordisk Folkeblad*, for example, bought *Minnesota*'s equipment and circulation list as the basis for founding *Budstikken* (The Messenger), which was the Cities' primary Norwegian American newspaper until 1894. The Nordic-language newspapers in the Twin Cities during the 1870s, like the American press generally at the time, were mostly explicitly partisan organs.[63]

The fourth common characteristic of Scandinavian American politics in the 1870s was the overrepresentation of Norwegians among the Scandinavian Americans elected to office. No Dane and only one Swedish American were among the Nordic city council members and state legislators of this period. The lack of Danish Americans in elected office likely resulted from their small numbers in the Cities and state. As Carl G. O. Hansen suggests, Norwegian Americans' greater assertiveness may have come from knowing that they composed almost twice as large a group as Swedes in the state as late as 1880. Earlier Norwegian settlement in the region resulted in a stream of men who relocated in the Twin Cities after acquiring familiarity with American conditions elsewhere. But these factors alone insufficiently explain the small degree of Swedish American representation on the municipal level, because Swedish immigrants outnumbered Norwegian Americans in both Minneapolis and St. Paul in the 1870s. Swedish American editor and local historian Alfred Söderström explained this apparent anomaly in 1899 as follows in his survey of Scandinavian American contributions to Minneapolis politics: "In regard to political affairs, our brothers the Norwegians, particularly in the early years, were better represented than the Swedes in every respect. Nationalist feeling among Norwegians played the most important role and aided their progress in politics, because they invariably supported the candidacies of their countrymen unanimously, regardless the political party involved."[64]

Conclusion

Between 1865 and 1873, the first crest of immigration from Norway brought many newcomers who settled in the rural Upper Midwest. A growing minority among these found opportunities in the rapidly expanding Twin Cities. Then the postwar agricultural recession, changes in farming methods, and insect plagues prompted both recent arrivals and longer-settled Norwegians to move to the river cities, where many stayed longer than they originally planned. The recession made many, in town and country, realize the interdependence of rural and urban economies. Women took positions as domestic workers in Minneapolis and St. Paul and sent money home to families in the countryside. In these years, seasonal migration of workmen in and out of the Cities was the rule rather than the exception.

Cultural interdependence between rural and urban communities also became evident in Norwegian American church life. A local congregation was often the first organization Norwegian immigrants established, in the city as well as in the countryside. Initially, rural Lutheran ministers came to town, preached, and helped form the first urban congregations. Then, as Norwegians moved into different city neighborhoods, these "mother" churches sponsored missions that became daughter congregations across the Twin Cities. With the founding of

Augsburg Seminary and the centering of the conference, one of the two largest Norwegian Lutheran denominations, in Minneapolis, a network of congregations whose pastors had been educated at Augsburg developed. Before the 1870s were over, a second network of the group's churches, this one formed by the Norwegian Synod, branched out over the region.

The growth of the Norwegian-born population in Minneapolis–St. Paul laid foundations for a many-faceted community life by 1880, when the group made up nearly 5 percent of residents of Minneapolis and almost 2 percent of the people in the state capital. Small-business, educational, and occupational leadership groups with a prominent number of Civil and Dakota War veterans appeared. In 1869, some of these men joined others of a similar status among the cities' Swedes and Danes to found the Scandinavian Society, which hosted the visit of Norwegian celebrity violinist Ole Bull and inaugurated the celebration of Norway's Constitution Day, May 17, in the Twin Cities. During the rest of this period, the growth of the Norwegian population led to the end of most pan-Scandinavian organizations and the rise of separate nationality-based institutions for Norwegian immigrants. A variety of secular voluntary organizations, shops, and services run by Norwegian immigrants lined the commercial streets in Scandinavian neighborhoods of both cities by 1880. Political groups centered on issues in the homeland as well as local, state, and federal politics in the United States mobilized Norwegian American opinion. Norwegian-language newspapers expressed partisan viewpoints and encouraged public engagement.

The main themes of this book—Norwegians' immigration to the United States and remigration into Minneapolis–St. Paul, the history of those cities, the changing forms of community among the Cities' urbanized Norwegians, and their relations with other local population groups—evolved into new stages between 1865 and 1880. As the following chapter reveals, in the years between 1880 and 1905, Norwegian Americans' nationalist inclinations would reach new heights—with regard to their participation in US politics and, even more, as support for Norway's full independence from Sweden.

CHAPTER FOUR

Expansion's Golden Age

The Flowering of Norwegian Immigrant Culture in the Twin Cities

[1880–1905]

DURING THIS GOLDEN DECADE OF GROWTH FOR NORTHERLY MISSISSIPPI River cities, the rate of population change for Minneapolis and St. Paul was unsurpassed in two senses. First, no other cities in America were growing so fast. Only Kansas City came close to their phenomenal demographic explosion, as Minneapolis rose through the ranks from the thirty-eighth to the eighteenth largest of the nation's cities, and St. Paul moved from the forty-fifth to the twenty-third largest by 1890. Second, in absolute numbers no other decade witnessed so many people taking up residence in the Twin Cities. Minneapolis grew three and a half times larger, adding nearly 118,000 people to reach a population of 164,738. St. Paul expanded only a little less rapidly, slightly more than tripling its size as its population jumped by more than 90,000 to 133,156. In fewer than thirty years the frontier villages by the river had become the Twin Cities, a major, internationally known urban industrial center.[1]

The foreign-born and their children made up a disproportionately large part of the newcomers in the Twin Cities during the 1880s, when the largest wave of immigrants from northwestern Europe reached its peak and immigration from eastern and southern Europe began to rise. By the decade's close, nearly two-thirds of the residents of Minneapolis and over three-fourths of St. Paul's population consisted of the foreign-born and their offspring. The epoch-making shift reflected an enormous influx of Scandinavians, especially from Sweden but also from Norway. In both cities, growing Norwegian American communities had to cope with whirlwinds of change, a significant part of which involved adapting to living in close quarters with other religious and nationality groups. Economic and political competition and maneuvering for influence with Irish and German Catholics while banding together with Swedes and other Lutheran voters became a common thread in local affairs. The Norwegian American community in its districts of greatest concentration won representation in local government and educational and social services. It achieved election to office more often than the larger Swedish American community and provided disproportionately to the ranks of police constables and firefighters. This influence was especially true in the Cedar-Riverside district of Minneapolis. Councilman Lars Rand effectively negotiated municipal laws in favor of Norwegian saloon interests for a decade. In St. Paul Scandinavians played a smaller role in local politics. Although both Norwegian and Swedish immigrants took office in these years, Swedes were more prominent in the capital city, and Irish Americans dominated civic affairs.[2]

In 1880 St. Paul was a small city of a little more than 41,000 people. Its five largest foreign-born nationality groups in order of size were German, Irish, Swedish, Canadian (both French and English), and Bohemian. The first-generation Germanic presence, strengthened by much smaller central European groups from Bohemia and Austria, accounted for some 5,800 people—about a seventh of the whole population and four-tenths of the foreign-born. The capital city's 3,000 Irish Americans ranked second among the local immigrant communities, and two-thirds as large a contingent of Swedes composed the third-ranking ethnic group.

Ten years later new arrivals had significantly altered the city's ethnic composition, although some features in the situation remained the same. The Germanic population had grown almost as fast as the city as a whole, and remained dominant. The Swedish, Norwegian, and Danish groups, however, had quintupled or more in size, far outstripping the increase in other elements of the population. By 1890 Swedes had become the city's second-largest group, with a population nearly twice the size of the Irish community; the Norwegians had displaced the Bohemians as St. Paul's fifth-largest population component; and the Danes had become its seventh largest. As a portion of the foreign-born, Scandinavians had become nearly equal in size with the Germanic groups. With their children, the older German, Bohemian, and Austrian American communities composed a much larger part of the city's whole population (about 28 percent compared to the 17 percent made up by Scandinavians), but they may have been less united because they included Lutheran, Catholic, and Jewish elements, while the Scandinavians were overwhelmingly Lutheran.[3]

In Minneapolis, the five nationalities that dominated the foreign-born population in both 1880 and 1890 were, from largest to smallest, the Swedes, Norwegians, English and French Canadians, Germans, and Irish. In even more pronounced form than in St. Paul, the significant change in the 1880s came with the huge influx of Scandinavian immigrants. Already the biggest foreign-born group at the start of the decade, the Swedish community more than sextupled in size and grew to 19,398 by its end. In 1880, Swedish Americans outnumbered the second-ranking Norwegians by only some 540 people, but in ten years, that

TABLE 4.1

Population Groups of the Emerging Twin Cities in Order of Size

ST. PAUL		MINNEAPOLIS	
1880	**1890**	**1880**	**1890**
German	German	Swedish	Swedish
Irish	Swedish	Norwegian	Norwegian
Swedish	Canadian*	Canadian*	Canadian*
Canadian*	Irish	German	German
Bohemian	Norwegian	Irish	Irish

*both French and English

SOURCE: US Census for Minneapolis and St. Paul, 1880, 1890. See also the extended population table for Norwegian and Swedish Americans in chapter one (pages 16–17).

gap had grown to more than 6,770, even though the Norwegian-born population had grown five times larger in the same years and reached 12,624. Danes, still by far the smallest of the Scandinavian groups at 1,542 people in 1890, had multiplied their number by a factor of seven in ten years. With their children, these Scandinavian groups composed nearly 30 percent of the entire population of Minneapolis and 55 percent of its first- and second-generation immigrants as the 1890s began. Here was a promising demographic basis for cooperation in municipal affairs. The Scandinavians, moreover, were the more easily able to capitalize on that potential because they understood each other's languages, shared the Lutheran faith, and in general were culturally more like each other than other groups in the city. Canadians, for example, split as they were between French and English backgrounds, even together made up a distant third-largest component in the city's population. Germans, who remained the fourth-largest group in 1890, were nearly as numerous as the Canadian population and culturally more unified, despite religious differences. Like the Canadians, however, the composite group of Germans was outnumbered more than four to one by the Scandinavians. The Irish community, which maintained its position as the smallest of the five leading groups in the city during the 1880s, was less than half the size of the German and Canadian populations. Even if French Canadian, German, and Irish Catholics could unite behind a cause, they represented together a much smaller local presence than the overwhelmingly Lutheran Scandinavian community.[4]

The signal change during the decade was the arrival of the Scandinavians, especially the Swedes. As striking as that seemed, however, the new Nordic cast of the recent immigrants confirmed rather than altered the Cities' overwhelmingly northwestern European population makeup. Nonetheless, by 1890 the size of the Polish and Russian populations revealed that rising immigration from eastern Europe had made a local impact. In St. Paul, ethnically the more diverse of the cities from its founding, Poles had already been noticeable at the start of the decade, and chain migration was the chief factor in the quadrupling of the group's size by 1890. At the same time, the city's Russian population became significant, and like the Polish presence included both Catholics and Jews. In Minneapolis, both central and eastern European settlement left its mark in the 1880s. While the Bohemian population grew little, the Austrian presence became sizable for the first time and the influx of Russians rivaled that of the Danes. Like the state capital, Minneapolis contained an eastern European Jewish community by 1890 largely because of newcomers from Russia, although some Polish Jews arrived, too. Southern European nationality groups, such as Greeks and Italians, remained very small in the Cities and Minnesota as a whole until after 1900.[5]

Negotiating Dissimilar Civic Identities in a Period of Galloping Growth

Historian Mary Lethert Wingerd argues persuasively that by the end of the 1880s each of the Twin Cities had acquired a civic identity that diverged significantly from the demographic profiles recorded in the census. Wingerd emphasizes the importance of cultural differences in negotiating the relationships among groups that came to represent the local understanding of the community's character. Through these largely informal negotiations, a "combination of social, political and economic positioning" in a particular place and time, she asserts, the two cities' peoples, especially their most influential leaders, evolved a local civic compact—a more or less accepted system which they used to grapple with problems and define a hierarchy among local populations in the distribution of the urban areas' resources. The priorities set by this customary practice shaped the local community identity more than the numerical size of demographic groups. In addition to ethnicity and religion, the cultural features most critical to the civic identity were class, race, time of arrival, and interethnic networking through social and political institutions. Together, these factors produced the bonds and attitudes by which people understood the local social landscape and determined economic and political advantage. This is a useful approach for exploring more closely the social environments that Norwegian Americans met in the Twin Cities in the 1880s and later. By the closing years of the nineteenth century, St. Paul had become the inland Northwest's only predominantly Democratic, Irish Catholic city, and Minneapolis was rapidly gaining the reputation of being its heavily Republican, Scandinavian Lutheran metropolis. Both characterizations were of course oversimplifications and amounted to a shorthand that identified and underlined a few of the Twin Cities' most noticeable differences. Still, as a convenient basis for attitudes and behavior, these popularly acknowledged community identities had considerable impact.[6]

The early arrival of large numbers of German and Irish Catholic immigrants in St. Paul before the Civil War, combined with the established presence of French Canadian coreligionists at the city's founding, resulted in an unusually full acceptance of Catholicism and a network of Catholic institutions while the main contours of the civic identity were still taking shape. The elite of the capital's founding fathers, relocated adventurers from Protestant New England, led the organization of Minnesota as a territory after working as traders for the American Fur Company and acknowledged the early French Canadian Catholic priests and institutions as the most effective organizers of community life among the heavily Catholic local population in the antebellum years. More than half of the adults in St. Paul were either Irish-born (26 percent) or German-born (23.5 percent) in 1860, and most of these people were Roman Catholics, even though the Germans in the city did include Lutherans and members of other Protestant denominations.[7]

Scandinavian immigrants also arrived in the 1850s but not in impressively large numbers until around 1880. By then, according to Wingerd's analysis, the early German immigrants' skills and capital on arrival, along with their success at founding business partnerships with old-stock Americans, had enabled them to penetrate all levels of the local economy and gain acceptance even in its highest social circles. It was a critical segment of the poorer, less-skilled Irish, however, who had achieved the most surprising economic mobility, she says, largely due to the aid they received from Catholic institutions established before the Irish arrived and to the status given to Catholicism by the most eminent of the city's religious and business elite. By 1880 St. Paul boasted of its grand Catholic cathedral and its energetic bishop John Ireland; Irish Catholic Democrats dominated local politics and municipal jobs; and railroad magnate James J. Hill, married to an Irish woman, favored her compatriots in his employment and business dealings, on which the local economy depended. Yet, even before the flood of Scandinavian newcomers in the 1880s, census statistics revealed that the city contained nearly as many Nordic as Hibernian immigrants. In

1880, it counted 2,759 foreign-born Swedes, Norwegians, and Danes compared to 3,013 Irish-born inhabitants. The longer-established and better-connected Irish leadership, supported by its economic and political advantages, nevertheless was on the way to imprinting its image on the local civic identity.[8]

In his "Historical Sketch" of St. Paul for the *Report on the Social Statistics of Cities* commissioned by the US Census of 1880, J. Fletcher Williams, then the secretary of the Minnesota Historical Society, states that the Irish population of the city reached its peak "in 1867, when there was occasion for a large body of laborers in the city for public improvements." After that, the Irish population declined, and by 1880, he asserts, "Swedes" had become the most common unskilled workers in the city. Although the Irish population remained large, by then "laborers' boarding-houses and other strongholds of the Irish population . . . [had] passed into the hands of the Scandinavians." Williams's contemporary account suggests that a significant part of the Irish moved out of the city or upward in its labor market when the amount of occasional day work in St. Paul became less and that later-arrived Scandinavians had replaced them at the bottom of the local occupational ladder by the start of the decade. Statistics concerning the national background of all common laborers in the city for 1880 are not available, but an analysis of all of St. Paul's employed adult Norwegians at the time shows that the men in that second-largest Scandinavian element in the population as often worked in the skilled trades (37.3 percent) as in unskilled labor (36.4 percent). Recently arrived Scandinavian immigrants might well have taken over a substantial part of the work done by Irish laborers earlier, but judging by the Norwegian example, a significant number came with skills they could put to use in better-paid work.[9]

In Minneapolis consequential divergences also existed between the city's demographic profile and its civic identity. Perhaps most significantly, in their early history St. Paul and Minneapolis had attracted quite distinct groups who came to dominate their social and economic elites. Rather than the old-stock American and Anglo-Canadian former fur traders who controlled affairs in early St. Paul, the members of the founding elite in Minneapolis were primarily industrial entrepreneurs from northern New England. More closely tied to their eastern connections, these men and their families maintained much more segregated economic and social elites than the parallel segment of St. Paul society. A year after its incorporation as a town in 1856, Minneapolis counted fully 60 percent of its residents as natives of Maine, and by the end of that decade the leaders of this Little New England on the Mississippi had established the Sons of Maine, Bowdoin College Alumni Association, and the New England Society—exclusive organizations that cemented the social solidarity in and perpetuated the influence of the Yankee elite. New England Protestant steeples, not the spires of Catholic institutions, marked the Minneapolis skyline in its first critical decade.[10]

The city's rapid growth before the 1880s was largely the result of the influx of those groups and large numbers of Scandinavian newcomers. Yet, in the same fashion as the earlier city directories, the sketch of the "social statistics" of Minneapolis in the federal census of 1880 (unlike the parallel study of St. Paul) made no mention of immigrants or migrant Blacks but concentrated almost entirely on the portrayal of the city as a successfully developing business opportunity. As the anonymous writer of the sketch noted, "The growth and prosperity of Minneapolis have been almost wholly due to the natural advantages of its site."[11]

Nonetheless, the political and social realities in Minneapolis at the start of the decade suggested a composite civic identity that acknowledged the status and contributions of immigrants and their children, especially those from Scandinavia. Although the mayoralty of Minneapolis remained in old-stock, Anglo-American hands, in that decade and the next the Scandinavian population steadily found representation on the city council. Norwegians and Swedes also held prominent positions in local civic life, serving as judges, commissioners of city agencies, engineers for city works, and leaders of the city and county school systems. In St. Paul as early as the 1850s, St. Patrick's Day became an emblematic occasion for the whole city, a celebration when the Irish embraced all immigrant groups and their contributions to the capital while drawing attention to their own importance as political brokers among the city's different subcultures. In Minneapolis, the Seventeenth of May, with its parade and associated program of public speeches and entertainments, played a similar role, becoming a general civic holiday to which the entire public was welcome during the 1870s and 1880s. From then until

1905, Syttende mai was the time for politicians of all stripes to recognize the group's—and all immigrants'—importance to the city and state by gracing Constitution Day events with their presence.[12]

The large Scandinavian immigrant presence, together with Minneapolis's essential role in processing the agricultural products of a hinterland heavily settled by the same Nordic groups, forged the civic compact of the city as the hub or population capital of Scandinavian America. The economic interdependence of the Mill City and its outskirts, the ongoing seasonal labor movements between city and countryside, and the accelerating urbanization of the region's country folk by 1903 led Lincoln Steffens to his famous characterization of Minneapolis as a "Yankee with a round Puritan head, an open prairie heart, and a great, big Scandinavian body." The Scandinavian middle and broad working classes epitomized the general population, Steffens continues, that moved in and out of the city lumbering and raising wheat; that ran the New England leadership's saw and flour mills, industries, and businesses; and that labored in all these enterprises in exchange for "one or two Scandinavians" on the local political "ticket." In politics, Blacks and Scandinavians were minority Republican groups in St. Paul. In the capital's sister city, Blacks were less numerous and constituted part of a Democratic political minority that included shifting parts of the city's Scandinavian residents.[13]

From Frontier River Towns to Gateway Cities

St. Paul benefited most directly from the great age of railroad development in Minnesota during the 1880s, when two transcontinental lines through the state and a network of spur lines bound the region's economy ever more closely to the Twin Cities. The mercantile economy of St. Paul rose to unprecedented heights on the strength of railroad magnate James J. Hill's accomplishments, which also provided the jobs that attracted a large working class. This situation drew not only Irish newcomers but large numbers of German and a wave of Scandinavian immigrants to the city. Rapid settlement of the region followed extension of the railroads, and the settlers' needs swelled the coffers of St. Paul's commercial houses. As the head and hub of railway travel leading into the interior Northwest, the city remained the jumping-off point for greenhorn immigrants and easterners, who spent time and money locally before boarding trains for other destinations.[14]

Emboldened by the buoyancy given the local economy by transportation construction, St. Paul capitalists launched meatpacking and marketing as an answer to Minneapolis's industrial superiority. Yet, as the decade went on, the Mill City by the Falls of St. Anthony increased its greater attraction as a field of opportunity for migrants and immigrants. This was the unparalleled era of productivity increases at Minneapolis flour mills. By 1880, the city had become the nation's leader in flour production. Although only a few new flour mills were built during the 1880s, production tripled and far surpassed the output of rival flour milling centers in the United States and abroad. Related tributary industries also boomed: the transportation, storage and trading of wheat; the manufacture of agricultural, elevator, and milling machinery; machine maintenance shops and cooperage and bag-making firms; and transportation networks for marketing the flour—all flourished and offered thousands of additional jobs.[15]

The largest employer in Minneapolis during the 1880s was sawmilling and lumbering, which was more labor intensive. A combination of factors led to the transfer of many sawmills, lumberyards, and related door, blind, sill, and sash companies from the central mill district to bankside areas in north and northeast Minneapolis. Local lumber production during the decade nearly doubled. The seasonal migration of thousands of men between logging in the state's northern white pine forests and sawmill work in Minneapolis took on gigantic proportions during these years. As the Twin Cities population soared, moreover, so did their public and private construction projects, and since St. Paul contained relatively few sawmills and lumberyards, most of the supply of wooden goods for both cities came from Minneapolis, which developed into a mecca for woodworkers of all kinds. The Mill City also became the world's leading financial market for grain and lumber. Its rise as a major banking center provided reserves of capital for other industries, such as metal foundries and machine works that gave jobs to many more by the decade's end. Minneapolis factories diversified as they freed themselves from locations by the falls by using steam and then electric motors. The city had much to sell, at home and abroad, and attracted hosts of people through immigration and urbanization.

All these developments show that Minneapolis and St. Paul changed from frontier river towns to "gateway cities" and that, simultaneously, the frontier moved west and turned into their hinterland. As William Cronon writes in *Nature's Metropolis*, using the terminology of central place theory in his study of Chicago's economic history, the Twin Cities became the "chief intermediary between newly occupied farms and towns in the West and the maturing capitalist economy of the Northeast and Europe."[16]

As we have seen, the specific situation of the metropolis on the Mississippi that secured its gateway status to the Upper Midwest between the 1880s and the early 1900s consisted in its mastery of the river's only falls with saw and flour mills. The waterpower's economic potential was secured by improvements in the milling of the region's winter wheat so that it became the finest white flour in the world at the time.[17]

The Roots of an Enduring Rivalry between the Twin Cities

In the 1880s, St. Paul and Minneapolis shared exceptional demographic and economic growth. They attracted a similar configuration of immigrants that, especially with regard to their own and their hinterland's Scandinavian presence, made them look more like each other and less like other American cities. They experienced the same growing social differentiation that accompanied technological change and territorial expansion in boom times. And all this occurred in the common circumstances of the startling speed with which the neighboring cities witnessed the close of their frontier period—the end of the timeframe during which they were catching up with the development of older US cities.

Yet perhaps the 1880s was the decade of greatest rivalry between Minneapolis and St. Paul. Knowledge of the success or failure of the local business community spread rapidly by word of mouth, letters, and newspapers—and thus affected the ebb and flow of migration to each city and made the people of each join in the championing of one of the Twin Cities above the other that filled the pages of local newspapers during the era. St. Paul was the more Catholic, Irish, and Democratic; Minneapolis the more Protestant, Scandinavian, and Republican—or third party. These, along with their economic differences, constituted the cornerstones of the Cities' civic identities as dissimilar twins in opposition and competition. With this foundation, a competitive boosterism and expressions of boisterous as well as bitter intercity rivalry were perhaps unavoidable. The emblematic role played by Syttende mai and St. Patrick's Day celebrations emphasized the different civic identities and competition between the Twin Cities.[18]

Attracting people, not only as customers during these events but as permanent residents, was the main point of the competition over civic festivals. As one Minneapolis patriot boldly expressed it: "Population is the true test of a city's greatness. . . . Population brings wealth. Men are so much capital in a state." Neither city was slow to include immigrant groups in promotional civic festivals. Farmers' Day at the Minnesota State Fair exhibited the agricultural products and cultural handicrafts of rural German and Scandinavian Americans, among others. Three times in the first five years of its existence the Minneapolis Exposition agreed to include large exhibitions and public sales of Scandinavian painting and sculpture under the auspices of the city's Norsk Kunstforening (Norwegian Art Association), which businessmen and professionals in the immigrant community organized expressly to promote the homeland's high culture and show the work of local Norwegian American artists.[19]

A more serious conflict concerning the national census of population in 1890 arose over how many residents each city had actually attracted during the 1880s. A US marshal from St. Paul and members of that city's police force tried to break up what he claimed was the fraudulent exaggeration of the population count for Minneapolis. The Mill City's civic leaders produced a formal denial of illegalities and then alleged exaggeration in the state capital's count. The stakes were well known. Federal census officials ordered a recount and found that both cities had overcounted their inhabitants. However, the "census war of 1890" demonstrated that the Mill City was rapidly outdistancing St. Paul in population and made clear the long-term winner of the demographic competition.[20]

Territorial Expansion, Technological Change, Social Differentiation, and Segregation

During the 1880s, the Twin Cities witnessed the increasing spatial segregation of urban functions, ethnic and religious groups, and socioeconomic classes. The many newcomers led contractors to erect housing divisions, tenements, and lodging house blocks to meet demand. Municipal leaders and property speculators urged the movement of city limits far beyond what was necessary in their eagerness to profit from the real estate boom. In 1883 Minneapolis roughly tripled its area by annexing large tracts on all sides of town but its eastern boundary toward St. Paul. The capital city moved its boundaries out later in the decade. With each legal extension of the city limits came demands for municipal services—platting and clearing residential, commercial, and industrial districts, grading and paving roads, implementing sewerage and refuse removal systems, providing police and fire protection—and these functions and others created ever larger numbers of jobs. In one decade, both cities built horsecars, cable cars, steam trains, and electric streetcars. New forms of transportation made expansion and more scattered housing additions practical. Business leaders and their families in the Twin Cities also began using telephones to speed communication and electric lighting to extend working and social life by the decade's end.[21]

Social differentiation and segregation accompanied the rapid pace of technological and territorial change. In St. Paul, the wealthy left the riverside lower town for the socially exclusive heights of Summit Avenue. The upper-middle class relocated in the nearby Crocus and Cathedral Hill neighborhoods. In Minneapolis, the old-stock elite abandoned the town center for streets near the city's chain of lakes. The downtown evolved into mill-industrial, warehouse, and commercial-retail districts. The more genteel retail stores and cultural institutions moved with their clientele. Much of the burgeoning working-class and immigrant population lived in a densely filled "walking city" near the industrializing segment of the town center where they were employed. These groups, especially the newcomers and transients among them, also filled the former homes of higher-class residents on the fringes of downtown as these decayed and were converted to apartment or rooming houses. In

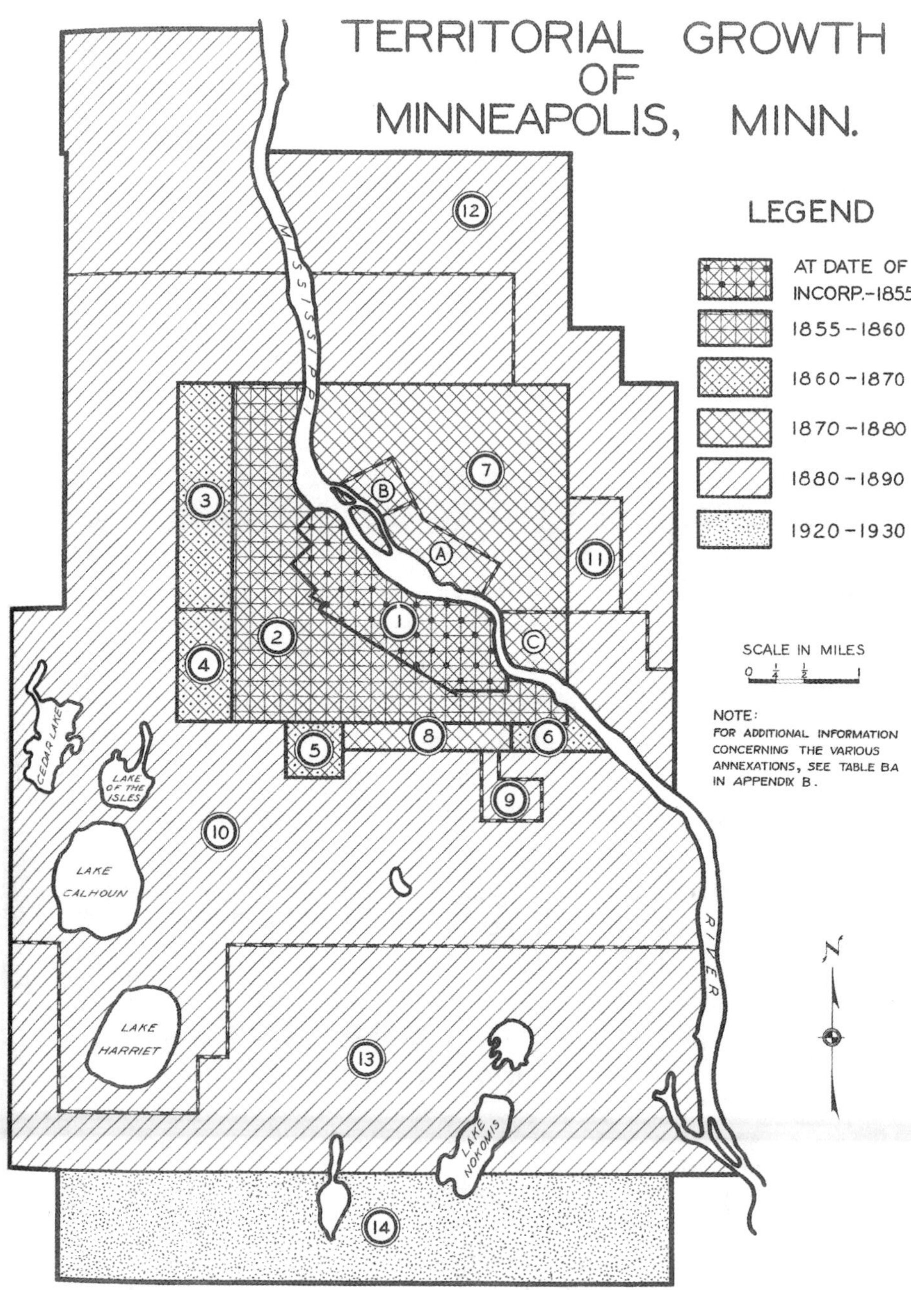

ABOVE AND OPPOSITE: From Calvin F. Schmid, *Social Saga of Two Cities: An Ecological and Statistical Study of Social Trends in Minneapolis and St. Paul* (Minneapolis: Minneapolis Council of Social Agencies, 1937)

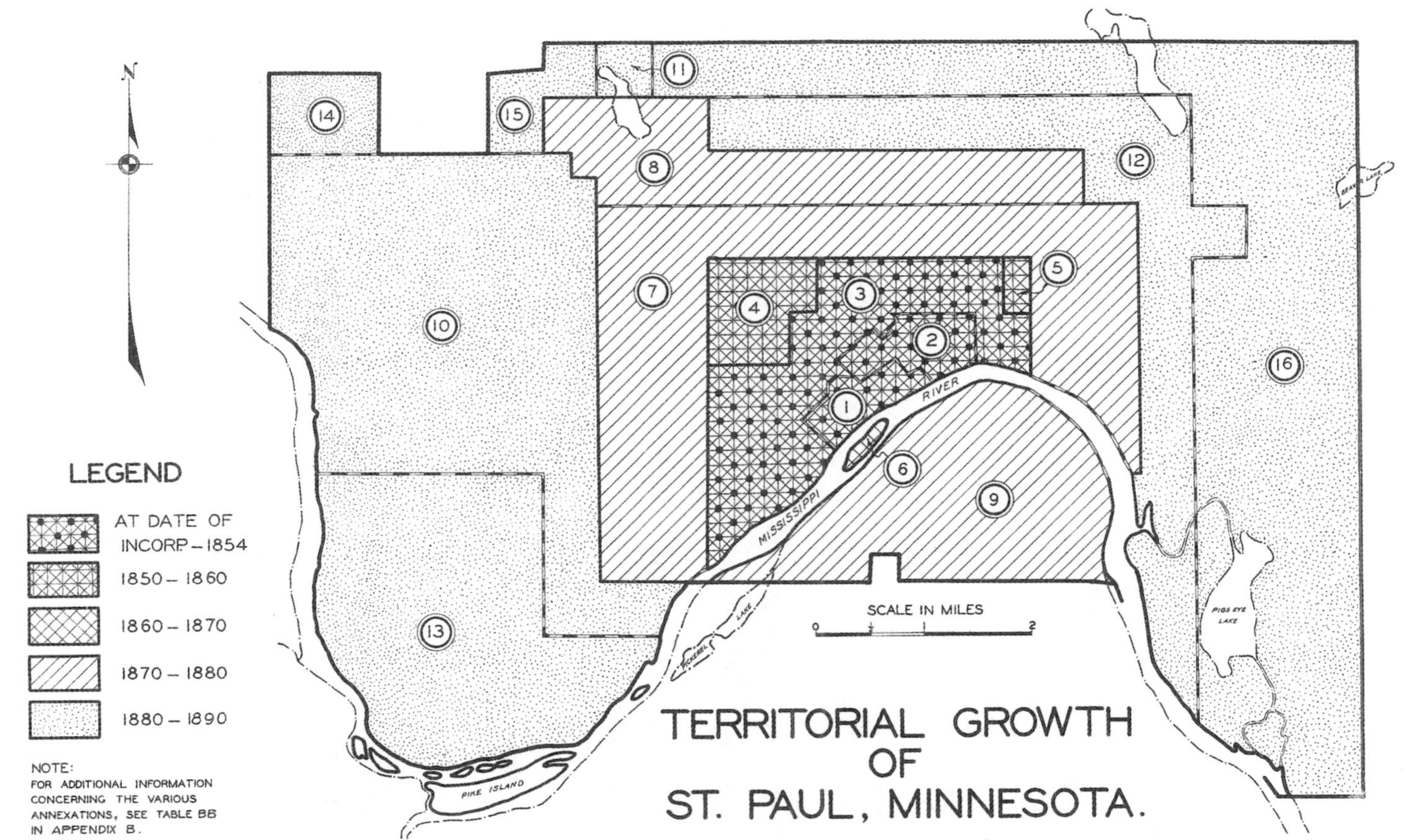
N
LEGEND
AT DATE OF INCORP. – 1854
1850 – 1860
1860 – 1870
1870 – 1880
1880 – 1890
NOTE:
FOR ADDITIONAL INFORMATION CONCERNING THE VARIOUS ANNEXATIONS, SEE TABLE BB IN APPENDIX B.
1
2
3
4
5
6
7
8
9
10
11
12
13
14
15
16
MISSISSIPPI
RIVER
PIKE ISLAND
PICKEREL LAKE
PIGS EYE LAKE
SCALE IN MILES
0
1
2
TERRITORIAL GROWTH
OF
ST. PAUL, MINNESOTA.

St. Paul, such quarters included city center districts and neighborhoods from Scandinavian "Swedetown" and Swede Hollow on the east, the mixed Mount Airy area north of downtown, and the largely German Frogtown and mixed housing divisions farthest west. In Minneapolis, immigrant and other working-class families moved north and south of Bridge Square as businesses, workshops, and a motley mixture of flop-house hotels, boardinghouses, and bars occupied the city's riverfront. In the 1880s, the Scandinavian community's center of gravity moved southeast down Washington Avenue to the Cedar-Riverside area and farther south to the Franklin Avenue neighborhood. The migration of the south-side German community, whose center remained somewhat farther west, followed a parallel route. On the north of downtown, the German neighborhood also remained in the interior, but moved farther out. On its west in 1880, developers opened the Oak Lake addition, a housing development for the upper-middle class. To the east of the north-side Germantown was the largely Norwegian but mixed Scandinavian community, many of whose men worked in the new sawmilling district along the Mississippi. On the east side of the river, in the former St. Anthony and the northeast quarter of Minneapolis, Scandinavians gathered in the east bank lumbering districts. From the later 1880s to 1914, both Scandinavian and recent arrivals from southern and eastern Europe clustered in what soon became known locally as the "Nordeast," one of the city's most "ethnic" neighborhoods. Working-class families of varying national backgrounds resided nearer the east-side flour milling district, and farther to the east toward St. Paul an upper-middle-class community expanded close to the University of Minnesota. The Irish in both cities during this period, although mostly residents of working-class immigrant neighborhoods, were less concentrated in particular areas and instead found homes in nearly all working-class districts.[22]

Two mostly working-class groups in these years, Blacks and Jews, lived a more segregated existence in the Cities, even though they resided very close to their socioeconomic equals. The established, increasingly middle-class German Jewish areas of St. Paul were downtown and on the bluffs above the state capitol building. Their later-arriving, mostly Russian coreligionists lived on the city's near west side. At the start of the 1880s, most of the roughly five hundred Jewish residents of Minneapolis lived on the south side close to the central business district. As the decade progressed, the first Jewish community moved farther west and south toward Tenth Street. Newer Jewish arrivals from Romania gathered nearer the Scandinavian community around Franklin Avenue, while the most recent newcomers in the years up to World War I, primarily from Russia and Poland, settled on the near north side to the east of the German and Scandinavian communities and between them and the city center. In this period, most of St. Paul's Blacks lived in the "Negro rookery"—old, shabby, single-family housing near lower Jackson Street in the central commercial district. The first settlement area of the Minneapolis Black community was close to the east bank of the Mississippi near Main Street in St. Anthony. After the merger of the towns by the falls, Blacks followed their jobs as cleaners and porters to downtown businesses across the river and relocated in the heavily Scandinavian Ward 6 and Cedar-Riverside areas or farther west on the fringe of downtown by the intersection of Tenth Street and Nicollet Avenue.[23]

As unhealthy and unsafe as the shabby locations that much of the Black community inhabited—and totally without municipal services—were the flats at the bottom of the gorges the Mississippi had dug near the Cities' downtowns and the ravine created by Phalen Creek in east St. Paul. There the poorest residents, mostly immigrants of different national origins but also some native-born Americans, lived. The public named the best known of these places the Bohemian Flats of Minneapolis and St. Paul's Swede Hollow with a half-informed disregard that suggested how separate the life of these pockets of poverty seemed.

In both cities, the Norwegian immigrants arriving in the 1880s and 1890s found themselves mostly in close contact with rather familiar northwestern European cultures, but they also confronted a mainstream American culture that for those arriving directly from Norway was unfamiliar. Less often but especially in south Minneapolis, whether they had prior American experience or not, Norwegians also adjusted to and acquired experience with living in close proximity to Jewish and Black communities. Many Norwegians in St. Paul and Minneapolis must also have at least heard about the conditions of life for the impoverished in Bohemian Flats and Swede Hollow, both of which counted a few Norwegian inhabitants and were adjacent to neighborhoods containing centers of Norwegian American community life in the Cities.[24]

How the Cities' Norwegian American Communities Became the Heart of the Heartland

The golden age of expansion saw more Norwegian immigrants and their children arrive in the Cities than any other period in the area's history. Altogether, close to thirteen thousand people came directly or by stages from Norway and took up residence in the Twin Cities during the 1880s. As they had in the fifteen years following the Civil War, a large majority of these people continued to migrate in from the surrounding region rather than arrive directly from Norway. Their adjustment was primarily to urban life in the Cities rather than to the United States. The population explosion within the Norse enclaves, like that in the metropolitan area as a whole, mixed people fresh off the boats and trains from Europe with a variety of individuals who had already begun their accommodation to American life. In the cities of the Upper Midwest, these "experienced" Norwegian newcomers included former pioneer homesteaders, veterans of the Civil and Dakota Wars, agricultural youth from the region, and people continuing the western movement from more easterly towns, cities, and farming districts. These groups brought to the tasks of urban life a greater knowledge of English as well as familiarity with American customs and attitudes. On the other hand, the 1880s also witnessed the arrival of a larger number of greenhorns who came directly from Norway's emigrant depots to the Twin Cities than any other decade. The homeland they left was more often urban, and because it was also industrializing, many of them had acquired occupational skills and social attitudes that diverged from those of earlier Norwegian immigrants. Thus, the stage was set—for a meeting of greenhorn Norwegian newcomers and more or less Americanized Norwegian immigrants from the surrounding countryside, as well as for meetings between these people, other immigrant groups, and the Cities' old-stock Americans.[25]

The compatriots coming from abroad were an additional presence—a second human wave cresting on top of the already established secondary migration of Norwegian Americans, especially single young people, from the countryside into the Twin Cities. The American custom of limiting farm women's work to household and family chores, along with the urban market for domestic workers, as we have seen, drew Norwegian American daughters to the city, where they could both support themselves and send money home. As Minneapolis and St. Paul's population and industrial diversity rapidly grew, the opportunities for young women as service and textile mill workers multiplied apace. Boys in their later teens composed a large part of the enclaves' single male group, and among them were many a Norwegian American farmer's son who had left the homestead for the city. Rural families often calculated that sons too could contribute as much or more to the family economy by leaving for town, especially when the introduction of farm machinery allowed fieldwork to be completed with fewer hands. In the Upper Midwest, as elsewhere in the country, mature couples and entire families also joined the tide of people moving to cities. Like international migration, however, urbanization was increasingly becoming a youth movement, the result of decisions made mostly by single sons and daughters.

The Norwegian American communities in Chicago and Brooklyn also experienced the arrival of countrymen both from the surrounding countryside and from Norway. But Brooklyn's Little Norway had only a very small Norwegian American hinterland in the other boroughs of the city and New Jersey. Most of its newcomers early in the 1880s came through seamen deserting in the port of New York or, late in the decade, from people fleeing the depressed shipping districts in southern Norway. Brooklyn's floating population of Norwegians consisted largely of seafarers in port between voyages. In Chicago, Norwegian American Great Lakes seamen made up a similar but smaller itinerant group than in the Brooklyn maritime colony. On the other hand, Chicago's Norwegian centers drew more people, especially the unmarried young, from a larger ethnic hinterland that included the country's oldest Norwegian American settlement areas in northern Illinois and eastern Wisconsin.[26]

Between the 1880s and World War I the distinctive features of Minneapolis–St. Paul with regard to immigration directly from Norway and urbanization became apparent. First, the Twin Cities then functioned as the only large urban magnet in the Upper Midwest. From the Canadian border south through western Wisconsin to St. Louis and west to the edge of European American settlement, no other urban center could compete with the Cities' entrepreneurial opportunities and job market. Second, precisely this area had since 1865 attracted the bulk of Norwegian immigrants and by the early 1900s had become home to the most populous and geographically extensive array of Norwegian settlements. In that decade the combined force of movement in from this huge hinterland and immigration directly from Norway began to give the Cities the largest *proportion* of Norwegian Americans of any metropolitan area in the nation. The two demographic movements led directly to the rise and enduring place of Norwegian Americans as one of the Cities' largest population groups. In Chicago and Brooklyn, on the other hand, Norwegian Americans never became more than a very small part of the general population.

Like the Twin Cities themselves in these years, their Norwegian enclaves claimed as their hinterland the American Northwest to the Pacific Coast. The Cities were the heart of this heartland, and through a dynamic interaction between immigration to this hinterland, secondary migration from it to the regional hub, and, from the 1880s through the 1920s, heavy immigration directly from Norway, Minneapolis–St. Paul became the preeminent urban center for Norwegian Americans in the United States. The 1880s witnessed the turning point, the critical shifting of weight, that made the Twin Cities—particularly Minneapolis—the ethnic group's center of gravity nationally. For Brooklyn, seamen who "went on land" in the city were the critical element in community growth. For the Twin Cities, the "seafarers of the prairies" were mostly young people with a double rural heritage, first from Norway's countryside and then from the farmsteads of the Upper Midwest. From the 1880s onward these youthful newcomers increasingly found themselves living side by side with young single people newly arrived by boat and train from Norway's cities.

The Enclaves that Welcomed Norwegian Newcomers during the 1880s

Compared to the many thousands of Norwegians who migrated into the Cities during the 1880s, the Norwegian American population already residing in the urban centers was quite small. Norwegian Americans composed only slightly over one in twenty people in Minneapolis and less than one of fifty residents in St. Paul at the start of the decade. By its end, the Mill City's Norse enclave had received a group three times its size at the 1880 census, and St. Paul's colony met six arrivals for each Norwegian already there at the decade's start. Certain characteristics of the Norwegian American population of Minneapolis and St. Paul assisted these greenhorns' adjustment to the Cities' rapidly changing urban environments.[27]

In 1880, the Twin Cities' residents as a whole, including the local Norwegian Americans, were relatively young. Over four-fifths of both the Norwegian-born and the general population of the Cities consisted of people under forty years old. The significant differences in the age of the immigrant community appeared in its exceptionally large group of adults in their twenties (40 percent) and unusually small group of children (7 percent). Weighted toward young adults, the Norwegian-born exemplified a relatively newly established immigrant community. The age of the general population was more evenly distributed. Adults in their twenties made up 27 percent and children composed 29 percent of the Cities as a whole. Looking at the size and age of the second generation in the Norwegian community helps explain its preponderance of young adults and smaller proportion of children. Only about a third of the immigrant community was American-born, but 81 percent of these people in Minneapolis and 86 percent in St. Paul were children under fifteen. Most of their parents had not begun childbearing until after they left Norway.[28]

Judging by the age and state in which their children were born, the large majority of the young Norwegian couples living in the local enclaves at the 1880 census had started their families elsewhere—in Illinois, Iowa, Wisconsin, and Minnesota—and later migrated into the Cities. The largest element in a community that was mostly foreign-born, these young parents had been brought up in the Norwegian homeland. Their strong inclination was to speak to their children in their native tongue and share, as Einar Haugen analyzed the situation, "All the lore that is natural for parents to transmit to their children. . . . the nursery rhymes, the proverbs, the anecdotes, the family sayings, the prayers, the songs . . . [are] woven into the very process of language learning in childhood." He stressed, "Only in Norwegian could the immigrant father and mother function as such, and they vigorously resisted any attempt to lessen their socio-cultural role." Haugen's words neatly explain why the Cities' Norwegian enclaves were foreign-language communities in 1880.[29]

If their compatriots' preference in marriage partners up to 1880 offered a guide to future behavior, these young adults were likely to choose mates within the immigrant community. Most young, single Norwegian adults in the Cities who were looking for a mate in 1880 sought out a companion with whom courtship and intimacy could occur with the ease that comes from using one's mother tongue and all the cultural nuances most easily expressed through it. They could select a mate from among the unattached Norwegian Americans already nearby or among the many single newcomers who arrived from Norway in the course of the decade. At the time of the census, an overwhelming majority of Norwegian immigrants and their children had married within their own community. In 1880 Norwegian-born couples led nearly 80 percent of the enclave households in Minneapolis and over 70 percent of the Norwegian American homes in St. Paul. Still, that also means intermarriage between Norwegians and other groups had occurred in nearly one-fifth of Minneapolis's and over a quarter of St. Paul's Norwegian American households. Most of these 160 families were first-generation Scandinavian American unions—with Swedish partners being the most common and Danish spouses next in number in spite of the small size of the Danish American population. In Minneapolis, Americans were most attractive as spouses after Scandinavians, but since the census did not indicate grandparents' national background, some of these couples may also have been Scandinavian American. In both cities there were only a handful of other mixed-background unions, and these were with diverse northwestern European groups, such as Germans, Scots, Scots-Irish, and English. Just one marriage in each city was an Irish Norwegian union in the first generation. Cultural similarity was clearly the most important factor in interethnic marriages. Over the next forty years, endogamy remained the rule in the Norwegian American communities of Minneapolis–St. Paul, although in the state capital, where the Norwegian-born composed a very small part of the population, marriage outside the group increased somewhat more.[30]

Few people in the second generation in 1880 were of marriageable age. In contrast to the first generation, there was a gender imbalance among the American-born: ten women to every seven men. This figure to some degree probably reflected the larger number of young single

TABLE 4.2
Intermarriage in Percentages:
Minneapolis–St. Paul, 1880, 1900, and 1920
(FIRST AND SECOND GENERATIONS)

	ENDOGAMOUS	TO SWEDES	TO DANES	TOTAL
1880 (100% sample) Minneapolis	79.5	9.0	2.6	91.1%
1880 (100% sample) St. Paul	72.1	11.9	7.9	91.9%
1900 (20% sample) Minneapolis	74.1	16.1	2.6	92.8%
1900 (20% sample) St. Paul	67.7	12.2	0.1	80.0%
1920 (20% sample) Minneapolis	74.2	15.2	1.8	91.2%
1920 (20% sample) St. Paul	65.3	18.4	0.4	83.8%

SOURCE: US Census samples, 1880, 1900, and 1920, for the Twin Cities History Project

women leaving Norwegian farmsteads in the region because women did less farm work in America and were less needed at home as the use of farm machinery increased. In St. Paul, the immigrant community included ten households headed by American-born couples of Norwegian ancestry, and only two of these had chosen a partner who did not share their national background. In Minneapolis, the number of second-generation marriages was somewhat larger (forty-five), although it still represented only one in ten of the total number of Norwegian American marriages. Norwegians had married Norwegian Americans in a little over 60 percent of these families—15 percent less than in the first generation, which seems to demonstrate an increased willingness to marry outside the community. Three marriages were between Swedes and Norwegian Americans. However, in nearly all of the other second-generation mixed-background unions (thirteen), the Norwegian's spouse was an American who, as mentioned above, may have been a Scandinavian American. Intermarriage rates in 1880 offer little indication that Norwegian Americans were intermingling with the Twin Cities' general population through marriage. In the enclaves that met the decade's wave of newcomers, marital mixing had occurred in only a small segment of the community and then primarily with other Scandinavian immigrants and their children.

Residential and Working Patterns among Norwegian Newcomers in the 1880s

Housing arrangements and in-home work in the Cities resulted in some important kinds of mixing between Norwegian Americans and other cultures during the 1880s. The two largest groups of young single Norwegian Americans of the Twin Cities at the decade's start had acquired housing as either live-in domestic servants or boarders. During the following years, these patterns would continue as young unmarried Norwegian immigrants and their American cousins found lodging through these inexpensive ways of settling into the city. For women with little money and no specialized job training, domestic service offered a convenient way to find paid work while adjusting to American urban life.[31]

As had been true since the 1850s, domestic service remained by far the most important source of wages for unmarried Norwegian American women in the Twin Cities. Thirty percent of the Norwegian-born working women in Minneapolis and 68 percent of their immigrant sisters in St. Paul were employed as servants. Among second-generation working women in the enclaves, nearly 40 percent in Minneapolis and 53 percent in the capital city were employed in domestic service. Although these domestic workers ranged in age from eleven to forty-four, most were around twenty—on average younger than both other Norwegian American adults and the general adult population. They were also on their own. Only four, all in their twenties, were married, and the large majority lived outside the enclaves in the homes of their employers in the better parts of town. A sizeable minority, on the other hand, worked in the immigrant quarters, living as help in family households or as residents in boardinghouses while they worked on the premises or elsewhere. The handful of women who described their work more exactly as, for example, "washing and ironing" seem to have made their living at home by taking in work from several customers rather than a single employer.[32]

In 1884, Norwegian-born Minneapolis resident Laura Bratager created the fictional working-class character Eleanora in the novel *Over Hav og Land*. Eleanora started life in the city with domestic employment in the local enclave. Her circumstances were common to many single female newcomers from Norway in the 1880s and 1890s. In a period when a woman's living arrangements easily exposed her to gossip and a ruined reputation, Eleanora arrived alone, young, and single, with no relatives to take her in. At her job in the largest of the immigrant group's centers in the Twin Cities, she could weather her first adjustments to American urban life while using her native tongue in the confines of a respectable home in a Norwegian American neighborhood.[33]

Eleanora soon discovered, however, that her wages were lower than the pay she could earn with an American family who lived far from the city's immigrant quarters. For her as for other immigrants, fiction writer Bratager emphasizes, the need to "make it" in America took precedence over the comforts of life in the safe haven of the immigrant community when she was more confident and better able to assess her situation. So that she could more quickly repay the relative in Norway who had lent her the cost of her "America ticket," Eleanora took a higher-wage house job with an American family on the far north side of the city.

Through her character Bratager indicates that servants evaluated what they chose to take with them from their experiences in American households by having Eleanora comment critically on the values she observed in her employer's home. While admiring the high respect and care accorded women and children, Eleanora remarks that these values seem limited to the domestic sphere and to secular, material interests, while the family shows no sign of the intimate comradeship and harmony she values. Like most of her countrywomen who worked as house help, Bratager's character viewed domestic service as a temporary phase in her single youth and left it armed with the lessons she derived from the experience when she married a fellow Norwegian the next spring, less than a year after her arrival.

The census manuscripts reveal a broad spectrum of households employing domestic servants in the Cities that ranged from elite family establishments to the homes of the lower-middle class. Not only wealthy business leaders and professionals but also many middle-class proprietors of family stores, agencies, and small businesses relied on live-in help to lighten household tasks before electrical appliances became commonplace. In Minneapolis, where the *percentage* of Norwegian American domestics was less than half that in the state capital, there were nonetheless nearly five times as many women doing this kind of work—reflecting the much larger Norwegian population in the Mill City. In its most elaborate households, the homes of flour mill magnates such as the Pillsburys and Pettits, Norwegian-born and second-generation Norwegian Americans met each other in the workplace and learned to cooperate in polyglot staffs that included Prussian, Swedish, Irish, and Irish American immigrants. At the same time, they learned the manners and tastes of northern New England, where most of the upper- and upper-middle-class couples who headed these households had been born. Well-to-do households varied greatly in size from the home of the extended Pettit family with its flock of children to the three-person household where eighteen-year-old Emma Johnson from Norway served New Hampshire–born carriage manufacturer James Pottle and his Maine-born wife, Phoebe.[34]

In less affluent middle-class homes, Norwegian American domestics learned to interpret a range of socioeconomic differences and nationalities that was about equally wide, largely because these households usually included boarders. Alice Johnson, for example, twenty-three and Norwegian-born, helped grocer Judson Higgins's wife, Mary, manage a Minneapolis home that included the couple's seven children, only two of whom attended school, and four American store clerks who had moved to the city from three different northeastern states and Wisconsin. Close by the west-side milling district, Julia Hanson served a flour mill worker and wife from more easterly states and their eight boarders—millworkers and several kinds of skilled workers in other fields who came from Ireland, Germany, Canada, and New England. Near the University of Minnesota, the boarders were often students from surrounding states and outstate Minnesota. The most usual work situation for Norwegian American domestics across the city was in middle-class households where a single servant performed household duties for a couple and three or more half-grown children. Distinctive kinds of live-in domestic work were available in the heart of the Cedar-Riverside and north-side Scandinavian neighborhoods. There numbers of young Norwegian American women spent their days employed in immigrant lodging houses and hotels whose residents were mostly their countrymen, Swedes, and Danes—but also Irish, Canadian, and, occasionally, Scottish immigrants.

In St. Paul, Norwegian American household workers experienced as wide a spectrum of situations as they did in Minneapolis, but the circumstances of their employment reflected the capital city's divergent socioeconomic and ethnic profile. The homes of wholesale merchants, railroad officials, financial figures, government officers, and lawyers provided more positions for Norwegian American domestic workers in St. Paul. American couples from northern New England, however, were also the tone-setters in most upper-class homes where Norwegian immigrants worked, and as in the Mill City, in many middle-class households old-stock Americans from other, more easterly states were their employers.

The difference in employers' national background appeared in the city's lower-middle-class and working-class areas, where first- and second-generation Irish Americans and German Americans more frequently provided work for Norwegian and Scandinavian immigrants generally. In the immigrant neighborhoods of east-side St. Paul, they also more often found positions with German and Irish Americans than in the Mill City. Anna Tollaas, for instance, worked for an Irish-born policeman in a household that included his wife, two small children, and fourteen mostly Irish and Irish American boarders, and Nettie Olsen served in a saloon and boardinghouse run by a couple from Germany who rented rooms exclusively to first- and second-generation compatriots. The combined saloon and rooming house or hotel was also common in the capital city's most Scandinavian immigrant district, but four of six such establishments there had Norwegian-born proprietors and housed either exclusively first- and second-generation Norwegian Americans or a Scandinavian mix in which Swedes predominated, as they did in the city as a whole.

Two Stories of Immigration and Urbanization: One in St. Paul and One in Minneapolis

The stories of how two families settled into the Twin Cities in the period, one in the Mount Airy section of St. Paul and the other in Minneapolis's Cedar-Riverside neighborhood, illustrate both the common features of the urban area's immigrant quarters and the typical migratory processes that augmented the population density of these sections of town. Public records confirm the family histories that tell how patterns of family chain migration ended in a common residence and occupation in one of the Cities' well-known immigrant neighborhoods.

According to their third- and fourth-generation relatives, for example, the three Larsen brothers from Ness in Romerike, Norway, all learned cobbling before emigrating at different points in the 1870s. Christian, the first to arrive in St. Paul, helped his brothers Johan (John) and Leonard get established in the city, and by the early 1880s they lived together as roomers on Thirteenth Street in the near-east-side Scandinavian neighborhood and worked together nearby at the Gotzian Shoe Company.

The stories preserved in family memory confirm the objective evidence of public records. John Larsen's experience provides an example of an immigrant who came directly to St. Paul from Norway and found a bride among the Norwegian American farm daughters who had moved into town through the ethnic group's regional urbanization. In 1885, he married Amalia Davidson, who for two years had worked as a domestic servant in the city after moving there from northern Iowa, where she and her parents had settled after the trip from Norway. John and Amalia lived in the Mount Airy district; near the foot of Oak Cemetery, John and a partner maintained a grocery store on 950 Jackson Street, where many Norwegian immigrants not only shopped for food but also exchanged news about home regions of Norway as well as about compatriots and events in the city, state, and nation.[35]

The Ofstie family history exemplifies how a series of relatives helped each other migrate to the Cedar-Riverside immigrant quarter of Minneapolis, which was a launching area for later moves to better parts of the city or other regional Norwegian settlement areas. During interviews, Lorraine Ofstie said that John E. Ofstie, an uncle of her grandfather, immigrated to Minneapolis in the late 1870s—and explained how the knowledge of his success in the city influenced five of his nephews and two of his nieces to follow the trail he had blazed. Edward Ofstie arrived in 1882 and found work as a teamster for the fire company in the heavily Scandinavian Cedar-Riverside section of town. Shortly after, his brother "Big John" came and soon patrolled the area as a district police constable. Their sister Albertina joined them a year or so later, sharing lodgings in Cedar-Riverside, where she worked as a laundress at mid-decade until she took a position as a domestic. Their

The chain immigration of family members over decades brought seven sisters and brothers in the Ofstie household to the Twin Cities between the 1870s and early 1900s. *Courtesy of the author*

younger brother Einar stayed with his siblings only briefly in the later 1880s before moving on to Sioux Falls. The youngest brother and sister did not immigrate to Minneapolis until the early 1900s, by which time their older brothers had found wives among the Norwegian American women migrating into the city and established homes outside the initial Scandinavian district in better residential areas, where these two latest arrivals made their start. Uncle John E. Ofstie had long since left Minneapolis for Eau Claire, Wisconsin, where he made his fame as a businessman and state politician.[36]

Boarding: Making Room for Our Own in Norwegian Neighborhoods

Renting a room or part of a room in a boardinghouse or family home—boarding—was the most common way the large group of young, single Norwegian Americans—usually men—found a place to live. Boarding was much more commonplace in American cities between 1880 and 1910 than at any time since, and the Norwegian immigrants in Minneapolis–St. Paul in the 1880s presented no exception to this general pattern. The single largest category of small business that local Norwegian Americans reported to census takers at the start of the decade was "keeping boarders." Moreover, an examination of the manuscript census responses shows that a large majority of Norwegian American households, regardless of socioeconomic class, included boarders, usually just a few but occasionally a half dozen or more—even though most of these families did not declare taking in boarders as an occupation. A typical enclave home included parents, children, boarders, and, not infrequently, a young female domestic servant, who may have helped out with the household work or have done domestic work elsewhere. The boarders in the Twin Cities' Norwegian American homes and lodging houses were so overwhelmingly youthful and unmarried that they gave the immigrant community as a whole a distinctively young, single character compared with the rest of the population. Nine of ten boarders were single, and their median age was twenty-three.[37]

Judging from personal memoirs and the family stories revealed in interviews, lodging represented an essential part of the varied ways through which people settled in and adjusted to their status in the Cities. For example, as a recently arrived unskilled worker, Andreas Ueland shared a room with two countrymen, a sailor and a cabinetmaker, in a boardinghouse near Minneapolis's west-side mill district in the early 1870s. A decade later, he was still a bachelor boarder sharing space, but by then he had become an attorney and roomed in a private home with his best friend, a young single physician born and trained in Norway. The family atmosphere of these new lodgings in more residential surroundings with a compatriot of a similar age and occupational class reveal the improvements Ueland had been able to make in his living arrangements. In his free time, he reported in his recollections, he and his fellow roomer spent "many evenings together at the theater, when a good play or opera was on the boards," which helped the ambitious young lawyer compensate for the cultural inadequacy he confessed to feeling as an immigrant, even after he had been admitted to the bar. A year later he ran for and won a seat on the Hennepin County bench as a probate judge, and in the mid-1880s he married a well-connected woman from Ohio whom he had met years earlier at the "young people's literary society of an American church" in the city.

Ambition, diligence, and prudence in personal contacts and living arrangements marked Ueland's rise to prominence. Like many people at the time, he set up his own household only after his marriage. Marital status rather than occupation was the clearest distinction between the male householders and lodgers in the Cities' Norwegian American communities. In 1880, another young Norwegian immigrant attorney told the census enumerator that he had been married, was now a widower, and currently lodged with his younger brother in a young American attorney's family home. This man's living conditions not only illustrate the likelihood of help in finding accommodations through occupational contacts but also suggest the support and comfort that was possible when lodgings could be shared with a close relative, especially after a death in the family. Boarders were about equally represented in all classes of Norwegian American workers, except among the unskilled, where they were somewhat more common.[38]

The strategy of rooming with relatives and workmates, combined with a preference for lodging with people of one's own national background, was common in both private homes and boardinghouses in

Minneapolis–St. Paul, particularly in the Cities' unusually young and single Norwegian American communities. Brothers born in Norway who worked together in one of the cities as carriage makers, as machinists, and in the building trades also took room and board together—usually in a "Norwegian" neighborhood, such as the Cedar-Riverside section of Minneapolis or the side streets of the near east side of St. Paul. Male relatives of different generations in skilled and unskilled occupations found the same solution to their need for inexpensive housing and companionship. The Norwegian American women rooming together in the Cities in 1880 included second-generation sisters from Iowa who were employed as domestics as well as pairs of sisters from Norway with jobs as dressmakers, laundresses, and servants. Three young immigrant sisters lodged together and reported that they all worked as "sewing girlies." Occasionally, one of two sisters sharing lodgings had been born in Norway while the other had been born in Wisconsin or Minnesota. The census records of people's housing and origins thus provide objective evidence of both family migration across the Atlantic as well as the urbanization of young women from the large Norwegian American settlement areas in the surrounding region. The living arrangements of boarders with Scandinavian names in the city directories of Minneapolis and St. Paul during the period, which include mostly listings of the male population, also reveal many instances of men with identical surnames sharing addresses and occupations.[39]

In *Over Hav og Land*, novelist Laura Bratager sketches an immigrant community in which taking in boarders was central to the success of family chain migration. In the later 1880s these practices, together with an unprecedented volume of new arrivals from "home," make privacy an impossibility for Bratager's newly wed protagonist, Eleanora, and her husband. They "did not exactly have a honeymoon," because they felt obliged to open their little apartment to three newcomers from Norway within a day or so of the wedding. "When the newcomers finally found work, they paid three dollars a week, which included having their laundry done as well as satisfying their other domestic needs," she reports. Eleanora's husband's wages only slowly increased, and he was often out of work, especially during the winter. They continued to live thriftily, and "many newcomers lived with them, once five at the same time, but by then they had four rooms, and a water pump in the kitchen." Bratager might seem to have exaggerated Eleanora's experiences for fictional effect, but the census manuscripts and city directories from the time demonstrate that her young wife's life represents a fairly accurate and vivid approximation, at least of the historical realities of living arrangements among Norwegian immigrant households in the Twin Cities during the 1880s.[40]

In contrast to the memories handed down in the Brooklyn colony, in which unattached men and transient sailors in particular dominated, Norwegian American narratives in the Twin Cities tell nearly as often about the boarding experiences of women as they do of men. An analysis of the census information supports this aspect of local oral history because it reveals very few women boarders in Brooklyn's Little Norway but nearly equal proportions of women and men among enclave boarders in the Minneapolis–St. Paul of 1880. Although seamstresses and dressmakers were common among women boarders in both the midwestern and New York Norse communities, female boarders in the Twin Cities enclaves also included needle trades employees not found among the East Coast Norwegian American women: a few shirt makers, factory or dress shop "sewing girls," and woolen mill workers. The relatively large group of female boarders in the Cities also held a large occupational group that was rare among Norse women boarders in the East Coast colony. Whereas nearly all unmarried domestic servants in late nineteenth-century Brooklyn lived outside the colony with their employers, in Minneapolis–St. Paul fully 40 percent of single Norwegian American female domestics lived in the midst of their compatriots in family homes or lodging houses in 1880. The greater balance between men and women altered the atmosphere of some immigrant boardinghouses in the Cities, replacing the bachelor society of the late 1860s and 1870s by enhancing the family atmosphere in some group-style housing arrangements. Comparisons with living conditions in the centers of Norwegian settlement in New York help us recognize the distinctive aspects of daily life in the Twin Cities for most of these immigrants at the time.

A Multifaceted Immigrant Subculture Emerges: Residential and Cultural Space in the Cities' Norwegian Centers

As the myriad links of family assistance brought many thousands of newcomers to the Norwegian neighborhoods in the Cities, the enclaves' pioneer era passed. When members of the group had located a boardinghouse or established a household in a section of town, they frequently found space for relatives and others who arrived later. Soon a duplex or apartment building or stretch of homes on a street held a cluster of Norwegian compatriots who had similar commercial and social needs. In the wake of this rising tide of newcomers, immigrant stores and taverns, churches and secular organizations multiplied. In the pioneer era of the 1860s and 1870s, daring individuals had opened the area's only "Norwegian" general store, pharmacy, hotel, or doctor's office. From the early 1880s onward, the newly arrived multitudes provided sufficient customers for *several* stores, offices, and services of each basic type—as well as specialty shops and commercial institutions. In similar fashion, Norwegian immigrant social institutions multiplied and diversified.

The age of pan-Scandinavian cooperation increasingly became a relic of the past, a matter for aging members of old settlers' societies and large-scale cooperation for influence in American politics. A fervent patriotism for authentic "Norwegian-ness" welled up among leaders in the Cities' Norwegian centers during the 1880s and 1890s. A local echo of the rise of national romanticism, the movement for a more liberal democracy, and rising tension with Sweden at home in Norway, this passion for the genuinely Norwegian came with the mass of newcomers directly from the old country but was also communicated in letters from home and through Norwegian American newspapers. Besides, by the 1880s and 1890s, Norwegians in the Cities were no longer a small group that had to band together with other Nordics to scrape together sufficient resources to establish basic community institutions. Now individuals both adjusted to American city life and defined their place *within* the nationality group by choosing among a spectrum of Norwegian residential areas, businesses, churches, secular organizations, leisure-time activities, and entertainments.

This abundance of institutions in turn attracted more population diversity within the group, full-fledged immigrant business districts, and an even greater variety of organizations. The nature of community for Norwegian Americans in the Cities crossed a significant threshold between the 1880s and early 1900s. In this period, the concentration of the group's population, activities, and institutions became so varied and complete that it supported a Norwegian American subculture that functioned as a kind of halfway house, a sort of haven that spared newcomers from facing the full force of mainstream American conditions. Opportunities abounded for feeling more at home in these spaces than in other parts of town.

Norwegian American Working-Class Neighborhoods

The local socioeconomic circumstances and traditions of familial migration and assistance that gave rise to the first settlement areas in the Twin Cities by 1880 were exactly the qualities that made these working-class neighborhoods the most attractive to the flood of newcomers. One Norwegian family often succeeded another when recent immigrants occupied the housing vacated by longer-settled residents who moved to secondary settlement areas. Meanwhile, in the old neighborhood, the families who remained often made space for relatives and compatriots whose payments as boarders helped keep the family economy afloat. The population density in the core immigrant districts rose even as those areas expanded. The number of boardinghouses and boarders in family homes increased as residents of all backgrounds helped new members of their groups find space in these cheapest first settlement areas of town.

Familial networks typify the ways that the Norwegian immigrant subculture developed neighborhoods in Minneapolis–St. Paul in the last decades of the nineteenth century. Informal self-segregation for mutual assistance determined the location for more formal institutions and activities. In Minneapolis these processes resulted in clusters of Norwegian settlement ranging from the extensive Cedar-Riverside community on the south side, through the next largest center of the group on the north side of downtown, to the small concentrations of Norwegian immigrants on the east side of the Mississippi River in north and southeast Minneapolis. In St. Paul, Norwegian immigrants offered each other mutual support in the Mount Airy and near-east-side districts of the city.[41]

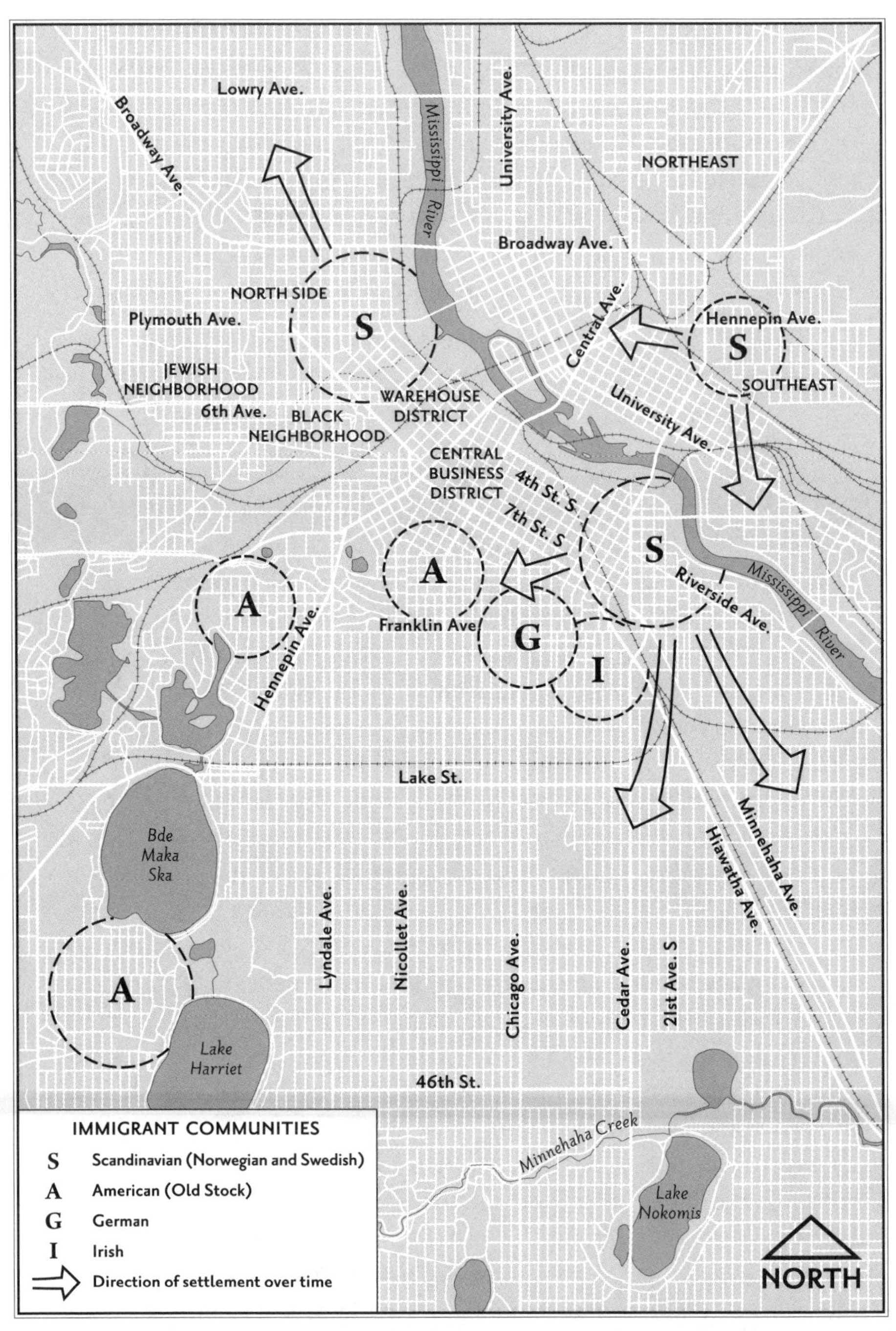

Immigrant Community and Migration in Minneapolis, 1880–1920. *Matt Kania, Map Hero*

By the early 1880s the center of the largest Norwegian settlement in Minneapolis had moved—along with the south-side section that experienced the transition toward commercial-industrial development—down the ten to twelve blocks of Washington Avenue South between the city center to the Cedar-Riverside district, which became the city's best-known and most densely populated immigrant quarter. The general area called Cedar-Riverside had parts in three city wards. The oldest centered on the lower section of Washington Avenue South and adjacent streets in the southeast corner of Ward 5. All of Ward 6, from Tenth Avenue on the west to Eighth Street on the south and the Mississippi on the east and north, was in the vibrant central section of the district. The last and newest part of the district filled the northern half of Ward 11, between Eighth Street and Franklin Avenue on the north and south and the river and Tenth Avenue on the east and west.

On the side streets were low-rent apartment buildings that housed many greenhorn immigrants, including the city's largest apartment complex at the time, a three-story half block of sixty flats with storefronts at its corners that lay two streets into Ward 6 to the southeast. This complex, starting on Washington Avenue, continuing along Twelfth Avenue, and ending partway down Second Street, boasted a size and population density so typical of the variety of polyglot peoples in the immigrant quarter that local residents called it "Noah's Ark."

The oldest section of the Cedar-Riverside immigrant district had the cheapest housing and was the first part of the community to become dominated by single or unattached boarders of many backgrounds. For Carl Gustav Oscar Hansen, who later became the long-term editor of the Cities' largest Norwegian-language newspaper, this part of the south-side immigrant district remained indelibly *his* Minneapolis, the part of town where he first touched foot as a ten-year-old in the spring of 1882 and the place that always most seemed like home. As the Hansen family story shows, the district was also a place where families reassembled and ties from abroad were reforged as friends and relatives stayed with each other while people got their start in the city. Hansen's mother, who was a widow, at first settled her family with relatives in a heavily Norwegian farming community in southwestern Minnesota. Like many another Norwegian newcomer, she "went up to Minneapolis" and sent for her children when she found that it provided more opportunities for work than smaller towns nearby. Other relatives in the city put her up in their flat in Noah's Ark until she got a job and rented her own apartment in the building. Her dependence on family networks for temporary housing and her secondary migration to the city show how neighbors and family who lived close together in the old country reestablished those living patterns in their adopted country.

A raw industrial boomtown met Carl Hansen and his four young siblings when they stepped off the train that March day at Milwaukee Station at Washington and Third Avenues. When no one came to meet them, they decided to find the address their mother had given them and walked the block east toward Second Street and the Mississippi River. At the corner of Second Street, they met an "endless maze of [railroad] trackage in front of the flour mills" between the unpaved street and the river. The sight was so discouraging that they reversed direction until the house number they had forced them back to Second Street to face the railroads and mills, where a recent thaw had converted the street to knee-deep mud. In the distance to the south they saw "some houses that might be human habitations," which proved to include 1211 Second Street on the eastern side of Noah's Ark, where the flock of Hansen children found their aunt.

When the Hansen children's mother arrived home later on that first day in Minneapolis, she installed them in a flat in the Ark. Meanwhile, Carl's aunt sent him out with one of his cousins to do some shopping for the enlarged family group. Along Washington Avenue, the young people found many Norwegian American businesses, many of them still housed in three-story wooden buildings with old-fashioned gabled facades from the 1860s and 1870s. Within a few blocks, they visited A. C. Haugan's business, the city's largest grocery catering to a Norwegian or Scandinavian clientele, and then walked on to two smaller Norwegian groceries, Olsen and Bakke's and then Tharaldsen's. Along the way they passed signs in Norwegian for the Thingvalla Line ("the only direct route to Scandinavia"), four furniture stores, a shoe repair shop, an undertaking business, a hardware store, saloons, and Petersen's Norwegian American commercial building containing both his dry goods business and a meeting hall where renowned visitors from the Nordic countries lectured, preached, or performed. Mixed among these stores Carl noted church spires, some of which marked the lingering presence of the immigrant community's first congregations in the oldest part of the district—Our Saviour's original building at Washington and Tenth Avenue and Trinity Lutheran's first edifice at Tenth Avenue and Fourth Street.

Hansen's family story is in several ways representative of the experience of many Norwegian Americans who moved into the Cities from the surrounding rural areas. They came because of the large number of jobs in the region's big cities. Here there was abundant work, especially for women and the semiskilled or unskilled of both sexes. Relatives, as well as friends and neighbors from the rural Midwest or Norway, lived in the Cities and helped newcomers find jobs and accommodations. In Cedar-Riverside, foreign-born Norwegian children found playmates who understood their language and culture as well as streets filled with Norwegian-speaking businesses and societies.

A Norwegian Village in Downtown Minneapolis

Decades later this setting seemed to a nostalgic Hansen "the very picture of 'a peaceful village'" and the most Norwegian part of the city during a period marked by a passionate interest in authentic *Norskdom* (Norwegian-ness). In the 1880s and 1890s, the national feeling this concept referred to was by definition intimately connected to foreign-born immigrants' need to honor their homeland culture during the flowering of national romanticism in Norway and the country's intensifying efforts to win complete independence from Sweden.

The small scale of the buildings plus green spaces around some churches and homes, together with the face-to-face knowledge of one's neighbors, created the small-town intimacy and sense of belonging that Hansen remembered fondly, but he also recalled a great diversity of population in the Washington Avenue section of the district even as he celebrated how "Norwegian" it seemed to a young boy recently arrived from the old country. Many nationalities resided in the Ark, he recalls, and the boys in the neighborhood, most of them greenhorn immigrants, revealed both their need to simplify because of the large variety of European origins among them and the largest groups in that mix by calling all Scandinavians "Swedes" and all non-Scandinavians "Irish." In the 1880s and early 1890s, young teenage boys formed groups that strutted around local streets, loudly proclaiming their presence and occasionally "pouncing on each other." A founding member of *Den Norske Gutteforening* (the Norwegian Boys' Society), Hansen reports that he and his friends spent evenings in the Ark's courtyard, playing ball, telling Norwegian jokes, and trading stories about school days in the old country. They also organized as a pseudo military troop and marched around the courtyard's woodsheds and outhouses as they sang "good old Norwegian patriotic songs" and shouted "left, right, left, right" in Norwegian—arousing both cheers and jeers from adults on back stoops and other youthful groups in the complex.

As the eighties continued, the south-side immigrant quarter centered increasingly on the Sixth Ward. Its business district and social institutions clustered along the intersections in the ward where the city's right-angled grid of streets shifted to the east at Cedar Avenue to follow the course of the Mississippi River. This alteration in the street grid produced a series of open areas similar to small plazas at intersections along the avenue between the river and Seventh Street. "Seven Corners," the largest of these and the liveliest meeting place in the immigrant quarter, appeared where Washington Avenue, the main artery from the city's central business center and its riverside mill district, met Cedar and Fifteenth Avenue South, which led to the rapidly developing new housing in the south-central part of town. Successful pioneer entrepreneurs in the Norwegian immigrant community used the capital they had accumulated in the 1860s and 1870s to establish Cedar Avenue from Seven Corners down to Eighth Street as the group's main commercial thoroughfare. According to Hansen, this movement began with the founding of Scandia Bank on the corner of Cedar and Fourth Street in 1883, which stimulated the erection of "one business building after another" on Cedar or adjoining blocks of Riverside Avenue. A. C. Haugan, once a member of the young Norwegian bachelor business elite in the late 1860s and 1870s, founded the bank with the proceeds of his large grocery on Washington Avenue. A. H. Edsten and Olaf Throbeck, other entrepreneurs from the first Scandinavian American business district on the edge of downtown, parlayed the profits from their early businesses into sufficient funding to put up commercial buildings close by Scandia bank. That financial institution's early officers included other long-established immigrant businessmen in the group, as well as pioneer scholar Rasmus B. Anderson, the first professor of Nordic languages in the Midwest at the University of Wisconsin, who engaged in various business activities and apparently viewed the emerging Cedar-Riverside section as a coming center of Scandinavian American life. Hansen claimed that practically every business starting up in Cedar-Riverside in the period was managed or owned by Norwegian immigrants. That estimate may well be inflated by an insider's local boosterism. In the booming economy of the 1880s and early 1890s, however, these new buildings soon filled with tenant shops that met the full range of daily needs of the swelling Scandinavian American clientele in the area.

The location was auspicious for a bank catering to Scandinavian immigrants. One early attraction of the area was the establishment of Augsburg Seminary just three blocks to the east in 1872, when Cedar-Riverside was a little-developed section on the city's outer fringe. The seminary was unusual in locating in an area that had not yet become a center of the group's settlement. Not only businesses but also meeting halls, other gathering places, and community institutions followed the movement of the population that made up their most likely customers or members. Educational institutions planning a campus of buildings and medical facilities looking for locations in healthier, less-developed surroundings were common exceptions to this rule. Aside from the building of Augsburg Seminary, the physical development of the newer sections of Cedar-Riverside closely followed the rapid increase in Scandinavian settlement farther southeast in the district.

In the early 1880s, the most popular meeting hall for Norwegian immigrants was Petersen's on Washington and Thirteenth Avenues in the oldest part of the immigrant quarter. In 1886–87, however, the location of most Norwegian American organizations and occasions followed the southeasterly movement of their clientele and shifted to the newly erected Dania Hall in the Scandia Bank block of Cedar Avenue, even though the building was owned and managed by members of another Nordic group. Through a building society called "Normanna," Norwegian American leaders had mounted a campaign to build a Norwegian-owned and -operated meeting place with a large assembly hall about a year earlier. So important was such a hall to the community that in 1888 and 1889 the centerpiece of the Norwegian Constitution Day parade and celebrations in the district was, first, the laying of the cornerstone and then the dedication of the completed building at Twelfth Avenue and Third Street in the old part of the district. Several Norwegian American organizations reserved space in Normanna Hall even before construction was finished, and for five hectic years the hall was the center of many of the community's voluntary associations. Yet, when that short span of years was over, the building society failed to meet its mortgage payments in the depression of the early 1890s, and the organizations moved back to Dania Hall. As Carl Hansen commented, "The deciding factor . . . was that the locality was no longer in the heart of the Norwegian District." The short-lived success of Normanna Hall illustrates how fundamental population movements were in the period when immigrant communities consisted of compact geographical areas within walking distance to the industrial and commercial enterprises that employed their members.

Cedar-Riverside: The Swedish Norwegian Sixth Ward

Two groups, Swedes and Norwegians, dominated the Sixth Ward immigrant community. In 1880, they and their children made up nearly two-thirds of the area's population. Norwegians established themselves here first, but from the late 1870s on Swedish newcomers increasingly outnumbered them. Their continuing high rates of urbanization and immigration assured that the needs, interests, and activities of these two groups continued to influence all aspects of life in the area well beyond 1905, when the first two generations alone still composed 60 percent of local residents. Swedish Americans were always the largest group in the ward and increased their demographic prominence there through the early 1900s. Danish immigrants, a very small presence, nonetheless contributed significantly to the area's overall Scandinavian character. The American-born, who may or may not have been of Scandinavian or other immigrant extraction, made up the third-largest group in the ward at under a third of the population in 1880 and over two-fifths in 1905. Irish and Bohemian communities were small but significant groups at the start of the period, and after 1900, growing numbers of Austrian, Hungarian, Romanian, Russian, and Italian immigrants joined them.[42]

From the mid-1880s to the mid-1900s, the middle section of Cedar-Riverside developed into the city's primary Norwegian and Scandinavian neighborhood. Not only did the opening of additional stores bolster the importance of Cedar Avenue as the main business street for Norwegians, Cedar and adjoining blocks of Riverside Avenue also became the site of many of the immigrant group's leisure-time activities. The informal gatherings among neighbors and friends in stores and the open areas created by the street grid gave the district's main thoroughfares the air of a village center. Three Norwegian drugstores put out tables with newspapers from the homeland and the newest books by its most famous authors, such as Henrik Ibsen, Bjørnstjerne Bjørnson, and the young Knut Hamsun, and thus became casual gathering places for people who wanted to discuss current events and ideas. Among the figures who may have joined in or been the subjects of drugstore discussion during this period were such newspaper and literary figures among Norwegian Americans as Kristofer Janson, H. A. Foss, Johannes B. Wist, and Hamsun, who lived in the district during two periods of residence in the 1880s. These journalists and authors had business in the shifting little beehive of a dozen or so Norwegian immigrant printing and publishing enterprises that were housed in neighboring blocks. A sober public also gathered in the district's coffeehouses and cafés, such as the meeting rooms of "Henrik Wergeland," a club for young Norwegian liberals, or the Scandinavian Coffee House, an alcohol-free alternative to local bars that was run by a Norwegian immigrant studying at the University of Minnesota.[43]

A much broader public patronized the saloons and bars that multiplied along Cedar Avenue from 1884, when mayor George Pillsbury won city council support for Minneapolis's infamous liquor patrol limits. This legislation aimed to facilitate the policing of public disturbances caused by drinking by excluding the sale of alcoholic beverages from most residential neighborhoods. It limited the location of bars and saloons to a few commercial areas of the city: the downtown, some German immigrant areas in the northeast section, and the main thoroughfares of the south-side immigrant quarter. By the early 1900s, Washington Avenue and the Cedar-Riverside district contained well over a hundred saloons. Carl Hansen remembered that these watering holes provided so plentiful a rendezvous that "to many thirsty souls [the idiom] 'å gå på Cedar' [go down on Cedar] meant just one thing: to tank up." Some local barmen became so well known that they earned colorful nicknames among district residents. One booming-voiced barkeeper was known as "Blaasaren" (the Blower), and the immigrant Norwegian who ran a saloon directly across the street on Cedar was called "Flisa" (an affectionate short form of Flisness, his surname). Several of the area's most prominent Norwegian-owned structures—Scandia Bank, Dania Hall, and the Throbeck building—contained saloons.

The local idiom, nicknames, and entertaining descriptions of colorful saloons and barkeepers that Hansen preserves demonstrate that these businesses were sites of informal gatherings for a Norwegian-speaking public, yet, as a proud insider who had grown up in the district, he maintains that few Norwegian immigrants were among the regulars at the local bars. Elsewhere in his memoir he offers a partial explanation for this claim by suggesting that Norwegian immigrants preferred to gather informally at home for drinks with family and neighbors. They did this, he says, through the common practice known as "rushing the growler," making use of the saloons' take-out business of filling dinner pails with beer for adults—or for the children who were often sent out to fetch it and "knew just where to go for good measure." Again, the overall effect of Hansen's memories is a convincing picture of drinking alcoholic beverages as an everyday part of life and not infrequently, as he says, a way of making life "just a little more cheerful" that usually did not call for police interference.[44]

Other informal gatherings further reinforced the sense that the common routines of life demonstrated the presence of a many-sided Norwegian immigrant community in the Cedar-Riverside district. One routine event occurred two times a day when local workers walked en masse up Riverside, Cedar, and Washington Avenues or the nearby railroad trackage to work in the mills and related industry along the Mississippi in the morning and back along the same routes to their homes in the evening. Another smaller branch of the work parade followed the Milwaukee tracks to the rail yards south of the district. An immigrant workforce in an age when most people lived so close to their jobs knew that little time was saved and too much money was spent by taking the streetcar to work. In an area dominated by Scandinavian immigrants, Norwegian Americans interviewed in later years took for granted that this parade prominently featured the sights and sounds of their countrymen and -women leaving for and coming back from work.

Swedish and Norwegian dialects, along with English, Irish brogues, and, less frequently, Italian, were audible in the passing ranks. Hansen and other community veterans recalled that around 1900 most in the lively parade were men carrying tin dinner pails that glinted in the sun. Few of the Norwegian immigrant men among them, according to federal census records, were walking with the crowds that labored in the nearby concentration of flour mills and railroads. Instead, they were on their way to construction jobs or to the wide variety of skilled and semiskilled positions available in smaller related factories that supplied products and services to the mills, railroads, and construction industry. Among the most important of these for Norwegian immigrants was probably Simonson and Newgord's, a sash and door factory a block or so off Cedar at the south end of the Sixth Ward that was owned and run by men from Norway. The small female minority in the mass of walkers, their lunch wrapped in a package rather than carried in a pail, were domestics, dressmakers, stenographers, and office workers.[45]

Looking back at the end of the 1880s in a speech given in Norwegian after World War I, Hansen noted a second routine event. "Most Norwegian churches," he reminded his listeners, "were then in the Sixth Ward, and on Sunday mornings one would meet a long procession of Norwegian-speaking church-goers" walking through the district. The procession was remarkable because it was a reliable weekly phenomenon that gave Norwegian immigrants the sense that the culture of the area was theirs, the place where one could regularly hear Norwegian on the streets and see people behaving as might be expected of their compatriots.

Norse settlers moved to Cedar-Riverside following the establishment of Augsburg Seminary. Business leaders among them seized the opportunity this population movement presented for a growing volume of customers and followed the settlers' migration. The immigrant churches, not slow to join the general movement, soon relocated to be closer to their members' new place of residence and thus gave rise to the churchgoers' weekly promenade through the district. In 1882 Our Saviour's Lutheran Church, the oldest Norwegian Synod congregation in the city, moved its building from the old Washington Avenue section of the district to a corner near the southwest boundary of the Sixth Ward. Trinity Lutheran, the first Norwegian immigrant congregation organized in Minneapolis, in 1896 left the old Washington Avenue settlement area to begin conducting services in a large new church building three blocks off Cedar Avenue just outside the southwestern boundary of the Sixth Ward. Having waited so long to leave the oldest part of the immigrant quarter, Trinity's leaders chose a location that was then fairly close to the newest, rapidly growing residential concentration of Norwegian immigrants in the Franklin Avenue section of Ward 11. By that time, one of Trinity's several daughter congregations had for four years been the first Norwegian immigrant church to be built south of Franklin Avenue. The old Washington Avenue settlement area lost with Trinity's departure the institution that had most made it seem the historic home of the city's Norwegian pioneers. With the church also disappeared much of the section's Norwegian character farther south to Cedar-Riverside and beyond.[46]

More formal secular or semisecular gatherings and organizations related to the concentration of Norwegian immigrant churches, jobs, and businesses in the Sixth Ward soon appeared. As mentioned earlier, many of the group's clubs and associations moved into Dania Hall in the mid-1880s and returned to the midsection of Cedar-Riverside in the 1890s after Normanna Hall closed. Many of these societies were short lived, but the range of interests they served almost always included the following: men's political clubs related to both Scandinavian and American affairs (sometimes with women's auxiliaries); paramilitary drill corps such as the Normanna rifle company; male choir and quartet societies such as *Nordmennenes* Song Association; thespian societies; athletic organizations including skiing, skating, and gymnastics; youth groups that were often associated with a church; mutual benefit clubs of workers such as the Scandinavian Sick Benefit Society and the Scandinavian Typographical Union; women's as well as men's literary societies; male debate societies; women's church circles and charitable societies; and organizations devoted to social or religious causes such as the women's rights or temperance movements. The churches and these organizations, together with meeting halls like Dania, kept Cedar-Riverside alive with enough activities and entertainments in Norwegian or other Nordic languages for anyone with the interest and resources to enjoy them. The broad range of wedding receptions and other family landmarks, meetings, concerts, performances, pageants, dances and holiday balls, and sports meets—and the bazaars and bake sales that were often a vital element in their financing—offered equally broad opportunities for different degrees of involvement, often at little or no expense.

Many of these events took place in Dania Hall's small second-floor auditorium, where local residents held wedding receptions, executive boards planned future activities, and local pastors and other of the district's public figures often spoke. In its elegant third-floor auditorium, a large public could assemble for a well-known lecturer, play, or visiting concert virtuoso. Similar if less-noticed occasions unfolded at upstairs halls in other buildings on Riverside and Cedar Avenues. Often a series of events—a speech on a current issue, musical performances, a play, and a dance into the small hours—made up an evening's entertainment at these halls.[47]

If, as has been estimated, only around 15 percent of Norwegian Americans were activist "joiners" of their group's voluntary organizations, perhaps twice as large a portion or more of these immigrants and their children took part within the large crowds of spectators or as occasional purchasers of tickets. Major occasions in Minneapolis, such as the annual Norwegian Constitution Day celebrations, the public procession and jubilation occasioned by the fusion of the three largest Norwegian church bodies in 1890, and the parade of choirs and concerts during United Scandinavian Singers of America *Sangerfest* in 1891, attracted a public of many hundreds or thousands who thronged the district.

The city had considered its designation of Cedar Avenue as a "wet" thoroughfare two years earlier and the multiplication of bars there since then when it rented the basement floor of the Scandia Bank building as the site of the south-side police station in 1886. Mayor A. A. Ames no doubt had the ethnic character of the local population in mind when he placed a Norwegian immigrant, Captain Louis Ness, in charge of the station and accepted the appointment of Ness's immigrant compatriots as a majority of the patrolmen under his leadership. Hansen lists by name a dozen of these Norwegian officers in Cedar-Riverside during this period, and the Swedish American local historian Alfred Söderström not only confirms these names but also demonstrates that

Norwegians were overrepresented among the Scandinavian immigrants in the municipal police force. Söderström, a strong supporter of the patrol limits ordinance that concentrated saloons along Cedar, also notes that Scandinavian saloonkeepers held over a third of the liquor licenses in Minneapolis in 1898. Both he and Hansen, however, resist drawing a connection between saloon ownership, the location of the patrol limits and police station, and the drinking cultures that immigrants from the Nordic countries brought with them.[48]

Until having a geographically defined "home district" no longer seemed vital for Norwegian Americans in Minneapolis, Cedar-Riverside remained the preeminent location of the group activities most vital for their cohesiveness as a subculture in the city. As historian Byron Nordstrom has noted, "The Sixth Ward exemplified all the characteristics of an area of ethnic dominance." One crucial effect of this reality was that, instead of facing the full force of mainstream American conditions at once, the majority of Cedar-Riverside residents could adjust more slowly within a largely Scandinavian section of the city. Here the majority of Norwegian Americans who moved in from the ethnic group's rural farm districts and settlements could adjust to urban life. The smaller group of immigrants arriving directly from Norway could focus more on accommodating themselves to each other while using their native tongue and helping each other preserve elements of their common cultural heritage in an urban American environment. The Swedes and Norwegians in Cedar-Riverside could understand each other's language and shared a broad range of cultural traditions. Nonetheless, the Sixth Ward held a diverse population.[49]

Non-Scandinavian foreign groups made up between 10 and 15 percent of the area population. Living closely together with some Danes, many Swedish Americans, and people from a variety of places in Norway, moreover, involved many complexities. Internal divisions among the Scandinavians resulted from their various regional backgrounds in the homelands as well as religious, economic, occupational, and generational differences. The large and many-faceted character of the local Scandinavian population in Cedar-Riverside itself was the foundation for the expression of both more cooperation and more inner diversity than anywhere else in the Cities. The significant numbers of each group, for example, allowed for a greater multiplication of the separate nationality-based congregations that began in the 1870s, along with churches aligned with each of the main varieties of Norwegian American Lutheranism, the appearance of separate Swedish and Norwegian Baptist and Methodist institutions, and a large population of unchurched Norwegians and Swedes.[50]

Nordic American Politics before 1905

Norwegian Americans in the Twin Cities had now become a large, well-organized community. They sustained a separate network of leisure-time organizations that allowed individuals to choose activities among a panoply of options without relying on pan-Scandinavian cooperation. Success in municipal, state, and federal politics, however, often depended on cooperation with Swedes and Danes to assemble a large enough voting bloc to win elections and affect public policy.

The Scandinavian groups' political attitudes became important when the part of the local voting public they composed grew potentially decisive in some election districts. Opinion in the Norwegian immigrant community, however, was far from monolithic. As we shall see in later chapters, these varied stances developed in part from political allegiances formed in Norway. To name some important examples, before emigration many had taken positions regarding temperance in the use of alcoholic beverages, women's right to the vote, and Norwegian independence from Sweden.

The political perspectives of the Cities' Nordic Americans evolved even more decisively in the context of larger economic and ideological issues in the United States concerning a fair distribution of economic goods. Common attitudes in the local Scandinavian centers included both support for the entrepreneurs who created jobs and criticism of middlemen and capitalists who appeared to deny economic opportunity to others. Working people in the Cities who were members of immigrant groups that were heavily rural in the region, particularly Norwegian and Swedish Americans, sympathized with the perspective of their relatives in the countryside. The region's Scandinavian American farmers, in all parts of the state but especially in the newer west-central and northwestern areas, increasingly viewed railroad monopolists like James J. Hill and industrial combines like Minneapolis

Milling as powers that deprived wheat growers and other farmers of a reasonable living from their labor by charging inordinate fees for the transportation, refining, and marketing of agricultural harvests. Partially because of that sympathy, during the hard times for Scandinavian American farmers in the 1880s and 1890s, significant numbers of their urban cousins deserted the pro-business Republican Party for the Farmers Alliance, the Populist Party, and less often the Democrats.[51]

In the course of the 1880s, as the numbers and organization of Scandinavian Americans made them politically important in Minneapolis–St. Paul, a paradigm shift occurred in the issues that preoccupied them most, their party loyalties, and the electoral roles they played. Scandinavian Americans' feeling of paying Civil War–era debt to Republican leaders for their free-soil, antislavery faith faded as larger numbers of newcomers arrived in the following decades, as another generation grew up, and as other concerns came to the fore. As local Scandinavian Americans reached political maturity, it seemed to many of them that Irish Americans, having gained an undue amount of political influence with party elites, dragged religion into politics, and become overrepresented in elected office, stood in their way. St. Paul was the nearest example of a place where Irish Americans controlled elections, the distribution of appointed offices, and decisions on public issues to the detriment of other groups. The two groups' political confrontation very likely contributed to increasingly explicit anti-Catholicism among the Cities' Nordics that was evident in their support for and acceptance in the American Protective Association in the 1890s. In the decade before, the temperance movement had gained great vitality among the Scandinavians in the capital and Minneapolis, and Nordic advocates of sumptuary law reform joined others during this period in stereotyping the Irish as heavy drinkers and blaming them for the failure of early proposals for prohibition of alcoholic beverages. These ethnic, religious, and social foci of dissatisfaction, combined with sympathy for the Farmers Alliance's ideological critique of financial and political leaders, made traditional Republican Scandinavian Americans willing to defect from the GOP. A close analysis of voting behavior in heavily Scandinavian wards in Minneapolis and St. Paul between 1888 and 1905 shows that Nordic voters became the most volatile part of the Cities' electorate, often playing the role of decisive "protest" or "swing" voters, third-party advocates, and supporters of particular candidates and programs rather than a traditional party line. According to political commentators on the Twin Cities' scene, one kind of candidate nearly always received many Norwegian American votes: members of their own or other Scandinavian groups.

The Farmers Alliance campaign across the state successfully circumvented the traditional Republican party apparatus (both in county seats and at party headquarters in the Twin Cities), chose its own leaders and speakers, and formulated an ideology based on opposition to the uneven distribution of wealth. In 1890 state elections, the Alliance and the Democrats routed the Republicans, and clearly the desertion of Scandinavian American voters was largely to blame. Judging from the greater independence Nordic voters—in the state but also in the Twin Cities—showed in party allegiance from then on, a key lesson they learned from the Alliance's success was to throw off unwavering support for the Republicans and instead use changes in party choice as a way to make political elites satisfy their concerns.

Conclusion

During these years, the first Norwegian settlement areas in each city filled up and burst their bounds because of the great in-migration. The immigrant quarters were transit areas. The increasing industrial and commercial enterprises that made those areas inexpensive for recently arrived immigrants at the same time led residents to move to more attractive districts as soon as they could afford something better. In St. Paul, the near-east-side Scandinavian community expanded farther to the east, and the Mount Airy settlement spread to the north and west. In Minneapolis, the nucleus of the Cedar-Riverside south-side Scandinavian enclave moved farther from the city center, and the Selbu colony on the north side expanded first to the south and later to the west. Nonetheless, Norwegians' residence remained mostly concentrated in sections of the Cities recognized as heavily populated by foreign-born speakers of Scandinavian languages.

Just as people from localities and subcultures in Norway had gathered in small towns and rural districts across the American heartland, so they assembled (or reassembled) in Minneapolis–St. Paul. In the largest of these colonies near the peak of Norwegian arrivals, Norwegian greenhorns—whatever their specific origins in the homeland or the Upper Midwest—stood a good chance of meeting someone who came from the same place, maybe even an acquaintance or friend, thanks to the networks of family and neighborhood chain migration that powered mass immigration from Norway and urbanization from the Upper Midwest. Here were buildings, stretches of houses, businesses, bars, and street corners where residents could discuss in their own language (or even one of its local dialects) the shared working conditions of the common occupational niches the group had found in the Twin Cities. Familial networks, such as those among the Larsens and the Ofsties described above, typify the ways that the Norwegian immigrant subculture developed neighborhoods in Minneapolis–St. Paul in the last decades of the nineteenth century. In addition to the colony from Selbu, on the south side of Minneapolis there was a gathering of people from Odal (a rural area just north of Oslo) and another from parts of the country's interior eastern valley (Østerdalen). In St. Paul's Mount Airy section, Norwegians from Nes in Romerike clustered together.[52]

Informal forms of self-segregation for mutual assistance provided the population base and determined the location for more formal institutions and activities. In Minneapolis, these processes resulted in clusters of Norwegian settlement ranging from the extensive Cedar-Riverside community on the south side, through the next-largest center of the group on the north side of downtown, to the small concentrations of Norwegian immigrants on the east side of the Mississippi River in north- and southeast Minneapolis. Local stores allowed immigrants to get goods and services from Norway and to do their daily business in Norwegian. Taken together, the core areas had institutions that offered a comprehensive range of religious, educational, social, and political institutions based on homeland cultural heritage and the immigrants' needs in an American city. The inexpensive "Norwegian" housing ranged from shared bunks in hotels for transient workers whose numbers were dominated by compatriots or at least Scandinavians to apartment houses, duplexes, multiplexes, and streets of single-family homes with the same ethnic complexion. In the largest of the enclaves, the mix of Norwegian Americans included a great diversity of ideological and social views, three generations of immigrants, and all socioeconomic classes, from well-off business figures and widely respected professionals and artists through a range of middle-class shopkeepers and skilled workers to the unskilled and unemployed. Here was a world within the world of the Cities, where people could devote themselves to the internal affairs of Norwegian America until they got their feet on the ground before venturing further afield in American society or, if they wished, for an entire lifetime.

In the 1880s, the Norwegian immigrant community of the Twin Cities achieved an institutional completeness as well as a diversity and variety *within* the group that led to a great cultural flowering. All the classic dimensions of a dominant big-city immigrant community were present. Surpassing a threshold of size and population concentration allowed them to support two networks of Lutheran churches and their seminaries, as well as a Methodist and a Baptist congregation of Norwegians. These religious institutions in turn supported growing charity efforts for the less fortunate in the group and, increasingly, the public at large. Entrepreneurs grown successful by catering to the needs of a burgeoning local population developed several banks and financed small businesses that employed compatriots; the most common of these were boardinghouses or taverns. Census records document this expansion, and that first-generation women found economic niches in domestic service, housekeeping, dressmaking, and cleaning. Norwegian-born men earned livings in a variety of metal shop, woodworking, railroad, and construction trades. Churches, taverns, coffeehouses, meetinghouses, auditoriums, and cafés provided sites for leisure-time activities ranging from informal gatherings to lectures, choral concerts, theatricals, sports events, and club meetings—all conducted in one's native tongue or dialect and the cultural forms to which one was accustomed. In these circumstances, three-quarters to four-fifths of the marriages that occurred were endogamous, between spouses who were both born in Norway.

By 1890, St. Paul's Norwegian American community contained 5,361 people, and 34 percent of these (1,840) were American-born. In Minneapolis by 1890, the immigrant community numbered 18,282, and the US-born (6,018) made up almost the same percent of the total as in St. Paul. The same census shows that the second generation consisted mostly of children fifteen years old or younger. By 1900, this large

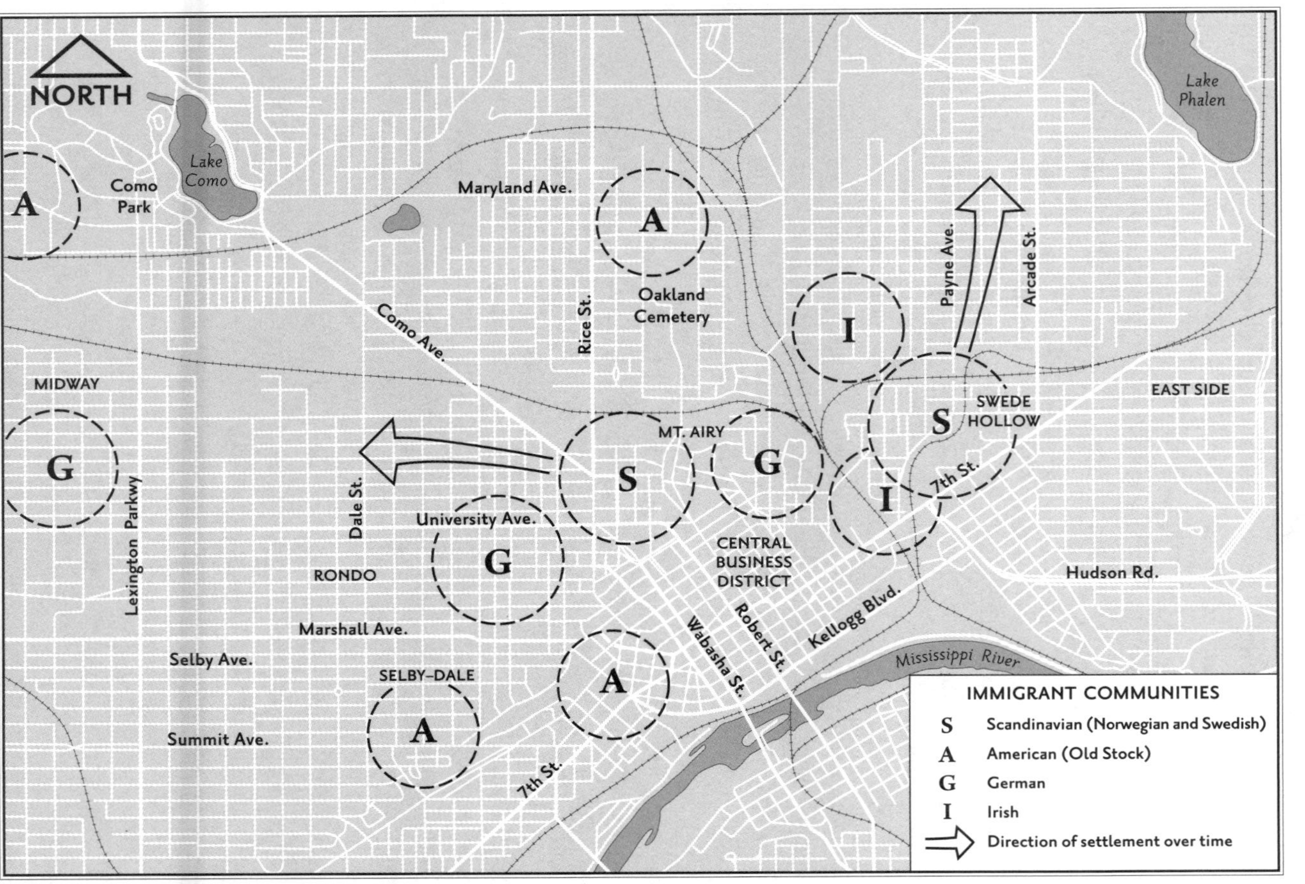

Immigrant Community and Migration in St. Paul, 1880–1920. *Matt Kania, Map Hero*

American-born generation outnumbered the Norwegian-born two to one in both cities and consequently was in the process of transforming the early immigrant subculture of foreign-language speakers into an ethnic community in which the predominant group increasingly consisted of people whose life experience was gained entirely in the Cities or at least in America. In Minneapolis, the large number of newcomers from Norway after 1900 would reverse that tendency, while in St. Paul the foreign-born part of the community would increase only slightly.

In sum, from 1865 through the second half of the 1880s, one significant continuing feature of the local Norwegian American communities was the different migratory history of elements in their population. The Norwegian Americans in these communities contained a shifting portion of greenhorns recently arrived from Norway, early urban pioneers—Norwegian-born adults—who had lived in St. Paul or (to a lesser degree) in Minneapolis for years or decades, their growing number of Americanized children, as well as many Norwegian-born or American-born members of the second generation who moved into the Cities from the upper midwestern countryside. A number of factors suggest that the migrants from the countryside, the group with both a rural Norwegian and a rural American experience before arriving in the Cities, had a greater and more lasting impact on the urban settlements' growth. Their influence in the society around them was larger than that of the first large contingent of American-born children in the Cities. Some, perhaps many, of those children were born in the region's rural districts and arrived in town with their parents. Their primary rural heritage was Norwegian American. Their Norwegian heritage, composed of memories handed down from earlier generations and adapted to recitals under American conditions, enshrined a Norway of the past with the sense of common origins that defined them as members of an American ethnic group.

CHAPTER FIVE

Social Issues in Expansion's Golden Age

[1880s–1920s]

OVER TIME, THE ACCUMULATED EFFECTS OF INTERNATIONAL MIGRATION FROM Norway and secondary migration into the Twin Cities combined to spur the development of a large, multifaceted segment of the urban population whose leaders took prominent roles regarding Progressive Era issues. At the same time this population evolved from a largely foreign-born immigrant group to become primarily an American-born ethnic group. The Norwegian American community integrated itself in the larger population of the Twin Cities between the 1880s and the 1920s. Through its many-layered involvement in several dimensions of the urban area's life, the community learned to know its neighbors and the relative size of the Cities' population groups in greater depth. Norwegian Americans' growing group size and diversity, along with the even greater increase in the number of resident Swedish Americans, led local Scandinavian Americans to realize that, taken together, their communities made up the largest segment of the Cities' population. As we have seen, that awareness supported their appointment and election to a range of municipal offices.

This chapter documents several ways that Norwegian Americans asserted themselves concerning social issues, building on the foundations of their growing integration and demographic prominence in these decades. Norwegians recognized causes of more general public interest and cooperated, especially with their Swedish cultural cousins, to carry more weight in debates and policy making. Leaders reached out beyond the nationality group and allied themselves with Swedes, Danes, Germans, and old-stock Americans who shared their views to push for common goals. They expressed their perspectives forcefully on controversial domestic and international matters through the ballot box, public lectures, newspaper commentary, literature, and the actions of organizations established to campaign for the relief of poverty, for women's rights, and against the abuse of alcoholic beverages.

Immigrant activists maintained networks of connections with compatriots in Norway who took part in political and social affairs that emigrants continued to be intensely interested in after their arrival in Minneapolis–St. Paul. Thus, Norwegian Americans in the Twin Cities developed transnational involvement in the homeland's politics, technology, music, arts, and literature. The urban area over these decades emerged as the "capital" of Norwegian immigrant life in the United States in the sense of becoming the preeminent center or headquarters of its political, cultural, religious, and social affairs.

The following pages examine the local Norwegian American community's growing importance regarding a wide range of issues—relations with members of Norway's visiting elites, the fight for suffrage for women in Norway and in America, and the homeland's struggle to gain independence from Sweden. Of consuming importance was also the renegotiation of relations with Norway's authorities through the centennial celebrations of the 1814 constitution as the Cities' Norwegian immigrant community became predominantly a second- and third-generation American ethnic group. Adjustments by that changing community to the nativist movements of World War I and immigration restriction by the federal government in the 1920s also inspired group members to critically examine the meaning of being both Norwegian and American.

Nonetheless, the Norwegian American community took positions on central issues of the Progressive Era, such as temperance and urban poverty (especially in the immigrant quarters of Minneapolis–St. Paul). Members of the established local American middle class as well as the Norwegian American working class and the ethnic community's leading religious institutions looked into the causes of economic hardship and launched a variety of initiatives, including charity associations, temperance lodges, fraternal mutual benefit societies, and a broad range of welfare organizations to deal with poverty. In 1925, celebrations of the hundredth anniversary of Norwegian immigration to the United States held in Minneapolis–St. Paul aptly reflected the social causes and processes of change that had occurred in the ethnic community of the capital of Norwegian America as well as in the transnational "greater Norway" of homeland and emigrated Norwegians in the twentieth century. Tighter bonds of familiarity and respect between these two "cousin" cultures of the same national background resulted from the commemorations, but simultaneously the centennial pageant revealed it was the group's shared historical experiences and future as Americans that unified it and earned it unreserved political praise from President Calvin Coolidge during his centennial oration.

The Twin Cities Emerge as the "Capital" of Norwegian America with Growing Ties to the Homeland

As the Twin Cities rapidly grew into a large urban industrial area between the 1880s and the 1920s, they became a regular stop on the national tours of performers and celebrities. Because of their unusually large Scandinavian American population, Nordic institutions, and strategic location in the nation's most Scandinavian region, Minneapolis–St. Paul became recognized as the unparalleled hub of Norwegian American life, an essential part of the itinerary of many visiting Norwegian Americans and prominent figures from Scandinavia. The Twin Cities also attracted the immigrant group's gifted and ambitious—influential elites who strove to raise the nationality's (and the Cities') status in both the United States and Norway. Among these were people who became famous as Norwegians engaged in issues, intellectual currents, and social movements on both sides of the Atlantic. They took sides in what historian Odd S. Lovoll has called the "war on orthodoxy" and made the Twin Cities a central site of the battle with what they perceived as reactionary conservatism in the late 1800s and early 1900s. Often champions of the American republic and its religious freedom, they frequently criticized the monarchy, class divisions, and the privileged status of the state church in the homeland. As social progressives, however, they also commented on the economic rapacity of the rich, materialism, and the unfulfilled ideals of the United States.[1]

The earliest visiting intellectual rebels from Norway in Minneapolis–St. Paul were Ole Bull, violinist and champion of the country's complete independence from Sweden, and Rasmus B. Anderson, professor of Nordic languages at the University of Wisconsin and crusading image maker for Norwegian Americans as modern Vikings. Anderson invited two prominent Norwegian authors, Kristofer Janson and Bjørnstjerne Bjørnson, to tour Norwegian American communities in the Upper Midwest in 1879–81. Janson, the first of these, returned to Europe until early 1882, when he brought his wife and their children to Minneapolis and stayed for more than eleven years. In the United States and Norway, he became famous as a talented writer, lecturer, freethinker, and Unitarian preacher. His equally gifted and socially liberal wife, Drude Krog Janson, published novels, short stories, poetry, and commentary on social issues such as women's rights, temperance, and religious tolerance during their residence. A year after his initial lecture tour in the Upper Midwest, with the help of Professor Anderson and Unitarians in Boston, Janson began his career as a Unitarian minister in Minnesota. He drew large audiences to his sermons and inspired the founding of Unitarian congregations, the first in Minneapolis and others in St. Paul and to both the east and west of the Cities.[2]

Janson also published his views on social issues in pamphlets and his Unitarian monthly *Saamanden* (The Sower). Drude Krog Janson not only wrote but also actively participated in the Cities' growing intellectual elite while managing the couple's household, caring for guests, arranging frequent gatherings of intellectuals, and meeting the needs of the seven Janson children. This couple made the liberal Norwegian American educated elite a force to be reckoned with during their time in the city. Their circle included leaders in the Norwegian-language press such as Luth Jæger and elected officials like Judge Andreas Ueland. Among the opponents of some of their liberal views were ministers at Trinity Church, professors at Augsburg seminary, and some Norwegian American journalists, even at *Budstikken*—until Jæger took over as editor.

According to Carl G. O. Hansen, both Rasmus B. Anderson and Kristofer Janson told how they had arranged to bring the soon-to-be famous Norwegian author Knut Hamsun to Minneapolis, with Anderson even taking credit for suggesting that the young man change his name from Pedersen to Hamsun, the name of the farm he came from. In his autobiography, Anderson reports that the young Pedersen arrived with a letter of introduction from Bjørnson and expressed his ambition to become a poet for the Norwegian immigrants in America. During his two periods in the United States, from 1882 to 1884 and 1886 to 1888, Hamsun traveled widely in the Upper Midwest and supported himself with a variety of manual work while observing and taking notes on American society. He treated Minneapolis and the Janson home there as his base of operations, forming lasting friendships in the city and giving many a lecture on literature and social topics at Dania Hall and other venues while he was in town.[3]

Norway's most admired and greatly controversial author Bjørnstjerne Bjørnson, who shared many of Janson's views, came to Minneapolis and St. Paul during a lecture tour of Norwegian centers in the Upper Midwest arranged by Rasmus B. Anderson in the winter and spring of 1880–81. Bjørnson's increasingly sharp criticism of traditional Lutheran theology and of the Norwegian American clergy led many pastors to warn their congregations away from his lectures during the tour, which provoked Bjørnson and attracted larger audiences. In Minneapolis, rival Norwegian-language newspaper editors fueled the controversy over Bjørnson's pronouncements and made his visit a matter of broad public debate. Jæger at *Budstikken* supported Bjørnson, and Sven Oftedal, Augsburg Seminary professor and editor of *Folkebladet*, opposed him. The chief resistance to Bjørnson's ideas came from religious conservatives of all stripes but especially the leaders of the Norwegian-Danish Conference and the Norwegian Synod, the two largest Norwegian American Lutheran organizations. The immigrant community's liberal set—notables including the Jansons, Ueland, the Jægers, and Hans Mattson and his wife, Christin (Peterson) Mattson, as well as local businessman-politicians such as A. C. Haugan, A. H. Edsten, and Andrew Tharaldsen—composed his strongest supporters. They arranged to have the first of Bjørnson's three lectures in Minneapolis at the city's most prestigious site, the Pence Opera House, where, according to Hansen, the visiting Norwegian drew the largest gathering of Scandinavian Americans seen up to that time locally.[4]

The visit, the controversy, and Bjørnson's proud nationalism, in which he believed the immigrants shared a sterling homeland legacy, raised the group's visibility and status in the Twin Cities. In the 1880s and later in this period, a growing stream of visitors from Norway stopped to speak publicly, further acknowledging the Twin Cities as the preeminent center of the immigrant group in the Midwest and that audiences for other notable Norwegians likely could be found there.

In the 1880s, Kristofer and Drude Krog Janson, shown here with their family, provided the Norwegian-language community with cultural leadership by writing socially critical accounts of life in America that were avidly read by an audience across the United States and Norway. *MNHS*

These prominent visitors and temporary residents knew that people in Norway were curious about life in the American republic and wanted to know how their emigrated compatriots fared under conditions in the United States. Even before he arrived, Janson wrote *Amerikanske fantasier* (American Fantasies), a play about the American ideals of individualism and self-reliance, which received widely varying reviews in Norwegian American newspapers. While on his tour of Norwegian America in 1880–81, Bjørnson wrote feature articles about his experiences for *Aftenposten,* the newspaper of *Venstre* (the Liberal Party) in Norway. The year after his first lecture tour, in Copenhagen Janson published *Amerikanske forholde* (American Conditions) based on his personal observations. Here he focuses on the salutary effects of free American institutions on Norwegian immigrants. However, his and Drude Krog Janson's fiction is also highly critical of the materialism, prudery, gender discrimination, and economic inequality found in American city life. After his first stay in Minneapolis, Hamsun wrote for Norway's major newspapers about his experiences in the United States. In the 1880s, when Norwegian migration to America was at its peak, these well-known authors spread news and opinion about events and social processes in the United States and life among emigrated Norwegians in Minneapolis–St. Paul. These were highly relevant topics of great interest in Norway at the time, and works by these authors contributed to controversial debates in the country's educated circles related to the desirability of religious and political change, women's rights, family life, and temperance in both countries.

Norwegian Americans in the Twin Cities Fight for Women's Suffrage

The fight for women's voting rights well exemplifies several features of local Norwegian Americans' engagement in social causes. Talented visitors and temporary residents from Norway like those mentioned above made the ethnic community more acutely aware of the international struggle to secure women's rights. For example, the fiction written locally by Drude Krog Janson and her husband Kristofer Janson likely helped change attitudes about discrimination against women in the educated elite. Becoming members of pan-Scandinavian and American suffrage organizations, socially engaged Norwegian Americans in their circle reached out to people of their national background and beyond to support woman suffrage.

Aasta Hansteen, the first woman to lecture publicly in the homeland and a prominent pioneer in its movement for women's rights, settled in Boston in 1880 and stayed for nine years. When she traveled west in 1882, she spoke twice in Minneapolis, and support for her appearances may well have included progressive local women such as Clara Ueland and Nanny Mattson Jæger (wife of Luth Jæger and daughter of Hans Mattson), who later became leaders of the Scandinavian Woman Suffrage Association (SWSA) of Minneapolis. The SWSA organized in 1907 as an auxiliary to the Minnesota Woman Suffrage Association, which operated across the state. The Twin Cities held many suffrage clubs at the time, but SWSA was unique as the only one in Minnesota organized along ethnic lines, which allowed it to make the most of the advantages gained by representing the largest ethnic group in the Cities and state.[5]

When the Scandinavian nationality groups unified behind a cause, they were an ethnic lobby much larger than the next-in-size local group, the German Americans. As historian Anna Peterson points out, "Scandinavian" was an ethnicity created for banding together related nationality groups for their mutual benefit in circumstances where the general population rarely distinguished the differences among them. In the Twin Cities and Minnesota, this large group could play a uniquely important role in giving the movement for women's rights access to local sources of economic and political influence that were not old-stock American. To attract larger audiences, the SWSA sponsored fund-raising events that featured its ethnic pan-Scandinavian allegiances in handicrafts, costumes, dances, foods, music, and literary and dramatic traditions. American suffragists saw prestige in being associated with the SWSA because of victories in women's voting rights in Scandinavia that predated successes in the United States. In Norway, for example, women won the right to vote in 1913, seven years before Americans in the movement achieved victory. The SWSA was not shy about drawing attention to the cause's progress in members' homelands, and perceptions of Norwegian American suffragists' connections with successful compatriots in Norway strengthened the organization's reputation.[6]

Until 1913 Jenova Martin, a Norwegian-born immigrant, led its activities in ways that reflected the strategies outlined above. She attracted a membership that was strongly of her own ethnic background and used that heritage to further the suffrage cause. Under the SWSA's auspices, she arranged Norwegian American activities such as the Norwegian Dramatic Society's production of *King Haakon the Seventh* and the lobbying of Scandinavian American lawmakers, especially those of Norwegian heritage, such as US senator Knute Nelson and state senators in the Upper Midwest. When Minnesota mobilized to vote on a suffrage amendment, she went on a two-week speaking tour, giving speeches in Norwegian and English.[7]

Martin's immediate successor as SWSA president, Mattson Jæger, was a Swedish immigrant. During her tenure, the portion of Swedish membership and ethnic events grew. The surviving membership cards in her papers, however, show a roster that, like the Scandinavian population of the Twin Cities in general, was overwhelmingly Swedish or Norwegian.

Mattson Jæger served through 1920, when women won the vote. She maintained the organization's interethnic nature and called on Martin's assistance in states like North Dakota, where Norwegian immigrants far outnumbered Swedes. Family relationships like Mattson Jæger's helped the suffrage movement's ethnic chapter take advantage of connections with local educated elites. Another prominent voice in the suffrage battle and in the Cities' Scandinavian American community, Clara Ueland was a well-educated Anglo-American married to a Norwegian-born judge in Minneapolis, Andreas Ueland. A cluster of other members, including Laura Bratager, Helen Egilsud, and Mary Tingdale, were members of leading local cultural families. Attracting and holding women like these with roles in other Scandinavian American organizations gave the SWSA a broad network in the biggest ethnic population group in Minneapolis–St. Paul during the turn-of-the-century decades.

That network surely helped the SWSA win a body of members from a wide range of classes, ages, and families in the pan-Nordic community. The surviving membership cards of the society, cross-referenced with census records and analyzed by historian Peterson, document the SWSA's appeal to subgroups in the community in ways that confute popular views about the women's suffrage movement. With an average

age of just over thirty-two in 1907 and forty in 1920, nearly half of the members were young women who were raising young children. Neither their youth nor their family responsibilities prevented them from taking part in the fight for the vote, as was commonly expected. What is more, perhaps partly because the society did not require dues, many members were wives of working-class laborers rather than spouses of middle-class skilled or professional men. Moreover, unmarried working women constituted a small minority that further diversified the SWSA's membership. Although foreign-born Norwegians and Swedes composed a large majority in the group, as they did among Scandinavians in the Cities then, women in Scandinavian or European American second or later generations also joined. A dozen Scandinavian American men joined as well. In gender, economic status, and family situation, the SWSA's membership revealed the breadth of the community's engagement in the woman suffrage cause.

Scandinavian women in the Twin Cities united in Minnesota's only suffrage organization based on ethnicity. Here they march for the vote in America at a time when the Scandinavian nations had already granted women voting rights. *MNHS*

By 1920, the range of the SWSA's activities demonstrated considerable usefulness to suffrage workers locally, regionally, nationally, and transnationally. In the Twin Cities, the SWSA was very visible through the cultural fundraising events it arranged for the cause. On the state level, it paid for the erection of the Woman Citizen Building that opened in 1917 on the grounds of the Minnesota State Fair. Nationally, the organization provided access to the movement for people fluent in a Scandinavian language but uneasy or illiterate in English. With little difficulty, Norwegians, Danes, and Swedes across the country understood each other's languages and the common elements of their Nordic cultures, which eased their shared efforts in the fight for women's political rights. Thus, the SWSA received and successfully carried out requests to assist in mobilizing support in centers of Scandinavian settlement, not only in neighboring North Dakota but across the nation.

The SWSA formed and operated as an American lobby. It relied on using members' shared Nordic ethnicity to consolidate as an interest group devoted to changing public policy in the United States. These facts illustrate the growing integration of Scandinavian Americans into the responsibilities of being citizens in their adopted country. As we shall see, like their increasing concern for social conditions in the United States regarding temperance and urban poverty, their engagement in the fight for women's suffrage showed their increasing assimilation into American life. Even the effort to construct a transnational "greater Norway"—that local Norwegian American elites led—centered on raising the community's status in America as much as in the homeland.

Progressive Reform and the Abuse of Alcohol

Temperance constituted one of the first social issues that most people in Minneapolis–St. Paul became engaged with in the Progressive Era. The range of views nationally on how to deal with alcohol abuse, from tolerance and regulation through various forms of restriction to total abstinence and prohibition, appeared locally by the early 1880s and divided the Cities' Norwegian American population until Prohibition became law in 1919—and beyond. In the best districts of the Capital City and the Mill City, many people in the economic, political, and educated elites enjoyed wine, beer, and distilled alcoholic beverages at home or in private clubs. These were largely native-born Americans, however, many of them with roots in New England or other more easterly regions, where temperance campaigns of various kinds had appeared as early as the end of the 1700s. Middle-class Progressives in both cities, whether native-born or immigrants, more often joined temperance campaigns. The largely foreign-born working class, especially its unionized elements, tended to oppose Sabbatarian and prohibitionist groups, especially when these worked to close the workingman's club, the saloon. Nevertheless, the immigrant quarters also harbored fervently pietistic communities who found common cause with Yankees on total abstinence.[8]

In St. Paul, tolerance of alcoholic beverages had support from most in the city's large Irish and German American Catholic communities as well as from its French and other smaller Catholic populations. The Church, however, strongly supported temperance. German Protestants differed in their attitudes to temperance, but most opposed sumptuary laws. Historian of the temperance movement among Scandinavian immigrants and Augsburg Seminary professor J. L. Nydahl asserted the ready availability of liquors in America combined with tendencies to drink ingrained from homeland cultures made *Scandinavian* synonymous with *drunkard* to sober-minded old-stock Americans. The historical evidence shows that distinct groups of Scandinavian immigrants advised different ways of dealing with drink—from government noninterference and broad acceptance of drinking at one extreme, to the moderate regulation of limited opening hours, high saloon licensing fees, and county option, to, at the other extreme, complete prohibition. Roughly speaking, the Nordic population divided into pro- and anti-drinking segments. Between 1890 and 1910, an electoral plurality in Cedar-Riverside kept pro-saloon councilman Lars Rand and his allies in office. In the early 1900s, however, total abstinence gained support from a widening variety of Scandinavian newcomers and Nordic American religious bodies. This trend was in line with developments regarding the issue in Scandinavia, attitudes in mainstream American society, and attempts by Scandinavian American leaders to make their subcultures more acceptable.[9]

The capital's biggest brewery, Hamm's, above Phalen Creek on the edge of Swede Hollow, became the east side's best-known producer of beer in the region around 1900. It and other makers of alcoholic beverages employed many workmen. Their products were on draft at local saloons, which lined the commercial streets in parts of downtown and the immigrant districts. In St. Paul as in other American cities, saloon keeping emerged early as a popular, low-cost avenue into entrepreneurship for the foreign-born. Often the saloon was combined with other entertainments such as a pool or dance hall and a mom-and-pop hotel or lodging and boardinghouse. Many establishments of these kinds—and eight of Hamm's St. Paul competitors—advertised in the 1880 Classified Business Directory of St. Paul and Minneapolis. The directory also listed two Protestant and five Catholic temperance societies in St. Paul. Within a few years, the local anti-liquor associations included the Union Lodge of the International Order of Good Templars, a Scandinavian immigrant total abstinence group whose members included twice as many Swedes as Norwegians and no Danes. In 1891 this lodge joined "Bernadotte," the first Swedish lodge in Minneapolis, and twenty-four other lodges in forming the Scandinavian Grand Lodge of Minnesota with headquarters in Minneapolis. Catered to by a local brewing industry and many small-businesspeople, drinking was a popular if much-debated pastime in the Twin Cities around the turn of the twentieth century.[10]

In Minneapolis, a situation similar to that in its sister city existed. In the early 1900s, the Mill City's four major brewers had plants near the Mississippi or its tributaries—from Orth's in the northeast to Gluek's near the southeastern city limits. Malt liquors were one of the city's largest industries at the 1900 census. In its heavily immigrant districts, such as the highly Scandinavian Ward 6 and the German Ward 3, where bars, saloons, and boardinghouses were commonplace, a mainly working-class electorate repeatedly elected aldermen who supported the saloon interest between the 1880s and 1910s. Minneapolis's much larger proportion of Scandinavian immigrant residents did not produce more unanimity of opinion in these groups about the issue of temperance. Against the pro-saloon advocates was marshaled a growing variety of church-related Nordic temperance forces centered on Augsburg Seminary and Trinity Lutheran Church in Cedar-Riverside, which was joined by the Swedish Augustana congregation nearby. In his history, Nydahl claims that the large Norwegian population in Minneapolis and the city's importance as the preeminent location of the group's educational, commercial, political, and religious activities made it also the main nerve center of Norwegian American temperance work. Since the Swedish population was significantly larger by the end of the 1880s and was equally split between pro- and anti-saloon opinions, there was ample room for a broader pan-Scandinavian participation in the temperance movement.[11]

Around 1880, temperance meetings on Washington Avenue South near Cedar-Riverside attracted large numbers of serious adherents but also "a lot of people who came only to have fun by heckling and creating chaos. This contributed to driving away the religious element and [led to] the organization's demise." Nordic support for temperance was strong in some quarters, however, and found an outlet among students at Augsburg Seminary and the University of Minnesota who opened a coffeehouse as an alternative to the saloons in 1883. Young working people in the community, including many housemaids, gave whatever they could spare to buy subscriptions that would open and maintain the coffeehouse, where they could respectably socialize with people of their own age who shared similar attitudes about drink. The venture, nonetheless, hovered near bankruptcy, even though its manager, Johannes J. Skørdalsvold, and other committed young men and women kept it going by paying out of their own pockets for a year or more.[12]

The low-church Lutheran clergy of the Swedish Augustana and Norwegian Conference church bodies in Cedar-Riverside provided the most energetic public leadership for total abstinence among Nordic immigrants through the 1880s. Their work was first publicly visible at Augsburg, Norwegian Trinity Church, and the Swedish Augustana Church in the district. Professor Sven Oftedal of Augsburg spoke at the grand opening of the Scandinavian Temperance Coffeehouse, where Trinity's pastor, Reverend Melchior Falk Gjertsen, also lectured. Later Oftedal joined the president of the seminary, Georg Sverdrup, on the list of speakers at mass meetings of Swedes and Norwegians at the two churches in the mid-1880s that resolved to found the Scandinavian Lutheran Temperance Society of Minneapolis. In the 1880s, the society held firmly to its explicitly Lutheran foundations and excluded speakers, such as Kristofer Janson, because of their unorthodox theological views.[13]

In time, however, the cause of abstinence assumed more importance than both national background and religious identification. To bring a wider audience, the word *Lutheran* was dropped from the organization's name. In the 1890s and later, according to Nydahl, public halls on the south side were again used for its temperance meetings, which became more like nonalcoholic socials than religious meetings. Immigrant Swedes left the society over time, and it became first "Norwegian" and then dropped any ethnic affiliation in its name. In the 1890s and years up to World War I, sister societies developed in other sections of the city, so that it contained the South, North, and East Minneapolis chapters, which in reality consisted of Scandinavian total abstinence societies in their most concentrated working-class settlements. The bylaws admitted any "decent" person, but the historical evidence does not reveal how that policy worked in practice.

According to Nydahl, the South Minneapolis Temperance Society in the twentieth century became the most influential among Scandinavians in North America because of its connection with Augsburg Seminary, with Trinity congregation close by, and to a lesser degree with other schools in Minneapolis. Professors and students at Augsburg frequently held membership at Trinity, but the congregation remained independent and included many members without affiliation at the seminary. Instead, Trinity became a "mother" church that allowed theological faculty and students to put their convictions in practice before they carried their messages, including those regarding temperance and other social issues, to sister congregations in the region. The South Minneapolis Temperance Society's speakers featured prominent professors and clergy who convinced students to ardently support temperance and total abstinence. Later these young adults set a good example of sobriety and social responsibility through abstinence when they returned to their home communities. The Augsburg-Trinity influence remained strong through 1914 with the Dano-Norwegian membership.

In Minneapolis politics, temperance became a central civil issue around the close of the 1800s. By the mid-1880s, temperance had found support in the city as a whole from three Catholic societies; ten Good Templar lodges, including a Norwegian one; a chapter of the Woman's Christian Temperance Union; and five local units of other, less well-known organizations opposed to intoxicating beverages. As Odd S. Lovoll has written, "The great breakthrough for the temperance cause among Norwegian immigrants came in the 1880s."

In the public arena, the deep divisions of opinion among immigrant groups over drink became evident. Several factors contributed to this situation. One of the most important was the city government's detailed six-page pamphlet entitled "Ordinances Regulating the Sale of Liquor and . . . Licenses in the City of Minneapolis," published in 1884. This document specified the conditions and costs required for receiving a license for wholesale or retail distribution of alcoholic beverages and for offering the entertainments commonly available in bars, inns, taverns, and saloons in the city.

The local law set the license fee at five hundred dollars, at the time a considerable amount of money, to discourage the too-easy opening of dispensaries of alcoholic beverages and to pay for policing the "active patrol districts" where alcoholic beverages could be bought and sold. Restricting the sale of alcoholic drinks to the commercial downtown and a few adjacent neighborhoods was another important means of controlling the effects of intemperance on public life. This became famous as the Minneapolis "patrol limits" that kept saloons out of affluent and better residential areas and concentrated their location on the commercial-industrial arteries of the central business district and nearby immigrant wards. The mayor drew up the geographic limits involved, and the city council had to approve them. Any change required the same procedure. All the immigrant districts at the time, including the heavily Scandinavian Cedar-Riverside, the near north side, and the northeast immigrant neighborhoods were within the active patrol zones and so had a lively traffic in alcohol on commercial streets. The law, moreover, banned the sale or giving away of alcoholic drinks on Sundays, election days, or within four hundred yards of a public park or school. In 1902 a public relations article in the *Minneapolis Journal* claimed that the patrol limits ordinance had become one of the city's most popular laws because it kept saloons to a relatively small number within inner-city areas. As a result, the anonymous writer explained, "There are no 'corner grocery saloons' in Minneapolis," a place whose "culture and public spirit is [founded on] the strong New England element in the population."[14]

The Norwegian-born Democrat Lars Rand, the longest-serving member of the Minneapolis city council in this period, successfully won reelection from Cedar-Riverside between 1892 and 1908. Rand staunchly defended the economic interests involved with the sale of liquor, saloonkeepers in particular, and the public's liberty to drink and otherwise enjoy itself in saloons and similar establishments. Forging an alliance with a German immigrant alderman from the near north side, in 1892 he successfully led the Democratic minority on the council in a battle to render ineffective the order prohibiting drinking on Sundays. The resulting ruling, popularly known as the "Rand ordinance," remained in force into 1900. Until he retired in 1910, he found Scandinavian candidates from the district who shared his views. Speaking a heavily Norwegian-accented English, he was always ready to put his political prestige behind a Scandinavian or Norwegian immigrant project. Regardless of his downplaying of religious motivations for temperance, Rand stood forth as the champion of pro-liquor forces and so as the enemy of both the Lutheran total abstinence groups among Scandinavian residents and the "Yankee blue-blood elite" that he claimed joined with them in Republican alliance that forced discriminatory ordinances against the working men through the city government.[15]

Most Swedish temperance activists, along with Americans and other immigrants who shared their views, chose to work primarily through the International Order of Good Templars (IOGT). Founded by old-stock Americans in New York State in the 1850s, the IOGT spread belief in abstinence from alcoholic drinks and worked to legalize prohibition around the world during the next forty years. By 1890, the order had split over women's and Blacks' participation, reunited, and accepted both groups. Laymen, not clergy, constituted most of the leadership elite of the IOGT. It offered a broader variety of meetings, other nonalcoholic social occasions, and a focus on women and youth beyond that of the cleric-led coalition centered on Augsburg and Trinity Church. The IOGT's secular approach meant that it also had to develop means of raising money to rent or to build temperance halls. The existing network of churches across the Cities and the state gave the Augsburg-Trinity coalition a wider scope of influence. Its religious approach, however, did not appeal as much to the young people who came to the city in the final wave of mass immigration between the late 1880s and 1914.

By the mid-1880s in Minneapolis, one of the city's ten IOGT lodges, Freya, named for a Nordic goddess, may well have been Scandinavian. In addition, another Protestant anti-drink lodge explicitly called itself Scandinavian. The first Norwegian IOGT lodge in Minneapolis, *Enighed* (Agreement) appeared in this larger pro-temperance Nordic context in 1889—around the same time as the Union lodge in St. Paul began operation. Two years later, the two lodges became part of the state's new Scandinavian Grand Lodge. Norwegian IOGT lodges appeared in succession in Minneapolis from then to the World War I years because the new wave of immigration from Norway brought many young people who had been active in the order at home between the late 1880s and 1914. The IOGT had spread from the United States to Norway and in this period returned with a later contingent of newcomers. Meanwhile, the earlier group of young Norwegian immigrants in Minneapolis who came in the 1860s and 1870s had developed a religiously based model of abstinence from alcohol through their churches. The temperance activists among the city's more recent arrivals had experience from a later stage of the abstinence movement in Norway that viewed drunkenness primarily as a social ill and cause for reform rather than as a sin or evil. Thus, a difference in generations, in the timing of people's departure from Norway, as well as in the resulting divergences in perspective about how to view and deal with alcohol abuse produced separate Scandinavian prohibition movements.[16]

The headquarters of both movements were in Minneapolis. The metropolitan district and the Minnesota Scandinavian Grand IOGT lodges and most of their officers were in the city. The vitality of the older, more Americanized cleric-led Scandinavian total abstinence movement continued to be evident in Augsburg's faculty, which offered courses to students and pastors about the dangers of drinking. In 1888 Theodore S. Riemestad sponsored a male quartet at the seminary that traveled across the region—and even to Norway—singing and lecturing at churches in the cause of complete abstinence. In the south, north, and northeast sections of Minneapolis, women's affiliates of the Total Abstinence Society developed in the 1890s. In the older organization, temperance work found its rightful place in the framework of the Scandinavian Lutheran faith and its congregations. Many a pastor said the local church was temperance society enough.

The International Order of Good Templars (IOGT), the era's most prominent temperance organization, established lodges across Minneapolis–St. Paul where Scandinavian Americans could enjoy a wide variety of social activities without alcoholic beverages. ***MNHS***

In the IOGT lodges, on the other hand, a shared belief in sobriety was the main foundation for a broader range of organizational responsibilities and activities. Its members could aspire to rise in the IOGT hierarchy or develop their interests and cultural talents. The order offered as broad a range of activities, excluding mutual insurance plans, as did clubs and others but did not make rejection of alcoholic drink its first principle. In Minneapolis, members of the Norwegian lodges also shared a common age group, migration experiences, and temperance movement memories (and perhaps personal acquaintance) from the homeland. These aspects of their lives separated them from longer-resident contingents of Norwegians who remembered the Norway of an earlier period and were now more integrated in American society.

By 1914, seven IOGT lodges had formed in the city: five in south Minneapolis, one on the city's north side, and one in its northeast section. Fulfilling a central aim of the order, the local Scandinavian IOGT also established a separate lodge for young people. As IOGT groups could not rely on an existent network of church buildings for housing their activities, they had to rent or build their own halls. If only they could raise the necessary funds, building their own hall would provide more options and more dependably available space. For five years, two lodges in south Minneapolis strove to finance a building without success and welcomed two new lodges in that part of town in hopes of bringing its realization. *Afholdfolkets Festskrift, 1914* proudly included a separate page with an artist's rendering of the three-story corner building they had planned in the south Scandinavian quarter, just off Cedar Avenue, the "Minneapolis' Karl Johan [main parade street], as it is called." Unfortunately, the four lodges did not manage to carry through their plan, and it fell to the city's first lodge, Enighet, to put up a hall on Cedar Avenue in 1924, which served many IOGT lodges and other temperance groups for several decades to come.[17]

Poverty and Community Reponses to Alleviate It

A dependence on alcohol often reduced individuals and families to poverty. The problem of poverty, moreover, became especially evident among the immigrant and native-born working classes during the boom years of the Twin Cities' explosive growth after the Civil War. Immigration and urbanization brought hundreds of thousands to Minneapolis–St. Paul in search of work. Their period of adjustment was often difficult. Even when settlers secured work and housing, the urban poverty they faced resulted from the low wages earned in many semi- and unskilled occupations. Working-class wages often barely met the necessities of food and shelter for a single person, let alone a family. As we have seen, pooling family incomes and taking in lodgers offered most of these people ways of making ends meet. If one or more family wage earners became sick, were injured through an accident, or suffered the consequences of social ills such as alcoholism or gambling, the situation quickly threw the group of relatives into peril. The transience of the large groups of young, single men, including many foreign-born or second-generation immigrants, who moved in and out from the surrounding countryside on a seasonal basis to work in the flour and lumber mills, aggravated their economic vulnerability. The end of the peak milling period often left them unemployed. Like most other groups, whenever possible Norwegian immigrants took care of their own and went to compatriots for assistance. Extreme circumstances sometimes overwhelmed the efforts of individual nationality and religious groups, however, so that larger cooperative organization proved necessary.[18]

By the mid-1880s, twenty years of accelerating industrial and geographic growth in the Twin Cities and the proliferation of human problems connected with it produced a variety of charitable institutions, public and private, to alleviate them. To assist transient and local young men through athletics and inexpensive housing in a Lutheran environment, Norwegian immigrants founded an independent YMCA in 1882. By 1892, the Norwegian Y had its own building in the middle of the Cedar-Riverside district. Faced with the "beggar and tramp evil" among single men as well as families ill with the "germs of pauperism," the city's civic leaders established a Friendly Inn for homeless single men in 1884 and consulted other cities' leaders for additional palliative initiatives they could take.

The Associated Charities of Minneapolis

By the end of that year, sixteen of these organizations joined together to form a coordinating umbrella institution named the "Associated Charities of Minneapolis," based on similar efforts in London, England, and Buffalo, New York. Charities representing ten Protestant congregations, a chapter of the Society of St. Vincent de Paul of the Catholic Church, two women's Christian organizations, a secular women's society, a neighborhood association, a city missionary society, and a hospital signed the catalog of founders. The oldest New England congregations in the city were represented, both in the list of founding institutions and as a majority of the leadership and board, where prominent members of wealthy milling families, such as George A. Brackett, George A. Pillsbury, and William D. Washburn Jr., took positions of responsibility.

This old-stock Protestant elite showed an openness to cooperation with Catholic, Protestant, and secular leaders, as well as with immigrant clergy. Norwegian American leaders connected to Augsburg

Seminary and its mother congregation, Trinity Lutheran, played a particularly prominent role in the founding and early work of the charities association. Reverend Falk Gjertsen, pastor at Trinity, called its inaugural meeting at city hall to order. Among the association's founding organizations was the women's charity group at Trinity, the Tabitha Society, whose first board of directors included Augsburg professor Sven Oftedal. The Tabitha Society dated from 1882, when Trinity congregation chose among its women members some who would lead its mission of helping the poor and needy, regardless of whether they were unchurched or belonged to another religious body.[19]

Working People Find Ways to Cope with Poverty and Scandal during the Panic of 1893

The Panic of 1893 receives only passing mention in standard histories of Minnesota. By contrast, local historian Carl G. O. Hansen, an insider who lived through the economic crisis in his early twenties, claims that it closed whole blocks of stores in the Cedar-Riverside Scandinavian business district, bankrupted all of the banks there, and left most residents unemployed. Normanna Hall and the Norwegian Y were only two of many immigrant concerns that closed for lack of funds in 1893. Leisure activities had to be as inexpensive as possible, and Hansen proudly notes how the community made the best of a situation in which living costs were low—potluck dinners at home or at the local church, backyard picnics, walks around local lakes, afternoons in the park, or club meetings in private family apartments. In the boom time of the 1880s, the Cities as a whole and ethnic enterprises in particular expanded rapidly because of the influx of a great many newcomers with all the needs of people getting settled. With the crash of the early 1890s, immigration rapidly decreased, credit dried up, and local real estate values plummeted. Some Norwegian immigrant entrepreneurs had moved into banking from smaller-scale businesses and used their financial institutions to invest in property. When the bottom dropped out of the economy, however, well-known Norwegian-owned banks in the district—Columbia National, Scandia, State, and the Washington Bank—closed their doors. Customers lost deposits, and investors saw their funds disappear. Between 1891 and 1897, moreover, local voters elected two Norwegian American bankers, A. C. Haugan and Kristian Kortgaard, city treasurer. Because of questions regarding their dealings with municipal finances during the depression, "the law laid its unrelenting hand on both of them," according to Hansen, who expresses concern that the scandal tarnished the ethnic group's good name in those years. Not until around 1900 did immigration to the Twin Cities and the local economy revive.[20]

In the dark mid-decade years when many people lost jobs and property, working-class men and women in the Norwegian community in north Minneapolis banded together for mutual support. Workmen in that section of the city habitually met to discuss current affairs and finances at Ingebret O. Rognaas's hardware store at Washington and Broadway Avenue. In January 1895, they resolved to form an organization along the lines of other mutual benefit societies. They chose to call their fraternal order *Sønner av Norge* (Sons of Norway), using a phrase from a patriotic song that had been considered for Norway's national anthem. By 1900, the order established lodges in the city's other Norwegian centers, and by 1914, its chapters spanned the nation. Meanwhile, in 1897, women formed the Daughters of Norway, a separate organization rather than an auxiliary to the men's order, in Minneapolis, and by 1914 it too had established chapters in areas of Norwegian settlement across the nation. Both orders raised funeral and sick benefits and continued their expansion into the 1920s, while they strove to gain states' approval as legitimate mutual benefit insurance institutions and won widespread acceptance among a broad class of Norwegian Americans. The Sons of Norway succeeded best in the early years as an insurance company, while the Daughters of Norway flourished most through cultural activities. Both orders grew in strength despite opposition in some quarters to "secret orders," to city-based organizations, to the consumption of alcoholic beverages, and to the idea of insurance generally.[21]

The Sons of Norway played an increasingly visible role in the community and pursued both of its primary goals. In 1897, its members marched in full regalia from the north side to take part in the first Syttende mai parade to the monument to Ole Bull in Loring Park, for which it had contributed a significant amount of money. When the order celebrated its tenth anniversary in early 1905, some three hundred

During the depression of the 1890s, Norwegian men in the working-class section of north Minneapolis banded together to give each other insurance benefits in case of injury or death at work. Their organization, the Sons of Norway, also devoted year-round efforts to preserving Norwegian cultural heritage. A separate benevolent organization, the Daughters of Norway, formed there soon after. *MNHS*

delegates joined in the gala banquet given by Nidaros Lodge Number 1. An alderman and the well-known city attorney Johan W. Arctander were important speakers. *Minneapolis Tidende*'s reporter found newsworthy Arctander's boast that the order had paid $4,600 in sick benefits during the previous year. The speech highlighted the lawyer's pride in the order's insurance and mutual benefits to members.[22]

During the week after the country's Constitution Day in 1905, people from "all the *bygd* [district cultures] in Norway" traveled home on a Sons of Norway excursion that departed on a special train by way of Chicago and Niagara Falls. The excursion exemplified the Sons' emphasis on maintaining contacts between the two countries and showed an awareness of how attractive returning home might be to some Norwegian Americans when the homeland's fight for full independence appeared to be intensifying. Including people from so many parts of Norway added to the feeling generated by the order that the entire ethnic group were sons of one homeland, thereby helping create a single nationality from many bygd subcultures. At home in the Twin Cities between 1905 and 1914, the Sons of Norway spearheaded efforts for large-scale public celebrations of the Seventeenth of May focused on the monument to Ole Bull that demonstrated a united Norwegian American community's patriotic devotion to the homeland's culture.

Women Lead in Founding Norwegian American Lutheran Benevolent Institutions

Group needs and the desire to care for one's own led to the founding of other benevolent institutions in the late 1800s and early 1900s. Women's charity groups formed in the community's earliest churches and in the congregations that appeared with the burgeoning Norwegian immigrant population. Among these were the above-named Trinity's Tabitha Society (1882), the Norwegian Christian Aid Society (1892) at St. Pauli Church, and the Lutheran Benevolence Society (1903) at Zion on the north side. In addition were organizations without a congregational tie, such as the Ladies Aid Society Dovre (1897). The Cedar-Riverside immigrant quarter also found representation in the Franklin Avenue Relief Association, a founding member of the Associated Charities listed without a religious affiliation that also served local people without limiting its clients according to their faith or background.[23]

The Norwegian Deaconesses Home and Hospital (1889), which aimed to meet the need for improved health services in the Cedar-Riverside section of Minneapolis, received initial leadership not only from the Reverend Gjertsen at Trinity and Professors Oftedal and Georg Sverdrup at Augsburg but most importantly from Lutheran sister Elisabeth Fedde, who created the model for the institution when she led the work to establish the country's first Deaconesses Home and Hospital in the United States in Brooklyn, New York, in 1883. With the help of businessmen and the ethnic community, Minneapolis Norwegians could boast that Cedar-Riverside sheltered a group of charitable medical sisters who offered outdoor relief and medical aid to the poor as well as a home for these women and a small hospital for in-house medical assistance that was open to all. Trained as nurses, the deaconesses also followed a Lutheran ideal of selfless service to others, offering help on a nondenominational basis but also speaking for their Christian faith to anyone who sought religious succor. Through the difficult mid-1890s, budgets were tight and staff made do with little, but the deaconess institutions withstood those trials. By 1910, they operated a three-floor hospital at Fifteenth Avenue South and Twenty-Fourth Street, a very central location for the south-side immigrant quarter. The deaconesses' institutions found reliable support from the regional religious network centered on Augsburg and the Norwegian-Danish Lutheran Conference.[24]

Around the turn of the twentieth century, the Norwegian American communities in the Twin Cities demonstrated the maturity and social capital necessary to launch a variety of social services successfully. The next venture to provide medical services to the poor and the community at large occurred in St. Paul with the founding of Luther Hospital in 1901. The institution operated under the auspices of the other major Norwegian American network of religious bodies—first with leadership from the Norwegian Synod, then from the United Lutheran Church, and from 1917 on from the Norwegian Evangelical Lutheran Church in America, the product of the last major Lutheran merger to occur before World War II. The Norwegian Hospital Society, the legal owner of the hospital and its attendant nursing school, stipulated in its articles of incorporation that five of the nine trustees on its board had to be members in good standing of a congregation in the above-named church bodies. Leading figures who met this requirement were Hans Gerald Stub, president of the Norwegian Synod, John Ylvisaker, and three other members of the Luther Seminary faculty in the Hamline section of St. Paul. In addition, Pastor Thomas Nilsson, Dr. Eduard Boekmann, Consul Engelbrecht H. Hobe, and Harald J. Lohrbauer were long-serving members of the board. A financial grant from Lohrbauer and the gift of a building from Charles Gilfillan enabled the institution to open as Luther Hospital at Tenth and John Streets at the beginning of the century. Expanded activity and concerted fundraising efforts allowed the hospital to move to a new building near the state capitol at Robert Street and East University Avenue as the St. Paul Hospital in 1914.[25]

Notices of the St. Paul Hospital's opening stress a combination of religious, social, and ethnic needs that the institution would satisfy. Many people of Norwegian background lived in the state capital, and many Norwegian Americans from the region visited it, *Decorah-Posten* noted in early 1902. At last, they could receive treatment from capable doctors at an institution under the control of the Lutheran church leaders. "All other nationalities in the city have their hospitals . . . but until now there has been none where we could place our sick *landsmenn* and give them suitable care. We have come so far as a nationality in this country that it should not be necessary to turn to other nationalities for medical help," wrote Carl G. O. Hansen, demonstrating his belief in Norwegian Americans' full establishment in their new home. As he notes in his local history, it was not until the early 1900s that Norwegian Americans "began to repose more confidence in doctors with diplomas from American institutions." The hospital's articles addressed its social purpose and ethical standards explicitly. No member of the Hospital Society or board of trustees was to receive profits from its operation, and free medical services to the poor were to consume all incoming funds beyond those used for maintenance and improvement of the facilities.

News articles state two purposes for the institution: caring for the sick and training nurses. When the hospital opened, it offered a three-year course of nurses' training. From the start, women played essential roles for the hospital, both as fundraising groups across the synod's congregations and as superintendent of the nursing school and chief surgical nurse. The first two superintendents were the daughters of Norwegian American doctors. Other women handled registration and cashier's duties at the hospital. In this period, all of the nurses were women. None of its doctors was female in the early years, but by 1916 Dr. Nellie Barsness was in charge of the period's version of electric shock therapy.

In Minneapolis, church and professional leaders founded a second Norwegian Hospital Society five years after Luther Hospital opened in

St. Paul. This group, rechristened as the United Church Hospital Association in 1907, established Fairview Hospital on the west bank of the Mississippi in the Cedar-Riverside section, not far from the Deaconesses Hospital. Prominent members of the association were among the hundreds of laypeople who left Trinity Church during the controversies related to the merging of Norwegian Lutheran institutions to form the United Church. Moving their allegiance from one of the two Norwegian American Lutheran networks to the other, in 1894 they and others organized Bethlehem Lutheran Church, which became one of the largest and most influential of the new church body's congregations in the Twin Cities. Hansen asserts that in time Bethlehem helped make the United Church the strongest of the Norwegian Lutheran organizations in the metropolitan area.[26]

Hansen was, however, a loyal member of Trinity and supported the institutions related to it. In a rare expression of personal feeling, he notes about the founding of Fairview Hospital that "A great many of the city's Norwegians were a bit peeved over the organization of this new hospital association. They held that support rather should be built up for the Norwegian hospital [that was] already a going concern." Reverend Carl Gustav Bjelland of Bethel Church, another United Church congregation, presided over the meeting to organize Fairview Hospital in the home of Dr. Henrik Nissen. As with the development of St. Paul Hospital, women's auxiliaries across the supporting church body made fundraising for building the hospital their project. South-side businesspeople provided a site and sufficient funds, so that an offer of a whole block from the Norwegian-American Commercial Club on the north side met rejection. After all, the people at Bethlehem and Bethel Churches were overwhelmingly south-side residents. By 1916, supporters of Fairview funded the construction of a large, several-story building on Sixth Street South, and Dr. T. H. Dahl, president of the United Church, dedicated it. Almost from the start, the hospital also trained nurses.

Assisting Other Unfortunate People in the Twin Cities

In the Progressive Era, Norwegian women played crucial roles in initiating, funding, and operating institutions for the old, the orphaned, the homeless, and the young from the countryside who fell on hard times in the Twin Cities. Lyngblomsten Home for the Aged (1902), the Norwegian-Danish Methodist Conference Elim Home for the Aging (1914), the Ebenezer Lutheran Home (1916), and the Scandinavian Union Relief Home (1925) provided food, housing, visitation, and varying degrees of medical help for the old and infirm. Large numbers of the Cities' early Norwegian settlers reached old age in this period, and the community mobilized in multiple ways to help those who faced privation in their later years. Growing proportions of the community were members of the second and later generations, in spite of the high rate of immigration from Norway between 1900 and World War I.[27]

Elim, Ebenezer, and the Union Home also offered shelter for the homeless and unemployed in the economic hard times of the 1920s. Other organizations focused their efforts on helping the unfortunate in younger age groups. The Lutheran Children's Friend Society operated an orphanage that by stages moved to Minneapolis (1922) from

The Wartburg Home for boys was one of several local Norwegian Lutheran institutions that offered a homelike Christian environment to protect young, rural Norwegians from vice and homelessness in the city. ***MNHS***

Winona (1900) and St. Paul ("several years later"). The Lutheran Girls' Home (1918) in northeast Minneapolis saw itself as an "institution of mercy." It aimed to assist unwed mothers and their "illegitimate" children in a "place of Christian atmosphere, comfort, cleanliness, and efficiency." The avowed purpose of the Wartburg Home and Hospice in south Minneapolis, a new inner-mission branch of the Lutheran Synod of Iowa and neighboring states in 1925, was to "guard homeless young men from the pitfalls and dangers of city life." Its constitution mandated that all board members had to be Lutheran and stated that its chief purpose was a defined kind of missionary activity among young males—to "bring them under Christian influence, and to save Lutheran young men for their church." Its founders, however, assumed that the hospice would serve needy men of any race or faith.[28]

Wartburg provided housing and clothes and appointed "big brothers" for transient men. When young men came to them for help, the home looked into their circumstances and tried to meet their needs. The hospice put its residents, whom it identified as often being orphans or from broken homes, to work maintaining its facilities until they could find paid employment. Facing the agricultural crisis of the 1920s and the shifting fortunes of seasonal work in logging by that time, many a Norwegian American youth from the rural Upper Midwest found temporary assistance at the hospice, where he was also likely to meet men from diverse backgrounds in a Christian setting.

Coordinated Charitable Efforts and Attitudes to Poverty in the Twin Cities

The Associated Charities of St. Paul did not begin operation until mid-1892. The profile of founding groups in the capital city's association reflected both the distinct size and culture of demographic divisions in its population and the timing of each population group's settlement in the city. Early on, Catholic French and especially Irish immigrants formed the body of the working classes. Many in the huge contingent of Germans who followed them were also Catholics. Scandinavians began arriving early but only in small numbers until the 1880s. As a result, the cadre of founding organizations of the Associated Charities in St. Paul found strength not in one but in eleven chapters of the St. Vincent de

Paul Society. They and the Irish or German Catholic charitable organizations far outnumbered the remaining institutions in the catalog of founding groups—the seven municipal institutions, which aided indigent and orphaned children, provided for widows and single women, supplied general relief, housed single men, or met the medical needs of veterans and the poor. Two Hebrew aid societies, two labor mutual assistance organizations, a relief group led by a Swedish American on the city's east side, and a miscellany of individual organizations completed the list of founders. In addition were a chapter of the Woman's Christian Temperance Union, the St. Paul Free Dispensary, and the Parish Settlement—all these efforts led by women. Wealthy German families such as the Weyerhausers and members of the early Protestant elite such as James J. Hill here too featured among the regular participants and contributors in the association. Rarities in the lists, the Danish-born banker's wife Mrs. L. C. Borup and the Norwegian American businessman A. E. Boyesen also donated funds. The charitable activities of Norwegian and other Scandinavian immigrant churches first find mention in the reports of the St. Paul Association in 1896, when the Swedish American Gustavus Adolphus Church joined the list of agencies offering relief and visitations to the needy.[29]

According to the Associated Charities of St. Paul's first report, existing charitable institutions completed "efficiently the relief work of the city, so that it was unnecessary to undertake any relief work." The umbrella charitable organization in Minneapolis made a similar claim. What was needed in each city was a clearinghouse organization that would help the constellation of institutions coordinate and document their efforts with the aim of avoiding overlap and people who approached one giving organization after another. The Associated Charities associations in the Twin Cities, like their parallels in big cities farther east, did not provide any relief themselves; rather, they investigated applications and referrals and then assigned these to the appropriate institutions within the umbrella organization.

In the decades around 1900, the Minneapolis and St. Paul associations also set out to educate their member institutions on the newest progressive methods of helping the poor out of their indigence. The foundation for this was the social science of the time, including values and programs from the settlement house movement, the "providential fund" savings plan, and the "friendly visitors" method of frequenting the homes of the poor, rather than the promulgation of a religious faith or attachment to a cultural background. Thus, much that individual church parishes contributed to charitable efforts, because it was directed inward to religious or ethnic members and mixed with the motives of conversion or holding allegiance, did not merit notice in Associated Charities reports. Minneapolis's association emphasized that the Norwegian immigrant Tabitha Society, an agency of Trinity Lutheran parish, was an exception to this general rule because its "methods are so systematic, broad and humanitarian irrespective of religious affiliations."[30]

Leaders of the Associated Charities stressed the necessity of prioritizing over religion or ethnicity the need to learn a willingness to work, honesty, foresight, thrift, and orderly habits of saving and consumption that would lift the poor to a stable, self-sustaining economic situation. Fathers had to fill the ideal role of reliable, robust breadwinners and devoted family leaders. Mothers had to keep a neat, hygienic home, serve nutritious meals, and raise the children in a wholesome atmosphere. Children, according to this contemporary consensus view, contributed part or all of their wages to the household economy at a time when their work was legal and needed. Low pay, illness, accidents on the job, overwork, and individual weaknesses kept hundreds of families in each of the cities from meeting these ideals and their own needs. In the 1920s, the Associated Charities became municipal family welfare services or children's services and later part of local community chest operations.[31]

The charity organizations in the Progressive Era viewed Norwegian immigrants as a typical group with regard to the causes of poverty. The roots of dependence on public relief, the organizations claimed, were the same regardless of nativity. In every category of assistance, not misfortune but personal character flaws and social conditions brought people into need, according to the associations' reports. In an "overwhelming majority of cases," defective character—insufficient industry, energy, persistence, efficiency, or self-control or lack of some other virtue caused some people of each cultural background to fail while other members of their group succeeded. Their tabulation of the causes of poverty between the early 1890s and first decade of the twentieth century sum up the most important causes of need for all population groups under the headings of "intemperance," "shiftlessness," or other traits among the personal flaws listed above.

Only in the depression years of the mid-1890s and in an occasional year after 1900 did the pattern of assigning blame for poverty to personal weaknesses change to recognizing citywide labor market structures as the most important origins of destitution. Viewed as a community-wide calamity beyond the control of the poor and the charitable organizations alike, the sharp economic downturn in the mid-1890s in St. Paul forced roughly twice as many families to apply for help and simultaneously cut donations to the Associated Charities in half. In general, the depression affected the individual ethnic communities with equal force.

A fire consumed the association records in Minneapolis for 1894–1900, but that led the author of the twenty-fifth anniversary booklet for the association to include a separate section of his narrative to explain the effects of the depression on the organization's activity in the city. Noting the drastic increase in need and loss of income to help the poor, the text emphasizes the "struggle to keep things a going and meet anywhere near decently the demands for help made on the organization." Programs were dropped or curtailed. Because of insufficient funds, the association could only manage for short periods to offer lodging for the homeless and a woodyard for people without enough fuel for heating. The number of friendly visits fell off, and the room for remaking used clothes closed. The employment bureau studied applications with more stringent methods to make sure that only the most "deserving" got help. Association agents advised women that "staying at home to take care of the children and letting husbands hustle for work" represented the best course.[32]

The leaders of the two charity organizations made a point of tracing poverty's effects. Inadequate housing and related health problems were among the results of poverty given most attention by the Associated Charities. The most concentrated residence of the poor lay in or near the most congested quarters in both cities, where the foreign-born found inexpensive housing near the commercial-industrial establishments that provided their work. Precisely these areas were the Cities' least healthy. As the St. Paul Associated Charities report for 1909 explained, the lack of sanitation resulted not so much from the fact that these areas lacked light and fresh air, as in more easterly American cities, but that the cheaply built housing in immigrant quarters was damp and drafty, "dilapidated and shed-like." Better housing cost more than the wages of immigrants could support, and to make ends meet financially, they "den[ied] themselves sufficient room" in the cheap housing they acquired by renting out space to lodgers. As A. W. Gutridge, then the general secretary of the capital city's association, analyzed the common situation, the root of many other causes of poverty lay in low wages and irregular employment—under- and seasonal employment as much as unemployment. The resulting situation of insuperable living costs for the classes without stable work represented a "social question which should engage us all," in Gutridge's view. The incidence of tuberculosis and other contagious diseases was highest in areas of low-cost, poorly maintained housing. Epidemics could potentially spread from these places to other parts of the urban area. Norwegian immigrants, like other foreign-born groups, suffered from these illnesses in proportion to the size of their group and its major settlement areas.[33]

The causes and effects of urban poverty in this period of most rapid expansion in Minneapolis–St. Paul concerned all residents. The social legislation of the time did not provide a publicly sustained social safety net, even though the workings of the country's capitalist market economy produced cyclical booms and busts. Norwegian Americans experienced the opportunities and trials of this situation as much as other immigrants.

Constructing a Transnational Greater Norway at Home and Abroad

As much as fighting for women's rights, temperance, and relieving poverty, local community activists fervently took up the cause of helping Norway win independence from Sweden. Allied with that goal was knitting bonds to the homeland by positioning the Norwegian community in the Twin Cities as the center of a transnational, greater Norway. Perhaps as much as a quarter of the locally resident group participated as part of the crowds of spectators at major occasions such as the fusion of the three largest Norwegian American church bodies in 1890 and the parade of choirs and concerts during United Scandinavian Singers of America Sangerfest in 1891. Most prominently, Norway's declaration of independence from the union with Sweden in 1905 and the centennial celebrations for Norway's constitution in 1914 brought much-publicized shows of gladness in the immigrant community. Hundreds or thousands thronged the Cedar-Riverside district and, in 1914, the downtowns of both the Twin Cities. Such events drew Norwegian immigrants from other parts of Minneapolis, St. Paul, and the surrounding region and solidified the Cities' function as the site of the nationality group's most significant occasions.[34]

This prominence was certainly the case with regard to Norway's fight for full independence. From the early 1880s to 1905, the prominent local Norwegian-language newspaper *Budstikken* included announcements and editorial support for amelioration or dissolution of the Scandinavian union. In 1882, a period of continuous Norwegian American activity for a fully independent Norway began when the more liberal membership of Our Saviour's young people's group left when it thought the church group had insulted Kristofer Janson and prevented him from speaking. This faction formed *Fram* (Forward), which mobilized liberal-minded members of the community to aid *Venstre* (the Liberal Party in Norway). One of *Fram*'s early projects was to raise funds for sending three hundred rifles to *Venstre* should military action prove necessary to preserve the nation from Swedish aggression. In 1884 its efforts to support the homeland's independence unified frequently opposed elements in the local Norwegian American elite through the founding of a second local association of supporters for Norway's Liberal Party, *Den Norskamerikanske Venstreforening* (the Norwegian American Liberal Association). Prominent Norwegian Americans in Minneapolis served as its first slate of officers. As much as Augsburg professor and editor of the low-church weekly *Folkebladet* Sven Oftedal might have disagreed with others in the association's leadership about religious matters, he took the lead by opening the founding meeting. He supported the cause of liberal politics in Norway in company with board members Andreas Ueland, Luth Jæger, and A. C. Haugan. Oftedal's close colleague at the seminary, Georg Sverdrup, had been a devoted Liberal in Norway and was the nephew of Johan Sverdrup, the party's leader. Andreas Ueland's father, Ole Gabriel Ueland, was for thirty-six years a member of the *Storting* (Norway's parliament) who led a caucus of members from rural districts that cooperated with Johan Sverdrup's urban liberals to pass democratic reforms. The Liberal Association in Minneapolis elected Andreas Ueland as its president and Nicolay Grevstad, formerly the editor of *Dagbladet* in Kristiania (Oslo), its vice president. Jæger, the liberal editor of *Budstikken*, became its secretary, and local businessman-politician Haugan its treasurer. In April 1884, the association sent four thousand crowns to Johan Sverdrup as aid for Venstre's cause, and local Norwegian-language newspapers printed Sverdrup's letter of thanks for the contribution. Personal, family, and professional ties to leading Liberals in Norway strengthened the association's determination to assist their ideological brethren in the homeland.[35]

Twelve female members of the association organized an auxiliary to help finance the liberal movement at home through a four-day bazaar. According to Carl G. O. Hansen, who assisted as an errand boy at the affair, many well-known liberals, such as Rasmus B. Anderson, Andreas Ueland, and Johan W. Arctander, took part. Through the bazaar, these men and women acted together as a liberal social set that argued for the homeland's greater or complete independence. The women set up a stage where the group's ideas and aspirations were aired through readings, guest speakers, and the occasion for meeting and mixing. Anderson, for example, presented his *fedrearven* (the national inheritance) lecture, which traced how Vikings originated democracy in their Norwegian homeland and brought it with them during the colonization of what later became Normandy and the United Kingdom. The full independence of the birthplace of democracy, in this lecture, becomes a goal fervently deserved and desired.

The blossoming of patriotic nationalism in Minneapolis next led to a Norwegian military company being founded. In the course of the 1880s, its name changed to the Norwegian Rifle Club and then the Normanna Infantry Company. Its membership swelled to a peak of 350 near the decade's end, when the company marched in splendid uniforms on Washington and Cedar Avenues leading the Seventeenth of May parade. On summer evenings, Normanna often paraded through the Cedar-Riverside district to military commands shouted in Norwegian, which led children in the area to call them the *hyre Venstrums* ("right lefters"). In the 1880s, Swedish immigrants in the city formed their own military company, the *Svenska Gardet*, whose friendly relations with the Norwegian community extended to participation in the Constitution Day parade. Norwegians in St. Paul also formed a military company, and the Twin Cities' two Norwegian groups visited each other for Seventeenth of May festivities. Normanna Company held target practices and debates and organized a men's chorus. Some of its and Fram's members weakened those organizations when they left to found the Scandinavian Labor and Sick Benefit Society and joined the Knights of Labor. These several changes illustrate the shifting organizational life and priorities among local Scandinavian immigrants in the Minneapolis–St. Paul of the 1880s and early 1890s.

The pan-Scandinavian harmony in the Twin Cities began to fray in the later 1880s. Hansen tells, for instance, how Johan W. Arctander, as the main Syttende mai speaker in 1887, allowed his Norwegian patriotism to overwhelm his Nordic feeling when he proclaimed from the balcony of the West Hotel in downtown Minneapolis how his landsmen had "thrown the Swedes flat on their faces back over the border" between Sweden and Norway. Odd S. Lovoll notes how relations between the two nationalities in the United States altered markedly in the course of the 1890s as the pan-Scandinavianism of the urban elite ended and Norwegian nationalistic feelings found strong expression.[36]

Like most Norwegian-language newspapers in the United States, the largest Norwegian journals in the Twin Cities, *Budstikken* and *Minneapolis Tidende*, sided with Norway's Liberal Party during the controversies over the nature of the Swedish Norwegian union between the 1880s and Norway's departure from the union in 1905. Regarding the homeland's political development, the editors of both Minneapolis papers were confirmed Liberals. They championed the party's demand for a separate consular service and free commercial dealings internationally. Strong supporters of its provocative line toward the Swedish king and parliament, they expressed extreme disappointment in 1895 when Norway's government backed down in the face of threats of military action from *storebror*, the country's Scandinavian big brother. A decade later, when Norway renewed its demands for greater freedom and unilaterally declared its own commercial relations and foreign policy on June 7, the local newspapers rejoiced. On July 14, 1905, *Minneapolis Tidende* splashed these headlines above five columns of its front page:

Norway's independence

It Appears that the Leaders in the Swedish Parliament now Feel that a Settlement will be Delayed until the Regular Parliamentary Meeting in January
In that Way the Question of Voting Rights for Elections Will be Avoided and Sweden Will also have Time to Arm
Prince Carl, Son of King Oscar's Daughter, Proposed as King of Norway
A French Friend of Norway Suggests France Act as Negotiator between Sweden and Norway

Becoming the Capital of a Transnational "Greater Norway," 1900–1925

As historian Daron Olson characterizes the cumulative effect of such coverage in the Norwegian American press, the "Norway in America concept" both asserted that "Norwegians in America had preserved their cultural traditions" and "articulated the ideas that emigrated Norwegians could still participate in celebrations of homeland Norwegian nationalism." During the teens and twenties, he notes, "this second idea would evolve into a much larger concept of a transnational Norwegian identity in which emigrated Norwegians were members in good standing." For Norwegian American spokespeople, taking sides on political struggles in the homeland became a means of showing loyalty through a willingness to defend and aid like-minded leaders in Norway. At the same time, the peaceful settlement of the Swedish Norwegian conflict raised the status of both countries in mainstream American culture.[37]

Around the turn of the twentieth century, the Twin Cities' Norwegian American communities developed by stages into a generally acknowledged status as the preeminent center of the ethnic group's life. Yet, all through these years, Chicago held a larger number of first- and second-generation Norwegian Americans. Moreover, between 1910 and 1920, the size of New York's Norwegian-born community surpassed that of both Chicago and Minneapolis. Three essential differences continued to make the ethnic group's situation in the Twin Cities unique. First, the other two cities were much larger. Second, Norwegian Americans made up a much greater *proportion* of the whole population in the Twin Cities: of Minneapolis—18.5 percent in 1890 and 10.8 percent in 1920; of St. Paul—6.4 percent in 1890 and 4.5 percent in 1920. Third, the

Twin Cities' hinterland, the Upper Midwest, included the nation's most densely settled Norwegian American region. Because of these factors, Minneapolis–St. Paul became the unparalleled organizational hub for Norwegian America.[38]

Acknowledgment of this unique status came in assorted dimensions of life in these decades. As the region's economic hub and the main destination of urbanizing Norwegian Americans, the Twin Cities were often the most convenient meeting place for convening regional networks—even if they were fundamentally rural in nature. For example, the *fellessråd* of the bygdelag, the common council of Norwegian rural district societies (lag) in the United States, was organized in Minneapolis. Some lag met in the city as early as 1909, and many organized in Minneapolis or St. Paul between then and 1920. The Scandinavian Singers Union held its national festival in Minneapolis over four days in 1891. Choirs from other Norwegian settlement areas across the country put the Twin Cities on the schedule of their interstate tours as often as possible.[39]

The Cities, moreover, were also the site of several fusions of the group's religious bodies. The larger St. Paul and Minneapolis area contained mother congregations of major Norwegian Lutheran denominations. The large auditoriums of these churches often provided space for religious bodies' annual meetings. Here, too, were the seminaries, faculties, and frequently the administrative offices of the ethnic group's largest diverging Lutheran denominations. Thus, in Minneapolis the United Church in 1890 formed from the three largest Norwegian Lutheran bodies. The negotiations soon broke down, however, and conference leaders at Augsburg and Trinity withdrew, taking many congregations with them to form the Lutheran Free Church in 1897.[40]

From an Immigrant Community to a Norwegian American Ethnic Group in the Twin Cities

Historian Odd S. Lovoll offers an insightful, multivariable analysis of the factors that around the turn of the twentieth century favored the movements for greater union among Norwegian Americans in their religious organization as well as in other aspects of group life. One factor was the experience of banding together for strength in their meetings with other population groups. Another side of this movement for greater unity was growing distaste with internal conflict among ordinary Norwegian American churchgoers. As increasing numbers of these Norwegians found a more comfortable degree of prosperity, they spent more leisure time together in secular associations. As urbanization continued, moreover, Norwegian Americans gained broader perspectives that involved them in American politics and social issues.[41]

These interests engaged them more than internal disagreement, which did not interest other Americans and simultaneously exposed these Norwegian Americans to criticism, as it prevented a pooling of their resources. Finally, in these years the last great wave of mass immigration from Norway arrived. The newcomers were unburdened with the historical sources of divisions in the group, which to many of them seemed both old fashioned and parochial. Norwegian Americans' changing circumstances in the United States added strength to their campaigns for public acknowledgment. Fortunately for the Norwegian American elites who led these efforts, the period from the late 1890s to 1914, unlike the decade and a half that followed it, was one imbued with positive attitudes toward a pluralistic society.

From 1900 to 1914, urbanization from the region to the Twin Cities continued, even as immigration soared. On a national basis in 1910, third-generation members of the group slightly outnumbered the Norwegian-born, who in that year reached their greatest number at 403,858. Ten years later, despite the large wave of newcomers, members of the third generation in America composed a group between two and three times the size of the population born in Norway, which declined to 362,862. This paralleled the development of demographic change in the Twin Cities. In the census of 1920, in Minneapolis the second generation outnumbered the first 24,901 to 16,389, while in St. Paul the preponderance of second- to first-generation Norwegian Americans was 6,732 to 3,818.[42]

As Norwegian American leaders' concern for the prospects of the younger generations in America grew steadily more important, they sought public proofs that the group enjoyed an honored position in the Cities' civic arena. Public monuments dedicated in civic ceremonies that marked Norwegian Americans' importance as an integrated and acknowledged mainstream community provided symbolic satisfaction of leaders' concerns. For example, in St. Paul, Norwegian Americans erected a bust of iconic dramatist Henrik Ibsen in Como Park in 1912. Later, statues of Viking voyager Olav Tryggvason and breakthrough Norwegian American politician Knute Nelson would be erected on the capitol grounds.

In 1920, the largest age groups of first- and second-generation Norwegian Americans in Minneapolis–St. Paul were children under fifteen and adults in their twenties. The group's pronounced youth presented a challenge to leaders who wanted to preserve the old-country language and culture. Between two-thirds and three-quarters of the married women chose a partner within the ethnic group, but spouses were often later-generation Norwegian Americans, rather than immigrants. Nearly as many Norwegian American women, moreover, were single as were married. Over half of these young women, most of them the daughters of former domestic servants, had made the change to white-collar office or store jobs. Nearly three times the number as in their mothers' generation worked as business and professional people, with the largest occupational clusters in educational or health positions. Overall, employment among the ethnic group's women paralleled that of the general female population in the Twin Cities. For a significant number, judging from the family histories related in interviews with community veterans, social activities and attitudes also paralleled those of local women generally. Lorraine Ofstie, for example, told of going to dances, nightclubs, and speakeasies with girlfriends who were not Norwegian Americans. There she found a group of men and women who became her friends. Her parents disapproved, but she did not stop going out. "I wanted to do what other people my age were doing and have some fun while I was young," she said.[43]

Norwegian American men were as often young and single as the subculture's women were. If married, and over half were, the men's spouses were three times out of four Norwegian American women. By then, the majority of Norwegian American men had moved into skilled manual work, mostly in the building and metalwork trades, although "laborer" remained among the largest single occupational category in the group. The number of businesspeople and professionals among them had roughly tripled since the census of 1900. Lawyers, doctors, and engineers composed the largest categories of professionals.

No longer primarily a foreign-language immigrant group, the community had evolved into an ethnic group—a community of Americans who shared a common cultural background. Now mostly later generation ethnics, Norwegian Americans, confident in their acceptance as Americans, could afford to look more closely into their ethnic background. Many Norwegian Americans had improved their material status and established contact with old-stock Americans, people in other immigrant groups, and other Norwegian Americans, frequently in secular organizations with memberships across religious divisions. They joined in larger causes such as political reform, the temperance movement, and the struggle for women's rights that crossed ethnic boundaries. These activities, combined with increased education and a greater variety of occupations, extended their world beyond the ethnic community.

The Responses of Older-Generation Preservationists

As the Harvard linguist and historian Einar Haugen pointed out, between 1890 and World War I, church leaders and other educated Norwegian Americans who wanted to preserve the Norwegian language experienced a "sudden, almost panicky realization." The forces that would replace the homeland tongue with English were "within the walls, determined not merely to demand a rightful place for English, but actually hostile to many of the values represented by the Norwegian language." Therefore, Haugen asserted, language preservationists mounted a "counterattack" by founding a series of religious and secular organizations on a national scale that aimed to maintain the ethnic group's institutions, culture, and language in America. Ethnic choirs, mostly male singing groups that performed in Norwegian, were the earliest to organize on a broad scale, first in the Upper Midwest in 1891 and then nationally as the Norwegian Singers Association of America in 1910. Between the 1890s and the 1920s, the Sons and Daughters of Norway, begun in north Minneapolis, expanded to national mutual benefit societies that not only provided insurance but also pledged to keep up members' interest in the Norwegian language and heritage.

The birth and spread of *bygdelag*, societies of Norwegian Americans from particular regions or local districts in Norway, occurred primarily between 1899, when people from Valdres held their first reunion or *stevne* in Minneapolis, and the mid-1920s. The principle of organizing according to loyalty to common cultural origins by place rather than nationality distinguishes the bygdelag from other Norwegian American voluntary associations. Yet broader goals link them to the ethnic group. They aim to preserve dialects of Norwegian and the subcultures from which the dialects arise, and thus share the common hope of maintaining an old-county heritage in the face of pressure to adopt English and assimilate to mainstream American culture. Norway's topography encouraged the development of rural subcultures because it divided settlements along fjords, mountains, and coasts with archipelagoes of islands. During the country's period of national romanticism, the conviction grew that these subcultures and their farming populations contained the "authentically" Norwegian language and culture rather than the country's towns and upper classes, which were more influenced by Danish and then Swedish rulers.[44]

The bygdelag, Lovoll notes, had a special relation to the group's urban settlements, especially those in Minneapolis–St. Paul. As he expressed it, "A description of how an association of a *lag* made up of Valdres Americans took shape may serve to introduce the societies as a whole. Indicative of Norwegian American organizational activity in general, the *bygdelag* first arose in an urban setting. The movement was, however, to be carried forward chiefly by the enthusiasm of rural membership."

The expansion of the lag and the Sons and Daughters of Norway occurred in the same years, and competition in recruitment and advocacy created considerable conflict at times. The rural clergy frequently controlled local lag and warned members against the Sons of Norway, which they belittled for its secret ritual and compared to the Masonic order. Although rivalry existed among the lag, they worked closely together and chose leaders across organizational lines to plan and carry out the Twin Cities' three-day celebration of the centennial of Norway's constitution (the so-called Eidsvoll Centennial) in 1914. Two years later, they formed the Common Council of the Bygdelag that met annually. Its leadership was crucial in managing the difficult cooperation between themselves and the wide range of Norwegian American religious and civic groups in St. Paul and Minneapolis that contributed to the four days of public festivities for the centennial of Norwegian immigration to the United States in 1925. Thus, the current of events and the ability to unite to carry out major projects for the whole of Norwegian America made the bygdelag a mighty force for unity between city and country in the preservation and public display of ethnic culture and achievements.[45]

In Haugen's view, *Det norske selskab i America* (the Norwegian Society in America) proposed the most important program of the initiatives to stem English language inroads and Norwegian cultural loss among Norwegian Americans. Its constitutionally stated goals were explicit and ambitious: to preserve the Norwegian language in the United States; to keep alive knowledge of Norwegian history and traditions among Norwegian Americans; to maintain interest in Norwegian literature, music, song, and art among them; and to pass on the unique character of the Norwegian people.[46]

The founders of the Norwegian Society in America, members of the ethnic group's educated elite, met in Minneapolis in 1903 to organize the society. From its beginning, the society attracted Norwegian American cultural leaders not only from the Twin Cities but also from Norwegian American centers across Minnesota and in neighboring states. The framework encompassed the whole nationality group and the preservation of its legacy from the fatherland. The society sponsored Norwegian speaking and essay contests in colleges and public schools and arranged concerts and lectures, many of them at Dania Hall in the Cedar-Riverside Scandinavian quarter of Minneapolis. It also sponsored a centennial festival in Minneapolis in honor of the great Norwegian poet and champion of civil rights for Jews Henrik Wergeland on Syttende mai in 1908. Perhaps the greatest accomplishment of the society was its sponsorship of the quarterly *Kvartalskrift*, which Waldemar Ager edited and managed in Eau Claire from 1905 to 1922. Well-known figures in the city's ethnic group organized the Norwegian Society of Minneapolis in 1908. Its activities paralleled those of the mother organization but also included receiving and entertaining notables from Norway, such as its minister to the United States, the primate of the country's state church, and the secretary-general of *Nordmanns-Forbundet* (the Norseman's Association).

By 1907, Norwegian American support for Norway's independence in 1905 and the many visits of emigrated Norwegians prompted members of the economic and political elite in Oslo to found Nordmanns-Forbundet to foster closer relations between the homeland population and the country's émigrés around the world.[47]

The foundation's creed and purpose developed from the notion that Norwegians had a unique national character marked by an especially strong individualism and self-reliance that grew in the soil of many separated settlements across the country's rugged terrain. That idea found an echo in the parallel of a "Norwegian America," which encouraged a diverse, multigeneration population in the United States to cohere around supposedly common origins and character traits in the old-country heritage. Although global in its reach, both historical and demographic realities caused the young organization to focus much of its attention and resources on Norwegian America. Nordmanns-Forbundet's origins were among high-level politicians and academics in Norway, yet the federation found its greatest early support in the largely working-class Sons of Norway in Minneapolis, which in 1909 provided the largest single source of memberships in the foundation—over a third of the total. The two organizations developed a close partnership. Both were devoted to maintaining Norwegian culture, and both built networks of lodges or, in Nordmanns-Forbundet's case, affiliated ethnic societies and, after 1909, Nordmanns-Forbundet chapters.

The Centennial of the Eidsvoll Constitution of 1814

Part of Nordmanns-Forbundet's planning for the 1914 Eidsvoll Centennial celebrations in Norway involved gaining approval to have a Norwegian American pavilion in Oslo among the large-scale exhibition halls for that grand occasion—and convincing as many emigrated Norwegians as possible to contribute to and attend the hundred-year constitutional jubilee. Speaking engagements at major public occasions where Norwegian Americans defined their later generation self-image provided a way that leading figures in the Norsemen's Federation could work toward this goal while cooperating with the ethnic group to strengthen ties with the homeland. For two years as the federation's editor, Ludvig Saxe traveled globally to increase the network, spending half a year of that time

In 1914 the one hundredth anniversary of Norway's constitution provided an opportune occasion for Norwegian Americans to visit their hometowns or districts in Norway. The Emigrated Norway Pavilion at the Eidsvoll Grounds in Oslo's Wergeland Park, with its exhibits celebrating the ethnic group's achievements, was a great attraction for American visitors. "Den Lutherske Frikirke," among other exhibits, inspired the creation of the Norwegian Emigrant Museum, suggested by individuals connected to the Norsemen's Federation. | TOP: *Courtesy Oslo Museum* | BOTTOM: *Courtesy of the Norwegian Emigrant Museum, Hedmark*

in 1912–13 in the United States. The Nordmanns-Forbundet magazine, *Nordmanns-forbundets tidsskrift,* reported that among the Seventeenth of May Constitution Day observations in the United States in 1913, the "largest single festival . . . was without doubt held in St. Paul, where all the Norwegian societies and congregations gathered at [one] large arrangement." Nordmanns-Forbundet's secretary general C. J. Hambro gave the Syttende mai address in the state capital that year, expressing his pleasure at speaking to a patriotic assemblage that made Norway larger and stronger than its national boundaries.

Nordmanns-Forbundet's efforts in bringing Norwegian Americans for the hundredth anniversary of the fatherland's constitution were enormously successful. Called the "Great Homecoming," the Eidsvoll Centennial hosted an estimated twenty thousand members of the ethnic group from America on Norway's shores. Many went to the exhibit in the Emigrated Norway Pavilion. Many also visited their places of origin around the country, which meant the Great Homecoming became part of the memories of a large number of homeland Norwegian families and communities.[48]

As far back as 1907, May 17 speeches in the Twin Cities included ambitious proposals for presenting Norway with memorial gifts from Norwegian America at the centennial constitutional celebrations. The Sons of Norway lodges in the city combined efforts for an impressive set of observances of Syttende mai at the Minneapolis auditorium. Johan W. Arctander gave the address on behalf of the organizers and focused on an appropriate memorial gift to the homeland in 1914, which in marked fashion revealed the prosperity and progress he felt emigrated Norwegians had accomplished in relation to the old country. His faith in their material well-being made him think it reasonable they could raise a million dollars, and he suggested that the givers tell the Norwegians at home what they needed to do with the money: Norway should use "a quarter million to dress the mountains, a quarter million to drain the swamps, and a half million to develop water power and industry." Arctander went into action at once, making so bold as to "appoint" a committee of twenty people, led by Senator Knute Nelson, to ensure that his plan was realized.[49]

Of course, this bombastic exhibit of Norwegian American bravado went nowhere, although the debates over what gift of aid and gratitude to give raised considerable interest over the next years. Emigrants traditionally sent remittances to their home communities in times of need, and by the early 1900s, by the best estimates these amounted to several million dollars annually. Norwegian Americans who had completed higher education at the University of Oslo, for example, between 1908 and 1911 set a precedent for the large-scale fundraising for the Eidsvoll Centennial. They supported the drive led by Consul General Engelbrecht H. Hobe and Dr. Eduard Boekmann in St. Paul and R. S. N. Sartz in Minneapolis to raise a large fund to honor their alma mater for its hundred-years' jubilee. By the 1911 centennial, 134 emigrated graduates, whose names and degrees appear in a tabula gratulatoria, had together donated 57,640.77 crowns, which the university used to build its elegant *aula* (public hall) on Karl Johan's Avenue in central Oslo. As Odd Lovoll notes, "Giving aid to the fatherland was a practice of long standing and one with wide appeal." After an unsuccessful year-long effort to mount a joint fund drive, in 1909 a central committee formed in Minneapolis under the leadership of state senator Lars O. Thorpe from Willmar. Proposals frequently combined the national dimension with interests that were more particular, however. Some devout groups proposed paying for the restoration of the country's national shrine, the medieval Nidaros Cathedral in Trondheim. Insufficient support led to that effort being abandoned. In the event, Norwegian American leaders presented the Norwegian government with close to $250,000, pledged in the tradition of the ethnic group's giving in times of need to charity and humane projects in Norway.[50]

Large and small Norwegian American communities across the United States arranged celebrations of the Eidsvoll Centenary. The acknowledged main event took place at the Minnesota state fairgrounds, midway between the Twin Cities. The bygdelag's leadership initiated the plans of those festivities, but competition among major ethnic figures and organizations in Minneapolis–St. Paul enlarged the committee in charge. The result, according to Hansen, was the "biggest 17th of May ever held in the Twin Cities." The first of the three-day affair consisted of bygdelag meetings in the morning, followed by grand parades of individual lag, contingents from Sons and Daughters of Norway lodges, and members of many other secular and religious organizations, each with banners and often with horse- or car-driven floats. Representations of image-making aspects promoted by Norwegian American elites also found space in the parade: Norwegian American elected officials in the lead with visiting notables from Norway, a float with Vikings in a longship, veterans of the Civil and Spanish-American Wars, and, reminiscent of Syttende mai parades in Norway, children waving Norwegian and American flags. As Orm Øverland and Daron Olson have emphasized, these were iconic presentations of the several mythical dimensions of the ethnic group's relation to the ancestral homeland and to its past and future in the United States. The public procession showed Norwegians as discoverers of America, people who had given their lives for their adopted country, and members of the coming generation absorbing American schooling.[51]

On the second day, the seventeenth of May, the program at the fairgrounds auditorium after church contained speeches by Norway's minister to the United States, a Norwegian American Lutheran pastor, and local Norwegian American lawyer-politician James A. Peterson. Hundreds of Minneapolis public school pupils clad in the common national colors assembled and sang "America" and then the Norwegian national anthem as they formed first the one and then the other flag. Massed ethnic men's choirs from the Twin Cities performed, and the St. Olaf College band played. That evening, visiting Norwegian American church choirs sang in concert at the auditorium and, as on the first day, individual societies held separate fest banquets. The planners had found a means of combining these events under the larger umbrella of a long weekend of commemoration.

On Monday, May 18, prominent figures from Norway, the region, and the state addressed an audience of thousands at the fairgrounds auditorium. The minister to America from Norway and the consul general from St. Paul proclaimed the group's acceptance on both sides of the Atlantic. The most prominent Norwegian American politicians in the nation at the time were the main attractions. The governor and US senator Knute Nelson of Minnesota and the governor and US senator Asle J. Grønna from North Dakota both spoke.[52]

The municipal authorities and the Cities' downtown merchants made their central districts available for the parades. Both city centers lavished attention on the centennial with enormous American and Norwegian flags on the sides of buildings along the parade routes. Stores

A memorable moment came during the centennial celebrations at the state fairgrounds, located between the Cities, when public schoolchildren dressed in blue, red, and white arranged themselves to display a massive Norwegian flag. ***MNHS***

displayed portraits of well-known Norwegian cultural figures, such as Ibsen and Bjørnson, or showed models of Vikings and the Eidsvoll building. One window held an enlarged reproduction of Christian Krohg's famous painting of Leif Erikson purportedly discovering America. The state allowed the fairgrounds to be the primary site for events on all three days. Mainstream society in the Twin Cities embraced the positive Norwegian American self-image the festival planners espoused. On display were traditional rural folk costumes and crafts from the Norwegian countryside.

The celebrations presented a selective, idealized version of Norwegian America—one that fitted well with the adopted nation's values and that seemed to best serve the ethnic group's prospects in America. Except for the Sons and Daughters of Norway, the women and men who made up the largest part of the ethnic group, the broad class of Norwegian American industrial and service workers, were absent from the celebrations. The labor unions they belonged to were nowhere in sight. The poor remained unrepresented. Only Norwegian American politicians in the mainstream center or conservative portion of the ideological spectrum found space in the festivities. None of the group's Nonpartisan Leaguers or Socialists were a part of its programs. Rather, similar to historian April R. Schultz's findings about the 1925 centennial celebration, the organizers of the Eidsvoll centennial in the Twin Cities "constructed a narrative of Norwegian American history that masked the many tensions and debates about ethnicity in their community. Their conservative vision was an effort to both regain and maintain their position as leaders in a viable ethnic community and to present their values to the larger culture as compatible with American culture, business, and politics."[53]

The Eidsvoll jubilee publications also intended to mold opinion in both the homeland and the United States—to strengthen the group's bonds to and status in both nations. The bygdelag organizing committee

To honor and publicize the centennial celebrations, Twin Cities municipal governments and businesses lavishly decorated their central districts with enormous Norwegian flags, bunting, and pictures of Norwegian subjects. *NAHA*

for the festival produced an official program book that not only held the schedule of events but also offered a history of the bygdelag movement, its activities, and its values. It also included a section focusing on the "Emigrated Norway" and its transnational technical and business elites. The civic leaders and educated elite of the Twin Cities and other urban centers in Norwegian America published an anthology of essays recounting the history of the ethnic group's accomplishments in its foreign-language press, Lutheran churches, educational institutions, literature, voluntary associations, and contributions to American public and political life. A third publication, also an example of "contributions history," records Norwegian Americans' part in developing the state of Minnesota and offers the widest range of Norwegian American subgroups and voices, including an ethnic labor union, *Det Uafhængige Scandinavian Arbeiderforening af Nord Amerika* (the Independent Scandinavian Workers' Association of North America).[54]

Countervailing Tendencies in Times of Radical Change

The centennial publications and celebrations make a case for the conviction that Norwegian Americans had successfully made their way to acceptance and prominence in the United States. At the same time, they also offered persuasive and manifold proofs that Norwegian America's links to the homeland and its cultural legacies remained strong and grew stronger because of the celebratory efforts. No fears of cultural and linguistic loss reached explicit expression to mar the congratulatory atmosphere. In fact, however, the transition to third and later generations in the Norwegian American community of the Twin Cities contained marked evidence of the continued struggle over how to negotiate the conflicting demands of integration into American society and the maintenance of Norwegian language and culture.

The founding purposes of two Lutheran congregations in the first years after World War I offer a striking example of polar opposite responses to Americanization and the encroachments of English language use in the Twin Cities. The leaders of Central Lutheran Church, on the edge of the business district of Minneapolis, chose to embrace modern American society wholeheartedly. In the bulletin for its first services, the congregation announced in 1919 that it existed because its founders recognized a need for a "down-town Lutheran" church, one that could attract the "number of our people" in that section of the city who were "as yet unaffiliated with any church." As other documents from the first years of the congregation indicate, the group of ten to twelve family heads that launched plans for the church defined its location precisely. They discovered that all the city's denominations except the English-speaking Lutherans had one or more large "representative" buildings in the downtown area—the section bounded by Franklin Avenue on the south, the Mississippi River on the north, Chicago Avenue on the east, and the railroad tracks on the west. Given the facts that Lutherans then comprised a population larger than "all the other Protestants combined in Wisconsin, the Dakotas and Minnesota and that Minneapolis was those states' preeminent demographic hub, [the] center of the city should reflect the region's 'actual condition as to church population.'" With this status in mind, the founding families started a "movement" to remedy the situation.

A materially resourceful and energetic group, the founders purchased the recently closed Baptist church in the midst of the district, renovated it, and called a suitable minister in time for Palm Sunday worship that same year. Jacob Aall Ottesen Stub, scion of one of Norwegian America's most distinguished clerical families, accepted Central Lutheran's call at the end of his term as general executive for the National Lutheran Commission for Soldiers' and Sailors' Welfare during the war. Within its first year, the church attracted so large a membership that the leadership agreed on an ambitious plan to build a new, larger edifice on a neighboring site. Central's leaders dedicated themselves to reaching out to all people in the area who dealt with the "temporal ills that man is heir to." The new "cathedral" of Lutheranism stood ready for occupation in 1928.

From the start, Central Lutheran defined its mission as ministering in English. It joined the English Association of the Norwegian Lutheran Church in America and soon became its most prominent congregation. In the thinking of those who mounted the building campaign, the new church would benefit the city and region as a whole. The leaders' analysis of the downtown population showed that it consisted largely of young women and men recently moved in from the vast rural area surrounding the Twin Cities. Part of the younger generation that left

Central Lutheran Church, the downtown cathedral of Lutheranism in Minneapolis. *MNHS*

farm and small-town life, these people viewed themselves as Americans whose native tongue was English. Often of Lutheran background, these mobile youths might become unchurched after arriving in the city. In their homesickness and loneliness, they were particularly vulnerable to the many temptations of city life. Central Lutheran sought to count members of this generation among its membership. "The New Central Lutheran Church: The Story of Central," the 1924 fundraising booklet for the building campaign, announces these fundamental points in the church's position:

> Central is a *democratic* church.
> It is a thoroughly *American* church.
> Although its membership, adherents and friends are descendants from nationals speaking many tongues, yet still all its services and meetings are conducted in the English language.
> It caters to no class but is all-inclusive. [italics in the original]

Its religious and social stance might seem a recipe for success in the context of the anti-foreign feeling and the Red Scare of the 1920s.[55]

The congregation that showed a diametrically opposite response to Americanization and the shift to the English language was *Den Norske Lutherske Mindekirke* (the Norwegian Lutheran Memorial Church). The proposal for the congregation arose not in St. Paul or Minneapolis but at a rural Lutheran conference south of the Twin Cities. In the fall of 1921, the president of the Norwegian Lutheran Church in America's Southern Minnesota District, the Reverend C. J. Eastvold, gave a speech at the district meeting in Montevideo that formally launched a movement to found a "completely Norwegian congregation in Minneapolis." A historical sketch made available by the Memorial Church notes that for some time there was a strong movement to found such a congregation because after World War I "most churches in the NLCA were completely English and the rest were moving in the same direction."[56]

The resolve to perpetuate the Norwegian language in a church setting "as long as anyone could understand it" was strong. Reaching agreement about the planned congregation's form became contentious, however, and finding the funds to rent and then to erect a building proved protracted. The effort moved against the mood of the times. Most Norwegian Americans invested their resources in other projects. After preparatory mass meetings in a downtown hotel, Dania Hall, and Central Lutheran's auditorium, twenty-two devout Norwegian speakers (including six pastors in the NLCA) decided to establish the Memorial Church to preserve Lutheran worship in the Norwegian language and tradition in the city. The founders gathered at Golgotha Norwegian Lutheran Church and, lacking the funds to acquire a building of their own, conducted services in other Norwegian American churches for the next four years. Heated disagreements about the proper size and ambitions for the structure delayed progress, and groups of people repeatedly left the congregation. Interest in and support for the memorial project continued to grow, however, and in early May 1930, more than a decade after the congregation's genesis, Dr. J. A. Aasgaard, president of the NLCA, dedicated the completed building.

Additional Movements toward Greater Group Solidarity and Recognition

During the negotiations that led to the formation of the United Church in 1890, elements in the two major Norwegian church bodies that remained separate, the Norwegian Synod and the Hauge Synod, expressed interest in an even broader union that they too could join. A groundswell of popular desire called for an end to sectarian disagreement and doctrinal bickering. The laity's views helped motivate continued discussion of means to surmount the differences among the Hauge Synod (a more lay-oriented body), the United Church (a middle way), and the Norwegian Synod.

The ethnic group's sense of nationalism and of patriotic solidarity after 1905 encouraged the majority of Norwegian American churchgoers to believe that a single Lutheran body for the whole group was a positive goal. In all likelihood, such unity appealed much more to laypeople than did seminarians' theological disputes. Ordinary worshippers found evidence of the common elements of their heritage in Lutheran hymns, liturgy, sacraments, and creeds from Norway. Twenty-seven years had passed since the last merger of Norwegian American Lutheran institutions when the United Church, the Hauge Synod, and the Norwegian Synod found amity in 1917 and joined to form the Norwegian Lutheran Church in America (NLCA). The three groups had held meetings throughout the Upper Midwest, from Madison, Wisconsin, on the east to Fergus Falls on the north and Willmar, Minnesota, on the west, and several times in the Twin Cities. Interest had waxed and waned through complex conferencing over the proper activities of laypeople, the doctrine of election, the call of clerics, and the structure of church bodies.

Agreement on these matters in 1912 prepared the way for a formal merger five years later, on the four-hundredth anniversary of the Reformation. By mid-June 1917, leaders had worked out the thorny details and published documents to carry out unification into one body. Delegates from the three constituent church bodies and thousands of interested laypeople gathered in St. Paul to witness the ceremonies that would make the NLCA a reality. Mounted police led an eight-person-wide public procession of clerics, church officials, and delegates through the downtown from the armory to the St. Paul Auditorium, where an audience of thousands, the St. Olaf College band, and a massed choir of between fifteen hundred and eighteen hundred singers welcomed them. A sacred concert that evening, a communion service the next morning, an elaborate commemoration of the Reformation's jubilee, and a group ordination of twenty-seven new members of the NLCA's ministry completed the weekend of celebrations. According to church historian E. Clifford Nelson, 3,276 congregations, 1,054 parish ministers, and nearly half a million Lutheran churchgoers were united in the NLCA. Norwegian American Lutherans had succeeded in finding commonalities that marshaled group strength in the competition with other Protestant denominations that made efforts to convert Scandinavian Americans.

The urge to demonstrate greater unity in a national identity had been growing for some time and early along also focused on honoring and memorializing iconic Norwegian cultural figures the whole group admired. In this way, the national rather than the regional or local in the homeland legacy became central. Norwegian Americans' increased self-awareness and belief that their cultural heroes deserved public recognition in the Twin Cities, where they composed such a large and influential group, also played a prominent role in their desire to elevate these countrymen.[57]

When Jacob Fjelde's statue of Ole Bull was unveiled on May 17, 1896, thousands of people attended at the Minneapolis exposition building, which became, as Carl G. O. Hansen expressed it, a "17th of May celebration, an Ole Bull festival, a Jacob Fjelde commemoration ceremony and a Sangerfest, all combined." Conceived to demonstrate that both the virtuoso violinist Bull and the local Norwegian American community held great cultural significance for the city at large, the program the organizers arranged was broadly inclusive. Nine men's choirs—two German, three Swedish, and four Norwegian—sang in competition, and no less a celebrity than Ignatius Donnelly, the nationally known radical Irish American politician from St. Paul, presented an oration. The statue was dedicated in Loring Park on the next Norwegian Constitution Day, and from then on it became an annual focal point of parades and patriotic song from all parts of the city and region. This constituted a major step toward the transformation of Syttende mai into everybody's day to celebrate national backgrounds, a festive public occasion to show respect for the commonly held values that bound together Americans of all heritages. In 1912 a similar adoption of Norwegian ethnic culture as everyone's public property took place when the city of St. Paul agreed to the Sons of Norway's proposal to mount Fjelde's bust of Henrik Ibsen on an eight-foot plinth in Como Park, its most prestigious recreational area. The mayor and parks commissioner were present, as were the governor and his staff. The event was the stuff that public recognition is made of.

Norwegian Americans and World War I

Less than a few weeks after the centennial celebrations in Norway ended, many Norwegian Americans in the Great Homecoming hurried back to the United States because of the outbreak of World War I. The flowering of activity in the ethnic group in the Twin Cities reached a climax with the constitutional celebrations depicted above. With the war and especially with American entrance into it in 1917, the dominant attitudes toward groups of foreign descent and ethnicity grew decidedly more negative. Until the declaration of war on Germany and the Central Powers, significant leeway existed for people who wanted to stay out of the war or who said it was not America's affair or blamed it chiefly on the interests of European and American capitalists. Many in the Twin Cities wanted the nation to remain neutral for these and other reasons. Franklin F. Holbrook and Livia Appel's history of the state's role in the war based on contemporary records collected at the Minnesota Historical Society (1928) views Scandinavian Americans generally as tending toward neutralist or pacifist positions. In 1914 a considerably broader segment of opinion in the state tended in the same directions. As farm and then urban economies in the state and region improved because of the increased needs for foodstuffs and other supplies in the warring nations, however, criticism of the war became more muted in many quarters, including Scandinavian American circles.[58]

In Minneapolis–St. Paul, *Minneapolis Tidende* early on endorsed the need to fight Germany and unequivocally backed President Woodrow

Wilson when he declared war. On the other hand, the local Norwegian-language Socialist-Labor newspaper *Gaa Paa* did not and suffered from state and federal government regulators' inhibitive rulings once the country was at war. Fears of divided loyalties made elements in American society view the hyphenated or hybrid identities developed by ethnic groups as a danger to national security. Those who spoke against becoming directly involved in the conflict often found themselves portrayed as pro-German—as supporters of America's chief enemy. Of course, German Americans found themselves suspected, often no matter what their stand on joining the war. Nonetheless, prominent Norwegian American institutions based in Minneapolis–St. Paul felt sufficiently endangered that several took protective action.

After the majority of the Norwegian American delegation in Congress, eight congressmen and two senators, voted against the declaration of war on Germany in early 1917, as Carl H. Chrislock, historian of the period, expressed it, Norwegian Americans had an "'image' problem." Shortly after, *Minneapolis Tidende,* along with two other major Norwegian American newspapers, published a letter from an anonymous but "highly respected" member of the ethnic group that urged its local organizations to avoid "demonstrative" celebrations on the seventeenth of May. For the duration of the war, the Constitution Day observances and almost all Norwegian American publications were notable for their unusually strong expressions of loyalty to America and the war effort.

The general atmosphere of repression and intolerance toward anything "foreign" in some quarters led Minnesota lawmakers to propose that the foreign-born be registered and to create the Minnesota Commission for Public Safety, which had almost unlimited authority to deal with "disloyalty." In this context, the Scandinavian American National Bank of Minneapolis chose to rename itself the Midland National Bank. The Norwegian Lutheran Church in America excised the ethnic identifier in its name by the overwhelming vote of 533 to 61 of its convention delegates. Very shortly after its founding, the NLCA formed an English Association for congregations, pastors, and young people's groups that operated in the tongue of mainstream America. Strong voices within the new church body wanted to ensure that clerical colleagues did not purposely block the "advancement of the church by insisting on the Norwegian language."

The church group, however, erred in judging it best to remove the word *Norwegian* from its name. Faced with a wave of protest from laity, pastors, and the Norwegian-language press, the NLCA resumed its original name at the first opportunity. In the Twin Cities, the Scandinavian Woman Suffrage Association (SWSA) also considered a name change but chose to keep its ethnic label.[59]

Most vulnerable among Norwegian Americans were those who vocally resisted America's entering a war footing, especially if their views appeared in print. Liberals who ran against conservative candidates on occasion found their chances of election thwarted by accusations or court actions based on their association with known Socialists or other opponents of the war or claims that their writings had violated the 1917 Espionage Act. An infamous case in point involved a well-known Norwegian American figure in Minneapolis, James A. Peterson, who engaged quite actively in the city's ethnic organizational life, became a successful lawyer in the community at large, and won election as Hennepin County attorney. By 1918, when he chose to run against Knute Nelson in the Republican primary for the US Senate seat from Minnesota, Peterson had become a La Follette Republican with a record of opposing the war. A grand jury found that Peterson had violated the Espionage Act in an article he wrote for an English-language journal in the Twin Cities. That conviction, although overturned by the US Supreme Court in 1920, was enough to weaken his candidacy against the popular prowar Nelson and to end his career in politics.

The 1920s: Immigration Restriction and the Norwegian American Response

With the war's end, the economy soured in Minneapolis–St. Paul and its agricultural hinterland. In the early 1920s, the value of farm products fell and urban employment in war production decreased sharply with disarmament. The Cities' Norwegian Americans and their rural cousins suffered these consequences in common with the general population. Like other groups, they mourned their war dead and honored their decorated veterans in homecoming parades and ceremonies to welcome returning heroes. Despite ethnic groups' service in the Great War, anti-foreign sentiments persisted and intensified with greater dissemination of information about Russia's Communist revolution in 1917. The political forces lobbying for severe restriction of immigration to the United States quickly triumphed. The 1921 Immigration Act imposed an emergency reduction of immigrant visas by roughly 50 percent to allay fears that millions would flee from war-torn Europe to American shores. In 1924, in spite of energetic lobbying by a wide spectrum of ethnic groups and their elected representatives, the government passed the Johnson-Reed Act, which limited the available visas even more, and enacted plans for "national origins quotas" that drastically curtailed legal immigration from Europe beginning in 1929, while banning Asian immigration. In the 1900–1914 period, an average of 14,332 Norwegians entered the country in a single year, more of them departing from urban centers and settling in metropolitan areas such as the Twin Cities than ever before. In 1903 alone, nearly 27,000 Norwegian immigrants arrived. Norway's quota under the national origins system was only 2,377, however. In the 1920s as these restrictions became law, a final though smaller wave of immigrants arrived, augmenting the growth of the foreign-born in Norwegian America by 8,852 a year.[60]

With this legislation, the ethnic group turned a decisive corner. Adjusting to community life with such successive and large reductions in newcomers, combined with the economic hard times in the Upper Midwest, placed Norwegian American organizations under considerable financial and demographic strain. Long-term effects of the nativist reaction against cultures of foreign origin and the generational shift in the local Norwegian American population were marked. Nationally, the use of Norwegian for church services declined startlingly from 100 percent in Norwegian American Lutheran churches in 1900 to roughly half of these congregations in 1925, when very few young people received religious instruction in Norwegian. In the early 1920s, the bygdelag and the Sons of Norway noted the inroads of English (or declining interest in the ethnic heritage in general) among their younger members as well. On the other hand, despite attempts by both state and local Americanizers during the war, classes in Norwegian language and culture continued in several public high schools in Minneapolis, even though the number of schools offering such courses fell from thirty-six nationally in 1917 almost by half to seventeen by 1940. As the centennial of Norwegian immigration to the United States approached in the first half of the 1920s, some leaders in these organizations and the NLCA feared that those celebrations could become the last mobilization of resources for the preservation of the Norwegian-language subculture.[61]

A Last Hurrah in the Twin Cities? The 1925 Centennial of Norwegian Immigration

Near the beginning of the 1920s, bygdelag leaders resolved to sponsor the main celebrations of the 1925 Centennial of Norwegian Immigration in Minneapolis–St. Paul. They planned an affair that would show what they had learned from arranging the festival in 1914 for the hundredth anniversary of Norway's constitution. The Common Council of regional societies extended an invitation to local and regional Norwegian American churches and secular societies to participate, and in November 1923 the joint effort got underway with an umbrella committee in charge. This committee worked to avoid the conflicts that attended early planning of the Eidsvoll celebrations in the Twin Cities. The state fairgrounds at Midway again became the site of the festival. Dual parades again processed through downtown business districts festooned with enormous flags and centennial effects. Again, many lag in the bygdelag met, and individual ethnic societies held their own evening events. Choirs sang, and Minneapolis children dressed to create huge flags while they sang American and Norwegian patriotic anthems.

However, the "Slooper Centennial" surpassed the impressiveness of the Eidsvoll jubilee. This affair continued through four days instead of three. A full-scale replica of *Restaurationen*, the iconic small sloop that carried the fifty-two original Norwegian immigrants to New York a century earlier, was on display. The organizers devoted an entire day to religious meetings and services. From the start, the women's committee developed activities, an exhibit, and a book to commemorate the contributions and achievements of Norwegian American women. The organizations that strengthened a national ethnic identity and a transnational Greater Norway appeared prominently in the program and on the speakers' roster. An idealized self-image centering on the distant Viking heritage and Leif Erikson's discovery of America, the immigrant pioneers, and Norwegian American sacrifice in American

Often called the Norwegian *Mayflower*, the *Restaurationen* was reconstructed and displayed for the centennial celebrations. Here descendants of those who came to New York on the sloop in 1825 pose on and around the ship. *MNHS*

wars appeared in parade floats and in an elaborate pageant with a thousand participants on the fairgrounds.

Costumed reenactors portrayed Native Americans, Abraham Lincoln, surviving Civil War veterans, and Colonel Hans Heg on horseback leading the famous Fifteenth Wisconsin Norwegian regiment. Spanish-American War and Great War veterans followed in full uniform. Professor Knut Gjerset of Luther College had collected and mounted an exhibition of the multidimensional material history of Norwegian Americans through their folk arts and crafts.

A catalog of exhibits and a historical essay for each part accompanied the exhibition. Other publications of the centennial included *Souvenir: Norse-American Women, 1825–1925*, an anthology of 454 pages; a special issue of *Minnesota History*, the journal of the state historical society; and a ninety-six-page, richly illustrated *Norse-American Centennial* program with essays by, among others, the historians Rasmus B. Anderson, Waldemar Ager, and Olaf Morgan Norlie. Inspired by his and the bygdelag's work on the centennial exhibitions and the resoundingly positive response they received, Knut Gjerset led the efforts that resulted in the founding of the Norwegian-American Historical Association at St. Olaf College in October 1925.[62]

The Twin Cities had never witnessed a greater assemblage of elected Norwegian American officials. The representatives from the homeland were impressive in number and notability, confirming official Norway's acknowledgment of its emigrated people and their descendants. Most affirming of all, President Calvin Coolidge and his wife walked up front in the Minneapolis parade, and in a speech at the fairgrounds, the president endorsed the ethnic group's claim that Leif Erikson discovered America and proclaimed that Norwegian Americans composed the immigrant group that best embodied American values. Two descendants of "sloopers" spoke to a huge audience on the same day as President Coolidge.[63]

The event appeared to satisfy Norwegian Americans' dearest hopes of acceptance and acknowledgment by the larger Twin Cities community, nation, and homeland. As historian April Schultz concluded about the centennial celebrations, a well-organized body of middle-class leaders had composed and successfully presented a safe, loyally respectable mainstream group without internal conflict or tension. Then, as Daron Olson has memorably noted, "All came to a crashing halt . . . when America passed the National Origins Act of 1929. . . . Moreover, it signaled the failure of the legacy myths approach, and it appeared that the Norwegian American identity had been dealt a blow from which it might never recover."[64]

Conclusion

As the next chapter shows, Norwegian American identity did recover and evolve after the effects of the National Origins Act. The acceptance and acknowledgment of Norwegian Americans by the general public in the Twin Cities continued to change in ways that could not be foreseen thanks to the passage of time and altered historical circumstances.

Norwegian Americans' active involvement in social issues between the 1880s and 1920s contributed to the range of Americanizing processes that integrated them into the local community and based a larger part of the history they shared on events in the United States, the place where they fought for women's rights, debated the abuse of alcoholic beverages, coped with urban poverty, and reached out to maintain a transnational connection with their ancestral homeland in centennial jubilation and war. During the next decades, the end of mass immigration from Norway, gyrating economic conditions, and a second world war would again test their group cohesion and continue their integration into American life.

As has been the case earlier in this study, investigating four central themes is vital for an understanding of the processes of change at work in these decades. The Twin Cities expanded in population and size, becoming a national and international economic power. In the early 1880s Norwegian immigration rose to its historic peak. Forty years later, when Norwegian Americans celebrated the centennial of their immigration in 1925, the dominance of the second and third generations in the local Norwegian community changed it into one of the Cities' largest and most influential English-speaking American ethnic groups. As a group, Norwegian Americans crossed a threshold of size and influence in this period. They confidently joined in citywide and national issues, forming broad coalitions with old-stock Americans and members of other ethnic groups who shared their point of view. At the same, the local Norwegian leaders reached out to the authorities in the homeland to mount grand centennial celebrations and support transnational organizations dedicated to strengthening an international "greater Norway." This represented a vibrant, new stage in community development, and in the process, Minneapolis–St. Paul became acknowledged as the "Heart of the Heartland" for Norwegian Americans.

CHAPTER SIX

Community Transformations

Boom, Bust, and War

[1925–1945]

THE FOUR MAIN THREADS OF THIS NARRATIVE, EACH CHANGED BY TIME AND historical circumstance, also wound their way through the next decades of local Norwegian American community life. Migration and remigration took new forms. From this point came the first twenty years with comparatively little immigration from Norway. Norwegian America's protests against the severe federal restriction laws of the 1920s failed. These immigration laws, a public mood inimical to foreigners, and the coming of the Great Depression and World War II led Norway to leave its quota of immigration visas to the United States incompletely filled. During the Depression years more Norwegians remigrated to Norway than left it for America. In these circumstances, local community leaders mobilized to pass on the group's cultural heritage to its youth through a multitude of public projects.

During increasingly hard times, family and community self-help became the order of the day. Labor unrest grew intense as the Citizens' Alliance of business leaders interpreted the New Deal Labor Relations Act to deny recognition and negotiation rights to hard-pressed union members. Near–civil war conditions erupted locally during the Teamsters strike of 1934. As internal resources became exhausted, many turned to public assistance, welcoming Governor Floyd Olson's and

President Franklin Roosevelt's relief programs. Urbanization continued, even increased, but its motivation was usually new. Beginning in the later 1930s people moved to the Twin Cities to take jobs in the military buildup that preceded America's entry into the war.

That buildup changed the Cities' economic profile, and the war years brought many Norwegian American women into previously male industrial work. With many men soldiering abroad, community women also more often managed ethnic group affairs. The Nazi occupation of Norway galvanized the ethnic group's activist core to send money and supplies to relatives in the homeland, support the free government in exile, and aid military efforts to end German control of Norwegian life. These became the new community projects.

The long-term processes of group change—an aging population, a reduced percentage of Norwegian-born, and the increasing proportion of third- and later generation members—also transformed the community. Community leaders energetically worked to preserve the nationality group heritage. Loss of Norwegian language competence, increasingly evident, motivated campaigns to maintain courses of study of the Norwegian language and culture in the public schools. However, no longer visibly different, local Norwegian Americans were increasingly indistinguishable from the overwhelmingly white, northwestern European American majority in Minneapolis–St. Paul.

A Church Suited to the Times and the Urbanization of the Young

In 1924, as part of its publicity to encourage donations to support erecting an impressive church building in downtown Minneapolis, Central Lutheran Church published a thirty-one-page pamphlet entitled "The New Central Lutheran Church: The Story of Central" by Seth Ernst Gordon. Viewed nearly a century later, Gordon's text suggests both aspects of the 1920s and common attitudes of the Depression years that followed. When he makes Central's case for contributions to build a downtown Lutheran cathedral, his rhetoric echoes the confidence in a self-regulating economy epitomized at the time by President Calvin Coolidge's remark that "America's business is business."

Gordon invites enlightened businesspeople to understand that the market—and American society as a whole—depends on a workforce molded by the Christian values of honesty and integrity. Certain that Christianity alone can imprint these values in the coming generations, he uses capital letters to loudly stress that

> Business—BIG BUSINESS—realizes that it is GOOD BUSINESS AND A SOUND INVESTMENT to give its financial as well as moral support to a church doing the type of work of, and so strategically located as, Central. Business has also come to the belated conclusion that it cannot neglect spiritual things with impunity.

The author's assertion is that donations to build this new downtown church are not charity but a certain investment because this financing will ensure "contented" workers for the Twin Cities. Central Lutheran offered both the appropriate denomination and the most relevant location. Its leaders' research confirmed that the large majority of those who were moving into the city looking for economic opportunity were young people raised in the Lutheran faith. Usually they settled at first in inexpensive housing in the church's neighborhood close to downtown, precisely when they were most vulnerable because of inexperience, loneliness, and homesickness. Their proving grounds in this critical time came when Central Lutheran was the closest congregation professing the faith of their ancestors.[1]

The benefit of investing in this new church was not only to the urbanizing youth and their employers, however, but also to the Lutheran community in the Twin Cities and their families in Lutheran settlements throughout the region. Gordon's argument succeeded in the boom years of the 1920s among the people in the city's business sector to whom he and the church leaders appealed. By 1928, before the effects of the Wall Street crash dashed the local economy, the Reverend Jacob Aall Ottesen Stub dedicated the imposing new stone edifice. The sense of urgency that motivated Gordon and Central's leadership to release the pamphlet resulted in part from their knowledge of continuing migration of Norwegian Americans (and other Lutherans) from the region to the Twin Cities.

Strikingly, the text makes no reference to ethnic backgrounds, as if those allegiances are already a thing of the past. The new church will rise in a time when an inherited religious Lutheran affiliation alone is relevant to Central's building project; as mentioned, the young moving to the city carried their family's faith. Moreover, the booklet explicitly states that Central accepts all nationality backgrounds and Christian denominations. The text offers no explanation for this pan-Christian stance. Unstated reasons might include knowledge of the large Scandinavian and German American Lutheran population in the region. Perhaps the intention that Central should be a haven for all Christian newcomers to the city was an indirect reflection of the congregation's conviction that the immigration restriction laws would end the likelihood that many of those newly arriving would be people direct from Norway. The underlying motivations remain unclear.[2]

The founding members expressed their sense of mission at this specific point in Norwegian American history through the congregation's motto and additions to it stated on the pamphlet's opening page:

> "The Faith of the Fathers in the Language of the Children"
>
> Twentieth Century American methods, but implicit obedience to Our Lord.
>
> The changing order, but the never changing Word of God.

The concluding section of the pamphlet's statement of purpose focuses on the threat the city and nation face. This section reflects attitudes common to the 1930s, when commentators blamed the prolonged economic crisis for the growth of radical ideologies to the far left and right—here termed "many isms and factions" that cause dangerous political unrest. The root problem, according to Gordon, is the present nadir of America's "spiritual life," which low church attendance documents. Falling from traditional faith destabilizes society and leads to "perilous times." However, businesses' donations to the building of a downtown church—the cooperation of religion and enterprise—hold the stabilizing promise of the application of Christian values in all dimensions of life.[3]

Effects of Prohibition and the Depression on the Norwegian American Community

Two major contexts framed the forms of Norwegian American community life in the Twin Cities of the late 1920s and 1930s: until 1933, the effects of Prohibition, and until the economic upswing brought by the approach of World War II, the trials of the Great Depression. Together with the passing of the Norwegian-born population and the end of mass immigration from Norway, Prohibition and the Depression brought transformations to the now largely old-stock, ethnic-American community.

Prohibition set fresh challenges for city authorities and private organizations. Crime levels rose throughout the 1920s and until the Eighteenth Amendment's repeal in 1933. Criminal activity grew more organized during these years as gangs of bootleggers responded to the greatest markets in the state for illegal liquor, which were in Minneapolis–St. Paul. Drunkenness increased. Kid Cann's bootlegger syndicate, named the Minneapolis Combination, competed, sometimes violently, with the Irish syndicate led by Tommy Banks to bribe municipal officials and control the local illegal trade in alcohol. FBI and local police raids, gang-style killings, and the trials of crime bosses filled many columns of newsprint in Twin Cities papers. In the immigrant quarters of both cities, parents worried that the underworld economy of speakeasies, vice, and bootlegging, concentrated in their neighborhoods by a long history of municipal ordinances, would entrap sons and daughters, in particular as legitimate work became scarce with the advent of the Depression. Lorraine Ofstie related seventy years later how she and young friends, some Norwegian American and others not, went to nightclubs and "after-parties" where they had illegal drinks and met men rumored to be involved in bootlegging and vice. "I never told my parents," she said. "They forbid me to go to those places, and I knew people who'd been caught in police raids."[4]

The strains of adjusting to rapid change and the deflation that occurred after World War I produced economic instability in the Upper Midwest and the Twin Cities throughout the 1920s. On the one hand, mergers and consolidations in the Cities produced fewer but bigger banks and such later well-known manufacturing giants as General Mills, Honeywell Regulator, and, in the latter years of the decade, Wilbur B. Foshay's holding company, a far-flung network of utilities companies. The first skyscrapers shot up in both cities in these years, the Rand and Foshay towers in Minneapolis and the First National Bank tower and new courthouse in St. Paul. Migration to Minneapolis–St. Paul for employment and educational opportunities swelled in the 1920s even though the rate of population growth in the state fell to half that in the previous decade. Film and radio spread knowledge about the possibilities of urban life with its jobs, conveniences, and entertainments. For many young people in the heavily Norwegian American region surrounding the Cities, farm-district or small-town life paled by comparison. The increased availability of cars and bus lines to the Twin Cities made urbanization or commuting into the Cities more practical and less expensive. All this supports Seth Gordon's analysis of the demographic situation around Central Lutheran Church during its fund drive.

On the other hand, the signature flour milling industry of Minneapolis began a long decline as early as 1916. By 1930, Buffalo, New York, replaced it as the nation's chief flour producing center. In the same years, depletion of the state's pine forests reduced and then ended logging that fed the sawmills of north Minneapolis and brought sharp reductions in the city's lumber and woodworking industries. For these reasons, when the Depression arrived, Minneapolis felt its impact even more than St. Paul. Until then, the local middle and working classes increasingly speculated in the commodities and stock markets, even as job prospects changed rapidly and became less stable. When the New York stock market crashed in 1929, many local investors doubted that events so far away would affect the upper midwestern economy anytime soon. The tendencies toward economic crisis suddenly became stark in Minneapolis less than a year later when bankruptcy receivers put Foshay's soaring monument to his economic empire at auction in May 1930. Many other enterprises in the Cities and state soon suffered a similar fate. As the lines of the unemployed rapidly grew longer, many families in the Cities felt hunger. As early as 1931, Governor Floyd B. Olson's relief committee began to dispense direct aid from the state to the poor and needy, and much of that relief went to Minnesota's large population of city dwellers.[5]

The desperate times Minnesota's farmers faced in the recession after World War I returned as the prices of agricultural products plummeted. By 1932, for example, dairy farmers' incomes fell to three-quarters less than their earnings in the 1920s. Commodity prices for wheat and corn also plummeted sharply. Migratory patterns among Norwegian Americans reversed because of the new circumstances: more Norwegians returned to Norway than immigrated to the United States. In travels across the rural Upper Midwest as ticket agent for the Norwegian America Line in the 1930s, Jacob Stefferud discovered the surge of Norwegian Americans who struggled to pay for tickets to return to Norway, not to visit, but to stay because of economic hardship in the United States. In "Memories," which he typed privately for his descendants, he wrote, "During the early 30's the conditions in the Dakotas were serious. . . . Farmers lost their farms and were starving. Many Norwegian farmers got help [from] their relatives in Norway who sent tickets and money to get back. . . . I remember one family with 5 or 6 children who had scraped together everything they had and got help from relatives in Norway to go back there. The whole family came to the Minneapolis office one Saturday morning for their tickets."[6]

The large majority of the Norwegian Americans who instead moved to the Twin Cities at this time were members of the second or third generation, people whose parents or grandparents had settled as immigrants in the rural hinterland of Minneapolis–St. Paul. In the 1930s, documents historian Elizabeth Faue, gendered regional migration of young adults within the United States occurred. Because the Upper Midwest held the nation's greatest concentration of rural Norwegian American communities, many among the young arrivals in the Twin Cities were members of that ethnic group. Unemployment in construction and factory work in Minneapolis–St. Paul rose to 25 percent during the Depression. Urbanization slowed down as a result. Nonetheless, Faue argues that migration to the Cities not only continued but became transformative in the course of the decade: "Over 75 percent of men and women migrating to Minneapolis and St. Paul between 1935 and 1940" left from farms. Furthermore, she notes, most of these migrants were in their late teens or early twenties. Remarkably, many more women came, and they were younger, traveled shorter distances, and more often arrived alone. Three of four men, on the other hand, arrived with their families.[7]

Like other population groups in Minneapolis–St. Paul, most Norwegian Americans did not want to accept public relief. People used up personal savings and sought help from their families and their own group's welfare institutions before asking for aid from the city, state, or federal governments. They turned to their churches and the inexpensive entertainments community ethnic organizations offered. The more economically secure, middle-class Norwegian Americans mobilized resources for relief and the strengthening of ethnic bonds. At the start of the decade, the authorities in the Twin Cities believed their umbrella charity organizations, by then called the Community Chest in each city, would be sufficient to meet local needs. By 1933, however, many private ethnic institutions, religious and secular, exhausted their funds, and municipal charitable efforts proved far from adequate. Therefore, between 1933 and 1936, increasing numbers of people relied on federal public assistance, and that commonly depended on President Franklin Roosevelt's New Deal.[8]

A Closer Look at Effects of the Depression on Norwegian Americans in the Twin Cities

The Norwegian American dimension of these general developments in the metropolitan area revealed the ethnic group's common experiences with many other population groups. In interviews that explored family history, old-timers remembered the 1930s and youngsters recalled the stories of parents and grandparents handed down from that time. Hilda Kringstad remembered, "I went to North High. This was during the Depression, and I couldn't afford the streetcar, so I walked to school every day. Oh, that was a long way! I remember that I wore the same dress every single day for the last year of high school. That was how poor we were at the time." Laughing, she commented wryly, "You wouldn't get by with that today!" On a more serious note, she concluded, "I had to find work because times were so hard. . . . My dad felt very sorry that he could not give me an education."[9]

Several people told how more fortunate family members helped relatives find work or lodgings or shared their own jobs, homes, and meals with people in the extended family who lacked the basics. Discretion and unspoken ways of relieving the needs of "our own" became the rule. Some Norwegians helped family first and then others from their home region in Norway. Others told how parents had improved the family's fortune through investments and the acquisition of property in the 1920s, only to suffer life-changing losses in the 1930s.

"My father lost forty-four thousand dollars," Ione Braak Kadden immediately announced when asked if her family felt the effects of the Depression in St. Paul. In her mid-eighties when interviewed, she explained that he was a builder and investor in local real estate and lost the money when relatives could no longer pay the home mortgages he had cosigned. "So, all of a sudden, these people, an insurance company in Minneapolis, came and told him that they were foreclosing on his property. . . . He had other property, but he thought he had reached retirement and was not going to build, but he began again at sixty years of age, building and remodeling more property to make up for what he lost."[10]

Some families fell out of the middle class, but most veterans of the era explained how working hard with the assistance of relatives and compatriots enabled them to struggle through some very trying times. Ione Kadden's immediate family "gave up when Dad lost the forty-four thousand; they moved back to their old home [a modest house] and moved out of a very lovely redstone mansion. . . . It never occurred to me that we were hard up or anything like that, but they did live frugally. They knew how to use what was available and got absolutely no help. A lot of people among the tenants owed them money. The tenants could not pay the rent . . . nephews on the other side of the family helped. They worked for my father. . . . Sometimes they were staying at our house and receiving board and so forth. . . . A lot more of the taking care of other people. My folks took care of many people."

Because he had other funds, and as he was well aware of the housing market collapse in St. Paul, Ione's father followed public auctions in the city closely, bought homes cheaply, employed relatives and other needy Norwegian Americans to repair them, and temporarily offered these people space in the buildings they were restoring. Meanwhile, for the duration, he and his family moved to more modest housing.

Urbanization and the 1934 Truck Drivers' Strike that Transformed the Political Scene

As noted earlier, migrants from the countryside were fewer in the thirties, but for some moving to town had a transformative effect. Joel Torstenson explained that he came to the Twin Cities in 1935 after teaching farm children in a one-room schoolhouse for three years in the Red River Valley. In that time the market for wheat collapsed. "Some farmers were losing the farms. Being foreclosed on. The insurance companies were taking them over. We thought that was terrible," he remembered. "My political ethos came partly out of the Depression," Torstenson said thoughtfully, confirming that he "lost faith in the market mechanism" as he watched these events occur.[11]

Many thematic threads in this history came together in the events of Torstenson's migration from northwestern Minnesota to the Cities and his activities there. He departed for Minneapolis because a Norwegian American friend who belonged to a Lutheran free church in the area told him about Augsburg College. The rural network of free church congregations connected to the college and the Norwegian settlement around it in downtown Minneapolis drew young Norwegian Americans into the city in the 1930s, just as they had earlier. This was another part of the urban magnetism of which Central Lutheran Church's promoters were so acutely aware. Secondary rural-urban Norwegian migration remained at the center of the story in the Depression years.

What prompted urbanization in the 1930s was the rising wave of agricultural discontent that followed the collapse of farm product prices and the subsequent wave of foreclosures that Torstenson's school families experienced. This was a recurrence of the straitened rural conditions that spurred the appearance of Populism in the late 1800s and the Nonpartisan League in the early 1900s. When he arrived to study at Augsburg College in the mid-1930s, Torstenson found like-minded friends there, men who had also moved into the Cities from the countryside. As he remembered much later, "At the college, there were many Norwegian American students that had come from rural areas. We shared a legacy of Norwegian background and on the campus, we organized a Farmer-Labor club. . . . Yes. I don't think there could possibly be any doubt about it. All my friends who came from rural life, Norwegian friends, I think all of them were farmer-laborites in those days."

Torstenson claimed that during the Depression the farm boys at Augsburg had a "pretty strong [farmer labor] club." One of the persons who was "very active," he asserted, was "Carl Chrislock. He was active in it. He was, of course, a farmer's son." The Augsburg students joined the Hennepin County Farmer-Labor Club en masse, "so we were part of the city organization." There, he said, "We did a foolish stunt . . . and took over the club," but at the next meeting the regular members turned out in force and "voted us out."

"The farmer-labor party in the city must have gotten quite a bit of their public leadership from the labor movement," Torstenson averred, but he went on to explain that in his experience many of these activists were young Norwegian American men who moved in from the countryside. Torstenson's sister was the first member of the family who left rural Minnesota for the Twin Cities. "I know when Marie lived here [in Minneapolis]," he recalled, "she came back to visit us and we went back to visit friends that she had made, and they were streetcar conductors. They, obviously, were farmer-laborites. So, I think when they left the rural area for Minneapolis, they had to get jobs. And they became members of unions."

A significant part of the agricultural workforce joined the ranks of city workers during these years. In the Twin Cities they learned that the lines of opposition between management and labor had hardened since 1900, with the rise of union activity, which was met by the formation of the Citizens Alliance (CA) against unions in Minneapolis in 1903 and the St. Paul Association of Commerce in 1911. Business leaders across the Cities had cooperated to control labor protests since 1901, when they formed the Twin City Association of Employers of Machinists to fight a strike in the metal industry of both cities.[12]

By 1930, there could be no doubt about who controlled the workplace in the urban area, especially in Minneapolis, where, as labor historian William Millikan explains, the CA's membership included all the local industries of significant size. In the Mill City, moreover, the organization enjoyed the full support of the police, the National Guard, and the municipal government. The CA also had spies inside local unions and, not least, its own heavily armed paramilitary force. At that point, after crushing failure during strikes and decades of being portrayed as Communist hotbeds of radicalism, most unions in the city were weak, including the "lifeless" General Drivers Local 574.

In June 1933, however, the National Industrial Recovery Act (NIRA) became the basis of labor relations across the nation as part of President Roosevelt's New Deal. It gave employees the right to organize in a union, to ask for its recognition by their employers, and to collectively bargain with employers through their own union representatives. All this was to happen without pressure or coercion from management. Local unions quickly responded to the opportunities the NIRA offered. They rapidly grew in membership and began to ask for recognition for negotiations over wages and working conditions. The CA and St. Paul Association opposed all of this activity and interpreted the new law quite differently.

At the Minneapolis–St. Paul Labor Relations Board, the regional office of the federal government's structure to implement the new law, local business leaders tested the government's understanding of the legal resolution of labor disputes. Clothing workers in Minneapolis struck for recognition of their union in July, and upholsterers at the city's furniture factories followed suit in October. The CA's lawyers successfully argued before the Labor Relations Board against these unions by early January 1934. The board called off the strikes and recognized the CA's interpretation of the new law.

During these months, however, the sleepy Teamsters local, General Drivers 574, awakened into new activity. After fruitless negotiations with management, the Twin City Coal Exchange, and the Regional Labor Board, the truck drivers responsible for delivering coal for heating in much of Minneapolis went out on strike on February 7. Over the next half year that the strike continued, to the CA's surprise, Local 574 grew stronger, gaining many members and winning elections among coal yard employees to be their representative in increasingly difficult negotiations with the coal dealers and the CA. Stiffening opposition to the union's demands led the CA to mount a radio and press campaign labeling the leaders of Local 574 as Communists. Governor Floyd Olson weakened the CA's position in April by proclaiming at a mass meeting that without unions the "status of labor would be pitiful."

Political support inspired many more drivers to join the union, which grew very effective at blocking truck traffic. The forces of law and order mobilized armed support against picketers. The Minneapolis police chief pleaded with the city council for more officers. CA members offered to be citizen deputies and recruited their clerks and salesmen to join them. These forces beat unarmed picketers with clubs and pipes as they picketed. A CA infiltrator set an ambush by sending unarmed male and female picketers to an alley where they were beaten bloody by CA deputies and police. From then on, the picketers carried clubs. The battle lines had formed.

On May 22 the situation exploded in armed conflict that soon left the "injured bodies of deputies, policemen, and strikers . . . littered" on the pavement. Several CA deputies and thirty policemen were hospitalized, and numbers of injured strikers, some with broken bones, got treatment at union headquarters. The strikers had forced the disorganized retreat of the CA army, which fled in panic while the police held their fire. The Battle of Deputies Run was a disastrous defeat for the CA, yet the conflict remained unresolved because the union refused to back away from its demand for recognition and the CA accepted no compromise offered by the governor or federal authorities. Another bloody clash, which left two picketers dead and sixty-seven wounded, took place on July 20, when union protesters ran in terror from police shooting machine guns. Governor Olson and President Roosevelt put strong pressure on the CA's financial backers. Still, only after four more weeks of evasive tactics by the CA could both sides consent to the compromise ordered by the National Labor Relations Board on August

During the 1934 Teamsters strike, Minneapolis police were often used as a standing army against strikers, but sometimes, as here, relations between law enforcement and picketers were friendly. *MNHS*

21. Neither the CA nor Local 574 got all the gains it desired, but each thought its members could build on the results.

"Of course, in 1934, the year of the truck drivers' strike," Joel Torstenson exclaimed, "that was a virtual civil war. I am very interested in that. That is when I became interested in the labor movement. I was watching it and reading about it. Following the news. . . . The labor people had . . . their headquarters. . . . The downtown people, the commercial leaders downtown, they would get their workers to come and join them in the struggle for the business people." Torstenson thought it was a turning point in the history of Minneapolis. "Out of that came Governor Olson's and FDR's involvement," he said. "It transformed the city from an anti-union city to a pro-union city. It was, I think, one of the most significant events in transforming the political scene in Minneapolis."

Stories about the strike traversed family networks in the Norwegian American community for decades afterward. Friends of Torstenson at Augsburg who came from Norwegian settlement areas in the Red River Valley of northwestern Minnesota were involved in union politics and shared their memories of the 1934 truckers' strike. Other urban Norwegian Americans did, too. A Norwegian American neighbor with whom Torstenson became "very good friends" in the 1950s told about being "a laborer up in the woods in northeast Minnesota before he came to Minneapolis. I supposed he came down here . . . Skid Row was the name. That is where he probably got started in Minneapolis." He had been active in the strike.

Jim Pederson recalled how these networks connected farmers and city laborers: His "cousin in Wisconsin was active in the farmers' union and as an official of the county agricultural establishment, he was very active. He had a weekly radio program where he talked farm issues, but he always rolled into a little bit about the interests of the farmers' union. He was a very, very vocal person."

Pederson continued,

> There was another uncle, and, interestingly enough, he came from Norway. He worked at Munsingwear in Minneapolis probably from about 1924 until his retirement in 1964. His name was Martin Strom. He lived in northeast Minneapolis, and he always went to union meetings. He told me some interesting stories about how he had been on the scene in

> the 1934 truck drivers' strike as a supporter. He said he was down there armed with a barrel stave, which, if you have read about it, was kind of a common weapon. At one point, shots were fired into the crowd and they all started running, the supporters did. He said he ran down an alley with the police or the deputized members of the Citizens Alliance right behind him. He must have been rather athletic in those days. He said he ran along and he would grab a garbage can and throw it out behind him and hope that these people would tumble over it. He was at least an enthusiastic supporter to the extent that he was there on the lines with the strikers in support of the 1934 truck drivers' strike, even though he could not have been a Teamster.[13]

The ideological legacy of Depression years migration to the Twin Cities remained vital in some Norwegian American circles long after the 1930s. In a subsequent interview, Carl Chrislock confirmed Joel Torstenson's view that these young men brought a rural Norwegian

Strikers and their supporters come into open conflict with the police. ***MNHS***

American populism with them to their compatriots' community in the Twin Cities. Torstenson became the father of the sociology department at Augsburg, a progressive figure of note in the Cities, and a leading scholar in his field. Chrislock went on to be a prominent historian of American Progressivism and continued his support for what later became the Democratic-Farmer-Labor Party. Pederson, a postwar student of his who became a DFL activist, said jocularly in an interview, "At Augsburg then, you didn't study history, you studied Chrislock." A solid part of the bedrock of the DFL in the Twin Cities was formed during the Depression years.[14]

An Era of Trials for Ethnic Institutions

Many Norwegian American organizations curtailed or dropped building plans and accepted reduced activity levels during the Depression. The history of these years at Trinity Lutheran congregation in Cedar-Riverside presents a representative example of how many of the group's churches in both cities managed their financial difficulties. Trinity put off maintenance and redecoration work. The pastor agreed to two salary reductions. The middle years of the decade, when financial reserves were gone, were the hardest. Bills and salaries went unpaid, and the congregation could not repay debts until 1939. To keep up its outreach, Trinity worked more closely with sisters from the nearby Deaconess Home and Hospital, who took on some visitations to congregants as well as people in the neighborhood. Women's charity groups at Trinity—the Tabitha Society, the Ladies Aid, the Sewing Society, and the Needle Guild—strove to meet growing needs for clothes and food.[15]

Most of all, Trinity Lutheran shared expenses through cooperating with other churches and organizations, not only with the deaconesses but by sending two delegates to the city's Lutheran Welfare Society, where representatives assessed overall needs and pooled resources. When Trinity and other NLCA churches in south-central Minneapolis found they no longer could continue outreach through open tent services separately in these years, they shared the work involved and staffed a summer tent ministry together. When Trinity could no longer run its traditional religion school on Saturdays, it and those other Lutheran congregations convinced Monroe School, the local elementary school, to release fourth through sixth graders for an hour a week for religious instruction.

The Great Depression left the Norwegian Lutheran Memorial Church unable to pay its bills or mortgage in the early 1930s. Membership dropped. Foreclosure on the building loomed. Intense disagreement about whether the language of the Sunday school should be English or Norwegian broke out. In hopes that a new minister could bring more unity in the membership, the Reverend Christian Munson resigned. In late 1933, the Reverend Elias Rasmussen accepted the congregation's call and engaged the church's difficulties with hard work and contagious enthusiasm. After an extensive effort, those who held bonds on the church mortgage agreed to donate them or settle for reduced payment. Most important, the Sons of Norway Grand Lodge lent the congregation the money needed to pay off all bondholders. Finally, in late 1945 Mindekirken paid the Sons of Norway the last installment on the loan. A much-cherished reminder of Norwegian Americans' cultural and religious heritage, the Memorial Church nonetheless labored through more than two decades before it reached firm financial footing. Pastor Rasmussen brought it clerical stability by serving until his retirement in 1958.

Educational institutions also grappled with tightened budgets. In his history of Minnesota, Theodore C. Blegen asserts that Minnesota's educational institutions served the public well during the Depression. Yet they did so at a cost. At Augsburg Seminary and College, the economic crisis led to salary cuts for faculty and drastic reduction of the budget for sports. One person served as athletic director and coach for football and basketball, and in 1935, the college limited football to an intramural activity. To save money, the music program focused on choirs rather than expensive instrument purchases. Its mixed-voice choir managed to gather the funds to tour regional Norwegian American centers. Student enrollment dropped and then rose to a new peak by the mid-1930s, despite academic changes, crowding, and limited maintenance on campus. Low tuition, generous financial aid for high achievers and impoverished applicants, and a location within walking distance of downtown part-time work permitted Augsburg to attract large numbers of undergraduates when other small colleges in the Cities and the region lost students. The college's academic offerings were somewhat

Minneapolis Tidende sendes hvorsomhelst i de Forenede Stater et aar for kun $1.50.

Minneapolis Tidende

Minneapolis-Ugeavis

Nr. 12. 49de aargang. Minneapolis, Minn., torsdag den 21de mars 1935. Pris 5 cents.

Hitler byr magterne aapen trods

Likesom de andre har overtraadt Versailles-traktatens militærbestemmelser vil Tyskland nu ogsaa gjøre det. Almindelig vernepligt. En tysk hær paa 500,000.

Hele Europa er pludselig blit opskræmt og frygter for krig som følge av en bestemt erklæring fra riksfører Adolf Hitler om at Versailles-traktaten forkastes og at Tyskland vil indføre almindelig vernepligt. Tyskland vil isaafald straks ha en hær paa 500,000 mand. Sir Eric Phipps, den britiske ambassadør i Berlin, blev kaldt til utenriksdepartementet og av Hitler personlig underrettet om at en tysk arme paa 500,0000 mand straks vil bli oprettet.

I sin proklamation erklærer Hitler ikke officielt og formelt at Versaillestraktatens militærbestemmelser skal ignoreres; men betydningen er den samme. Han indleder proklamationen med en henvisning til at da det tyske folk i november 1918, i tillid til president Wilsons 14 punkter, nedla sine vaaben efter en 4½ aars krig, som de aldrig hadde ønsket, trodde de at de tjente en stor tanke. Lidende under følgerne av denne vanvittige strid klamret millioner tyske folk sig til den tanke at der nu skulde bli en ny ordning blandt nationene, at det skulde bli forbi med de hemmelige diplomatiske forhandlinger og at de frygtelige krigsredskaper skulde bli ødelagt. Ingensteds vandt tanken om et Nationernes Forbund varmere tilslutning end i Tyskland. Den tyske regjering og det tyske folk trodde fuldt og fast at opfyldelsen av Versailles-traktatens avrustningsbestemmelser vilde indlede en almindelig international avrustning. Tyskland, sier Hitler, opfyldte de betingelser som blev paatvunget det. En international kontrolkommission paasaa at den tyske avrustning fandt sted. Tyskland hadde da ret til at vente at ogsa de andre nationer vilde opfylde betingelsene. Men det blev hos dem ingen almindelig nedrustning i forhold til den tyske. Tvertimot. De andre oprustet. Det var derfor klart at Tyskland maatte forlange at de nationer som hadde seiret i verdenskrigen la for dagen sin hensigt og vilje til at nedruste i overensstemmelse med Versailles-traktaten. Isteden blev der bare lagt an paa at skaffe mere ødelæggende og dræpende krigsvaaben. Hitler henviste blandt andet til at Moskva nylig meldte at Rusland hadde næsten 1,000,000 mand under vaaben, og at Frankrike har øket vernepligten for sine borgere fra et til to aar.

"Der er et skrik paa krig idag, som om der aldrig hadde været nogen verdenskrig eller en Versailes-traktat," sa Hitler.

Gang paa gang, sa kansleren, har Tyskland vist sig beredt til at samarbeide om nedrustningsplaner; men disse planer er altid blit forkastet av de andre.

"Tysklands hensigt med at væbne sig," heter det i proklamationen, "er at bevare freden for sig selv og det øvrige Europa."

Hitler minder om at Stanley Baldwin nylig bemerket at "den nation som ikke sørger for sit eget forsvar aldrig vil bli en mægtig nation."

De nye militærforanstaltninger blev lørdag godkjendt som lov av det tyske kabinet. Loven gjælder almindelig vernepligt og inddeler den tyske fredsarme i 12 armekorps og 36 divisioner. General Werner von Blomberg, forsvarsministeren, blev bemyndiget til at træffe de nødvendi-

(Fortsættes paa 2den side.)

Til Minneapolis Tidendes abonnenter.

Med dette nummer tar Minneapolis Tidende avsked med sine abonnenter. Bladet er blit slaat sammen med det mest utbredte norske blad i Amerika, den velredigerte Decorah-Posten og Ved Arnen, Decorah, Iowa, som altsaa med næste uke vil bli sendt til alle Tidendes abonnenter. Decorah-Posten og Ved Arnen utkommer to ganger om uken, hvilket utentvil særlig vil glæde dem som fra tid til anden har henstillet til Tidende at utkomme oftere end en gang om uken.

Til sine mange trofaste venner frembærer Minneapolis Tidende hermed en hjertelig tak. Abonnentene er venligst anmodet om at overføre sin velvilje og støtte til Decorah-Posten og Ved Arnen.

Med venlig hilsen til alle læsere av Minneapolis Tidende.

T. Guldbrandsen Publishing Co.

McCarrans amendement forkastet

Senatet gir med 83 mot 2 stemmer presidenten myndighet til at bestemme lønningene for nødsarbeide. Senatet forlanger forsorgsadministration et aar til.

Washington, 19de mars. Fredag kom senatet endelig til en løsning av konflikten om "herskende lønninger" for nødsarbeide. McCarrans amendement, som for næsten en maaned siden med 44 mot 43 stemmer blev vedtat av senatet, som kort efter besluttet at opta det til fornyet behandling, blev nu forkastet med 50 mot 38 stemmer. Da McCarran-amendementets skjæbne saaledes var beseglet vedtok senatet med 83 mot bare 2 stemmer administrationens kompromis, som gaar ut paa at presidenten faar myndighet til at bestemme lønninger som ikke vil sænke det nuværende lønsnivaa, men utsatte med at fatte nogen bestemmelse om at fortsætte med de offentlige arbeider to aar til. Denne forandring i presidentens planer blev vedtat som et amendement til billen om $4,880,000,000 til offentlige arbeider og forsorg og vakte paa visse hold adskillig forandring, eftersom presidenten tidligere sa at det var meningen at avskaffe nødhjælpen fortest mulig under den nye ordning. Forandringen har maaske sin aarsak i at det kan komme til at vare en god stund før det blir noget av samfundstrygd i forskjellige former.

Senatets justitskomite godkjendte mandag Blacks forslag

Anklagen mot brødrene Insull strøket.

Staten Illinois har opgit sine forsøk paa at faa nogen av familien Insull straffet for formentlig svindel i forbindelse med driften og salget av aktier i de nytteverk som tilhørte familien. Hverken Samuel Insull eller hans bror Martin menes at kunne bli holdt kriminelt ansvarlig for det sammenbrud som kostet folk der anbragte penger i deres foretagender utallige millioner. Dommer Cornelius J. Harrington i Chicago avviste mandag anklagene mot Insull'ene.

Samuel Insull, som nu er 75 aar, sies at være beredt til at gaa ind i forretningslivet igjen i raadgivende egenskap hos et eller andet industrifirma. Martin Insull, der er 10 aar yngre, skal ha akceptert et forretningstilbud fra Canada, hvortil han som utlænding maa vende tilbake under betingelsene for utleveringen.

Assisterende statsadvokat John O'Hara erklærte, idet han foreslog sakene avvist, at staten hadde gjort sit bedste for at faa brødrene Insull dømt for underslag, og at han betragtet det som umulig at opnaa domfældelse i de gjenstaaende saker.

Mangel paa surstof tvang Post ned fra stratosfæren.

Med forsyningen av surstof paa det nærmeste opbrukt steg Wiley Post ned fra stratosfæren 100 mil østenfor Cleveland, O., fredag eftermiddag. Dermed avsluttedes hans andet forsøk paa at flyve over kontinentet fra Los Angeles til New York gjennem det øvre luftlag Han steg op fra Los Angeles kl. 8 om morgenen. Post satte en ny uofficiel rekord for

virksomheten. Det viste sig at mænd hadde den største møie med at forsørge flere hustruer og mange barn. Det blev antydet at flergifte — uten kirkens sanktion — fandt sted i avsides strøk av staten. Ingen paastod at de som saaledes forbrøt sig var mormoner.

Landsvid jagt paa organiserte forbryderbander.

En hel hær av 12,000 regjeringsagenter begyndte fredag en utryddelseskrig mot organiserte forbryderbander, ifølge ordre fra finansminister Henry Morgenthau. Mandag meldtes 2,389 personer at være arrestert, og det ventedes at mindst 3,000 vilde være bak laas og lukke inden offensiven avsluttedes. I mindst 100 byer hadde regjeringsagentene foretat sine razziaer. Jagten gjælder væsentlig falskmyntnere, peddlere av narkotika, smuglere og personer der vrir sig undav at betale skat paa rusdrikke. Flyvere og kystvagten tar del i jagten. Eiendom for flere millioner dollars blev konfiskert, og flere hundrede tusen dollars i bøder blev betalt.

Næsten 2 milliarder i frihetsobligationer indkaldes.

De Forenede Staters skatkammer har indkaldt til indløsning den 15de juni hele emissionen av utestaaende First Liberty loan bonds lydende ialt paa $1,933,000,000. Denne obligationsemission, som forfalder 1932—1947, bestaar av tre serier: $1,392,226,250 til 3½ procent rente, $5,002,450 konverterte 4 procent obligationer og $535,981,250 konverterte 4 procent obligationer. Det er regjeringens hensigt at faa indløst alle sine obligationer der har guldklausulen, og denne

Et britisk flaatebudget paa $268,000,000.

Det britiske underhus vedtok fredag med 158 mot 48 stemmer flaatebudgettet for 1935 beløpende sig til 60,050,000 pund (omkring $268,000,000). Det er 3,500,000 pund mere end flaatebudgettet ifjor. Avstemningen fandt sted efter at Sir Bolton Eyres-Mousell, første admiralitetslord, hadde forsikret at Storbritannien fremdeles er villig til at forhandle om at avskaffe undervandsbaater og gjøre krigsskibene mindre. Han sa at man ikke maatte ta for tragisk Japans opsigelse av Washington-flaatetraktaten.

Richberg foreslaar elimination av 537 coder.

En plan om at eliminere 537 av NRA's mindre coder ved at slaa dem sammen under én tøielig code for de "smaa industrier" blev forrige onsdag forelagt for senatets finanskomite paa administrationens vegne av Donald R. Richberg. Skjønt Richberg ikke personlig anbefalte planen, forela han den for komiteen som et middel til at forenkle NRA administrationen, saa dens arbeide kan samles om de store industrier, om kongressen skulde ønske det. Hvis planen blir gjennemført vil coderne bli reducert fra over 700 til 181.

Gjenreisningsloven igjen erklært konstitutionsstridig.

I Newark, N. J., avgav føderaldommer Guy L. Fake forrige onsdag en kjendelse som gik ut paa at gjenreisningsloven er konstitutionsstridig naar det gjælder regulering av indenstatlig forretning. Dommeren efterkom Ac-

The closing of *Minneapolis Tidende*, the Twin Cities' largest Norwegian-language newspaper, in 1935 made the toll of the Depression painfully evident for the Norwegian American community. *Courtesy MNHS collections* curtailed as foreign language and social studies changed from majors to minors. In mathematics, the college strengthened standards, but only via an arrangement through which the University of Minnesota took over teaching some courses. Augsburg kept its strong faculty, however, as many academics took advantage of reduced teaching duties to continue their graduate studies. Most important for Augsburg's future as an urban college, the Depression brought the end of plans for moving to a suburban campus in Richfield, south of the city.[16]

By far the largest Norwegian-language newspaper in the Twin Cities, *Minneapolis Tidende* did not survive the economic trials of the Depression. In 1932, it suspended publication of its daily edition. The continuing depression brought additional declines in circulation. The death of the paper's founder-publisher, Thorvald Guldbrandsen, and the inability of its business manager to solve its financial crisis brought the situation to a head: *Minneapolis Tidende*, one of the "big three" in the Norwegian American press at the time, stopped publication with its March 21, 1935, issue. As Odd S. Lovoll writes, the announcement evoked in readers "deep sadness in witnessing the departure of a cherished institution."[17]

Maintaining Norwegian Language and Culture as Academic Subjects

Throughout these two decades, concerted efforts continued to make instruction in Norwegian language and culture available to the American-born youth in Minneapolis–St. Paul. As Theodore C. Blegen emphasized in his history of Minnesota, in the 1930s "schools, public and private, and the colleges and university functioned across the decade with astonishing vitality, notwithstanding financial troubles." Augsburg and St. Olaf Colleges offered extensive courses of study in both Norwegian and Swedish that continued to attract full classrooms. The University of Minnesota's adult classes in Norwegian at its Center for Continuation Study remained popular, drawing on the exceptionally large population of people of Norwegian extraction in the Twin Cities and vicinity who wanted beginning or refresher classes in the language. The University's Scandinavian Studies Department flourished in the late 1920s, supported by strong student interest and the inspired leadership of Gisle Bothne, who served as chair of the university program until 1929. Enrollment in Norwegian courses and Scandinavian studies decreased sharply after his retirement.[18]

In the late 1930s, the university regents responded to complaints about the program's decline from community leaders by putting two professors of history, the Swedish American G. M. Stephenson and his Norwegian American colleague Theodore C. Blegen, as well as the Norwegian American Martin B. Ruud, professor of English, in charge of the Scandinavian Studies Department. In addition, the university hired another professor and secured a series of visiting professors from universities in Scandinavia to maintain the revived program. During World War II, the university offered a new program in spoken Norwegian for members of the US Army, designed with a textbook by Einar Haugen for people with the wide diversity of cultural backgrounds whom the army might send to occupied Norway.

The campaign to include Norwegian and Swedish language and cultural electives in Minneapolis's public high schools achieved success in 1910 when a citizens' committee chaired by Bothne persuaded the city's board of education, which included Trinity Church's pastor, M. Falk Gjertsen, to institute Scandinavian studies as a part of the secondary school curriculum. By the second half of the 1920s, South, East, Central, North, and Roosevelt High Schools offered classes in Norwegian and Swedish language as well as clubs and foreign-language school newspapers dealing with those two Scandinavian cultures. At the peak of nativism in the war years and early 1920s, anti-immigrant activists agitated unsuccessfully for the elimination of these programs, which continued at several local high schools until well after World War II.[19]

With the support of municipal resources for secondary education and devoted teachers, the Norwegian American ethnic group mounted a campaign to pass on its heritage to English-speaking generations. Perhaps the most inspiring mentor, Maren Michelet, taught Norwegian language and culture at South High as well as at the university, published an often-reprinted textbook that laid foundations for her colleagues across the urban area, and arranged traditions of community leaders as guest speakers and public speaking and essay competitions in Norwegian for students. The ethnic community responded by including high school students in the programs for the Henrik Ibsen,

Roald Amundsen, and Leif Erikson festivals. Community leaders and teachers created school programs aimed at transmitting a knowledge of and respect for the Norwegian heritage to all the group's youth—both those born in the Twin Cities and the school-age Norwegian Americans who migrated into the urban area during the 1930s.[20]

Mobilization: The Norwegian National League and the Leif Erikson Movement in the 1930s

The movement for public acknowledgment of Leif Erikson's early voyage to North America mobilized important elements of the ethnic elites in the 1930s. The Norwegian National League led the campaign to convince the state legislature to enact an official Leif Erikson Day and succeeded when Governor Floyd Olson signed the law in 1931. Around the same time, the Nordkap Sons of Norway lodge in St. Paul began promoting the project of putting a statue of Erikson on the state capitol grounds, and leaders in the Norwegian American communities of the Twin Cities founded the Leif Erikson Monument Association. In Minneapolis, the national league again arranged its annual Erikson festival—this time with the governors of Wisconsin and Minnesota, the first state executives to establish Leif Erikson Day, as principal speakers. Local leaders took part in the efforts of the Leif Erikson Memorial Association of America across the nation in these years. In 1935, President Franklin Roosevelt crowned their efforts with success when he joined Congress in making October 9 the official National Day of Recognition for the Viking explorer. In jubilation, the monument association and the league marked the victory with a combined celebration, including a parade and a mass meeting of an estimated five thousand listeners to an address by Wilhelm Morgenstierne, Norwegian minister to the United States. The league and other local ethnic organizations arranged banquets and excursions in Erikson's honor annually for the rest of the 1930s and 1940s.[21]

In retrospect, the years from 1925 to 1931 might seem a period of adjustment to the immigration restriction acts of the 1920s and a prelude to the Depression. The public acknowledgment and approval showered on Norwegian Americans during the 1925 centennial conflicted sharply with the congressional votes and presidential signatures that reduced

Ingebretsen's Model Market on Minneapolis's Lake Street in the 1930s. *Courtesy of the author*

the stream of newcomers from Norway to a trickle by decade's end. The prestige of Norwegian America and its legacies to the group's adopted homeland had not swayed the weight of anti-immigration opinion. The ethnic group adjusted to the end of community renewal through immigration. As noted previously, its counterattack shifted the community focus to passing on cultural heritage to the American-born generations through a series of anniversaries and prestigious visits. These events heightened the status of the Norwegian homeland in the Twin Cities and refreshed public memory about the legacy of one of their largest local population groups.

From 1925 to 1945, the ethnic community experienced in some senses an unexpectedly energetic level of mobilization. In late 1927, the rebirth of *Det Norske Nasjonalforbund* (the Norwegian National League) in Minneapolis, first founded in 1920, did much to bring about a renaissance of community strength. The organization's renewal occurred through the efforts of the same leaders who had carried the most responsibility at its first founding and later at the 1925 centennial. The league marshaled resources and united diverse elements in the community for public displays of devotion to Norwegian American heritage. The movement to restart the organization developed from a meeting of Norwegian American leaders in the Hennepin County commissioners' office in April 1927. Reflecting on the manifold evidence of the city's large number of people with a Norwegian background and the host of Norwegian American voluntary organizations, the group resolved that it was time for Minneapolis to have a permanent overall structure where all member organizations would have representatives. Chicago, New York, and San Francisco already had this kind of associational congress. The preeminent site of the 1914 and 1925 centennial celebrations could surely also benefit from more coherent and democratic organization considering the likelihood that it should be a location of future events involving all of Norwegian America.

A committee from the group invited delegates from the city's Norwegian American organizations to a mass meeting in early May. The representatives (around a hundred people) chose Professors Gisle Bothne and Lars Lillehei to lead the assembly, and under their guidance, a unanimous list of supporters for the establishment of such a league took the floor. No one opposed the plan. The assembly elected temporary officers—Bothne as president, Lillehei as secretary, and a full slate of lesser officers and committees—until a constitutional meeting confirmed them in late June. Names among the initial list of officers, including Bothne, Lillehei, and Laura Bratager, showed the overlap between the 1925 centennial's and the national league's leadership.

The founding organizations included representatives from two Daughters of Norway and two Sons of Norway lodges, four men's choirs, three IOGT temperance lodges, seven bygdelag or local district associations, a University of Minnesota literary club, *Norrøna Leikkarring* (a folk dance society), the Norse Sports Club, Zion Mandsforening (a Lutheran men's society), and the Norse *veiledningsbureau* (an employment bureau). The bureau, folk dance society, and men's group represented recent developments in the constellation of associations, while the large number of men's choruses showed the staying power of that tradition. The continued vitality of the lag, the sons and daughters mutual benefit societies, the temperance cause, and literary and sports clubs in the city is evident. The program showed the active participation of a wide range of the league's constituent organizations.[22]

The league's activities for 1927 centered on reviving the event it staged in 1920, the Leif Erikson festival. It was already somewhat of a tradition in Minneapolis—with the first celebration in 1906, the next in 1918 under the auspices of local Sons of Norway lodges, the third sponsored by the league in 1920, and the fourth in 1923. This time the league gave itself just three months to complete the planning. Since no less a public figure than President Calvin Coolidge had endorsed Erikson as the original discoverer of the continent at the festivities in the Twin Cities in 1925, continuing the local celebration of Erikson's achievement may have seemed highly appropriate, especially considering recent events. The organizing committee chose September 26 as the date of the festival—one year and a day from the first official Leif Erikson Day in Norway, September 25, 1926. The committee invited Captain Gerhard Folgerø to come in his ship, a replica of a Viking vessel he built and named the *Leif Erikson*. Between April 1926 and June 1927, he sailed the ship from Nordland County in Norway to Duluth. Following the example of other Norwegian American urban communities, the league in addition strove to have a park, lake, or main traffic artery in Minneapolis named for Erikson. Both ambitious efforts failed, although Captain Folgerø himself came, participated in the festival, and showed a film and lectured about his adventures "In Leif Erikson's Wake" at Norway Hall in late October 1927.

At the Erikson festival in September, Rasmus B. Anderson, long the most prominent proponent of Erikson's place in history and Viking Norway's gift of democracy to the United States, served as the main speaker. The city's mayor, as well as representatives of each of the Scandinavian nationality groups, offered welcoming words. Folgerø greeted the public on behalf of Norway and the Norwegian king. Then Professor Bothne welcomed the audience to the memorial festival in honor of the "first white man to set foot on American land." A musical program inspired by the Vikings' heroic feats and performed by massed choirs followed. Under the direction of Norwegian language retention advocate Pauline Farseth, high school students in the city's Norwegian language and culture electives staged a tableau of Erikson's landing as witnessed by Native Americans and Valkyrie, with stirring background singing. Folk music groups danced and sang. The climax of the evening came with Folgerø's narrative about experiences on his trip while four members of the Daughters of Norway dressed as Viking goddesses stood guard. The details of the evening's program preserved in the league's annual report offer a revealing picture of the resurgent Norwegian American ethnicity in Minneapolis in the later 1920s.

Despite economic privations and faced with a public mood that continued to support severely restrictive immigration laws, Norwegian Americans in Minneapolis–St. Paul publicly celebrated the versions of history that most enhanced their rightful status as first-class Americans—precisely because of their Norwegian background. Their Viking ancestor Leif Erikson arrived in America before Christopher Columbus did and brought with him his people's tradition of democracy. As Daron Olson, historian of the group's evolving ethnic identity, has written, "The tangible voyage of the *Leif Erikson* . . . provided powerful reinforcement for the ideological constructs centered on the Viking explorer, whose legacy greatly enhanced the self-image of Norwegian Americans as well as the national identity of Norway."[23]

In the Twin Cities, at once the generally acknowledged capital of the ethnic group and the preeminent urban magnet of the Upper Midwest, group leaders acted with particular urgency to achieve this enhancement. In 1928, in a gesture that highlighted the ethnic group's elevated status in the homeland as well as in the United States, Norway shifted its Leif Erikson Day to October 9. The United States marked that date as both the day modern Norwegian immigration began with the arrival of *Restaurationen* in New York and the day to recognize the Viking adventurer. The Cities' Norwegian American community had reason to be proud of the international agreement over which day to set off for honoring Leif Erikson.

In 1928, the most important league-sponsored event consisted of a three-day observation of the birth of Henrik Ibsen in March. The planners designed the celebration in an appropriate fashion for the preponderance of later-generation English speakers in the ethnic group and the playwright's status as a world-renowned dramatist. The committee printed the programs in English as well as Norwegian and scheduled separate speeches in each language. It selected public rather than ethnic arenas for the entire festival—the downtown Lyceum Theater for the opening ceremonies and the following evening's performance of Ibsen's first drama of social criticism, *The Pillars of Society*. The third night's banquet took place at the Nicollet Hotel in the city center. At the high point of the opening cultural evening, the singers who performed music composed for Ibsen's plays gathered around his bust, each bearing a flag indicating a nation in which his translated work existed. The closing of the first evening consisted of what since the war years had become the usual explicit patriotism of singing both the Norwegian and the American national anthems.[24]

The league also designed the affair to appeal to the region and the Twin Cities' vicinity. Through its broad range of contacts and announcements in *Minneapolis Tidende*, the organizers promoted an open contest to write a lyric poem in honor of the Ibsen centennial. Among the thirty-eight poems submitted, a panel of judges awarded the prize to the one written by P. O. Bugge, a pharmacist in North Dakota. The poet came to the opening, where he heard his work performed as a song by the festival choir and band. And, although located about 40 miles from the Twin Cities, St. Olaf College increasingly became part of their larger vicinity in these years, often offering academic and cultural contributions in the urban centers. During the Ibsen centennial, the college's band and orchestra provided music. Otherwise, the league made effective use of the choirs and actors in its own ranks. According to its annual report for 1928, the "amateur thespians performed mostly, and at times, thoroughly well." Consul General Engelbrecht H. Hobe, then stationed in St. Paul, commented to the league that in his forty-five years in the state capital he had never experienced a Norwegian festivity that surpassed the Ibsen centennial.[25]

The polar explorer Roald Amundsen came to Minneapolis and lectured at West High School in 1927. He died in the Arctic only a little over a year later, in mid-June 1928, while attempting to find survivors of another explorer's expedition. The league invited as wide a range of people as possible, whether members or not, to take part in planning the Amundsen memorial to give it appeal beyond the bounds of the Norwegian-speaking part of the ethnic group. For the same reason, the planners asked the mayor, members of the city council, the governor, and the Norwegian consul general to participate as honored guests. To further increase attraction to the occasion, the league offered the program free to the public and held it in Central Lutheran's new auditorium.

These efforts met success. The city council agreed to fly flags outside public buildings at half-staff to honor the world-renowned explorer. Some three thousand people filled the auditorium. The governor sent a greeting, which the state treasurer read. The mayor came, gave a short speech, and presented a wreath to Roald Amundsen's memory. Slides illustrated events in the explorer's expeditions. The assembly rose to its feet and sang the Norwegian national anthem. Speeches in English and Norwegian praised his courageous adventures. Choirs sang secular and sacred music in both languages. Consul General Hobe's closing address brought greetings and thanks from the Norwegian monarch and people.

The league thus drew public attention to three of Norway's most iconic figures and the qualities they embodied during the year. Performing Ibsen's play and demonstrating his place in world literature highlighted the progressive nature of the society that produced a dramatist of such social-critical power. Celebrating the courage and daring of Viking and modern Norwegian explorers enhanced the homeland's reputation as a culture that produced such heroes and strengthened the recognition that Norwegian Americans greatly admired brave fastness of character. The league had effectively summoned its resources to share what it considered the best of its heritage with American publics, and in the process identified with that set of values. The only disappointment the organization faced at year's end was the fact that the Ibsen jubilee, the Leif Erikson festival, and the second performance of *The Pillars of Society* all lost money. Only the Amundsen memorial, which donors funded, broke even. As the annual report noted, the "exception" to the league's satisfaction with its work was the low attendance of Norwegians in the capital of Norwegian America.[26]

Perhaps a partial explanation for the disappointing attraction of these celebrations was that later generation ethnics, people of the third or fourth generation, by the late 1920s composed a large segment of the community that identified as Americans involved with their local lives as Twin Citians and nationally as Americans. For them, events such as the jubilee of Norway's greatest playwright and celebrations to honor its greatest past and present explorers may have seemed appropriately mounted and most appreciated by a smaller core of ethnic activists.

At the time, stationed on the margins of the larger Twin Cities area, Ole Edvart Rølvaag, the most admired of Norwegian American authors, meditated and lectured at St. Olaf College on the dilemma of the younger generation's increasing assimilation and the pressing need to preserve their ancestral legacy. In *Concerning Our Heritage* (1922), he published his message to Norwegian American youth, adamantly disagreeing with the many "Pauls and Pers" who claimed that the assimilation of the young was inevitable. Instead, he asserted, the youth should emulate the mythic Ash Lad figure (*Espen askeladden*) of Norwegian folktales and successfully attempt the impossible. At the time of his writing, Rølvaag said that emulation meant striving to maintain their homeland heritage, the *fedrearven*, in America. He wrote: "'Norwegian heritage in America? What kind of nonsense is that?'—Many a Per and Paul among us has asked this question and reasoned this way. And yet an organization promoting the Norwegian heritage in America has come into being. Last summer at its annual meeting there were about 2,500 interested people in attendance. Admittedly, this organization has not yet won the princess and half the kingdom, but who knows? Espen might reach his goal." Rølvaag went on to note, in an allusion to the efforts at the college and in the Twin Cities to maintain fluency in Norwegian among the young, that there was unprecedentedly wide interest in the Norwegian declamation contests held the previous winter.[27]

Norwegian Ethnicity Rebounds Despite National Restriction and the Great Depression

The resurgence of ethnic pride that the Norwegian National League's activities represented continued unabated, undiminished by insufficient support from the local ethnic group, the 100 percent Americanism of the war years, and the anti-foreign feeling that supported the increasing restrictions on immigration through the 1920s. In 1929 the league began an annual summer picnic for the Cities' Norwegians that it called St. Hans Fest and that continued for decades after as Norway Day in various Minneapolis parks. It organized *Den norske Storfest* (the Great Norwegian Festival) in Minneapolis in June 1930 in cooperation with the Common Council of the Bygdelag, the Sons and the Daughters of Norway, the Norwegian Singers Association of America, the NLCA, and the Lutheran Free Church. Local historian Carl G. O. Hansen termed the arrangement the "Norwegian Festal Week." As he viewed it, the celebrations encompassed the commemoration of the nine-hundredth anniversary of the Christianizing of Norway by Olaf Haraldsson, the Viking king who after his death became St. Olav. Minnesota's governor, Theodore Christianson, gave the keynote address at the opening, which also included speeches by Dr. T. O. Burntvedt, president of the Norwegian Free Church, Hansen, and the presidents of the major sponsoring organizations. On Sunday, church services led by the city's highest-ranking Lutheran clerics preceded a massive parade of marching Sons of Norway and a historical pageant. The celebration brought an estimated forty thousand people to the city, including participants in the parades, lag meetings, pageants and tableaux, concerts, entertainments, and, Hansen stresses, three whole days devoted to the singers' sangerfest.[28]

St. Olav's ninth centennial witnessed a second great homecoming of Norwegian Americans. Arrangers of the religious ceremonies honoring St. Olav and the uniting of a Christian Norwegian people expected so many returning compatriots from abroad at the end of July that they erected a pavilion next to Trondheim's Nidaros Cathedral to receive them. Thousands of emigrated compatriots journeyed to Trondheim, and many more in the Twin Cities and across Norwegian America listened to the ceremonies through a simultaneous radio broadcast from the Nidaros Cathedral. Concerted use of the era's most advanced communication technology made it possible for many in the ethnic group to hear Bishop Johan A. Aasgaard of the NLCA, who had traveled from Minneapolis, speak as he delivered Norwegian Americans' gift of a silver crucifix mounted on a black marble altar to the homeland's national shrine. The event represented another climax in the strengthening of

During the Depression, leading Norwegian organizations mobilized their human resources in a show of strength for *Den norsk Storfest* (the Great Norwegian Festival), which lasted for four days. *NAHA*

the bonds between emigrated and homeland Norwegians in a Greater Norway during the twenty-five years between Norway's full independence in 1905 and the celebration of St. Olav in 1930.

In July, simultaneous transnational celebrations across the Atlantic occurred again when the league arranged two days of festivities to mark the festival of St. Olaf at the city's Norwegian Memorial Church. Augsburg Seminary professor Rasmus Malmin served at the altar and gave the blessing, during which he commented on the spiritual union between Norwegian America and the homeland. The Norwegian vice consul, Harry Eberhardt, delivered greetings from the Norwegian government and the cathedral in Trondheim, and a prominent member of the league read aloud its telegram to the celebrants in Trondheim. The combined Norwegian men's choirs of Minneapolis performed. They and the congregation sang American and Norwegian patriotic anthems. At the same time, homeland Norwegians celebrated *Olsokdagene* (St. Olav's Days) in the Trondheim cathedral. Earlier that year, leading members of the league joined with other activists in the ethnic group to establish a Twin Cities chapter of the Norsemen's Federation, which also expanded the local ethnic group's participation in the federation's transnational efforts for a Greater Norway.[29]

During the remainder of the 1930s, despite the economic crisis of the Great Depression, vibrant Norwegian American activity continued in the Twin Cities. In 1932 the Norwegian National League, the University

of Minnesota, St. Olaf College, and several of the group's literary, dramatic, and fraternal societies sponsored events to honor the hundredth anniversary of Bjørnstjerne Bjørnson's birth. No longer viewed as a foreigner with liberal social ideas who sparked radical criticism from the immigrant group's clergy, by the 1930s Bjørnson had gained the international reputation of an early progressive and a literary master.

At the grand opening in Minneapolis's Northrop Auditorium, Governor Floyd Bjørnstjerne Olson, university president L. D. Coffman, and the former league president Professor Gisle Bothne addressed a large audience. The university orchestra and the Nordraak Twin Cities Male Singers' Association performed excerpts from Edvard Grieg's incidental music to Bjørnson's epic play *Sigurd Jorsalfar*, about the Viking king and crusade traveler to Jerusalem. Governor Olson praised Bjørnson's verse as having the strength and democratic foundations of Walt Whitman's work. In his address in Norwegian, Professor Bothne in similar fashion admired Bjørnson's services in improving the status and freedom of the common people of Norway. The community remembered the poet's career and views through recitals, readings, translations, and musical performances of his songs and poetry. Young people staged two of his plays—one through the efforts of the local junior chapter of the American-Scandinavian Foundation, and another as part of the program of the Norwegian Department at St. Olaf College.

Norway Day 1933 and later in the decade continued to gather thousands of Norwegian American picnickers. The Norwegian men's choruses in the Twin Cities remained active. In 1933, they sent a singing delegation to meet the home country's naval training vessel *Sørlandet* (the South Land) at the Chicago World's Fair, and later in the 1930s, they visited "brother" singers at other places in Norwegian America. A stream of notable visitors from Norway also buoyed ethnic activity among the Cities' Norwegian Americans during economic hard times. In the fall of 1930, Captain Gerhard Folgerø returned, sailing up the Mississippi in the *Roald Amundsen,* another Viking replica vessel, to St. Paul, where the local Sons and Daughters of Norway lodges arranged a reception during which Governor Christianson and Consul General Hobe addressed the gathering. Then Folgerø sailed on past Fort Snelling to a rousing salute fired from its ramparts and an airplane escort to Riverside Park in Minneapolis, where a men's chorus greeted him and public officials, a cleric, the league president, and Folgerø made public remarks. Festivities continued as thousands viewed the docked ship during the fall and winter. Two years later, another famous modern voyager-adventurer, Magnus Andersen, who sailed a Viking craft to the Chicago World's Fair, visited the Cities and captivated local Norwegian Americans with his maritime anecdotes, regaling them with the ideals of their seafaring heritage.[30]

Between 1933 and 1936, the Norsemen's Federation worked with various partners to send homeland Norwegians to Minneapolis–St. Paul on a tour of the United States. The visitors included a folk high school principal; University of Oslo professors, among them immigration historian Ingrid Semmingsen; twenty-six "tourists" from the Oslo area elite; journalists; and an Oslo Boy Scout troop. The federation's primary mission was to strengthen relations between homeland Norwegians and the country's international diaspora, the largest part of which was in the United States and centered on the Twin Cities and the surrounding region. The intention of "the Joint Journey to America 1935" (*Fellesreisen til Amerika 1935*), for example, consisted of bringing Norwegians for a three-weeks' vacation tour in the United States. The federation cooperated with Oslo's main newspaper, *Aftenposten,* which publicized the tour, and the Norwegian America Line, which arranged the voyage on the SS *Stavangerfjord.* After visiting New York, Niagara Falls, Detroit, and Chicago, the Norwegians spent a weekend in the Twin Cities.

On the visitors' arrival, the federation's local convoy of fifteen chaperoned automobiles drove them to their lodgings in the homes of local

Norwegian Americans. The next day the convoy gave the visitors a guided tour of the sights, brought them to lunch at the Norwegian consul's residence in St. Paul, and then ferried them to Nokomis Lake Park in Minneapolis. There the Norwegian National League had arranged an outdoor program with a male choir concert and speeches by Governor Floyd B. Olson, Viking ship captain Magnus Andersen, and Oslo city council member Alf Bjercke. In the evening, the local chapter of the federation hosted a banquet at which Norwegian American cultural leaders talked about their activities. On the way back to Norway, the overseas visitors toured Washington, DC; Atlantic City; and New York.[31]

The First Royal Visit, an Unparalleled Boost to Ethnic Pride

The most significant and precedent-setting visit came in June 1939 when Crown Prince Olav and Crown Princess Märthe of Norway arrived in the Twin Cities for an extended three-day visit after touring other centers of Norwegian America. The royal visit represented a culmination of the growing acknowledgment of Norwegian America by official Norway. Preparations began a half year before the royal couple's arrival. Consul General Hobe and staff took charge of the initial planning meeting, to which they invited all recognized Norwegian American organizations. Hobe made editor Carl G. O. Hansen his recording secretary and appointed an executive committee under the leadership of the Norsemen's Federation with Hansen and prominent figures from the consulate, the Norwegian America Line, Minnesota banking, and the NLCA. The committee represented the business, educational, social, and religious elites of the ethnic group and conferred with the consulate and Norwegian legation in Washington about every important decision. A separate committee from among the wives in these groups designed a schedule of activities for the Crown Princess.

The working classes, their organizations, and political groups outside the mainstream found no place in the planning for nor presence at the royal visit. As historian April Schultz wrote about the portrait crafted for important visitors at the centennial celebrations in 1925, "organizers made concrete choices about what and whom to include," to present a narrative of a Norwegian American-ness that suited their interests on the occasion. Those interests did not include the unions that had mounted lengthy strikes earlier in the decade. In the context of the late 1930s, the purpose was to show that Norway could count on the United States and a united Norwegian American community in the Twin Cities.[32]

During their stay, the royal couple resided with their entourage and Minister Wilhelm Morgenstierne at Dr. Egil and Rachel Boeckmann's mansion on Summit Avenue in St. Paul. Additional personnel from the government and palace in Norway stayed at a nearby hotel. After the royals' arrival early on Saturday evening by train, the executive committee met the prince and princess and their entourage at a reception in the Boeckmanns' recreation room, where the royal couple then gave a press conference. Americanized, the executive committee of Norwegian Americans did not expect the two royals to be approachable and talk naturally to commoners, as they did at the opening reception. Their first encounter with the royal couple whetted local ethnic leaders' appetite for another meeting.

Changes in technology transformed some aspects of the royal visit. Many members of the ethnic group drove their cars from the surrounding region to the Midway neighborhood, located between the Twin Cities, to attend church services with the prince and princess on Sunday at the Hippodrome on the state fairgrounds, just to the north of the St. Paul city limits. Out of respect for the Norwegian visitors—and because organizers thought this occasion might well be the last time a massive public might worship in the Norwegian language in the Twin Cities—the leading NLCA and Lutheran Free Church clerics conducted the services entirely in Norwegian. Some ten thousand people attended, and ushers circulated printed translations to those who could not understand the spoken language they heard over the Hippodrome's loudspeakers. After lunch with Minnesota governor Harold E. Stassen, his wife, Esther, and more than four hundred invited guests at the St. Paul Athletic Club, where the prince and governor exchanged toasts, the royal party rode to the fairgrounds and the afternoon "People's Celebration" (*folkefest*) began before grandstands filled with a crowd of an estimated twenty to twenty-five thousand.

Some parts of the program showed much greater democratization by including a broad public, large numbers of participants from the working classes, and visits to institutions for ordinary people. The fairground folkefest was the most important event designed to have broad appeal—expressed primarily through spectacles of sound and sight. Marching National Guard troops paraded into the stadium, and a military band announced the royal visitors' arrival behind them. When the royals had reached their places and shook hands with notables on the platform, the brass band led the public in singing the national anthems, followed by the firing of a twenty-one-gun salute. Immediately after, drill teams, flag squads in formation, singers, and folk dancers filed onto the field. With the drill teams in the formation of an American flag, Norwegian and Swedish American groups offered a series of short greetings to the crown prince and princess. The president of Luther Seminary in St. Paul welcomed Prince Olav and Princess Märthe on behalf of the Norwegian American Lutheran churches. The Grand Lodge presidents of the Daughters and Sons of Norway gave them honorary memberships in the mutual benefit organizations. As the drill teams transformed their formation into a Norwegian flag, massed choirs from Minneapolis and St. Paul sang well-known Norwegian national hymns, while the drill teams spelled out the letters of the royal couple's names. Swedish American representatives gave the princess bouquets of flowers and sang the Swedish national anthem. The greetings continued with brief talks and gifts from the choirs, the Common Council of the Bygdelag, the Norsemen's Federation, the Leif Erikson Monument Association, and the Norwegian-American Historical Association, whose president, Professor Theodore C. Blegen, gave the crown prince a bound set of all the association's publications. *Norrøna leikarring* and a troupe of junior folk dancers performed before the royal party and other notables. Governor Stassen and the crown prince addressed the gathered throngs, each warmly offering public greetings to the other, their nations, and the large public. The two-hour affair concluded with the audience singing the patriotic hymn they had in common, "My Country, 'Tis of Thee."

It had been a grand public ritual of mutual acknowledgment and recognition, of gift-giving and patriotic display, a mighty affirmation of how to be proudly binational. Private exclusivity returned to the royal couple that evening at dinner at the Boeckmanns' country home in the St. Paul suburbs. Monday morning brought a series of calls and receptions with local and state officials—the governor at the state capitol, the mayors in their city halls, and crowds hoping to see and greet the royals outside. At lunch with some six hundred Twin Cities businesspeople, a relaxed prince spoke even though the event was to include no address.

Meanwhile, the women's committee arranged an elegant hotel luncheon for Crown Princess Märthe with six hundred middle-class clubwomen. The governor's wife and the wives of Consul Hobe and Vice Consul Eberhardt met the princess and escorted her to the dining hall, where the assembled women sang the two nations' national anthems and ate between a series of welcome comments and speeches. Two young girls curtseyed as they gave the royal guest American Beauty roses, and a young woman sang solo. Delia Ylvisaker gave the principal address, which delineated the ideal traits of "princesses of old" and paid Princess Märthe the tribute of saying she embodied the contemporary version of these qualities. At the end of these remarks, Johanne Muller Hobe presented the royal guest with a vase of silver and gold. The program concluded with the assembly's singing of "America." The occasion was a gendered version of the exclusively "polite" side of the program for the royal visit.

That evening, the American hosts held a formal banquet for the prince and princess with selected members of the Twin Cities elite. Governor Stassen, the president of the University of Minnesota, the crown prince, and Carrie L. Fosseen, a champion of woman suffrage and a former Republican chairperson for the state, addressed the gathering. With implied compliments to the royal couple and the state's Norwegian Americans, Stassen asserted that the Norwegian government could not have chosen a finer way than the royal visit to "re-establish and re-quicken" the connections between Norway and Minnesota's pioneers and current residents. The future king thanked his hosts for their hospitality and said this inaugural trip to Norwegian America made it "vividly real" to him. While Fosseen spoke, fourteen teenage girls came in with bouquets of prairie flowers for Princess Märthe and Esther Stassen, after which each of the flower-bearers met the princess personally. After Carl G. O. Hansen directed a short concert by the Norwegian Glee Club, the assembly adjourned to a reception, during which many guests found the opportunity to meet the royal couple.[33]

On Tuesday, the crown prince made informal visits to a range of Norwegian American institutions. His first stop in Minneapolis was to greet elderly residents at the Ebenezer home, where he spoke with individuals and presented greetings from his father and the people "at home," leaving signed portraits of himself and Princess Märthe. At the end of the round of visits, the princess joined him for a similar stop at the Lyngblomsten Home for the Aged in St. Paul. Between these brief appearances, Prince Olav called at the NLCA headquarters, Augsburg Publishing House, and Augsburg College and Seminary in Cedar-Riverside. The stop at the Augsburg campus included an appearance and exchange of speeches at the opening of the Lutheran Free Church annual convention. His entourage drove slowly past the nearby Norwegian Memorial Church before

The impressive main entrance of Luther Seminary in St. Paul. *Courtesy of the author*

moving on to the University of Minnesota, where the royal couple met the president and board of regents. In St. Paul, the prince met the Luther Seminary president and faculty. The seminary's president emeritus took his royal guest to the Muskego pioneer log church on campus. Dr. Johan A. Aasgaard met them there and related the old, rustic building's place as the first church built by Norwegian immigrants in America. The two clerics gladly received the prince's heartfelt remarks and his gift of a Bible for the church.

Prince Olav's speeches, delivered in English, educated many in his invited audiences and the local newspaper-reading public about the development of a modern constitutional democracy and the modernization of industry in Norway. The royal couple repeatedly affirmed their support for Lutheranism among Norwegian Americans. They warmly and publicly showed respect for the religious, social, and educational institutions the ethnic group had sustained in Minneapolis and St. Paul. At the same time, they presented an understanding of the binational nature of the culture they visited. The contributions the royal couple made to local knowledge about Norway added to a distinguishing mark of the Twin Cities—the size of its educated population that was familiar with these topics. Previous and future visits from the highest level of Norwegian society had characterized and increasingly would come to characterize the general populace in the capital of Norwegian America.

Sixty years later, when interviewed for this history, several community veterans told how participating in the royal visit remained an indelible memory. Hilda Kringstad's face lit up as she remembered how the folk dance group she belonged to performed for the prince on a high stage: "It was a big affair with a huge program, and I knew it was held over there [at the state fairgrounds] because they didn't know where else to have it at the time that would hold as many people as they thought would come." Mary Ann Olsen exclaimed, "But what I really remember the most is when Crown Prince Olav came. He came to Minnehaha Park. I think it was in 1939. There was a huge, huge assemblage of people. I can remember my dad having my brother up on his shoulders and then I knew it was a wonderful place to be that we were seeing this man from Norway. And, oh, we did see him. Oh, yes."[34]

The Depression affected individuals, families, businesses, and institutions differently during the decade. The people who worked at

Norway's consulate general, for example, suffered little because they received salaries from the home government throughout the 1930s. Most people working in the public sector—in government, education, and medical services—at most had to deal with salary reduction, even though employment openings were few. Overall, the prosperous middle and upper classes, except for those whose income depended on real estate or investments, managed to maintain their socioeconomic status. They composed the core of people who sustained the series of ethnic anniversaries and celebrations of these years. The poor or nearly poor in the working classes and the young trying to continue education or begin employment felt the crisis years most. Most institutions recovered by the decade's end. In 1940, for example, Central Lutheran Church was able to make a seven-year plan for paying off the $600,000 in debt it accumulated though its ambitious building project. Lutheran Brotherhood, the largely Norwegian American insurance company launched in 1919–20, not only expanded rapidly in its first ten years but, after a significant dip in the early thirties, successfully sold increasing amounts of insurance for the rest of the decade. The Sons of Norway found that the organization's assets, the number of lodges, and its cultural activities increased, even though it faced competition and opposition from the Lutheran Brotherhood. The fraternal organizations did, however, report that membership totals suffered decreases in the first half of the 1930s. The Depression hit the Daughters of Norway much harder. Funds ran short for many lodges, and membership dropped by 21 percent. Nonetheless, the daughters remained a highly visible part of the ethnic group's public celebrations.[35]

World War II and the Norwegian American Community in the Twin Cities

In 1938, the local economy began to improve as national preparedness for war resulted in rapidly increasing numbers of defense contracts and as industries across the country retooled to produce military equipment and supplies. In addition, by 1940 the New Deal's Work Projects Administration found jobs for more than forty thousand people in the state in addition to the many other Minnesotans it employed in other parts of the nation. That same year the WPA spent more than

$44 million within Minnesota. The economic times were improving, but for tragic reasons. The Twin Cities public responded with horror to newspaper and radio reports as the Nazi war machine rapidly took power in Denmark and Norway on April 9, 1940. Confronted by the German emissary who demanded unconditional surrender, Norway's foreign minister, Halvdan Koht, steadfastly proclaimed that the war of opposition was already underway. The German forces smashed open resistance and quickly occupied major Norwegian port cities from Oslo to Narvik in a blitzkrieg that sent the royal family, the Norwegian parliament, and the country's huge maritime fleet fleeing abroad during the following weeks. Pursued north from the capital by bombers and storm troops, the king and crown prince received daring assistance to escape. Norway's military forces continued fighting until the nation capitulated on June 7. From then until liberation after five years under Nazi control, the occupiers killed or sent members of the Norwegian underground resistance to Grini, a concentration camp near Oslo, and deported other resisters and Norwegian Jews to death camps on the occupied continent.[36]

In Norwegian America, and not least in Minneapolis–St. Paul, people told and retold narratives of the events of April 1940, praising the courage of endangered family and friends in the homeland. Activists in the ethnic group hurriedly mobilized to aid Norway in any way possible. As local historian Carl G. O. Hansen noted emphatically, "no single event" before the occupation so powerfully unified and "deeply stirred" Norwegian Americans "still conscious" of their ethnic background. In the energizing shock of the first days after April 9, leaders of the many nationwide Norwegian American institutions with headquarters in the Twin Cities met to discuss how the ethnic group could most effectively organize relief for Norway.

In the office of NLCA president Johan A. Aasgaard, the presidents of the Lutheran Free Church (LFC), Augsburg and St. Olaf Colleges, and the Daughters and Sons of Norway met and evaluated what was best to do. Board members from the bygdelag's common council, the Norwegian-American Historical Association, the northwest chapter of the Norsemen's Federation, and the Minneapolis chapter of the American-Scandinavian Foundation joined in the group meditations. The meeting chose a committee headed by Aasgaard to confer with leaders in the rest of Norwegian America in late April in Chicago, where Relief for Norway, Inc., was formally founded.

At the behest of the US State Department, to recognize the American origin of the aid and to conform with the names approved for other ethnic groups' relief efforts, Relief for Norway consolidated with several Norwegian American associations and became American Relief for Norway (ARFN). In June 1941, Norwegian American leaders from the Twin Cities visited Camp Little Norway north of Toronto, where Norwegian refugees trained to join the allied air campaign. Shortly after their return, they founded the Camp Little Norway Association. Chicago remained the location of ARFN's headquarters. Although residing in Minneapolis, Aasgaard continued as ARFN president and E. B. Hauke, president of the Sons of Norway, continued as its vice president. In the course of the war years, other men from the city joined the ARFN board, including Jacob Stefferud, regional agent for the Norwegian America Line since 1930 as well as acting consul general in the Twin Cities from April 1941 until the summer of 1944.[37]

Across the United States in 1940, Norwegian America read daily coverage of events in Norway in the ethnic and mainstream press. In the coming months, in the Norwegian American population centers of thirty-six states, the ethnic group formed committees to aid the homeland. Uncoordinated efforts multiplied and quickly became a problem among these committees. By 1941, the federal government faced the same difficulty on a much larger scale and so announced a set of rules. Norwegian Americans chose the ARFN office in Chicago as the only officially licensed organization to send relief to Norway. Like other such organizations, it was responsible for collecting all the contributions from subgroups and sending them to America's National War Fund by a set date each fall. The largest of the Norwegian American relief groups, including Norwegian Relief and the Camp Little Norway Association in Minneapolis, became members of ARFN. Between April 1940 and December 1941, US neutrality laws strictly restricted the kinds of aid ARFN could offer.

Meanwhile, in Minnesota the federal Selective Service Act took force in September 1940. Many thousands of young Norwegian American men and women enlisted or joined the various military services through the draft. Serving their country and contributing to the liberation of Norway and the rest of occupied Europe motivated them and many other Americans to risk their lives. In December 1941, a day after the Japanese attack on Pearl Harbor, the United States entered the war. More than three hundred thousand Minnesotans served, and thousands died overseas by its end. In contrast to conditions during the First World War, little anti-German and foreigner hostility marred state and local wartime preparations.

From 1939 onward, the state's industry shifted to war production, which greatly increased employment opportunities in the Twin Cities and vicinity. During World War II, movement to and from Norway nearly ceased, military service took many young people out of the Twin Cities, and Minneapolis–St. Paul's wartime jobs brought a surge of urbanization, especially of young women. The state's farmers redoubled production, sending many crops to the Cities to be processed and shipped as war supplies rather than consumed domestically. People in the Twin Cities cultivated "victory gardens" for food. Local women—many of them through their organizations in Lutheran congregations—sewed, knitted, and gathered shoes and clothing for the troops as well as for people in Norway. Other women and the metropolitan population generally found expanded work opportunities at 3M, International Harvester Company, or Northwestern Aeronautical Corporation in St. Paul, all of which produced important materials for the war effort. In Minneapolis, the same was true of General Mills, Munsingwear and North Star Woolen Mills, Minneapolis-Moline, Northern Pump Company, Honeywell Company, and Minnesota Onan Corporation. In New Brighton, north of Minneapolis, and Rosemount, south of St. Paul, the federal government built huge ordnance plants that hired thousands during the early 1940s.[38]

After America joined the Allies' war effort, the ARFN and the Camp Little Norway Association broadened their efforts. Norwegian American groups across the Twin Cities collected shoes, clothes, and food, while a corps of volunteers, including Jacob Stefferud and his two daughters, sorted and packed these goods for shipment. The Norwegian government-in-exile and its representatives in New York and Washington, DC, sent a series of elected officials and resistance fighters to keep the ethnic community informed about conditions in occupied Norway. Among these were the president of Norway's parliament, C. J. Hambro, who in September 1940 provided a firsthand account of the attack of April 9 to a local audience. In 1942, the former city council president of Narvik, who had escaped the attack on his city, set up a Norwegian Press and Information Agency in Foshay Tower. Other visitors who also stirred local publics with moving descriptions of the trials in the homeland included famed novelist Sigrid Undset, Norway's director of public health, its minister of church and education, and Halvdan Koht and Trygve Lie, successive foreign ministers of Norway. Ole Reistad, commander of Camp Little Norway, came several times to talk about the training of pilots there, on occasion introducing young men who had fled from Norway and managed to reach Canada.[39]

Crown Prince Olav made a second visit to the Twin Cities at the end of April 1942. This time his address to local leaders emphasized the crucial importance of Norway's merchant fleet in delivering "supplies to United Nations forces all over the world" and the daring bravery of teachers and clergy at home who faced the Nazis' intimidation. A photograph in the *Minneapolis Star Journal* showed his royal highness shaking hands with a woman munitions maker at the New Brighton ordnance plant. Afterward he told a journalist for the Norsemen's Federation that he had succeeded in raising the funds he sought in the Twin Cities. Johan Nygaardsvold, Norway's prime minister, served as the principal speaker for Norwegian Constitution Day observances in Minneapolis that same year. He expressed understanding for the reasons people once emigrated from Norway to find greater freedom and praised Norwegians for not forgetting the homeland in its hour of need. Visiting Norwegians also urged the ethnic group to make the homeland's case in the United States as well as to continue their campaigns for relief aid. This assistance persisted, but as long as the occupation went on, Norwegian American organizations faced dilemmas in finding means to get goods into Norway without the German forces seizing them.

In late 1940, the Twin Cities again had a Norwegian-language press outlet when *Duluth Skandinav* arranged with the Norwegian National League in Minneapolis to give the fourth page of each issue to Minneapolis events and release that as *Minneapolis Posten*. Until 1956, the new Twin Cities newspaper served useful local purposes. During the war years, when so much was at stake and the mails interrupted, Norwegian Americans in the Twin Cities hungered for local perspectives on news

In exile in America during the Nazi occupation of Norway in 1942, Crown Prince Olav visited the Twin Cities ordnance plant in New Brighton and spoke to a capacity crowd at the Minneapolis armory, where he and Crown Princess Märthe received a bouquet from eight-year-old Ruth Stefferud. Minneapolis Star Journal, *April 30, 1942, courtesy MNHS collections*

from home and visits from compatriots who were in Norway to experience events firsthand. In January 1941, the newspaper reported that the Minneapolis Auditorium hosted a meeting to aid Great Britain and her allies. In mid-February, it reported a severe lack of meat in Norway. On February 21 and in many later issues it accounted for the activities and income of ARFN. In March, it reported facts from Norway's health director on nutritional conditions in the homeland. Throughout April, it reported in detail about the German attack on Norway. Further, it announced the views of Jacob Stefferud, Wilhelm Morgenstierne, and other prominent figures that, as the headline proclaimed, "Norway Will Reclaim Her Freedom."

The repressive German refusal to allow May 17 celebrations prompted outraged responses in the newspaper. Local Norwegian American observances received detailed coverage in energetic repudiation of what happened in the homeland. In August, *Minneapolis Posten* reported enthusiastically about the visit of eight Minneapolitans that resulted in the Camp Little Norway Association. In September, it announced and reported on Ole Reistad's visit from Camp Little Norway. In November it jubilantly told of Swedish Americans' campaign to help occupied Norway through Wings for Norway, an organization that supported the Norwegian pilots camp north of Toronto. December issues reported optimistically about the hope US entry into the war gave occupied Norway. At St. Paul's Leif Erikson celebration in 1942, the keynote speaker, Norway's former prime minister Johan L. Mowinckel, told of his escape to Sweden and of conditions for Norwegian refugees there. A month later the paper reported that the Service Center for Norway had opened in the Foshay Tower, where a corps of women knitted clothing for people in the homeland, in Norwegian shipping, and at Camp Little Norway. It also informed readers about the Ninety-Ninth Infantry Battalion, then stationed at Fort Snelling between the Twin Cities, explaining the plan to develop a unit of soldiers with Norwegian birth or heritage who spoke the language and so could effectively infiltrate and help liberate the homeland. The article assured readers that these compatriots worshipped in the mother tongue at the Norwegian Memorial Church and received assistance for their social needs from the metropolitan area's large Norwegian American community.

During the rest of the war, *Minneapolis Posten* continued its detailed coverage of similar topics but paid increasing attention to the closing of universities and arrest of faculty and students in Norway, as well as to the imprisonment, torture, assassination, and execution of Norwegian resistance heroes by the Nazi SS. In 1944, the newspaper focused on D-Day, the Allied armies' progress, the participation of Camp Little Norway fliers in the fighting, and the accumulated supplies ARFN readied for sending to Norway. In banner front-page headlines the paper jubilantly followed in detail Germany's surrender, the liberation of Norway, and the return of the royal house and parliament in May and June 1945. During the year's remaining months, it focused on the war's toll on the country, on the trials of traitors and treatment of collaborators, and, repeatedly, on cataloging contributions made to ARFN. On November 30, *Posten* announced plans for an American summer school at the University of Oslo after the war.[40]

Overestimating the degree to which the war years galvanized the self-identifying Norwegian American community in the Twin Cities is difficult. As historian Daron Olson correctly notes, the leaders of Norway's government-in-exile made the nation's wartime trials an experience it shared with Norwegian America. The historian of Mindekirken asserted that the Norwegian Lutheran Memorial Church became the preferred place where visitors from Norway and Camp Little Norway worshipped and held talks about affairs in the homeland. This decisive factor, the historian claimed, made the church well known and enabled it to pay its debts. The records of the consulate general in Minneapolis–St. Paul resonate with the deep concern of individuals, families, and metropolitan area institutions in their intense search for ways to help people at home in Norway. The consuls in the United States received copies of circulars from Norway's government in London, which stated the policy it expected them to follow. One circular sent to Minneapolis announced the government's resolution to dispatch several ministers and the president of its parliament to the United States "above all to bring about a systematic propaganda about Norway's situation and especially, to create support for the collections of 'Relief for Norway.'"[41]

Commodore Per Askim at the Norwegian Embassy in Washington, DC, corresponded with the Norwegian Information Agency in Foshay Tower to guide public opinion to a more correct appraisal of how many and what kind of relief collections were appropriate. Askim felt that in their urgent wish to help, Norwegian Americans had already started too many aid collections. In the spring and summer of 1946, the Teachers' League of Minneapolis arranged through Norwegian authorities to send funds for teaching materials to the teachers of Oslo. In February 1946, the consulate received instructions from CARE, the Cooperative for American Remittances to Europe, about what CARE packages should contain and how to send them and remittances to Norway, information it made available locally as long as the program lasted. In August 1946, the consulate received and sent financial gifts from Norwegian Americans in the Twin Cities and Upper Midwest "to assist Norway where help is most needed."

All through the war years, on the anniversary of the attack on Norway, the Camp Little Norway Association held Liberation Rallies, in coordination with the Sons of Norway and other local organizations.

Prominent refugees from the homeland and representatives of the Norwegian government-in-exile addressed large publics at the rallies and vividly recalled the invasion and brutalities committed against Norway and her people. In 1945, a service of thanksgiving at Central Lutheran Church attracted some three thousand people for a bilingual program of sacred and patriotic music as well as a speech in English by the president of Luther Seminary and one in Norwegian by the president of the LFC. These public observances through the war years and celebrations of Norway's liberation contributed greatly to unifying the ethnic group in the Twin Cities and solidifying its ties with the homeland.[42]

Conclusion

A series of major challenges had to be met by the ethnic group between 1925 and 1945. Nativism triumphed after 1925. Restrictionists in Congress outlawed mass immigration from Norway and all of Europe except Great Britain by the end of the 1920s. Over the next fifteen years, Norwegian Americans made initial attempts to adjust to that future-changing reality. In Minneapolis–St. Paul, memorial jubilees for homeland cultural icons Bjørnstjerne Bjørnson, Henrik Ibsen, Roald Amundsen, and St. Olav exhibited energetic broad-based efforts to teach the younger generation to know and share the richness of their ethnic heritage, not only for themselves but also for the Twin Cities as a whole. Passing on a historical legacy was a major attempt to maintain the group's identity despite the end of large-scale immigration. Preservationist campaigns also sought to strengthen the teaching of Norwegian language and culture in the Cities' secondary schools and at Norwegian American colleges.

Unifying the group and pooling its resources represented another means of dealing with the end of immigration. The creation of a "big-tent" structure for the broader urban area's Norwegian American organizations in the Norwegian National League (*Nasjonalforbundet*) is a prime example of group members recognizing the usefulness of uniting various subgroups and activities in common efforts such as celebrating the era's cultural jubilees. Local leaders also strengthened transnational organizations based in Norway, such as the Norsemen's Federation, by founding chapters in the Cities to promote an updated knowledge of the homeland as well as homeland Norwegians' increased appreciation of Norwegian America's loyalty and manifold ties to Norway. The trials of the Great Depression further brought members of the community together, as they helped their own cope with economic difficulties and fostered inexpensive ways to entertain each other.

The occupation of Norway gave new, more desperate meanings to these transnational efforts. This threat was hugely greater than earlier disasters that had prompted local Norwegian Americans to mount fundraising efforts to assist the homeland. The consulate staff and family collected vast amounts of clothing, shoes, and canned goods to send to relatives facing shortages in Norway. Many individuals, congregations, and ethnic associations joined these communal efforts. So many in the Cities wanted to reach people they loved who were enduring the occupation and be assured of their safety. The consulate and people with resources contributed to the funding of Camp Little Norway in Canada, where pilots from Norway trained. The Norwegian government in exile and its representatives in Washington, DC, knew of these manifold efforts in the Twin Cities and across Norwegian America. They sent homeland officials, resistance fighters, and people who escaped occupied Norway to inform the Twin Cities community, provide firsthand accounts of conditions at home, and thank Norwegian Americans for their assistance. On many a Sunday, visitors from Norway spoke at the Norwegian Memorial Church in Minneapolis and satisfied a grateful public with news from the homeland. As we shall see in the next chapter, these bonds of transnational mutual assistance continued into the postwar decades.

CHAPTER SEVEN

A Later-Generation Ethnic Group during the Postwar Decades

[1945–1975]

THIS CHAPTER FIRST EXPLORES HOW THE NORWEGIAN AMERICAN COMMUNITY changed in the postwar period. It traces the lingering effects of the war years on ties between homeland Norwegians and the Twin Cities community. Then it examines how the passage of time created a later-generation, more Americanized ethnic group. That enclave received a small wave of immigrants directly from Norway in the 1950s, people who founded their own immigrant organizations and strengthened the older community's institutions. Meanwhile, a surge of urbanization and suburbanization swelled the enclave by bringing an even larger number of rural newcomers who shared a Norwegian heritage, though of a more distant sort.

Then, in chronological order, the chapter looks closely at the series of challenges the Twin Cities' white ethnic groups—in particular the Norwegian and Scandinavian Americans—faced between 1945 and 1975 in efforts to answer minority protest and ameliorate socioeconomic inequalities and discrimination. As the Reverend Paul A. Boe confirms below, these efforts brought a turning point in his life. This chapter argues that the same may be said about the evolution of the local Norwegian American community and life in Minneapolis–St. Paul as a whole. The first challenge involved binding together

Lutheran divisions across sectarian and ethnic boundaries. The second required engagement in ecumenical cooperation to ease the integration of postwar immigrants and displaced persons (DPs), largely from Baltic nations that had been occupied by Germany during World War II.

Liberal Lutherans in the Twin Cities, whether in formulating religious social services or making policy for municipal government, confronted the same dilemma. Old-stock German and Scandinavian Americans alike searched for ways to live up to their values in their dealings with each other and displaced refugees. The arrival and settlement of Blacks and urban Indians in the postwar decades presented two more challenges to the Twin Cities and their establishment groups. Norwegian Americans played central roles in negotiating relations between the haves and the have-nots in the Twin Cities. Their position in the status hierarchy of Minneapolis–St. Paul could hardly have been higher from 1945 to 1975. The public perceived them and Scandinavian Americans generally as "old" immigrants whose early arrival and white Protestantism by then had assisted their integration into the mainstream white majority. In Minnesota that meant they had participated in historical events and processes that earned them a place among the "founders" of the state and Twin Cities. They had played prominent roles in the original land-taking from the Native Americans and the organization of farming-district and small-town governments, and they constituted a major component of the people who between the later 1860s and 1970s either immigrated directly to or left the countryside for Minneapolis–St. Paul.

The brief quotation below comes from an interview with Boe, the social services director of the American Lutheran Church. He remembered vividly a decisive meeting with representatives of the minority groups the ALC wished to assist in the 1960s. The church body had allotted a half million dollars for that purpose. His realization of a turning point came in that meeting when he and church representatives faced an unprecedented demand: ". . . the Blacks were saying, 'Look, you can't any longer just do things for us; we want to do it ourselves.' And the Indians were saying this, and the, the poor people were saying this. We had people in welfare who were beating down the door saying, 'We want a voice in our own destiny.'" The church's client groups resolutely insisted that church welfare deal not with charity but with "participating democracy." His interviewer, Gjermund S. Thompson, inserted that term and Boe agreed. The dilemma was that the representatives of the minority "clients" asked for a voice by demanding the right to decide how best to spend the money. The passage exposes the underlying problem that not only the ALC but also the larger established European American community faced throughout this period. How should an overwhelmingly white, well-situated church—and the metropolitan majority—act if it wants to "minister among all people" and behave "inclusively" in social services and political rights?[1]

Later-generation Scandinavian Americans constituted the largest segment of the old-stock white population in the state and Twin Cities, and Norwegian Americans had a record of being the most politically active among them. A public majority, therefore, expected that leaders of this ethnic group would formulate and marshal public support for policy to deal with these social problems. In cooperation with others, local Norwegian Americans and their leaders in fact rose to the occasion, actively working to meet the internal and metropolitan challenges outlined above, especially the protests of growing African and Native American minorities in the 1960s. By the end of the decade, however, as a prominent part of the old-stock white establishment, Norwegian Americans repeatedly elected conservative Charles Stenvig mayor in Minneapolis during a backlash against liberal social policies that was both local and national.

A Predominantly Third- and Fourth-Generation Ethnic Community after World War II

Since the turn of the twentieth century, Swedish and Norwegian Americans have together composed a uniquely large portion of the Twin Cities' residents. In 1910, however, the number of foreign-born Norwegian residents of both Minneapolis and St. Paul reached its peak, and their percentage of the Cities' general population went into decline a decade earlier. The second generation reached its high point in absolute numbers in 1930 but had been falling as a percentage of each city's residents since 1890. Foreign-born Norwegian Americans and their children, nonetheless, still numbered nearly 34,000 people or 10.6 percent of the entire population of Minneapolis in 1930. The first two generations in

St. Paul comprised a little over 9,000 residents or 4.6 percent at that point. By then the multigenerational Nordic ancestry group was likely as much as a third or more of the people in Minneapolis and a quarter of the population of St. Paul.[2]

The stark realities of World War II strengthened ties between ethnic groups in the United States and their European homelands. The forced separation caused by the breakdown of transportation and communication systems during the war years and the enormous effort put into helping the people at home who suffered through war and occupation created intense psychological needs. As was the case for other European American ethnic groups, the war brought a resurgence of unity and solidarity among local Norwegian Americans, both those who served in the military and those on the home front who engaged in relief for Norway. Many who perhaps viewed their ethnic heritage as a private matter or something they had taken for granted found it thrust into the headlines and public commentary because of the occupation of Norway and the Norwegian people's courageous defense and resistance. No less a public figure than President Franklin Roosevelt had elevated their homeland as the prime example of how a people could stand up to Nazi aggression. For years after the war, the intensity of that experience and the memory of visits from Norwegian refugees—prominent representatives of the government in exile and ordinary people fleeing or bravely facing death—continued to bring homeland Norwegians and members of the ethnic group in the Twin Cities closer together. The experience of World War II, in contrast to the oppressive suspicion felt during World War I, made the Cities' Norwegian Americans prouder of their background and rewarded them with an enhanced status in mainstream American society.[3]

The best-informed estimates stated that third-generation Norwegian Americans made up the largest part of the group as early as 1920, but the census did not count them as such. In 1940 and 1950, the federal government published no information about the size of the second, third, or later generations. The severe limit put on Norwegian immigration by the end of the 1920s (2,377 visas annually), the greater return migration than immigration during the Depression of the 1930s, and the occupation of Norway and danger of ocean navigation during the war meant that very few Norwegian immigrants arrived for fifteen years or more. The increase of the group's size from urbanization related to war industries involved mostly third- or later generation members of the ethnic group. In the postwar decades, therefore, one component of the metropolitan-area ethnic group consisted of a small number of people born in Norway—divided between people near retirement and postwar newcomers, who together accounted for less than 2 percent of each city's population. Tens of thousands of people in the largely middle-aged second generation, and many more who were uncounted—their descendants in the third, fourth, and later generations—made up the rest of the community. In 1960, nonetheless, the first two generations of Norwegian Americans composed 7 percent of the population in the Minneapolis–St. Paul metropolitan area. With Swedish Americans, Scandinavian-born people and their children made up nearly 17 percent of people in the Cities and suburbs. Odd S. Lovoll, in his study of postwar immigration from Norway and postwar Norwegian American life, concludes, "when one ignores the flurry of activity and individual efforts on special occasions, such as jubilees and prominent visits from Norway, it becomes clear that there [was] an obvious decline in ethnic community life." (See Table 1.1 in chapter one, pages 16–17.)[4]

In several senses, the classic community of the past was gone. The shift to a mainly later-generation ethnic group—together with a larger Swedish American ancestry group and a smaller Danish American presence—constituted a Scandinavian American community that was a distinctive part of the Twin Cities' "white establishment." After the war, Norwegian Americans appeared indistinguishable from other American whites. Integration into the larger community, over decades or generations, had Americanized their attitudes and outlook. They spoke English as their native tongue. They no longer lived together in Scandinavian immigrant sections of town. Their schooling and occupations revealed that they were an integrated segment of the general population.

Yet, after World War II, the significant differences for Norwegian Americans in comparison to local whites generally were several. The large size and long-term residence of the Scandinavian group in Minnesota, along with their ancestors' efforts to win public acceptance, earned them status, broad mainstream community participation in their holidays and jubilees, unusual awareness of their religious affiliation, knowledge of the culture and events in their homelands, and the selection of Scandinavian Americans to positions of public trust and responsibility. Since the 1930s, state and local voters often chose to elect Scandinavian Americans as governor of Minnesota and mayor of Minneapolis. Since the 1890s, moreover, Norwegian Americans won elected office out of proportion to the number in their group compared to the greater size of the Swedish American community. Observers noticed the unique predominance of Swedes and Norwegians in the local population mix as early as 1903, when Lincoln Steffens wrote of the "great big Scandinavian body" of Minneapolis. In 1961, popular historian of the Twin Cities Carol Brink characterized the distinctive metropolitan situation: "We have come to think of ourselves as a Scandinavian community, and I am sure that we are looked on in that way by outsiders . . . because our Scandinavian complexion is one of the things that distinguish the Twin Cities from other large cities in the United States." Recognition of the unusually Nordic quality of life in Minneapolis–St. Paul certainly contributed to different community roles and kinds of activity for leading people of Norwegian extraction—many of whom did not appear as overtly ethnic.[5]

Urbanization and Immigration to the Twin Cities after the War

The state and region, both heavily settled by the same Scandinavian nationalities, reinforced the groups' influence on the urban centers. The continued urbanization of Swedes and Norwegians from the region into the post–World War II period maintained their strength in the Twin Cities long after large-scale immigration directly from the homelands ended in the 1920s. During the war years, some refugee visitors from Norway stayed in the Cities. In the postwar decades to 1975, more than 49,500 Norwegians immigrated to the United States, many of them well educated and meeting relatives who would help them make a life in America. Between 1945 and 1960, Minneapolis–St. Paul attracted significant numbers of newcomers from Norway because of the extensive personal connections available in the Twin Cities' large Norwegian American population and thanks to opportunities to complete educations interrupted by the occupation. Others, especially people with technical professions, found very limited employment at home compared with prospects available in the Twin Cities. People in

Norway had heard about Minneapolis–St. Paul for many years. They knew about the metropolitan area's opportunities and its reputation for offering a positive reception to Scandinavian immigrants. Nonetheless, the portion of these newcomers who returned home after two or so years was higher than in any previous period. In the postwar world, the highly educated class in the West showed increasing levels of geographic mobility, regardless of national background.[6]

The latest wave of Norwegian newcomers, despite their small number, established a few new voluntary associations and added vitality to many organizations and activities founded earlier. A few examples illustrate the variety of these associations. Engineers and architects educated in Norway formed the Norwegian-American Technical Society (NATS), in which they shared educational experiences, occupational knowledge about their professions and employment in the metropolitan area, a lecture series, and a social calendar. The society had twenty-six members in 1973 and reported its date of origin as 1926. A chapter in a nationwide organization, the local NATS sponsored the two-day national convention—and its own thirty-fifth anniversary party—in 1962 at the Sons of Norway Building in Minneapolis and the St. Olaf College campus in Northfield. Keynote and banquet speakers included famous designer of New York City's river tunnels Ole Singstad and Kenneth Bjørk, editor of the Norwegian-American Historical Association and author of *Saga in Steel and Concrete*, the history of Norwegian engineers and architects in America. The postwar members designated NATS as a first-generation organization and decided that members' children who completed technical degrees and worked as engineers or architects in the United States could not join.[7]

Carl G. O. Hansen associates the Kontakt social club with some seven youth clubs organized in the early 1900s by recent newcomers from Norway. He notes, however, that some of the many young immigrants who arrived after World War I founded Kontakt in 1935 and, unlike the other youth clubs, it survived into the decades after World War II, welcoming newcomers and helping them feel at home in the Twin Cities through its social events. In 1973, however, Kontakt reported its founding year as 1953 to Minnesota Historical Society researchers and claimed that ninety to a hundred people commonly attended its events, which offered opportunities to "speak Norwegian, exchange ideas, and maintain cultural traditions." One of Kontakt's officers characterized the club as "a social group of young people who perceived their problems and experiences as different from Norwegian groups already established in America." The newcomers departed from a later stage of Norwegian society and met a different Norwegian America and mainstream American society. In this sense, NATS was akin to Kontakt in the postwar years in providing mutual support and understanding for new arrivals in what they perceived as their unique situation. Newcomers' sense of having a different homeland identity and meeting an American society distinct from that experienced by earlier Norwegian groups in Minneapolis–St. Paul had a history of motivating the formation of a new constellation of immigrant societies after every sizable contingent of arrivals.

In the early 1970s, state historical society researchers gathered information for the encyclopedic multiethnic history *They Chose Minnesota.* In their study of Norwegian Americans in the Twin Cities and vicinity they found (in addition to NATS and Kontakt) a range of contemporary ethnic organizations. Among them were nine Sons of Norway lodges and the order's headquarters. There were also three women's, three men's, and one mixed-voice choir. In addition were six bygdelag and the headquarters of the organization's common council, three folk dancing societies, and chapters of organizations devoted to strengthening bonds with Norway, such as the Norsemen's Federation, the American-Scandinavian Foundation, and the Norwegian National League. These organizations published or distributed several periodicals, among them the Sons of Norway *Viking,* the national Norwegian American choir magazine (*Sangerhilsen*), and *The Norseman* and *Norge's Jul* from the Norsemen's Federation.

Norwegian American activists, recent immigrants among them, planned and carried out public Seventeenth of May, Norway Day, and Leif Erikson Day festivities annually during the first three decades after World War II. At Augsburg College, plans for local celebration of the sesquicentennial of Norwegian immigration to the United States were already underway by an association founded for that purpose. One Norwegian-language weekly newspaper, *Minnesota Posten,* served the local and regional ethnic group. In addition, dozens of Lutheran (and a few Methodist and Baptist) congregations maintained ethnic traditions—although in English instead of Norwegian, with the exception of religious services at the Norwegian Memorial Church. Norwegian language lessons were available at the Sons of Norway headquarters on Lake Street in Minneapolis, in several public high schools, and at local colleges and the University of Minnesota. Starting in 1963 schoolchildren could study the language during the summer at Concordia College language camp, and *Skogfjorden* Norwegian Language Village, which offered immersion summer school study of Norwegian language and culture, opened in 1970. Although this level of activity could not match the lively ethnic community life of the prewar years, for the portion of the local population that was interested, the options for involvement in the ethnic community were still many.

In relative terms, the metropolitan area's Norwegian American population decreased less in these decades than did the numbers in other European ethnic groups. The small postwar wave of immigration directly from Norway was a contributing factor. Continued urbanization, however, was more important. It brought more Norwegian than Swedish Americans into the metropolitan area because of the greater number and size of the Norwegian American settlements across the Upper Midwest. The negative experience of the world wars greatly reduced the civic visibility and influence of German Americans, the single largest nationality group in the Cities and region. Scandinavian ethnic groups in many ways filled the public gap left by the German ancestry group's retreat.[8]

Circumstances in Minneapolis–St. Paul and Norway molded Norwegian Americans' responses to the postwar situation. Growing membership in the local chapter of the Norsemen's Federation reflected the active interest of later generations of Norwegian American leaders in learning more about the ancestral homeland and its significance for their history as part of its emigrated population. The rapidly increasing number of visits exchanged among Norwegians and their relatives across the Atlantic from 1946 onward offered striking evidence of pent-up needs for personal contact and persistently strong bonds. The resumption of Norwegian America Line sailings from New York and the inauguration of Scandinavian Airlines System flights between the two nations in 1946 resulted in an immediate spike in transatlantic visits. In the following years, air travel became both more convenient and less expensive. From its founding the Norsemen's Federation assisted travel between the United States and Norway. In the later 1940s and 1950s, it responded to growing interest in and convenience of travel by expanding that service and opening a separate travel division. Organizations such as local Sons of Norway lodges, the bygdelag in the Cities and region, and other ethnic institutions soon arranged group trips to Norway. These and the federation offered charter flights in the 1960s. The Twin Cities' international airport naturally became the point of departure and arrival for the rising tide of contacts between Norwegians and Norwegian Americans in the Upper Midwest.

Immediately after the war, colleges and universities in the United States learned that Norway's universities, deprived of financing, faculty, and students during the occupation, found it impossible to provide housing and courses of study for all its people who wished to pursue higher education. American colleges and universities in parts of the country with strong traditions of Norwegian settlement eagerly offered to make space for Norwegian students. By 1947, more than five hundred Norwegians were studying at institutions such as St. Olaf and Augsburg Colleges and the University of Minnesota. After almost two years of planning on both sides of the Atlantic, in that year the Oslo Summer School for American Students at the University of Oslo gave 221 young Americans, a fifth of them later-generation Norwegian Americans, the opportunity to spend six weeks learning about Norway. They studied Norwegian language, literature, history, and society with the help of university faculty and guest lecturers from the highest echelons of government and cultural life. Over the next ten years, the academic strength of the school grew, the size of the student body increased, its reputation steadily rose, and it attracted larger numbers of applicants, many of them from countries other than the United States. In 1958, it adopted a new name, the International Summer School of the University of Oslo. In spite of the name change and a greater proportion of non-Americans in its student body, the school continued to contribute to a corps of Americans with deep, up-to-date knowledge about Norway, many of them residents of Norwegian American centers such as Minneapolis–St. Paul.[9]

Scandinavian Americans' Role in Meeting Postwar Challenges

A number of interrelated processes engaged and changed the Twin Cities' Norwegian American community in the postwar period. Between 1945 and 1975, the Scandinavian Americans (largely of Swedish and Norwegian extraction) in Minneapolis–St. Paul exercised significant influence on transformative processes of historical development because of the status they held as large local and regional ancestry groups, related ethnicities, and segments of the population with well-established traditions of political and social leadership in the Twin Cities. At the time, American society as a whole wanted to make the most of the opportunities presented by the transition to peace. Across the nation, moreover, leaders focused on lessons that would help America avoid repeating the traumas of the Depression and world wars. Because of Scandinavian Americans' continued demographic dominance in the Twin Cities metropolitan area, it was not unusual that Norwegian Americans and their Swedish American "cousins" were visible in local approaches to the issues of the time. An interview with Paul A. Boe, the ALC social services director in this period, excerpted above, reveals one of the ways Norwegian Americans became involved in difficult intergroup relations.

Central issues for Twin Citians included receiving and resettling tens of thousands of returning veterans, helping them find education, work, and paths to a satisfying future. Norwegian Americans made up a large part of the returning servicepeople, and the local community, formally through its institutions and informally through family networks, pooled resources to reintegrate their own into community life. Like people in the Twin Cities generally, the ancestry group and its veterans wanted to find ways to establish stable prosperity. Traumatic experiences at home and abroad led them to eschew the ideological extremes that had been encouraged by the hard times of the thirties and that ended in the racist bigotry and holocausts of the war. Norwegian Americans successfully implemented means of strengthening connections with their ancestral homeland and unifying their religious institutions along broader transethnic Lutheran lines. Local politicians with Norwegian American roots, such as Hubert Humphrey, found support for moving the Democratic-Farmer-Labor (DFL) Party toward the moderate center and for creating a municipal regime of equal civil rights in Minneapolis.

Leaders searched for a consensus that realized American egalitarian ideals and economic freedoms. Humphrey and other liberal leaders asserted that a generous tolerance of cultural pluralism, combined with the programs promoted by modern political and social science, offered the best means of achieving these goals. The postwar decades in addition posed new challenges in the Cities because of the need to organize for the arrival of displaced Europeans. The immediate and desperate problems of the millions of displaced persons (DPs) in the ruins of Europe faced most of the American ethnic institutions that had striven to help during the war with a new challenge to reach out to uprooted compatriots and coreligionists in the later 1940s and 1950s. In the same years, a rapid increase in the size of the Native American and African American communities, in both cities but especially in Minneapolis, gave rise to new intergroup conflicts and negotiations.

The Scandinavian dominance in the Twin Cities' population profile after 1945 and group relations between Norwegian Americans and other populations in those years revolved around four related processes that shaped Norwegian American adjustments and responses to changing circumstances. One accelerating process was the decline of central-city Scandinavian immigrant neighborhoods. Second, migration to the suburbs by Norwegians and other established groups greatly reduced the inner-city Scandinavian American presence near the downtowns. Third, new interstate highway systems carved through historical immigrant neighborhoods. Fourth, the in-migration of African Americans and Native Americans to, as well as the later settling of Latino and Asian immigrants in or near, those same sections of the Cities transformed the first settlement areas of Scandinavian newcomers a century or more before.

These processes modified the ethnic identity of many Norwegian Americans as they journeyed to the outskirts of the metropolitan area. On the one hand, their ethnic community grew much more dispersed and, as Herbert Gans has theorized, became a largely voluntary and symbolic dimension of life in the multiethnic suburbs. On the other hand, the ease of travel on metropolitan freeways and an "ethnic core" of activist Norwegian Americans maintained close relations with the old neighborhoods. Ethnic activists kept memberships in historical ethnic institutions and took part in outreach activities to the recently arrived populations now surrounding these monuments to Norwegians' past residence in the central city.[10]

Several paths of historical development illustrate how Norwegian (and Scandinavian) American leaders mediated among segments of their own groups as well as between these and other communities in Minneapolis–St. Paul. The first example focuses on local Norwegian clergy's part in efforts to unite different strands of their Lutheranism into one body and then on further efforts (now increasingly ecumenical) to create a pan-ethnic American Lutheranism in the form of the American Lutheran Church (ALC). The closely related cultures of Norwegian and Swedish Americans facilitated their cooperation in this phase of the ecumenical movement in the United States.

The second example, to some degree building on the achievements of the first, involved a broader ecumenical, public-private cooperation between the federal government and Protestant, Catholic, and Jewish social service agencies to help DPs from various European nations migrate to and integrate into the metropolitan area. Although the headquarters of Lutheran Social Service in Minneapolis worked specifically with Lutheran DPs, these refugees were not necessarily ethnically Norwegian, and a larger pan-religious effort brought Norwegian American church and civic leaders into much more contact with other ethnic groups' religious traditions. A series of interviews with members of historically Norwegian congregations that sponsored DPs consistently indicates that this participation had the overall tendency of making these Norwegian Americans view ethnicity in more tolerant and socially engaged terms and laid the foundations for continued cooperative assistance to groups in need.

The third and fourth interlocutory, mediating efforts in these years—Norwegian (and Scandinavian) Americans' relationship with African Americans and urbanized Native Americans—resulted for the most part from Scandinavian American politicians who were local leaders and carried on liberal traditions in DFL circles. When growing unrest in predominantly Black sections of both cities erupted in race riots for three consecutive years in the mid-1960s, this leadership elite in municipal and state government played a critical mediating role across racial, cultural, and economic lines. Before, during, and after the crisis years, other Norwegian American civic and religious leaders—as well as members of the ethnic group who lived in or were members of Norwegian American institutions nearest the areas of unrest—found their attitudes and approaches to race-based inequality and conflict deeply affected by local events. Protest, conflict, and subsequent negotiations with Native Americans followed a largely parallel pattern, but here the leadership and activism of ALC social services director Paul S. Boe and Clyde Bellecourt of the local American Indian Movement (AIM) played unique roles.

Norwegian American Interethnic Relations: An Overview of the Postwar Decades

As noted previously, many Norwegian Americans in Minnesota settled first on or near the frontier or in rural districts where they encountered Native Americans or common American attitudes toward Native Americans before they or their children later moved to St. Paul or Minneapolis. After the Dakota War of 1862, contacts between Norwegian and Native Americans soured and remained distant into the post–World War II years. Krista Sande Johnson, for example, explained how she absorbed stereotypical attitudes toward Ojibwe people—and Native Americans in general—when she was young. As a small girl in the late 1940s in Detroit Lakes, Minnesota, she saw Native Americans only on Sundays when her family walked past the Becker County Jail on their way to church:

> the jail would be littered with Indian men, hanging from the windows in all kinds of weather, dangling things out, and their women and their children would be outside wailing with their meagre possessions. And they'd be passing things back and forth through the window—liquor or food or candy or whatever. And that was one of my earliest recollections: these Indian men hanging out of the jails, and the women outside. People didn't want to drive by there. My mother would make comments about "Oh, they're doing it again, they're hanging out the windows." And my father would make comments about "Indians and liquor do not match."[11]

When asked if anyone discussed how the Native Americans got in that situation, she said, "No, it was all blaming, their own fault. Oh, yes, and if they didn't live like that, they wouldn't have such a life of misery. And if they'd stop drinking, and if the women wouldn't hand them liquor through the bars. It was taught to me as being disgusting and demeaning." As we shall see, only gradually—through *shared* neighborhoods, social needs, outreach by Native Americans, and the positive responses of historically Norwegian religious and social service institutions—did segments of the groups reapproach each other.[12]

Krista Johnson's experience provides a closer look at how individuals could acquire bigoted views toward other population groups, and how these attitudes, learned from their rural midwestern experience, could migrate with them when they joined the ongoing urbanization into the Twin Cities. Patterns of acculturation continued in an urban setting from the 1890s to 1930s, as Norwegian Americans in Minneapolis found their place beside small but growing groups of southeastern Europeans there. Significant parts of these contingents belonged to Jewish or Slavic Catholic cultural groups, who settled in the near north and northeast of Minneapolis or in St. Paul's lower east side and near west. Most Norwegian Americans lived to the north and east of the growing Jewish community in north Minneapolis, but the two communities lived in close contact around and north of Plymouth Avenue and in the public schools.

In northeast Minneapolis the older Norwegian settlements close to the Mississippi River lumbering district and the Norwegian and Swedish Lutheran churches in the central part of that section of the city became surrounded by the homes and institutions of Catholic immigrant communities from, for example, Greece, Italy, and Poland. Patterns of group concentration and segregation limited interaction between Norwegian Americans and these new groups. But the student bodies of the main high school from different sections of town revealed the background of the largest groups, and the sometimes hostile rivalries that developed between the schools' students, according to most interview subjects, had ethnic, religious, and racial dimensions that gave vent to attitudes acquired at home. At the same time, some students formed lasting friendships across these ethnic and religious divides.

In St. Paul the influx of Catholic groups was even larger, and its multiethnic character permeated residential patterns more than in Minneapolis. The capital city's lower east side became predominantly populated by southern and eastern European newcomers. In interviews, some longer-settled Norwegians claimed that the streets and schools became rougher because of tensions among group cultures between 1910 and 1930. Members of the Scandinavian American communities that could relocated near the city's edge or in suburbs.[13]

Meanwhile the marginally small Black community in each city continued to expand, moving into new areas as Jews and others moved to more attractive neighborhoods. In Minneapolis, for example, the result was that the city's largest Jewish and African American sections of town lay beside each other along an east-west axis near Plymouth Avenue and the Olson Memorial Highway, while Scandinavian, German, and Finnish American neighborhoods lay in stretches from a few to many blocks farther north in the city's north side. During both world wars, but especially the second, Blacks migrated to the Cities, some in response to labor recruiters. Nevertheless, the Twin Cities' Black community remained very small compared to those in other northern industrial cities until fifteen to twenty years after World War II, when it grew rapidly. Race riots occurred in both cities in the mid-1960s. Self-segregation and discriminatory restrictive housing contracts (real estate documents with clauses prohibiting renting or sales to non-whites) had kept the Norwegian and African American communities at some distance throughout their history in Minneapolis–St. Paul.[14]

Between 1945 and 1975, institutionalized segregation gave way to first local and then national civil rights legislation. The initial result was greatly increased school integration, so that the young in each community more often met at school, if not so commonly in their free time. Then, the response of leaders in both groups to the race riots of the 1960s brought political negotiation with the city government and attempts to improve relations through civic, religious, and educational institutions. Finally, as discriminatory housing contracts were abandoned, the movement of Blacks into formerly all-white districts of town occurred with greater frequency—which increased tension in parts of the two communities as housing values changed and the attractiveness of public spaces declined.

Near the end of World War II, a small number of Japanese Americans, relocated from federal internment camps, broadened the Cities' tiny Asian American (mostly Chinese American) enclave. In the mid-1970s the Twin Cities witnessed the beginning of the transformation of their Asian communities through the resettlement of large numbers of Vietnamese, Hmong, and Cambodians in areas previously home to African Americans or, before their arrival, Germans or Scandinavians. Lutheran churches operated a range of social services to assist Asian immigrants in their accommodation to local life, but most Americans had very limited direct contact (sometimes as urban landlords or social workers) with the Cities' new populations.[15]

Encouraged by the federal Bureau of Indian Affairs, thousands of Native Americans left desperate conditions on reservations across the country, including in the Upper Midwest, to find industrial work in the nation's metropolitan areas, including Minneapolis–St. Paul. Like other newcomers from minority groups, most of them selected homes in districts that historically housed Scandinavian immigrants and their community institutions.

A Transformed Ethnic Community

At the end of World War II, Scandinavian American servicepeople returned to ethnic communities that were largely relocated from concentrated ethnic neighborhoods in central areas of the Twin Cities to more dispersed locations in better parts of town nearer the city limits or in the first ring of suburbs. This second-stage migration in the metropolitan area increased rapidly from the early 1900s through the 1920s, stalled temporarily for many in the 1930s, and accelerated again from the later 1940s through the 1970s. From the north-side warehouse district to Bridge Square and south to Cedar-Riverside and beyond, parts of the downtown core and adjacent districts became run-down commercial-industrial areas. The real estate values in residential streets near these areas fell greatly. Anyone who could tried to move away. After passage of the Servicemen's Readjustment Act (the GI Bill) in 1944, millions of veterans became a huge bloc among those who could acquire the resources to leave. They not only received aid for higher education but also low-cost loans for housing—which frequently provided the opportunity to move from the inner city or to leave the city entirely.

The exodus to the suburbs gained force in the mid- to late 1960s because major highway projects for Interstates 94 and 35 sliced through downtown neighborhoods, making large areas of adjacent housing unattractive and obliterating landmarks of community history. One of these was the "cathedral" of the Norwegian Lutheran Free Church in Cedar-Riverside, the Trinity congregation building that since the 1870s had held so many memories for Augsburg Seminary and later Augsburg College faculty and students. If the damage caused by the interstate highways hastened the decline already well underway in the traditional Scandinavian neighborhoods, the new transportation systems also facilitated commuting in and out to jobs and historical ethnic institutions.[16]

On Minneapolis's north side, second-stage migration meant that more Norwegian Americans relocated to housing spread across the city's middle or far north toward the city limits. Some of this outward movement can be characterized as "white flight." Here, as elsewhere in the metropolitan area (and nation), for the most part the older generation or the less prosperous remained behind in the first settlement areas and older neighborhoods. In the northeast section of the city, a dispersed Norwegian and Swedish American community meant living in working-class neighborhoods farther north and relatively distant from downtown with a mixture of southern and eastern European nationalities or in more largely Anglo-Scandinavian communities in middle- or lower-middle-class parts of St. Anthony. South of downtown Minneapolis, Norwegian American residential patterns spread from the far eastern edge of the city to its western boundary. Working-class and lower-middle-class Scandinavian Americans congregated farther and farther below Lake Street in the extensive subdivisions of modest housing between Lake Nokomis and the blocks just inland from the Mississippi River. The southeasterly diagonals of Minnehaha and Hiawatha Avenues became lined with Scandinavian shops at intersections to the residential side streets where many Norwegian and Swedish Americans lived. On the city's far southwestern side, more affluent Scandinavian Americans lived in homes lining or near the Chain of Lakes. Minneapolis's older suburbs—Bloomington, Richfield, Edina, St. Louis Park, Golden Valley, Robbinsdale, and Columbia Heights—became home to growing numbers of Scandinavian Americans from the 1920s onward but especially to the younger generation of families founded after the war.

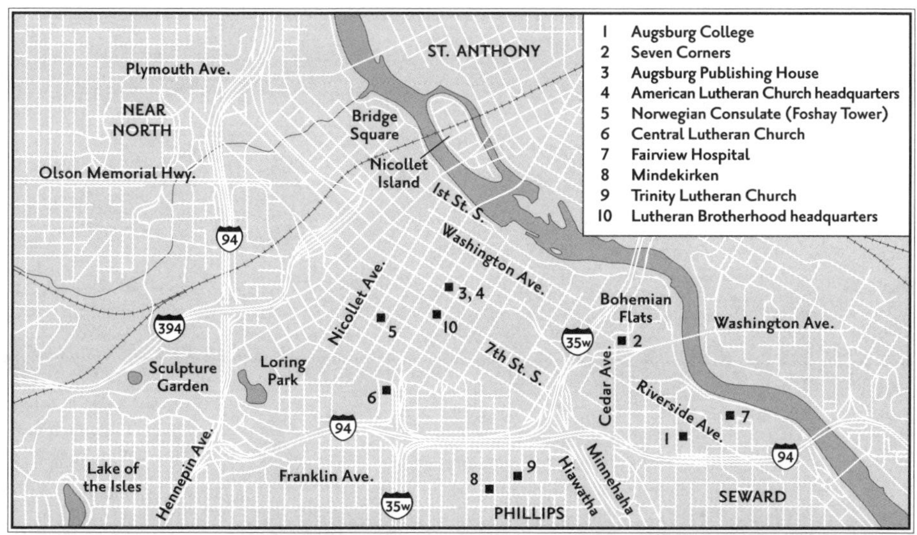

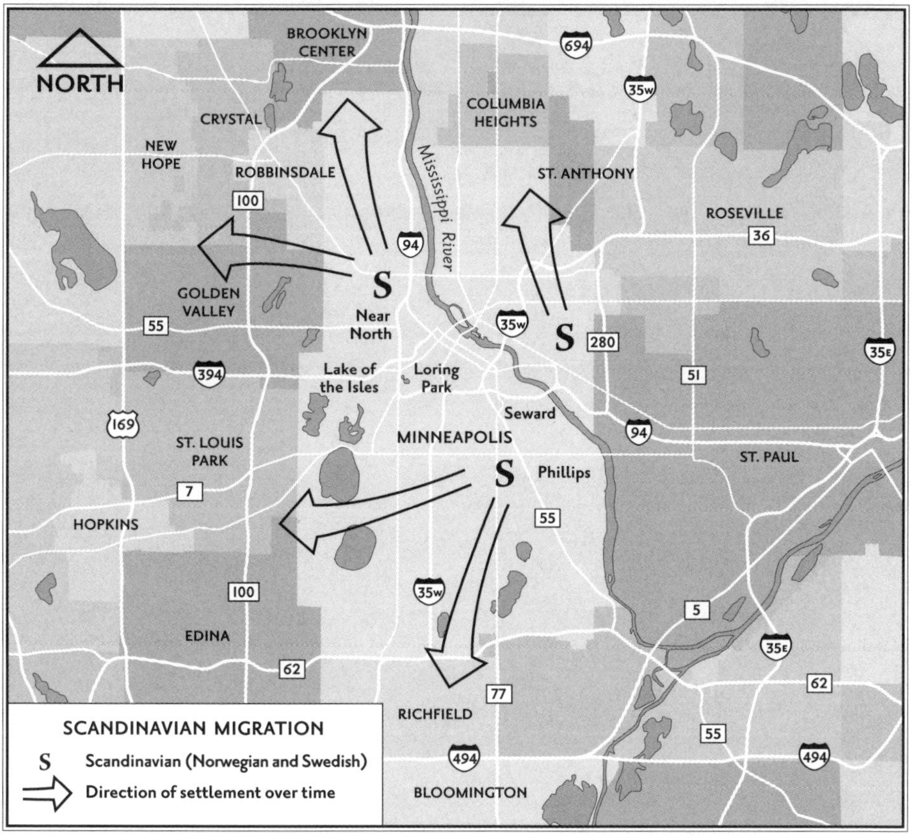

Norwegian American Community and Migration in Minneapolis, 1955–2020. *Matt Kania, Map Hero*

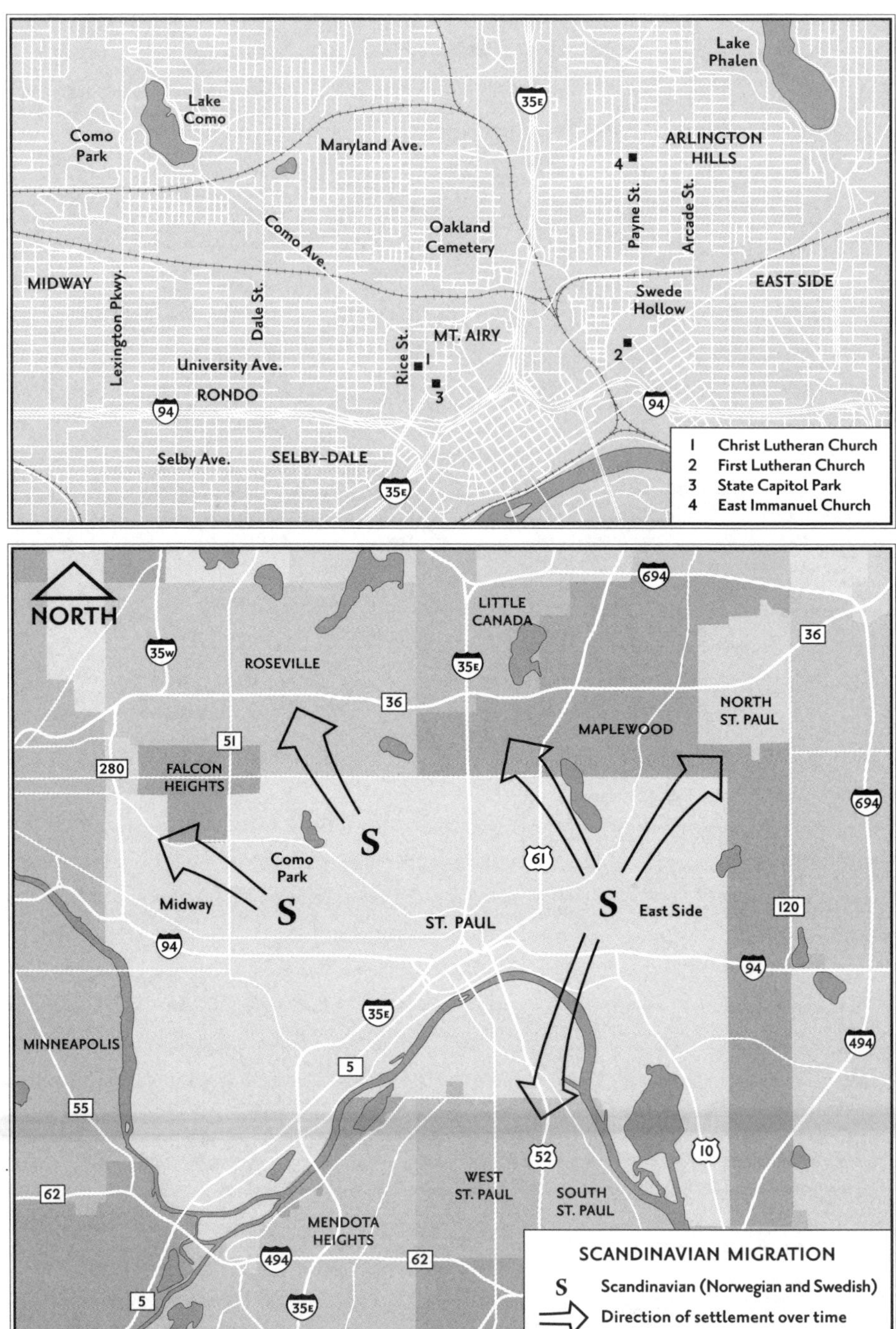

Norwegian American Community and Migration in St. Paul, 1955–2020. *Matt Kania, Map Hero*

In St. Paul, the process of migration to the outer parts of the expanding city and the nearest suburbs was parallel. The capital's Scandinavian Americans became an urban and suburban diaspora across the Como Park and Midway sections of western St. Paul as well as the northernmost reaches of Lake Phalen and Arlington Hills areas to the east. They also joined the suburban movement into the suburbs of Falcon Heights, Roseville, North St. Paul, Maplewood, and South St. Paul. As early as the 1880s, portions of the educated Norwegian American elite kept summer residences in rural districts west of Minneapolis in exurbia on Lake Minnetonka, and toward the 1970s, more and more middle-class Norwegian Americans moved into second-ring suburbs such as Plymouth, Brooklyn Park, Arden Hills, White Bear Lake, Eagan, Apple Valley, and Burnsville.[17]

In many of the newer sections of the Cities and their suburbs, Scandinavian Americans in these decades lived with diverse, Americanized populations, where their ethnicity became transformed by their second- and third-stage journey into what sociologists have called "voluntary" or "symbolic" ethnicity. The term denotes a dimension of themselves that they could choose to don on some public occasions like a style of clothing but otherwise keep as a matter of private family tradition. For voluntary ethnic communities, no longer did a foreign language or accent, "outlandish" dress, recognizable niches in the job market, cultural patterns perceived as exotic by the American mainstream, or residence in immigrant neighborhoods readily identify their members. They could freely decide how ethnically recognizable they wished to be and when, and if they were active in the Norsemen's Federation or the Sons of Norway, that involved no social cost.

In a few areas of the Twin Cities, however, Swedish and Norwegian Americans, now mostly of the third or later generations, resided so closely to each other that into the postwar period their culture—holidays, foods, even history and language—played salient roles in the public schools, community religious life, and voting patterns. This was true, for example, in the more northerly parts of St. Paul's east side and the southeasterly section of Minneapolis's Lake Nokomis–Hiawatha neighborhood. Retired minister and Lutheran author Reverend Hoover Grimsby remembered how every four or five square block area of this section of Minneapolis was so thickly populated with churchgoing

Norwegian Americans during this time that it resembled an ethnic Lutheran parish, each with its own Norwegian American church. Grimsby and others asserted that this part of the city also provided a reliable core of voters for Scandinavian American candidates.[18]

In practice, in the Twin Cities there existed a sliding scale of ethnic involvement and identification rather than the two polar alternatives of disinterest or active participation. A few examples illustrate the complexity of the situation. Eunice Baker recalled a vibrant east-side St. Paul community with a full set of ethnic stores as well as Scandinavian seasonal and religious festivals among Swedes and Norwegians between the 1940s and 1960s. Some Norwegian Americans she knew involved themselves with these phenomena more or less than others. Religious and civic ethnic identification meant much to Eunice in her upbringing and adult life. She remembered with keen nostalgia a Scandinavian quarter that was largely gone by 2000. Those who prospered sufficiently from 1945 to 1975 usually moved to residential side streets further up Payne Avenue and Arcade Street, Baker noted. Jim Stolpestad confirmed this tendency in 2012 as he told the story of his own family. When his father, a medical doctor with offices above a store on lower Payne Avenue, could afford it, he moved his family to a comfortable residence near the higher end of the avenue.

South Minneapolis resident Marilyn Sorensen fondly remembered growing up with lots of Swedish and Norwegian families in a neighborhood around Forty-Fourth Street East and Forty-Fifth Avenue South in the vicinity of Hiawatha Avenue, where the family owned and operated a bakery. The area's elementary schools, Marilyn said, honored both Swedish and Norwegian traditions. When she went to a south-side secondary school, she could choose to study Swedish or Norwegian and join a club connected to either language elective. The Norwegian club was open to pupils of her national background, and its activities included speaking and essay contests judged by community authorities, such as longtime Norwegian-language newspaper editor Carl G. O. Hansen.

Tom Thompson also grew up in south Minneapolis, but unlike Marilyn, he did not think pan-Scandinavian ethnicity played a significant role in how he viewed himself or his development. He became an interview subject but warned his ethnicity meant little to him. In the course of the interview, however, he recalled that as a boy, for more than a year, he voluntarily went to Norwegian language lessons sponsored by the Sons of Norway on Saturdays. As a college student, he attended the International Summer School at the University of Oslo. Further, he married a Norwegian American in a historically Norwegian American church. When confronted with the likelihood that these choices might suggest that in Minneapolis his ethnic heritage had played a formative role in his life, he remarked in irritation, "This is aggravating. It suggests more significance than I have given these circumstances. I just don't think about it. Does a fish think about the water?" The last comment capped the interview because it so succinctly expressed the pervasiveness, the apparent everyday naturalness of the influence of a Norwegian heritage in some parts of Minneapolis—even when one persuaded oneself that this was not the case.[19]

An Interlocutor within and between Demographic Groups

A long-established part of the municipal leadership elites and electorate, Norwegian Americans played critical roles in relations among the urban area's diverse communities in the postwar decades. When much of the Norwegian American population moved away from the areas of their earlier concentration, the buildings their organizational efforts had financed remained behind. Most of these institutions were churches, but monuments to the group's ethnic past as late as 1955 also included Normanna and *Enigheden* (the Agreement) IOGT temperance halls; the Norwegian Lutheran Deaconess, Fairview, and St. Paul Hospitals; and the *Lyngblomsten* (Heather Blossom) and Ebenezer homes for the aged. Augsburg Publishing House as well as Augsburg College and Seminary never relinquished their location in central Minneapolis.

Nearby on Cedar Avenue stood Dania Hall, the most notable monument to the community role the city's Danish immigrants played for themselves and their Scandinavian neighbors. The headquarters of the Sons of Norway (and several of its oldest lodges) and Lutheran Brotherhood insurance companies, as well as the home offices and lodges of the Daughters of Norway, also remained in or close to downtown. Not far away was the elegant American Swedish Institute, a mansion donated by Swedish immigrant newspaper owner-editor Swan Johan Turnblad to house the city's Swedish American activities and history.

For many decades Norway's consul general for the Upper Midwest kept offices in St. Paul, but after the war, the Norwegian government placed them in Minneapolis in the Foshay Tower, where they offered a stable presence for the rest of the century.[20]

The home offices of the American Lutheran Church and its Lutheran Social Service were also in central Minneapolis, even though its theological school, Luther Seminary, was in St. Paul. Loring Park in downtown Minneapolis featured the statue of Norwegian violinist and Seventeenth of May celebration promoter Ole Bull. St. Paul's Como Park displayed a bust of Henrik Ibsen, and the state capitol grounds displayed heroic oversized statues of the legendary Viking discoverer Leif Erikson and the breakthrough Norwegian American politician Knute Nelson. The original Scandinavian quarters of both cities housed a large number of Swedish, Norwegian, Danish Norwegian, and Danish churches, most but not all of them representing strands of Nordic Lutheranism.

The above outlines but a part of the densely woven Scandinavian American cultural canvas against which the Norwegian American religious officials joined in and partially led negotiations to meet challenges in intergroup relations during the postwar years. The first of these was to achieve ecclesiastical union among ethnic branches of American Lutheranism in the American Lutheran Church (ALC). The Norwegian Lutheran Church in America, renamed the Evangelical Lutheran Church in 1946, resulted from two earlier mergers among different wings of Norwegian immigrant Lutheran bodies. In 1960, these merged with one Danish and several German American Lutheran synods, which were spread geographically from New York State to Texas and the Upper Midwest (the "old" ALC). Just two years later, the process of merging brought Swedish, Finnish, Danish, and Scandinavian Lutheran bodies into the ALC. Through all these unifying changes, Norwegian American clergy played major interlocutory roles, and the combined ALC headquarters and church publishing company remained in Minneapolis, where an essential part of its leadership consisted of Norwegian Americans.[21]

Most of the individual churches in the Twin Cities stood where they originally were erected: in Minneapolis, near downtown in Cedar-Riverside or the Seward and Phillips neighborhoods or in the city's near north or northeast; in St. Paul, the historical buildings were to be found mostly on the east side near East Seventh Street and lower Payne Avenue, but some historical congregational edifices were also located on the capital city's near west side. Between 1945 and 1975, downtown congregations and other ethnic institutions deliberated, sometimes repeatedly, whether to sell their buildings and relocate. As noted, Augsburg Seminary, College, and Publishing decided to stay where they were. In general, churches considered whether to move nearer their younger membership in secondary settlement areas or to redefine their mission to become inner-city congregations that ministered chiefly or at least more than previously to the population surrounding them.

Among others, Central, Trinity, the Norwegian Lutheran Memorial Church (Mindekirken), and Our Saviour's Lutheran in Minneapolis and First, Christ, Immanuel, and East Immanuel Lutheran in St. Paul chose to develop extensive programs for serving the people nearest them—embracing their neighbors while maintaining as much as possible their historical ethnic character. The Memorial Church, for example, kept its tradition of services in Norwegian. In many cases, these churches represented the oldest congregation of different branches of Norwegian American Lutheranism in Minneapolis or St. Paul. Their migrating members had usually received aid from the "mother" church and its larger Lutheran body to establish daughter congregations farther out from the center of town and then in the suburbs. The generations in families and generations in congregations kept the bonds between older and newer churches strong for some members.[22]

Civic-minded young couples who were brought up in such downtown congregations frequently chose to move away to have a family and attend church in "healthier surroundings" until the children were grown. Then some—members of what might be called the group's liberal, activist core—returned to active membership in the mother congregation, commuting so that they could become personally involved in the history and community programs of inner-city churches again. In addition, Norwegian Americans from the entire Upper Midwest and nation returned to these historical buildings or institutional headquarters on the occasion of regional or national conventions. Thousands of Norwegian American Lutheran Free Church youth and hundreds of the denomination's pastors spent the years of their undergraduate (or perhaps seminary) studies at Augsburg in Cedar-Riverside. The segment of the Cities' Norwegian Americans that maintained contact with the central-city institutions also contained most of the ancestry group's liberals regarding social issues and outreach to the less privileged in the central districts of the metropolitan area.[23]

Displaced Persons and Norwegian Americans

Norwegian Americans who were active members in such historical institutions tried to establish amiable, mutually helpful relations with new population groups that greatly altered their historical first settlement areas. The first of these groups, Displaced Persons (DPs), refugees who escaped their homelands when they fell under the control of the Soviet Union after World War II, included Poles, Ukrainians, Latvians, and smaller numbers of Estonians and Lithuanians. During the war, many local Norwegian Americans were deeply involved in helping their home nation. Many in the ethnic group contributed to homeland resistance to the Nazi occupation and supplied whatever material assistance they could to people in Norway. Immediately after the war, three Minneapolis daily newspapers sent Norwegian American journalists to report on conditions there, and one of these, Brenda Ueland, helped hundreds of Norwegian Americans reestablish contacts with family and friends. But at war's end, Norwegians who wished to could return home; they did not become displaced persons.[24]

The Minnesota refugee agency and religious organizations such as the National Catholic Welfare Council and the National Lutheran Council sponsored the resettlement and integration of DPs across Minnesota and in the Twin Cities, where the majority who came to the state wanted to live. Their numbers locally were small, a few dozens or hundreds of each background in each city. While they mostly did not reside near the Cities' central business districts, many received the "assurances" of aid that the federal government required from downtown congregations and administrators at the headquarters of the (Norwegian American) Evangelical Lutheran Church in Minneapolis. The Lutheran Resettlement Service, established by the denomination's national council, recruited area committees who in their turn found congregations and individuals to sponsor Lutheran DPs. The state and Minneapolis–St. Paul helped more DPs than the government-interdenominational religious cooperation set as a goal for these geographical units. In the process, the Cities' synagogues and Protestant and Catholic churches learned more about each other, and their interest in ecumenical efforts grew.[25]

Members of historically Norwegian Lutheran congregations in both cities recalled that their churches and individual families within them "adopted" DP Baltic families, providing housing, employment, and whatever was needed, frequently for two years or more, until the newcomers were securely settled. Over the course of a few years, Lutherans of the Baltic nationalities congregated on the south-central section of Minneapolis and St. Paul's east side, strengthening their already predominantly Lutheran character. Less than half as many DPs settled in St. Paul as in its sister city. Most eastern Slavs, such as Poles and Ukrainians, built communities in the northeast section of Minneapolis. By all accounts, cooperation among federal and state authorities and private ethno-religious institutions in resettling these northeastern European refugees functioned well to integrate them into the Cities. Norwegian American Lutheran clergy and church members, judging from comments in interviews, discovered that their sponsorship of DPs brought a deep personal involvement that broadened their outreach to other nationality groups and their experience with their own faith's and other faiths' cultural variants. Eugene Fevold, a church historian at Luther Seminary, asserted, "Outreach took on a whole new meaning in these years. We stopped any pretense to limiting our activity to Lutherans or Scandinavians." The Reverend Keith Olstad, at the time responsible for congregational outreach at Our Saviour's in downtown Minneapolis, echoed Fevold's views. Ione Kadden said about her St. Paul church's "adoption" of families from the Baltics, "They became our relatives and we shared what we had and cared for each other. Now we're all in one family as long as we live." Long-term individual and family ties between Norwegian and Baltic Americans who resettled in the Twin Cities through the DP effort, according to lay people and clergy involved, altered both groups' outlook on themselves and the larger idea of helping and relating to DPs and, by the 1970s, southeast Asian refugee newcomers to the community.[26]

Blacks and the Scandinavian American Establishment

Black Americans, whose communities grew much larger after World War II, in many cases settled in or near the historical first settlement areas of Scandinavian immigrants. In the Twin Cities as elsewhere in the nation, restrictive housing covenants had created ghettoes with dilapidated housing and a wide range of urban problems. In Minneapolis, these Black sections of town existed in the near north around Plymouth Avenue and the beginning of the Olson Memorial Highway and in the near south from Seven Corners in Cedar-Riverside to the Seward and Phillips neighborhoods to its south. Middle-class Blacks lived farther south or in the better-maintained vestiges of the Homewood community on the north side. In St. Paul, Blacks were concentrated in areas more distant from traditional Scandinavian American sections of town. The principal Black ghettoes were in a tenement district not far from the state capitol, on the river flats, and on the east and west sides of Dale Street near University Avenue in Rondo, the best-known Black community in the city. The Black population of the Twin Cities more than quadrupled in the 1950s and 1960s; its least-skilled workers concentrated in the near north and south sections of Minneapolis and the Selby-Dale section in St. Paul.[27]

The African American community in Minneapolis grew to nearly twice the size of its counterpart in the state capital by the 1970 census (19,005 to 10,930), by which time Minneapolis's Black enclave had also become the leading of the two Black communities, according to local African American historian David Taylor. Noting how the city's National Association for the Advancement of Colored People (NAACP) and Urban League chapters functioned as the most important mediators with city authorities and politicians on municipal and state levels, Taylor praises the civil rights legislation, including fair housing and employment laws, passed due to this biracial cooperative effort. He asserts, however, that these organizations' efforts and their cooperation with liberal whites to enact local ordinances between the 1940s and 1960s mostly benefited middle-class Blacks in the Cities. The Black community's much larger—and rapidly growing—working class remained poorer, less educated, younger, and more often unemployed. It also had more repeat juvenile offenders, and more often lived in lower-standard housing than was average for residents of the Twin Cities throughout the period. Unfortunately, as urban renewal projects got underway in some parts of the north-side ghetto, their displacement of local residents increased the population density in neighboring districts and contributed to dissatisfaction with housing conditions.

Since 1946, Minneapolis's political elites had striven to repair the damage done to the city's reputation for protecting civil rights by Carey McWilliams's essay that declared it the capital of antisemitism in America. The Democratic (DFL) municipal administration, led by Mayor Hubert Humphrey, conducted a survey of participation in the city's civic life by minorities—Jews, Blacks, Japanese Americans—published the discouraging results, and set a municipal Commission on Civil Rights in action to attempt to rectify the situation. Humphrey also made the city more visible as a delegate to the Democratic Party's national convention by convincing the party to write a civil rights plank into its 1948 platform. The mayors following Humphrey (1945–48)—Democrat Eric G. Hoyer (1948–57), Republican Paul Kenneth Peterson (1957–61), and Democrat Arthur Naftalin (1961–69)—continued efforts, with limited success, with established African American organizations to improve conditions in low-income, inner-city Black areas in the near north and near south.[28]

Norwegian American and Scandinavian political figures played important roles in the liberal response to changing the city's civil rights record. The Norwegian and Swedish American ancestry groups stepped forward, as elected officials, party leaders, and voters, to develop responses to African American grievances in the Twin Cities. The mayors listed above were typical of the Scandinavian American liberal political establishment in Minneapolis. Humphrey, whose mother was a Norwegian American; first-generation Swedish American Hoyer, who spoke with a pronounced accent; and Norwegian American Peterson made the most of their ethnic background politically and received strong support from the demographic weight of Scandinavian American voters in Minneapolis. Naftalin, a Jew who later became a professor of political science at the University of Minnesota's downtown Minneapolis campus, was known locally as one of Humphrey's protégés. At Augsburg College, Carl Chrislock assumed leadership of the history program in 1963, integrating his scholarship in midwestern progressivism and liberal principles into his teaching, inspiring a generation of students, among them several prominent Norwegian American Democratic politicians, including Larry Sabo and Jim Peterson, to say, as noted earlier, that at Augsburg one studied not just history but Chrislock's progressive views and political activism. Ethnicity did play a role in the local complexion of politics and helped members of the Cities' largest ancestry groups get elected, judging by the number of Scandinavian Americans put in office in these years.[29]

Humphrey set the course for later municipal administrations through his Self-Survey of Human Relations in Minneapolis in 1946. In the late 1930s, Humphrey finished his bachelor's studies in political science at the University of Minnesota and then spent a year in Baton Rouge, Louisiana, completing a master's degree in the same subject. A year in the Deep South awakened him to the effects of inequality and segregation. That experience convinced him that it was essential to address civil rights and race relations on the local level on his return to Minneapolis. According to the report of a team of researchers who studied labor relations in the city in the mid-1940s, its Jewish and African American minorities met systematic discrimination and segregation in employment and housing. As part of the federal government's relocation program for interned Japanese Americans, moreover, an estimated 1,000 to 1,500 resided in the city by the war's end. Despite efforts to help them settle in and find work, the report noted that fewer apprenticeships and job opportunities opened for them than for the resident white population.[30]

Minneapolis's demographic profile at the war's conclusion revealed an overwhelmingly white, Christian population. The city contained fifteen different European nationality groups, but Swedish and Norwegian Americans were by far the largest of these. As John Hope II wrote emphatically in his report for the study, "so widespread is the Swedish and Norwegian strain and so influential the citizens having these ancestral backgrounds that in Minneapolis these groups are of the dominant group rather than the minority." Hope reported his primary findings about intergroup relations and Scandinavian American dominance in 1946 as follows: "One is told with parallel derision and futility by Negro, Indian, and Slav that 'The Swedes run this town.' Yet some

Swedes and Norwegians still feel the burden of their accent in some circumstances."[31]

Of the approximately 600,000 residents of Minneapolis at war's end, about 4 percent were Jewish. That was four times as large a population as that of the largest racial minority, African Americans. Less than 2 percent of the population were non-whites, a small segment of the population that included 304 Chinese, 147 Filipinos, and 145 Native Americans. The report aimed to analyze the degree of employment opportunity available for Jewish, Black, and Japanese American minorities in the city during the prewar, wartime, and first postwar years. Its primary finding was that all three of these groups had traditionally suffered from significant employment discrimination, African Americans most, followed by Japanese Americans and then Jews, whose entry to some unions and most professional associations was denied. Because of the wartime demand for labor, all three groups found a wider range of better-paid work available, but with the return of peace, signs of reversion to traditional employment patterns appeared. The report's purpose was to document the under-utilization of the labor potential of these groups and the damage that did to the community as a whole.

Humphrey chose to become politically active during the war, running for mayor unsuccessfully in 1943 and again in 1945, when the voters put him in office. Only days after taking the oath of office, he met with the mayor of Chicago to discover how that city had managed to pass and implement a fair employment ordinance. Immediately on his return, he proposed an even tougher law to the city council of Minneapolis. The majority of council members opposed him, however, and referred the bill to a subcommittee that voted it down. In response, Humphrey marshaled support through a large committee of prominent citizens, including leading Scandinavian American clerics, which publicized the mayor's effort and lobbied for it. Then he organized a smaller Committee on Human Relations under the leadership of the Swedish American minister at Mount Olivet Lutheran Church, Reuben K. Youngdahl, whose brother Luther Youngdahl became Minnesota's governor in 1946.

Throughout that year, the mayor's committee carried out the Self-Survey on Human Relations. A team of sociologists from Fisk University organized the survey. The team set up ten committees of community leaders to organize and manage collecting and systematizing data. The membership of each committee included an academic expert as well as leaders from the full range of ethnic and religious segments of the population. Bradshaw Mintener, vice president and general counsel for Pillsbury Mills, led the overall sponsoring committee. Professor Theodore Blegen, the Norwegian American historian who was then dean of the graduate school of the University of Minnesota, served as one of the vice chairs, as did, for example, the German American Elizabeth Bradley Heffelfinger and the Swedish American Gottdfrid Linsten. Bernhard Christensen, president of Augsburg College, succeeded Youngdahl as general chair of the survey project.

Ethnic and religious backgrounds among the leadership and those interviewed, though evident, remained assumed rather than explicit. The committees used a small army of volunteers to persuade businesses, unions, religious bodies, educational institutions, civic organizations, welfare services, law enforcement officials, real estate concerns, public health and hospital services, and recreational organizations to evaluate whether they included minorities and to document how many and in what capacity on forms provided by and returned to survey leaders. Given the structure of the survey, the entire range of Norwegian American institutions became involved in collecting information and documenting it.

As the survey work went on, the publicist and lawyer Carey McWilliams visited the Twin Cities. Afterward, he published an article in *Common Ground* asserting that Minneapolis was the nation's most antisemitic city and contrasted its prejudice with the religious tolerance of St. Paul. Humphrey, Youngdahl, and the various committee heads of the community survey publicized the need to improve rights equality and implement fair housing and labor practices. They recognized, criticized, and attempted to correct the ways that the white majority enjoyed a privileged position and benefited from discrimination against non-white minorities. The mayor's survey prompted local businesses to hire more Jews and African Americans. Before the end of 1946, in response to outrage over a property owner's use of a restrictive housing covenant to exclude a Japanese American veteran from renting an apartment, Humphrey convinced the city council to approve an ordinance forbidding the use of discriminatory housing contracts. In 1947, the city council passed a strong fair employment practices law. Gradually, over the 1950s and early 1960s, the exclusive business clubs of Minneapolis invited a few members from minority groups to attend their social affairs.

Meetings Between Blacks and Nordic Whites in the Racial Disturbances of the 1960s

Against this local context, the Watts ghetto of Los Angeles exploded in riots in the summer of 1965. The Minneapolis city council, much influenced by its liberal members, some of them Scandinavian Americans, quickly moved to strengthen local civil rights efforts to avoid disturbances in its Black neighborhoods. Nonetheless, during the summers of 1965, 1966, and 1967, incendiary conflicts erupted on the near north side along Plymouth Avenue between teenage Blacks, Jewish merchants, city police, and members of the National Guard. In 1965, a brutal arrest in mid-July resulted in rioting among Black youth on the avenue. The National Guard restored order, and Mayor Arthur Naftalin established a commission to study and report on the city's needs to prevent further riots. When rioting broke out in the same area on August 2, 1966, Naftalin with key support from two Scandinavian Americans—city council president Glenn Olson and Governor Karl Rølvaag—worked with Black community leaders to return civic calm to the area.

Mayor Naftalin and this biracial leadership kept the police and guard members in check, making sure they did not use their batons and guns but moved nonviolently in groups of four at every intersection in the riot area to disperse the crowds. The police stopped Blacks casting Molotov cocktails and calmed the many spectators, both white and Black, who reacted to the arson and other violent actions of the smaller number of activist protestors. The same restrained, nonviolent response from the city and state authorities characterized events in all three years. The local political establishment and press openly claimed the response was calmer and more restrained than what occurred in Newark, Philadelphia, and Los Angeles, but did not posit that those distinctive qualities resulted from the Twin Cities' Scandinavian American heritage.[32]

Nonetheless, Scandinavian American and Norwegian American

leaders in particular were prominent among those who negotiated with the Cities' African Americans to restore order and who sought to improve conditions for Blacks. Leaders of the ancestry groups held positions of responsibility locally and represented not only public opinion generally but the views of the electorate that most shared their attitudes and cultural background. In 1966, after the previous night's vandalism and burning, Naftalin and council members met with leaders of north-side Black factions. Later that same day the mayor and Governor Rølvaag answered questions and made statements at a public meeting with north-side residents, where city officials promised to establish a $50,000 fund to improve conditions along Plymouth Avenue. Council president Olson appointed a fact-finding committee, which convinced local businesses to pledge the money in less than a month. Yet from 1966 to 1967, most of the Plymouth Avenue businesses that suffered damage during the first riots, the large majority of them Jewish American, closed or moved away. Norwegian Americans had earlier run a food store, a pharmacy, and a furniture outlet on the avenue but had sold these to other entrepreneurs some years before. The businesses and others nearby in the decade of the riots reported that loss of customers, theft, intimidation, and vandalism not associated with the disturbances made store and inventory insurance expensive or impossible to buy.

The commission report Mayor Naftalin asked for after the 1965 riot, entitled *Decision 1967*, recommended that the city apply for federal funds under President Lyndon Johnson's Great Society programs to add to the local funding pledged, stipulating that the north side would be best served by a Pilot City Program that would offer services directly to local residents. Near-south Black neighborhoods were pointed toward the Model Cities Program, with money earmarked to rehabilitate housing and repair damage to communities caused by highway construction. Minneapolis's Model Cities application met with refusal from the federal Office of Equal Opportunity, but the Pilot City project for the north side received $50,000 in funding on July 1, 1967. A month later race riots broke out in the Cities for a third time. In 1967 the crowd involved in the riot on Plymouth Avenue doubled in size to an estimated seventy-five to one hundred who took part on the first day of disturbances. Naftalin and Black leaders conferred immediately on the scene that night, and the mayor followed their advice to make a measured, calm response. The next night Blacks in the Selby-Dale area of St. Paul joined the unrest. All but one of the thirteen Blacks arrested in 1967 were residents of St. Paul.

The Twin City riots occurred in the context of violent disturbances in many other American cities, and local papers contained reportage and analysis of the causes of those other riots. In 1966 one commentator in the metropolitan-area monthly *Twin Citian* remarked that in contrast to the "abrupt show of force" from other city governments in response to riots, which had brought on more violence, the local authorities' "extremely moderate" response and immediate openness to dialogue had brought "an eventual response in kind." A second commentator in the same issue of the monthly, Native American writer Gerald Vizenor, recounted the state's and city's progressive civil rights legislation as well as the problems faced by the populations on the north side displaced by urban renewal. He characterized the social disorder as the selective violence of a class conflict between specific Jewish merchants and local teenagers. His conclusion was that the "bright response from leaders of the political and economic community" gave promise that Minneapolis might one day become the "model city" Mayor Naftalin said he hoped for when he spoke on the day after the 1966 riots.[33]

A year later, without mentioning the spread of racial turbulence to St. Paul streets, the *Minneapolis Tribune* editorialized that the city's second racial disturbance was the "Riot That Wasn't." The newspaper noted that the "minimal" material damage and personal injury, as well as the lack of police brutality contrasted with what occurred in such cities as Newark and Los Angeles. Compared with the riots that marked other cities in those years, the racial disturbances in the Twin Cities were demonstrably less violent and destructive. Local reportage of the events in Minneapolis suggested that while the elimination of racial inequality and discrimination in the city was necessary, its problems were not nearly as challenging as elsewhere in urban America.[34]

Meanwhile, with the seed money for the Pilot City project in near north, Minneapolis officials negotiated with local residents to specify the community services they lacked and their cost. Repeated applications to the Johnson administration through the rest of the decade brought more than $1.1 million to make needed improvements. Some of those funds helped establish the Pilot City Regional Center, whose programs aided Blacks, Native Americans, the foreign-born, and poor whites—all the groups who lived in the near north. At the same time, however, real-estate values fell over widening areas of the north side and parts of the south side in response to claims that, following the movement of Blacks onto a street or block, there were increases in vandalism, theft, arson, and public disorder. In interviews, former Norwegian American residents reported incidents of racial hostility in schools, libraries, and parks that prompted their movement to other districts of the Cities or suburbs. "They didn't keep up their houses or yards, didn't repair broken windows. The whole street soon looked shabby," said retired high school teacher John Futcher. "After Blacks moved in, the price we could get for our house fell through the floor. Then it wasn't even safe for my wife to walk home anymore. We are not racists, but we didn't like what happened to our neighborhood after they came," he continued. The departure of growing numbers of whites, including Scandinavian Americans, from these areas increased throughout the era.[35]

Relations between Old-Stock Norwegian Americans and Urban Indians

An "old-stock" ethnic group, the descendants of early-arriving immigrants and white Protestants, Norwegian Americans became thoroughly integrated into the mainstream white majority both in the countryside and in the Twin Cities after urbanization. The Native American communities of the Twin Cities, on the other hand, continued to suffer from debilitating stereotypes and institutionalized prejudice after their relocation to the metropolitan area. Pushed by appalling reservation conditions and pulled by the federal relocation program of 1953, the urbanized Native American population grew rapidly in the 1950–70 period—from three to four hundred to eleven to twelve thousand. The Bureau of Indian Affairs, as part of the Department of the Interior, developed a postwar change in Indian policy enacted by the federal government. As a new attempt to relieve conditions on reservations and integrate Native Americans into mainstream American society, BIA agents set up individual and family plans for reservation Natives who were willing to move to a nearby urban area where they could theoretically assimilate by becoming blue-collar industrial workers. The BIA provided financial aid for travel, lodgings in the city, and expenses while it assisted these Natives in finding employment. Adjustment to urban and industrial conditions proved difficult and disheartening for most of the relocated Native Americans. Compared to the Black population, the number of Natives in the Twin Cities remained small, but by the 1970s, their Native American communities had grown to be among the largest in American cities.[36]

Minneapolis's urban Indians, like its Blacks, resided in low-cost housing areas just north or south of downtown. On the north side, urban Indians lived on the northern edges of the old warehouse district and up to Central Avenue, an area that long ago had housed Norwegian immigrants from Selbu in Trøndelag County of mid-Norway. This same area became home to Blacks who moved to the city around 1950. The Seward and Phillips neighborhoods on the south side, once centers of the city's Scandinavian immigrant community, became largely Native and Black sections. The Native American population in St. Paul, much smaller and ethnically very diverse, was also located in low-rent, downtown areas near African American neighborhoods.

Shared experiences in the city weakened allegiance to individual tribal cultures and gave rise to a pan–"urban Indian" sense of community in both cities. Starting in the 1950s, downtown churches, including historically Norwegian American congregations, shared space with Native American groups. Natives added elements of their spirituality to services, held their own services, hosted dance clubs and powwows in church gyms, and organized independent organizations in educational wings. Native American leaders and Norwegian American ministers marched around a local liquor store in Cedar-Riverside until it closed. The clerics and Natives in addition founded a neighborhood patrol to prevent police profiling. Under the leadership of the American Indian Movement (AIM), the Upper Midwest American Indian Center, and the Minnesota Council of Churches—and some funding from the city and state—the Native American community of Minneapolis founded a series of group mutual benefit institutions in the 1960s and 1970s. These included a legal rights center, a church and community center, a housing project, and Native American–controlled "survival" schools to take Native children out of public schools.[37]

The Reverend Paul A. Boe's long-term dealings with Native American leaders in the Twin Cities is a dramatic instance of a relationship of trust that grew up between a Norwegian American minister and Native American activists who local, state, and national authorities were convinced were dangerous radicals. Boe became director of social services for the American Lutheran Church when the Norwegian Lutheran Church, Scandinavian, and German American Lutheran church bodies merged in 1961. Although he resided with his family in St. Louis Park, a suburb west of Minneapolis, he worked at the ALC's downtown headquarters in a neighborhood then dominated by Native Americans. He visited area congregations that were opening their doors to Natives and invited activist Native leaders to his office for discussions. Convinced that the most committed of these leaders—Dennis Banks, Vern Bellecourt, Clyde Bellecourt, and Russell Means—deserved help to establish a national network to fight for urban Indians' rights, in 1968 Boe persuaded the ALC to allocate funds to help launch AIM. During a telephone interview in 2012, Clyde Bellecourt said he founded AIM with his brother, Banks, and Means at a near-north-side bar.[38]

Over several years Boe and these Natives, especially he and Clyde Bellecourt, developed a relationship of trust that deepened as AIM carried out increasingly publicized direct-action protests. Boe told Bellecourt he felt their cause was just and vowed he would "stand with" them but admitted that he found it difficult to see American society as they did. Therefore, when federal marshals surrounded AIM during its occupation of Wounded Knee, South Dakota, in 1973, Bellecourt called Boe and asked him to come as an observer who would personally experience their situation. Boe arrived at the Pine Ridge Reservation the next day, and local Natives sympathetic to AIM ushered him into their besieged camp at Wounded Knee. AIM's occupation of Wounded Knee was to protest against what it called the "trail of broken treaties" left by white governments and the resulting misery of reservation life.[39]

When Boe left the camp, FBI agents detained him, and a federal judge found him in contempt of court when he refused to answer a grand jury's questions about his two five-day stays with the surrounded AIM occupiers of Wounded Knee. With the aid of the ALC and defense lawyers, including the famous defender of dissidents and protestors William M. Kunstler, Boe appealed. An hour before the deadline to

The Reverend Paul Boe (right, with wife Carola), an observer from the American Lutheran Church, with AIM leaders (from left) Dennis Banks, Vernon Bellecourt, and Russell Means. *Image courtesy of Concordia Historical Institute, Department of Archives and History, The Lutheran Church—Missouri Synod, St. Louis, Missouri*

turn himself in for fourteen months in jail, an appeals judge reversed the contempt charge in mid-January 1974. Thus freed, Boe returned to the Twin Cities. As a minister and Lutheran social services director who had counseled the AIM leaders over a long period, he claimed that the privacy of pastoral conferencing prevented him from reporting about his experience in the Native camp. The ALC approved Boe's visit before he left the Twin Cities, and he reported to it and ALC congregations on his return. He found that two-thirds of the responses he received from congregations and individuals to his reports opposed his visit to Wounded Knee and the ALC's financial support of AIM. Only his stand on the privacy of ministerial counseling won near universal support. A minority of members and the ALC president voiced strong support for greater justice for Natives. As part of a previously arranged reorganization of the ALC, Boe devoted the rest of his career to a "special ministry to Indians" that began in St. Louis Park and developed into a nationwide social service sponsored by the church body.

Fred J. Nichol served as the federal district court judge in the trial of Dennis Banks and Russell Means for alleged "conspiracy to commit crimes against the United States" during AIM's occupation of Wounded Knee. The list of specific charges in the government's case included burglary, theft from the Pine Ridge Reservation trading post, presenting a list of demands to federal officials, and impeding FBI agents and federal marshals during a civil disorder. In early 1974, due to the high level of controversy in South Dakota, Judge Nichol moved the case to St. Paul. The federal authorities planned to prosecute Clyde Bellecourt and other AIM leaders after the initial trial.

Conflict surrounding the case quickly mounted in St. Paul. AIM supporters arrived and held rallies highlighting speeches about Native rights by Reverend Boe with sympathetic publics including students at the University of Minnesota. Their conflicts with opponents produced headline articles in Twin Cities media outlets. Reverend Boe's stance on the privacy of pastoral counseling became the subject of local public debate as he spoke out on the Natives' right to justice under treaty and current civil rights law. The drama of the trial continued for eight months, until mid-September 1974, when Judge Nichol dismissed the charges due to illegalities in the prosecution's collection and management of evidence. Meanwhile, Boe began his special ministry to Natives. Norwegian Americans and Native Americans in the Twin Cities were generally self-segregating and held critical views of each other. Still, Lutheran Social Service, its employees (such as Boe), DFL activists, and some historically Norwegian congregations in downtown Minneapolis have developed cordial relations and engaged in mutual assistance with the Native American community.[40]

A Norwegian American Leads the Backlash against Protest

From the mid-1960s, a crescendo of protest actions by minorities against discrimination and students against the Vietnam War rose in the Twin Cities. Near the end of the decade, a backlash against public disorder had political consequences. In 1968, the president of the police federation in Minneapolis, Charles Stenvig, stood as an independent mayoral candidate. Making himself the standard-bearer for mounting popular displeasure in the city over its liberal mayors' handling of public disturbances, Stenvig also appealed to the feeling in the working and middle class that public officials and their academic allies at the university paid too little attention to their needs while showing too much sympathy to the protestors. Stenvig proudly pointed to his third-generation Norwegian roots and membership in an ethnic group known for its respect for law and order. His position in the police department won him a strong following among police officers and support for his critique of Mayor Naftalin's approach to the racial disturbances. Stenvig campaigned on the promise that as mayor he would treat all protestors the same—as criminals if they broke city ordinances. As a self-proclaimed law-and-order candidate, he attacked liberals for their permissive attitudes toward social protest. He asserted that liberal politicians bore the responsibility for increases in crime the city had experienced in recent years. Naftalin had wrongly handcuffed the police during the north Minneapolis riots, Stenvig proclaimed. Negotiations with local Native Americans and students, he declared, would only begin when they no longer danced on desks in offices and instead behaved like civilized people.[41]

One of Stenvig's main arguments as a right-of-center populist was that a few influential members of the local political and educated establishment exerted undue influence and power at the expense of so-called regular citizens. Showing open hostility to schooling, he claimed in an interview that he "hated school." In answer to a reporter's comment that he had received a bachelor's degree from Augsburg College, he remarked, "my mother said one of us kids had to go to college, and I was it. So I got done in three years [and] got [out] of there fast." Much of Stenvig's support in the 1969 election came from people without higher education. During the 1971 campaign, he admitted, "I'm no brain, I don't know everything, but I'll dig and I'll do my best for the city." His populist views and criticisms of previous administrations, coming when law-and-order candidates handily won elections in Philadelphia and Los Angeles, succeeded in Minneapolis in 1969, 1971, and 1975. He consistently won with large majorities, enhanced by solid support in the most heavily Scandinavian working-class sections of the city. These voting patterns may signify that many Norwegian Americans in the city held views like those espoused by a majority of white, working-class Americans in Minneapolis and other big cities in the country.

Conclusion

In 1968, demonstrations took place in African American sections of both cities yet again, but this time the protestors, thousands of them, both Black and white, marched in harmony. They were grieving in nonviolent silence in response to the assassination of the Reverend Martin Luther King Jr. The biracial action built on the efforts of urban civic and religious organizations, among them the city council and churches that included historically Norwegian, Scandinavian, German, and old-stock American as well as African American congregations who had joined in mutual action to improve race relations after 1967. In the months that followed Dr. King's death, private groups, among them the heavily Scandinavian ALC, its division of social services, and Augsburg and St. Olaf Colleges, worked together to put in practice a "crisis colony" of students, clergy, and faculty in the near north of Minneapolis, where they took up residence and received instruction from their neighbors. The primary goal of the crisis colony, notes Augsburg historian Carl Chrislock, was to "provide a 'feeling' knowledge of communities and conditions" that these more privileged groups had known only "intellectually" before. Augsburg also revised its curricula and admissions policies so that "minority history and culture [would] be given more stress."[42]

The racial disorders made more Scandinavian American leaders, as well as a broader population of Norwegian and Swedish Americans, realize in several ways how the situation of less privileged local population groups, such as African Americans and urban Indians, affected their own community. Those in seats of power in the Cities, especially in Minneapolis, where these minority communities were largest, struggled to improve the situation generally and restore peace. As noted earlier, our focus here is not the racial violence and the effects of the riots themselves but rather the representatives of so-called "old" immigrant groups who attempted to deal with minorities' rights and demands. In the Twin Cities the negotiators from local authorities were in many cases Americanized third- or fourth-generation Scandinavian Americans. The local commentators cited in this chapter, none of

ABOVE: A backlash against public protests by minority groups and university students helped elect and reelect conservative Norwegian American Charles Stenvig as mayor of Minneapolis in the early 1970s. Minneapolis Star*, April 30, 1969, courtesy MNHS collections* | BELOW: Following two years with summer race riots, when people in the Cities heard of the assassination of Martin Luther King Jr., Blacks and whites responded by marching together in honor of his memory. *MNHS*

them Scandinavian Americans, proposed that more moderation, less physical force, and immediate and greater willingness to engage in dialogue more quickly brought reconciliation and an end to violence in Minneapolis–St. Paul. They did not say, however, that what made the difference was the predominance of Scandinavian American figures involved in local negotiations and policy making. Perhaps the most that one might assert is that the sheer demographic predominance of Scandinavians and their high degree of active participation in local politics meant that they frequently held decisive positions or influenced others who held positions of responsibility for deciding and carrying out policy locally. Many Scandinavian Americans in Minneapolis–St. Paul during the 1960s became more empathetic and understanding with regard to the situation of non-whites. Other Norwegian and Swedish Americans grew less tolerant of minority protest. Events between 1969 and the mid-1970s, when law-and-order candidate Norwegian American Charles Stenvig was repeatedly elected mayor of Minneapolis, reveal a backlash against public disorder related to causes such as minority civil rights, which considerable numbers of other Scandinavian Americans worked to support.[43]

Further, negotiations on behalf of peaceful relations with African Americans that Norwegian and Scandinavian American leaders helped lead or were deeply engaged in represented but the latest in a series of quite distinct and challenging efforts that opened their ethnic communities to increased contact with other local cultures; in that way, their local journey in America transformed them. Recently relocated in large numbers in the suburbs, "old" ethnic groups (such as Norwegian Americans) rediscovered and "watered" their roots in America at the historical institutions founded by their forebears in central-city districts. In the postwar decades, they learned to maintain historical ethnic institutions in the city center and rededicate those institutions by sharing them with groups that had arrived more recently. They unified different ethnic Lutheran organizations into the ALC, and through a multidenominational religious effort assisted Baltic DPs in resettling in the metropolitan area. All of these efforts occurred as dimensions of larger national processes: suburbanization and white flight from inner-city districts; the implementation of postwar DP legislation through public-private sector cooperation; the self-searching of the Humphrey administration's ambitious civil rights campaign; the upheavals and mixed success of the African American and Native American civil rights movements; and the Stenvig law-and-order administration's reaction to protests. All of these wrenching changes altered individuals' and groups' sense of identity. Participating in these events and historical trends made the ethnicity of Scandinavian and Norwegian Americans in Minneapolis–St. Paul carry new meanings and function in new ways.

When asked in interviews whether the Norwegian American ethnicity of prominent figures played significant roles in the intergroup relations discussed in this chapter, those figures or their families and associates assured the author that ethnic allegiance was only one of a complex of important factors. Socioeconomic class, political party, place of residence, and degree of religious devotion also affected their choices. Perhaps most of all, Norwegian American opinion locally reflected shifts in the national mood during these decades, a sign of the ancestry group's growing degree of integration into American society generally by this point in the twentieth century.[44]

CHAPTER EIGHT

The Norwegian American Ancestry Group in the Metro Area

[1975–2000]

DURING THE LAST TWENTY-FIVE YEARS OF THE TWENTIETH CENTURY, FOUR thematic threads remained central to the ongoing story. Types of migration were still significant. Arrivals from Norway became a trickle of a dozen or so mostly well-educated people who often had family connections in the metropolitan area. Urbanization to Twin Cities suburbs continued, from both the Cities themselves and surrounding rural areas. The influx was less than in the immediate postwar decades but nonetheless made Norwegian Americans the metropolitan area's largest Scandinavian ancestry group by 2000.

The second theme, the development of Minneapolis–St. Paul, also entered a new stage. The Cities grew into a multicounty metropolitan area with several rings of suburbs—where most people in long-established European ancestry groups, such as Norwegian Americans, lived. The third theme, the evolution of community forms within the group, showed new historical developments as well. The community became a diaspora of people across a large area who chose to maintain signs of the common ancestry they shared. The elements of cultural legacy in which the group's activist core took part varied greatly in substance and intensity. Being a part of the ancestry group had become a matter of individual choice and carried no cost in social status.

Finally, these years brought a new phase to the relations between Norwegian Americans and other local population groups. Asian and African immigrants, especially Hmong refugees from Southeast Asia and Somalis escaping conflicts in northeast Africa, made their new homes in historically Scandinavian first settlement areas in the Twin Cities.

Former *Star Tribune* journalist Chuck Haga is a second-generation Norwegian immigrant whose father left the Stavanger area in 1924 for east-central North Dakota, where Chuck grew up. Chuck's migration to the Twin Cities parallels the urbanization that is a major theme in this history of Norwegian American life in Minneapolis–St. Paul. Like many others over the last century and a half, Chuck knew the rural and small-town Upper Midwest before living and working in the Cities. As part of the metropolitan news corps—in particular, as a journalist who for thirteen years wrote about the evolving ethnicities he observed in the Cities—Haga commented about the achievements and attitudes of the local Norwegian and Scandinavian communities by the end of the twentieth century.[1]

According to Haga, through size and long-term residence, these ancestry groups have earned leadership roles. They "run" aspects of urban life. They became the owners of businesses, homes, and ethnic institutions of many kinds. They are a well-accepted part of the whole community. In Haga's view, they are self-aware of the identity they have within the Twin Cities' public as an essential part of what it means to be "Minnesotan." This awareness involves dangers as the journalist assessed the end-of-century situation for Norwegian and Scandinavian Americans.

Some members of these groups developed feelings of "entitlement" to the roles they have. As a large, comfortable, and accepted segment of the population (a "residual established majority," Haga terms it), some in these ancestry groups assume they have a right to be in charge and thus adopt a "smug" attitude. A deeply concerned member of the Norwegian ancestry group himself, Haga concludes his statement with a catalog of the attitudes he asks his "fellow Norwegians" to avoid. He asserts that old-stock ethnic groups must approach signs of change in the community and their position in it not defensively or by "retreating into their ethnicity" but rather with a welcome to other, sometimes vulnerable groups, with an openness that should be possible for people in their secure position. The twenty-five years of Norwegian American life in the Twin Cities considered in this chapter give evidence of continued outreach to other populations, a sense of obligation to serve the general community, and a devotion to maintaining transnational ethnic traditions and celebrating ethnic anniversaries and, in some circles, a degree of retreating into a segregated ethnic fellowship.

Defining the Later-Generation Ancestry Group

To begin, we consider the definition and the multidimensional nature of a post-ethnic phenomenon, the Norwegian American "ancestry group" in the larger urbanized area of Minneapolis–St. Paul. In these twenty-five years, the people who claimed "Norwegian" as their ethnic *background* during personal interviews and at the federal censuses constituted one of the largest and longest-established white population groups in the metropolitan area. This population chose to maintain self-identification as Norwegian American when the large majority in the group were in the third or later generations and in a period when that decision was, as sociologist Herbert Gans has famously said, "voluntary," a nostalgic choice they "indulge mainly in a familial and leisure-time" dimension of their lives. For nearly all of these self-identifiers, nothing in their appearance, occupation, language, or place of residence made their chosen ethnic allegiance self-evident to the public. In Minneapolis–St. Paul, where both of the presidents of central workers' coalition unions were men of Norwegian ancestry at the end of the 1990s, for example, neither these men nor the union membership thought ethnicity played a significant role in the labor movement any longer. Rather, Norwegian Americans' private family memories and customs, maintenance of membership in ethnic organizations and institutions, furnishing of their homes with ethnic objects, private preservation of elements of an ethnic cuisine, and participation in the group's ethnic celebrations together revealed their choice to retain an identity as part of the ancestry group.[2]

The definition of the Norwegian ancestry group in Minneapolis–St. Paul in the first instance is the 303,450 people in the Twin Cities and surrounding counties (what the census called the Twin Cities Standard Metropolitan Statistical Area) who in 1990 identified themselves as primarily or secondarily of Norwegian ancestry or ethnicity. With that number, the Twin Cities metropolitan area contained the highest urban density of Norwegian American ancestry in the United States at the time. In other words, the area retained its preeminent position as the demographic "capital" of the group that it had held throughout the postwar period. In the last decades of the twentieth century, however, most local Norwegian Americans lived in the Cities' several rings of suburbs, rather than within the city limits. Near the end of the twentieth century, a considerable number of later-generation Norwegian Americans commuted to the metropolitan area from surrounding towns and cities—from Rochester and Northfield in the southeast, Mankato in the south, Milan in west-central Minnesota, Plymouth north of Minneapolis, and Eau Claire, Wisconsin, to the east.[3]

The phrase "multidimensional nature" refers to factors that led to separate groupings among Norwegian Americans in these years. Which generation in America a person is represents one significant dimension. Here the first generation signifies the foreign-born who emigrate from Norway to the United States and remain long enough to make accommodations to American society. Their American-born children are the second generation, and so on. From 1975 to 2000, the largest part of the ancestry group was in the third or fourth generation, as it was when Odd S. Lovoll published his epic "portrait" of Norwegian America, *The Promise Fulfilled*, in 1998.[4]

This chapter about Norwegian Americans in the Twin Cities from 1975 to 2000 relies on hundreds of in-depth oral history interviews, analysis of newspapers and census materials, and recent scholarly models for understanding the contemporary experience of "old" ethnic groups. One might assume that the later the generation, the more integrated or assimilated—the less ethnic—these people might perceive themselves as being. This has been the conventional view, especially regarding "old" ethnics in big cities, where contact with other cultural groups is more frequent and supposed to have worn away their "foreign-ness" over the generations. This expectation has proven to be only partially true. The small but continuing immigration after the war, surviving ethnic institutions and customs, royal visits, the presence of other prestigious figures from Norway, the sesquicentennial celebrations of Norwegians' immigration to the United States, the ongoing "roots" and family history phenomenon—all these and other events and processes have repeatedly renewed ethnic awareness for parts of the ancestry group.[5]

A second dimension in the ancestry group developed because of the greatly varying degrees of involvement in activities and concerns that Norwegian Americans perceived as ethnic or part of ethnic maintenance. The people who for various reasons were uninvolved or unconcerned about their ethnic background represented one extreme on a continuum that ran to the ethnic core, defined here as individuals, families, and organized groups that maintained a relatively high level of explicitly ethnic activity. The uninvolved or minimally involved constituted the large majority of Norwegian Americans who very likely did little more than indicate Norwegian ancestry on census forms. As the number of generations between the foreign-born immigrants and the present-day majority increased to the fourth and beyond, the lack of the mother tongue and cultural knowledge generally, combined with intermarriage, shifting religious choice, and accommodation to mainstream American life, made ethnic allegiance tenuous. That the minimally or uninvolved made up such a large group in the last quarter of the twentieth century was evident from historically Norwegian American institutions struggling to stem declining membership and funds and the small size of the core of activists and members who kept ethnic customs and institutions alive. In interviews the largely uninvolved told how specifically Norwegian elements composed only small and occasional dimensions of their personal sense of identity, their Lutheranism, leisure-time activity, occupational life, and social networks. Works by Herbert Gans, Mary Waters, Richard Alba, and other scholars who study "later generation ethnics," LGEs for short, indicate that the changes underlying the trend toward decreasing ethnic involvement among people whose ancestors arrived between the 1870s and 1920s was general rather than limited to one group.[6]

The ethnic core, as delimited here, consisted of two small groups. One was composed mostly of devoted and involved members of the third or fourth generation. Not infrequently, their family involvement in Norwegian American associational life stretched over two or three generations, with roots that went back to ethnic involvement in the rural countryside of the Upper Midwest. Between 1975 and 2000 this part of the core constituted the backbone of such organizations as historically

Norwegian American congregations and the bygdelag (associations based on district cultures in the homeland), the supporting membership of the Norwegian-American Historical Association, the practitioners of ethnic folk arts, and the friends of the national ethnic museum (Vesterheim) in nearby Decorah, Iowa. They composed the core membership of the Norsemen's Federation in the metropolitan area and region and the active participants in lodges for the Sons of Norway, the group's largest fraternal insurance and cultural organization. These people researched family lineage, maintained ethnic celebrations and family customs, and cherished the ethnic pictures, papers, and objects that embodied ethnic tradition. For many in this part of the ancestry group, "ethnic activity" became a leisure-time pursuit during a later phase in life—when the children had grown and left home or during retirement.[7]

The other major segment of the ethnic core consisted of first- and second-generation immigrants—the Norwegian-born who arrived after World War II and their immediate descendants. In the first fifteen years after World War II, only around two thousand Norwegians immigrated to the United States annually. After the 1950s, only a few hundred Norwegians settled in the United States per year, and only some dozens came to the Twin Cities. Between 1975 and 2000, these people were typically highly educated professionals—who frequently moved directly to affluent suburbs—or were their close relatives who joined them later under the family reunification provisions in the federal immigration law of 1965. During interviews, it often surfaced that trans-Atlantic connections to the Twin Cities had eased the immigration of both the professionals and their relatives. These people most often belonged in the ethnic core because they openly identified as Norwegian. They actively participated in new and older ethnic organizations. They frequently viewed themselves as the most authentic Norwegians in the area, contrasting their knowledge of contemporary Norway and their cultural attitudes with those of "veteran" Norwegian Americans, with their old-fashioned picture of the homeland, preference for dated ethnic markers such as lutefisk church suppers, and distaste for modern Norway's social democracy. As discussed in the last chapter, postwar-arriving Norwegian Americans in the Twin Cities founded notable organizations aimed to meet the needs of their own segment of the ethnic group.[8]

Lovoll calls these two groups in the ethnic core "newcomers and old-timers." Key individuals in both parts of the core bound it together, serving in central leadership positions and negotiating a public image favorable to the whole group. Old-timers were most often Sons of Norway, bygdelag, and historic congregation members. Newcomers and notable old-timers mixed at consular affairs for visiting celebrities or royalty from Norway and in meetings of elite clubs. These included the Norwegian-American Chamber of Commerce, Norsemen's Federation chapters in each city and Northfield, and a "cod club" for businessmen and male professionals in each of the cities—*Torskeklubben* (1933) in Minneapolis and *Den Norske Torskeklubben* (1966) in St. Paul. All these social events became sites for finding people to interview for the Twin Cities History Project. Women professionals in the ancestry group formed *Lakselaget*, a mutual support society, in 2002, which like the two men's business-professional clubs meets monthly to eat fish, hear guest speakers, and build contact networks across the metropolitan area and nation. All three of these clubs aim to keep knowledge of and contacts with Norway up to date. The schedule of speakers and scholarship programs of all three function as primary means of maintaining transnational communication and deepening the group's awareness of contemporary issues and events in the ancestral homeland.[9]

Performing Ethnicity

In the last quarter of the twentieth century the Norwegian American ancestry group in some senses had become a postethnic phenomenon. While members engaged in activities bound explicitly to their ancestral heritage in one dimension of their lives, most had passed into the mainstream and become integrated into middle-class American life economically, residentially, and socially. Like other later generation white European American ethnics (LGEs), most of the time they acted out a largely "symbolic ethnicity," as defined by Herbert Gans. In choosing undemanding ways of feeling that they had a distinctive background, for a fringe minority of Norwegian Americans the special ethnic markers in the late twentieth century were distant, mythic stories of an ancient Viking past that made them descendants of the discoverers and earliest European residents of North America. A few of these people resided in the Twin Cities and, for example, continued to argue that the narrative carved in runes on a large stone by Vikings in Minnesota in the 1300s provided material proof of Norwegians' pre-Columbian presence in what later became the heartland of Scandinavian immigrant settlement.[10]

For a much larger number of LGE Norwegian Americans, in the Twin Cities as well as the countryside, some sort of participation in an annual ethnic occasion satisfied the need for a shared, visible heritage to feel and express a voluntary Norwegian American identity. The event might be Norwegian "national day" celebrations on May 17, joining in the Norway Day picnic, or an annual *lutefisk* (cod cured in lye) and *lefse* (Norwegian flatbread) dinner at a historically Norwegian immigrant church. The most involved LGEs might attend and be involved in the planning and work of carrying out several or all of these—as well as other observances. On Syttende mai, core members of the ancestry group could choose from several daylong menus of events, selecting the courses that best suited their skein of interests, contacts, and felt obligations. In the Twin Cities at the end of the century, these activities could begin with an early rising for a festive breakfast with speeches at a hotel or the Norwegian Lutheran Memorial Church. Mindekirken offered religious services and a potluck meal followed by a parade in the Franklin Avenue neighborhood streets. Norwegian Americans of all ages, many in folk costumes, waved flags, marched, and cheered while a local, largely nonwhite audience of curious African and Native Americans looked on. The parade ended in a nearby park, where children of all these groups played together and enjoyed grilled hot dogs and snacks while the adults mixed and conversed. Others met at the statue of Ole Bull in Loring Park in Minneapolis or by the mounted bust of Edvard Grieg in St. Paul's Como Park to hear speeches and choir music. Individual Norwegian American organizations arranged celebratory lunches and evening meals with prominent Norwegian guests and Americans serving as keynote speakers. With concerts and theatrical performances, the marking of Norway's Constitution Day could continue until late in the evening. It was voluntary and in practice varied as greatly as the individuals and families involved.

Attendance at several lutefisk and lefse church dinners and listening to stories about many others made clear that common to them all was a menu featuring the main varieties of cured cod known to attract the largest pool of customers. These dinners showed the Americanization of old-country foodways in the production-line serving of identical picnic plate dinners and the exaggerated emphasis on lutefisk, which did not establish cultural identity *in Norway* in these years. As scholars have noted, this LGE identity was voluntary and rested in whatever generated a person's *feeling* of being ethnic, so it could also be individualistic. Those interviewed included a man who expressed identity by painstakingly making lutefisk in a suburban garage, a couple operating a part-time business in rustic-style furniture from Norway, and a man who installed a Norwegian-style grass turf roof in a southeastern Minneapolis residential district. One businesswoman sold high-quality reproductions of classic Norwegian oil paintings to members of the ancestry group. Several of these people's activities exemplify the commodification of ethnic culture. However, all these individualistic markers of LGE identity shared a large dose of nostalgia combined with varying degrees of Americanization and a sense of satisfaction in expressing what seemed to these individuals an authentic part of the group's cultural heritage. For many in the ethnic core these expressions were, as Gans and others have noted, a source of leisure-time diversion.[11]

Later-generation Norwegian Americans in the ethnic core were rather easy to contact as Lutheran churchgoers and members of the remaining ethnic organizations and institutions in the metropolitan area, but it was not so easy to find the unchurched and ethnically uninvolved. Communication through organizational networks and well-connected people in the know helped a great deal. In such a situation, however, the sample of people interviewed remained unrepresentative. Of course, a larger population could be identified through public records that required little or no effort on the part of the respondent, such as the census and public surveys. These consisted of statistical, quantitative sources and, except for the census's questions about self-perceived ancestry, usually contained information about unnamed members of the first and second generations who in the last decades of the twentieth century composed under 1 percent of the group. For the most part the likely much-larger group of LGEs for whom ethnic background no longer was significant remained outside the Twin Cities History Project study.

Norwegian American Ubiquity

The situation in Minneapolis–St. Paul nonetheless presented an unusual case, which became apparent in that incident at a local barbershop, when the author was faced with the riddle about the difference between an introverted and an extroverted Norwegian. The spectators all knew and enjoyed the joke. The point is that the stereotypical profile of the Norwegian American was public property in the Twin Cities at the end of the twentieth century. The typical Norwegian American was reserved and modest to a fault, a man with hat in hand before those in power. Based on a very dated picture of countrified peasants that lived only in the Cities' urban humor, the joke was about an ancestry group that was so large, well established, and accepted that it could laugh with others about its supposed foibles. Norwegian jokes in the environment of the still heavily Scandinavian Minneapolis–St. Paul metropolitan area posed no threat to a group that held leading positions in the state legislature in St. Paul and in the municipal leadership and cultural life of Minneapolis.[12]

The long-term accumulated presence of so large a Norwegian American ancestry group in the Twin Cities delayed the twilight of the group's ethnicity that Richard Alba and Herbert J. Gans metaphorically call the coming "darkness" among European-origin "old" ethnic groups in other places in the United States. While their ethnicity grew increasingly tenuous and showed many of the characteristics these scholars attribute to LGE groups in general, Norwegian and Scandinavian Americans were still ubiquitous in the Twin Cities. Their public celebrations represented everybody's celebration of ethnicity's role in local society—as St. Patrick's Day and Cinco de Mayo do in St. Paul and in other metropolitan areas.

Nordic Americans filled visible and influential roles in the metropolitan area's political, economic, religious, and cultural life. In politics, not only were Scandinavian Americans prominent among officeholders but popular opinion has asserted that candidates with the "-sen" names common among Scandinavian-origin residents had a better chance of election even if they were otherwise not well known. When the flamboyant Independent Jesse Ventura was elected in 1998, local politicians of Norwegian American background quipped "this was the end of 'lefse politics,'" the demise of dependable Scandinavian American control of state government. After one term in office, however, the Ventura episode soon ended while the Scandinavian influence endured.

Scandinavian-name firms and businesses were many and prominent in the local yellow pages of this period. The headquarters of the Sons of Norway and several lodges in downtown Minneapolis and suburban Sons lodges on all sides of the metropolitan area made that fraternal insurance company and instrument of cultural preservation a notable presence. At that point, the impressive new skyscraper of Lutheran Brotherhood Insurance in Minneapolis's business district presented towering evidence of a firm with Norwegian roots, a pan-Lutheran business success, and a devotion to engaging in social welfare projects.[13]

In religion, the Norwegian and Scandinavian American presence found expression in the Cities' many Lutheran churches, the American Lutheran Church's headquarters in downtown Minneapolis, and Luther Seminary in St. Paul. Lutheran Social Service locally grew largely out of a shared Scandinavian American history of each group's care for its injured, vulnerable, sick, orphaned, and aged. In secular culture, Minnesota Public Radio and the stage and orchestral performances of the Cities showed a disproportionately high degree of attention to Scandinavia's most admired authors and composers. In popular culture, Garrison Keillor's radio program *A Prairie Home Companion*, with its humorous tales of rural Norwegian Americans and other ethnic Americans, was broadcast weekly from downtown St. Paul.[14]

In interviews, reactions to living in a metropolitan area so strongly marked by this Scandinavian presence varied greatly. Most took it for granted as an environment in which they could be proud. Some stated that they avoided having others identify them in terms of their Nordic origins because they did not want any special favors on that basis. Instead, they were determined to assist the newest foreign-born groups and their children. After admitting that ethnicity had influenced his education, religion, and choice of a mate, Tom Thompson claimed he felt provoked by the interview questions because he found the local Scandinavian American atmosphere so enveloping that he never gave it a thought, calling it similar to the water in which fish swim without considering its importance to life's basic functions. A minority asserted they felt so overwhelmed that they needed to get away from the Cities' claustrophobic Scandinavian American atmosphere. They moved abroad or to other parts of the country for some years before returning with a broader perspective or greater appreciation for the metropolitan area's Nordic complexion. In many interviews, reactions to the veracity of the Cohen brothers' film *Fargo* dependably presented diverging perceptions, according to whether the person involved had lived outside the Twin Cities area for some time or not. Those who had never left the area roundly criticized the film's portrait of the ancestry group, while those who had lived elsewhere felt the picture of the group and its values and even the actors' Scandinavian brogue captured kernels of truth about LGE Norwegian Americans in the region and Twin Cities. No one, however, questioned the plausibility of the story line including a trip to the Twin Cities.[15]

Celebrating the Sesquicentennial

This preponderance of institutions, customs, and cultural support constituted one of several factors that sustained the vitality of the Norwegian American ancestry group's core in the last quarter of the twentieth century. Another was the 150th anniversary that led the community to recall the historic events that centrally involved Norwegian Americans. The transnational celebration of the sesquicentennial of Norwegian immigration to the United States took place in 1975. Preparations began years before. About a year in advance, the home office of the Norsemen's Federation in Oslo arranged for two national chairpersons of the Norwegian American national coordinating committee to fly to Norway's capital. While there, they had an audience with King Olav V and met with his personal secretary and the two countries' ambassadors to confirm plans for the royal visit to North America a year later. Members of the Norwegian and the Norwegian American national committees agreed on mutual plans. At a press conference, they gave information about the royal trip, announced the attendance of two state church bishops at the Norwegian American celebrations, and previewed a sesquicentennial medal to be issued by Norway's royal mint.[16]

In the United States, the national committee allotted responsibility to chairpeople and local committees they recruited for geographic stops on the royal tour. In the Twin Cities, under the chairmanship of John

Ryan Groettum of Minneapolis, the committee made plans for festivities throughout 1975. It promoted art exhibits at the Lutheran Brotherhood building and the Sons of Norway headquarters. It and local groups also set up "sesqui" observances for May 17, Sankt Hans (Midsummer Day), Norway Day, and "Snoose Boulevard Days" in Cedar-Riverside. It arranged local concerts by the famous Norwegian popular singer Erik Bye and the Danish balladeer Birgitte Grimstad, as well as a concert by the Augsburg College choir, which later in the year sang at sesquicentennial events in Norway. It publicized the bygdelag's decision to hold its sesqui conference of lags in Minneapolis and the plans of the International Institute in St. Paul for a series of events displaying Norwegian foodways and crafts. It invited the bishop of Oslo to preach at Central Lutheran Church a week before the arrival of the royal party.

The primary festivities in Minneapolis–St. Paul, those lasting the longest and with the most prominent guests—including Norway's king and queen—took place October 11 to 14. During the first evening, the royal party joined the audience for Saturday's "Norwegian-American 1975 Sesquicentennial Concert" by the Minnesota Orchestra—a public event performed by the state's premier orchestra. The repertoire consisted of Edvard Grieg's *Peer Gynt Suite* and his *A Minor Piano Concerto* and Arne Nordheim's *Epitaffio for Orchestra and Magnetic Tape* from 1963—a program evincing respect for Norway's greatest classical music and one of its highly praised recent composers. It was a grand evening of high culture in the Cities' most appropriate setting, Orchestra Hall in Minneapolis—a convincing tribute to the king and a sound acknowledgment of the ancestry group's attainment of the highest levels of local prestige.

The next morning King Olav and his party worshipped at the Norwegian Lutheran Memorial Church. Princess Astrid had attended services there during her visit in 1958 at Minnesota's state centennial. King Olav had first come to services in 1968. The next generation of royals, Crown Princess Sonja and Crown Prince Harald, worshipped there in 1978—and in 1982 when they came for the "Scandinavia Today" events and the church's fiftieth anniversary. Participating in worship and speaking at the Memorial Church became traditional, as royal visits to the Twin Cities grew more frequent in the last decades of the 1900s. King Harald and Queen Sonja returned to Minneapolis–St. Paul and the church in 1987 and 1995. In 1999, Prince Haakon told the Norwegian American congregation, "It is important to take care of our traditions and history. But, at the same time it is important to bring in modern Norway." Periodic visits by royal family members, sanctioned by the Norwegian state, have helped strengthen the cultural bonds between two closely related peoples, the homeland Norwegians and their American cousins, keeping those bonds resilient despite the passing generations since mass immigration to the United States.

Later in the visit of 1975, the king and his party joined a large audience at the Minneapolis Auditorium for an evening of music and tributes, appropriately named "A Salute to Heritage." The St. Olaf College Orchestra played short pieces by Edvard Grieg, Johan Svendsen, Morton Gould, Knut Nystedt, Rikard Nordraak, and John Philip Sousa.

From 1939 onward, Norway's royal family increasingly recognized the importance of the Twin Cities' Norwegian community by visiting its leaders and institutions. King Olav came to Minneapolis in fall 1975 to commemorate the 175th anniversary of Norwegian immigration to America. Minneapolis Tribune, *October 14, 1975. Courtesy MNHS collections*

Everyone sang as the orchestra performed the national anthems. Harold L. Enarson, president of the Ohio State University, presided, introducing a greeting from the governor of Minnesota, Wendell Anderson, and a response from Professor Einar I. Haugen, the most prominent Norwegian American scholar at the time. The world-famous modern adventurer and explorer Thor Heyerdahl delivered the evening's keynote address. The national chair of sesquicentennial planning in 1974, Gordon M. A. Mork, offered concluding remarks. Displays of the evolving cultural legacy from Norway and of the ancestry group's reverence for the values embodied in that heritage framed the occasion. On Monday, the royal party toured St. Paul and Minneapolis before a gala farewell banquet at the Leamington Hotel Hall of States. In the same fashion as during the centennial of Norwegian immigration fifty years before, exhibits and displays in both cities highlighted the history, foodways, home crafts, and folk arts of the local Norwegian American ancestry group. On Tuesday, the royal party departed for its visit to the St. Olaf College campus.

Ethnic Revival

The Seventeenth of May celebrations in 1975 provided a boost for continued public Norwegian Constitution Day parades in downtown Minneapolis in the 1980s. In some interviews, the author heard how these public displays of ethnic allegiance depended on a small leadership group who "burned out" by the later years of the decade. In the 1990s the marking of May 17 became a largely neighborhood affair, centered on Mindekirken (the Memorial Church) on Franklin Avenue and national romantic choir music by an aging men's group at the statue of Ole Bull in Loring Park in downtown Minneapolis. However, when Norwegian royalty was in town, these and other Constitution Day events grew in size and number. Chuck Haga, the seasoned Norwegian American journalist, wrote feature articles about visits by members of the ancestry group's royal family or the meaning of May 17 in 1987, 1994, 1995, 1996, 1998, and 1999. The articles explain the historical context and significance of Norway's Constitution Day, the history of local connections to the royals dating back to World War II, and the schedule of events for each royal visit to the Twin Cities, in 1987, 1995, and 1999. Each article and the events it presented strengthened the ethnic core. One or more times a year prominently placed, multicolumned articles in the region's largest newspaper reminded the ancestry group and general public of the special importance of Norway and Norwegian Americans to Minneapolis–St. Paul and the Upper Midwest.[17]

The ethnic revival, prompted by the "roots phenomenon" of the 1970s as well as by increasing longevity and retirees' use of their leisure time for research into family history, further maintained interest in the ethnic past by the Cities' LGE Norwegian Americans. The Norwegian-American Historical Association, the Minnesota Historical Society, the Norwegian-American Genealogical Society of Minnesota, the Sons of Norway, and local media encouraged family history projects. These institutional archives, the expertise of their librarians and archivists, and their willingness to collect and store the completed histories laid foundations for the roots phenomenon. As dean of Norwegian American historians Odd S. Lovoll concludes in *The Promise Fulfilled* (1998), "What is clear from this study is that a combination of overt and subtle forces in the late 1960s and 1970s triggered a revival—a new ethnicity—among segments of the many generations of Norwegian Americans." Lovoll continues, "This urge remained strong toward the end of the century."[18]

LGE Norwegian Americans Meet New Asian and African Immigrants

Continuing immigration and regional migration between 1975 and 2000 also lent strength to the ancestry group. Foreign-born Norwegians were few in number, but the Twin Cities was one of a handful of locations that disproportionately attracted members of the first generation. Most new arrivals, moreover, came with substantial social capital in their education, occupational experience, and up-to-date familiarity with current Norwegian institutions and attitudes. Frequently, their network of contacts included people in the Twin Cities. The concentration of the ancestry group in Minneapolis–St. Paul and vicinity attracted newcomers from Norway and for some immigrants presented opportunities. In this period, the small minority of immigrants frequently became active members and leaders of the group's ethnic organizations.[19]

Other groups, some of them very unfamiliar to LGE Norwegian Americans, also migrated into the Twin Cities during these decades. In St. Paul, rural Hmong farmers from the hill country of Laos and Thailand started arriving in the early 1980s with the help of voluntary agencies (VOLAGS) in Minnesota that had assisted the settlement of refugees in the state since the late 1940s. These VOLAGS, in cooperation with the US government, initiated the migratory flows that brought displaced persons and families from the Baltic nations to Minnesota after World War II. Similar cooperative efforts assisted early contingents of Hispanic settlers. Norwegian Americans were long involved in these settlement processes through the family assistance programs of the Lutheran church. Encouraged by VOLAGS, municipal politicians helped the initial wave from Southeast Asia to grow. With a delegation of professionals and educators, many of them Hmong, the mayor of St. Paul traveled to Thailand in 2004 to assess the possibility of expanding the community of Hmong refugees in the city. In 2000, the local Hmong community already numbered 40,707, and by 2010 it had grown to 66,000, which made it the largest *urban* Hmong population anywhere.[20]

The largest and most dense areas of Hmong residence were on St. Paul's east side and near the state capitol in the University Avenue area—both districts of early Norwegian settlement in the capital city. Smaller numbers of Hmong settled in Minneapolis and the Cities' suburbs. Vietnamese, Laotians, and Asian Indians also formed clusters of settlement across the metropolitan area between the 1990s and 2014. People from the northeast horn and Mediterranean coast of Africa—Somalis, Ethiopians, Eritreans, and Libyans—immigrated to the Twin Cities in this period, too.

Somalis, the most numerous of these groups, established their largest community in the once mainly Scandinavian districts of the Cedar-Riverside and Franklin Avenue areas of Minneapolis. Their arrival began with migrating individuals in the 1980s and increased with the help of VOLAGS after the start of a civil war in the early 1990s. The growing community attracted and assisted Somalis coming directly from the homeland as well as from the global Somali diaspora. By 2014, between 40,000 and 50,000 Somalis resided in the metropolitan area, making it the largest Somali community in an American big city. As some families improved their economic status, they moved from the concentrated first settlement areas to the suburbs, just as Norwegian and Swedish immigrants had done earlier.

Both Somalis and Hmong founded a variety of business enterprises and voluntary community associations in the Twin Cities. St. Paul's oldest Hmong organizations, Lao Family Community and Hmong American Partnership, date from the early 1990s. They act as umbrella associations that host the annual Hmong New Year's celebration and Fourth of July soccer tournament. By 2014, the city had over ten Hmong voluntary groups, including the Center for Hmong Arts and Talent and the Hmong Cultural Center. The community's economic activity centered on West University Avenue and in the hundreds of merchants and score of restaurants located in Hmong Village marketplace.

Somali entrepreneurs have likewise founded hundreds of businesses in Minneapolis. The group's traditional marketplaces, offering all kinds of goods and foods, share space along a street or pathway near downtown. The city named one such Somali commercial center "Samatar Crossing" in 2018 to recognize the efforts of Somalia-born civic leader Hussein Samatar to enhance business life in the downtown. The city is home to two umbrella Somali organizations, the Confederation of Somali Community in Minnesota and the Somali American Parent Association, which provide a variety of community social services in the city and across the state.[21]

A portion of the next chapter discusses how Hmong and Somali leaders became engaged in the larger community and then the state and nation by running for political office. Like Norwegian immigrant leaders before them, they represented their community's interests and simultaneously helped their compatriots learn about and become more integrated into American society. Repeatedly the Twin Cities witnessed a form of ethnic succession in politics as members of these recently arrived groups won election to public offices previously held by Nordic Americans.

The growth of the metropolitan area in these years resulted not only from the movement of people out of the Cities to the suburbs but also from the continued urbanization of rural residents, including LGE Norwegian Americans, who moved not to the Cities themselves but to their suburban rings. The Upper Midwest was historically so heavily settled by Norwegians and they urbanized in the Twin Cities so much that by the 1990s the Norwegian ancestry group for the first time became the largest Scandinavian American group in the metropolitan area. But perhaps most remarkably, in interviews Norwegian Americans told how later generations of family and neighbors from specific districts in Norway who had clustered in neighborhoods of the Cities resettled near each other in inner and then outer suburbs. The maintenance of latter-day homeland ties through private relationships—and despite suburbanization—occurred on the south, west, and north of Minneapolis and on the northwest, northeast, and southeast of St. Paul. Residence in bedroom suburbs, exurbs, and outlying towns and cities also led to commuting in pools of people connected by their LGE networks. All these varieties of migration and occupational travel reinforced the ongoing vitality of LGE identity among Norwegian Americans.[22]

Although in attenuated "symbolic" form among aging mainstream white LGEs, much remained preserved in the Twin Cities' Norwegian American ethnic core. The continuing vitality of voluntary associations formed by post–World War II immigrants in 2000 provided examples of this. *Kontakt ungdomsklubb* (contact club for youth) set up a regular schedule of dinners, dances, and other social activities for young people who arrived in the first decades after the war. In 2000, the membership and activities were still largely the same, but most participants had gone from youth to retirement age. Spending their adult lives together as people who shared the experience of adjusting to life in Minneapolis–St. Paul during the same decades strengthened their sense of community in the club. The Cities' Norwegian-American Technical Society, organized in the same period for recently arrived engineers and architects, in time consisted of mostly older men who refreshed their ties with Norway's technical circles by inducting the trickle of later arrivals who met the society's membership requirements of birth and education in Norway. As it had resolved earlier, however, even when members' children completed degrees in engineering or architecture in the United States, the society left its bylaws unchanged and excluded the second generation. In 2000, NATS remained an organization for the foreign-born and old-country-educated in the local Norwegian American ethnic core.[23]

Through proliferation of classes in Norwegian folk arts and respect for the work of generations of folk artists, this segment of the ethnic core continued to be energetic in the last years of the twentieth century. Craftspeople and artists moved in networks in and around the Cities, meeting there, in the region, at Vesterheim museum programs for folk arts in Decorah, Iowa, and at craft fairs and folk culture festivals in Norway. Practicing a high level of expertise in creating forms of material culture and in performing the homeland's folk music and dance demonstrated the dedication and skill of these transnational folk artists and the liveliness of tradition among LGE Americans.[24]

A series of interviews and visits to folk artists and the premier historian of Norwegian American folk art, Marion Nelson, between 1998 and 2000 revealed the vitality of several forms of material culture and performance. Wood sculptor Fred Cogelow's work leaves an indelible impression of the ways that a deep knowledge of different sorts of woods and how best they may be worked in expert hands produce strikingly realistic or symbolic pieces of art. Cogelow credited the quality of his work to generations-old traditions of Norwegian woodworking. Dick Enstad assiduously studied and later taught how to make the bentwood household objects of Norwegian folk culture, such as elaborately hand-painted oval dairy and festive food carriers called *tiner*. Shirley Evenstad so successfully specialized in this traditional hand-painted decoration, *rosemaling*, that she became renowned as a prize-winning artist in both Norway and the United States. These are but a few examples of practitioners of material folk arts. In addition were LGEs who played folk Norwegian instruments, such as the Hardanger fiddle, or were accomplished performers of traditional folk dances from Norway. The interview with Carol Sersland was particularly interesting because she explained how her father (Harold Sersland) had been a well-recognized dancer before immigrating and that teaching dance traditions necessarily changed because of the move from rural district society to big-city life in the United States. He taught Carol and she grew skilled, but folk dance and dancers, while preserved in the ethnic core and passed down through the family's generations, could not regain the place they held in the rural life of the Norway he left.[25]

The ethnic core also maintained the whole panoply of institutions cataloged above. The aging original Sons of Norway lodges in downtown Minneapolis and the later-generation suburban lodges continued their engagement in traditional activities and made increased efforts to attract younger LGE Norwegian Americans by welcoming suggestions for new initiatives. The consulate general and the elite clubs, such as the Norsemen's Federation, Torskeklubben, and Den Norske Torskeklubben, dedicated themselves to preserving and bettering cultural ties with Norway. Not least, Mindekirken, with religious services in both Norwegian and English, offered a wide range of cultural activities and receptions for visiting notables and royalty from Norway. The Sons of Norway expanded its cultural programs in the last years of the century, featuring programs in dance and the folk arts and placing less emphasis on its fraternal insurance policies.[25]

Norwegian folk artists Dick Enstad and Shirley Evenstad (at left) made a rose-painted, bentwood "tine" (traditional food and cake carrying box) for the author and his wife, Marit Dale Mauk (at right). ***Courtesy of the author***

Family Tales

The combination of several of the above factors played an important role in family histories recorded in interviews for this research. Talking with families revealed the complexity of networks that developed between the United States and Norway when their central focus was the concentrated Scandinavian American population centers of the Twin Cities and the Upper Midwest. Kåre and Helen Faber and their two children, Karen and Harald, presented such a case. Like many a Norwegian of college age after World War II, Kåre came as a foreign student from Oslo when the capacity at universities in Norway was limited. He studied engineering along with a group of Norwegians at Case Western University in Cleveland, Ohio, in the later 1950s and took a job in Minneapolis in 1959 after graduation. Helen, a third-generation ethnic American of mixed Norwegian and Swedish-speaking Finnish heritage, had roots in northeast Minnesota. She and her sister participated in the widespread urbanization after the war, moving to the Twin Cities to further their education. Kåre and Helen met there. In typical fashion for people of Kåre's education in the postwar decades, although he was a first-generation immigrant, he and his family moved directly to the suburbs. The children lived from birth in pleasant suburban surroundings close to their father's place of work, first in Cleveland Heights near Case Western and then in Fridley and Minnetonka outside Minneapolis.[26]

The Fabers, moreover, had historic connections with Minneapolis and Minnesota. In both Kåre's and Helen's grandparents' generation, members of the family left Norway (or Swedish-speaking Finland) for Minnesota. As early as the 1880s three family members on Helen's side of the family were residents of Minneapolis. Kåre's grandfather's brother lived in northwest Minnesota for some time during the same period. Interestingly, in 1999 it was the adult Harald who had become the family genealogist and researched both public and private family records. He and his sister recalled how they earlier had "resented" or "resisted" being drawn into connections with their Norwegian American background. They resisted the bonds available to them through family membership in Sons of Norway and attendance at Skogfjorden language camp. Their interest in the family's ancestries in young adulthood, however, had grown stronger through visits to Scandinavia and family reunions in the United States, Canada, and Norway. They could regard themselves as second or fourth generation, as Norwegian or Swedish-speaking Finnish Americans, a combination of these, or simply as American. Karen perceived her situation this way: "I think when I was younger, I kind of resented the fact that I felt like I was pushed—felt different because I was the first generation, basically, so to speak, and so I didn't want that. I just wanted to be a normal American kid like everybody else who had generations and generations of people in America."

Harald's sense of his situation fitted Herbert Gans's picture of a voluntary, individualistic ethnicity very well. Here is how he expressed how important ethnicity was to him:

> HARALD: It's strange. It almost varies with the situation. . . . I see myself as a Norwegian American, with a Norwegian and a Swedish background, but when I'm around Americans who have a Norwegian background and are so into it, I find myself pulling away from it.
>
> INTERVIEWER: Why?
>
> HARALD: I think they overemphasized their Norwegian history and confused it with their American present.
>
> INTERVIEWER: Are you trying to say that they're sentimental and nostalgic?
>
> HARALD: To the point that the Norway they dream of isn't there in Norway, and they will argue with people from Norway on how to get from point A to point B . . . in Norway.

Not only Harald but the whole family considered the situation in Minnesota exceptional. For example, when asked if they thought of their Norwegian-born father as an immigrant, Karen and Harald responded in unison, "Not in Minnesota!" and laughed. People from Norway and Scandinavia in Minnesota were near or distant family. As Helen put it, "No, I always think of myself as an American. I have a strong interest, strong ties to the family in Norway—we've had contact with them, but we just think of them as the family. But I don't think of myself as being Norwegian."

Ethnicity to the Fabers was a private, international web of family connections that in Minnesota's dense Scandinavian demography did not seem at all foreign. The population they spoke of was for the most part the Cities' long-established whites. Only through mentions of his work as a teacher of children with learning difficulties did Harald broaden the interview's perspective to include the more recently arrived, non-white immigrant groups of the Twin Cities.

Conclusion

This chapter documents and discusses a new phase of community among people of Norwegian descent in the Minneapolis–St. Paul metropolitan area. In these years, the large majority in the group were, as scholars have called them, later generation ethnics—in their case, people three or more generations distant from ancestors born in Norway. Superficially indistinguishable from other white Americans except in family history and cultural ethnic markers they voluntarily chose to honor, they self-identified to the US Census as primarily, or secondarily, people of Norwegian ancestry.

In a diaspora across the multicounty metropolitan area, they "performed" their membership by traveling into the central cities to take part in ethnic occasions and activities and by maintaining family foodways, holidays, and folkways in music and the arts. At the same time, LGE Norwegian Americans again adjusted to the concentrated settlement of new immigrant populations—this time Africans and East Asians—in city districts that once had mostly housed Norwegian and Swedish immigrants. Once again their leaders learned to acknowledge, accept, and cooperate with newcomers, as we will see in the next chapter. The activist core of the group also cooperated with the small number of newcomers from Norway to update the local community about contemporary life in the ancestral homeland. They chose to define a distinctive variety of American ancestral culture: the "Norwegian American" seemed ubiquitous in Minneapolis–St. Paul. The general public shared Norwegian jokes, stereotypes, holidays, jubilees, royal visits, and cultural icons. As a result of the group's uniquely large size and long settlement in the Twin Cities and region, the "twilight" of this old white population's ethnicity came very slowly and late in the metropolitan area.

CHAPTER NINE

A Glance Forward and Concluding Remarks

[2000–2020]

THE CHAPTER THAT FOLLOWS FOCUSES ON THE CHANGING STATUS OF NORwegian Americans during the final years of this history. The ancestry group now lived in a metropolitan area where the dominant communities in the historically Scandinavian districts in the Cedar-Riverside and Franklin Avenue section of Minneapolis and the east-side Payne Avenue area of St. Paul were Somalis and Hmong. Intergroup relations between these recently settled communities and Norwegian Americans is a major theme of the chapter. Also prominent is discussion of signs of decline and renaissance in the Norwegian or Scandinavian American character of the Twin Cities during the first two decades of the twenty-first century.

The migratory patterns of local Norwegians, a third theme of the book—either from their ancestral homeland or through urbanization to Minneapolis–St. Paul—manifested themselves in a cumulative fashion in these years. A century and a half of moving into adjacent urbanized areas along the river taught local Norwegian Americans how to adjust to life in close contact with other cultural, religious, and racial groups. Successive waves of other peoples found the booming towns along the Mississippi an attractive destination.

To a degree, Norwegian American movement to the Cities' suburbs amounted to participation in white flight from multiracial urban districts, but members of the ancestry group also migrated to the suburbs from outlying rural areas. As becomes clear in this chapter, Norwegian American political and social leaders left first settlement areas and lost elective offices to Asian newcomers. They shared the new Norway House with other ethnic groups. The Norwegian ancestry group seemed to understand that, just as Norwegian Americans had many decades earlier, Asian Americans and African Americans were benefitting from integration into the Twin Cities.

Signs of a Coming Post-Scandinavian Era and Yet of Ethnic Renaissance

For a considerable time, some signs marked the decline of Minneapolis–St. Paul as the "capital" or preeminent hub of Norwegian America. The change became apparent in the ethnic press; the larger Lutheran religious bodies to which most Norwegian Americans belonged; prominent, historically Norwegian businesses; and the ethnic background of the people elected to offices long held by Norwegian Americans. This history provides detailed accounts of the lasting vitality of institutions and traditional events within the Norwegian American community of Minneapolis–St. Paul. By the early 2000s, however, there were indications that the metropolitan area was perhaps entering "a post-Scandinavian" era.

An early sign of a changed epoch came with the demise of the metropolitan area's Norwegian American, mixed-language press. When *Minnesota Posten* stopped publication in 1979, it shuttered an institution of major importance to the core of the Norwegian American ancestry group. Since 1956, *Posten* had provided a bilingual Norwegian and English outlet for news from the metropolitan area's dozens of Norwegian American organizations. The weekly took up issues of concern to the group in editorials by editor Jenny Alvilde Johnsen and columnist Brenda Ueland. It covered events in Norway and relations between the homeland and Norwegian America in an up-to-date, informed fashion. All these news sources became much less accessible with the newspaper's demise. Instead, latter-day Norwegian American newspapers in New York and Seattle, in place of the Twin Cities, competed to produce a national voice in print for the nationality group. In the Twin Cities, from that time a generation of Norwegian Americans had no newspaper, in Norwegian or English, written for and addressed to them as its primary audience. *Posten*'s disappearance seemed to some in the ancestry group another sign of a different cultural era in the Twin Cities.[1]

The primary Lutheran denomination to which the ancestry group belongs, the Evangelical Lutheran Church in America (ELCA), formed from a fusion of three Lutheran denominations centered in the Midwest in 1988, left its headquarters in Minneapolis for a new national home in Chicago. The location of church publications and administration also shifted out of the Cities in following years. As ethnic and ancestry groups continued integrating into American society, their attachment to religious institutions formally reflecting their origins grew less important. The urbanization out of strongly ethnic rural communities into diverse metropolitan areas that this study traces also contributed to the feeling that Scandinavian and German Americans had more in common as people with a shared Lutheran heritage than they did as members of historic, ethnic church bodies.

In a somewhat similar fashion, another iconic institution in the Cities also gradually lost its direct connection to a Norwegian immigrant background. The largest financial services concern founded by Norwegian Americans, Lutheran Brotherhood, began in 1917 as a fraternal mutual benefit insurance company. In its first year of business, the firm limited benefits to members baptized in a Norwegian Lutheran congregation, a requirement meant to counter conservative ministers' opposition to all insurance at the time. Originally called Luther Union, the fusion of three Norwegian Lutheran denominations in that year inspired two Norwegian political entrepreneurs, Jacob Aall Otteson Preus and Herman Ekern, to explore the business opportunity. They also followed the successful example of another fraternal insurance company, Aid Association for Lutherans, founded around the same time by Lutheran laymen in Wisconsin.

Men's clubs in Norwegian immigrant churches were the first local branches of the Lutheran Brotherhood, but three years after its founding, the common heritage of all Lutherans became its stronger, broadened base. By 1970, when longtime Chief Executive Officer Arley Bjella moved to Minneapolis from North Dakota, the Brotherhood provided not only life insurance but also financial planning and administered a large charitable foundation. In Bjella's time the foundation aided many a Norwegian American project, but increasingly merit unrelated to ethnic attachments determined the distribution of Brotherhood charity. Then, in 2002, the Brotherhood's Norwegian Lutheran beginnings became submerged in the renamed Thrivent Financial, which advertised services for all Christians, regardless of denomination. Though its ancestral background was no longer evident, its headquarters remained in the landmark skyscraper built for the Brotherhood in downtown Minneapolis.[2]

Yet another monument to Norwegian ancestry in the Cities disappeared in 2008 when Norway's foreign ministry closed its full, professionally staffed consulate for the Upper Midwest. Since 1944—for more than half a century—the country had sent a career diplomat to Minneapolis to maintain relations with the region. Before that, from 1870 onward, a local businessman who was a leading figure among the Cities' Norwegians had served as an honorary consul general, and the consulate had its office near his full-time business in St. Paul. The consulate strengthened the Cities' and the region's ties to the homeland by settling inheritances for families on both sides of the Atlantic. It encouraged increasing political, economic, and cultural contacts over the decades by managing the visits of homeland elected officials and members of Norway's royal family. And after 1944, a consular staff member acted as an international impresario, arranging for artists, musicians, authors, and other notable figures from Norway to visit and perform or hold lectures and exhibitions.

Thus, it seemed to many latter-day Norwegian Americans that their community and region had returned to its earlier, lower level of importance to the homeland when an honorary consul general replaced the professional emissary. Until 2010, former vice president Walter Mondale served in the position in Minneapolis, after which Eivind Heiberg, the chief executive officer of Sons of Norway and Sons of Norway Foundation, succeeded him. Both men's selection testifies to the continuing prestige of the consulate among the region's Norwegian American leaders. However, Paul Bjarne Grindem, former inspector general of Norway's Foreign Service and Consul General in Minneapolis–St. Paul, in 1999 characterized the local diplomatic station in the Twin Cities as "an anachronism," a quite modest post in Norway's diplomacy because it no longer served commercial relations but only cultural contacts between the two countries, while an array of other institutions also fostered those connections. Grindem knew that others disagreed with this assessment. They thought Minneapolis–St. Paul, still the capital of Norwegian America in the eyes of leading members of the ancestry group, ought to keep the professional diplomatic station as an indication that Norway's government remained concerned to show that the "Norwegian-American community is still considered important" and that "Norway is still interested in maintaining the connection with the immigrants and their descendants."[3]

The long-term accumulation of voters from other ethnic backgrounds and the increasing voting power of Asian, African, and Latino Americans, among other factors, signaled the end of the postwar era of Scandinavian American dominance in metropolitan politics. As noted in the previous chapter, to some Norwegian Americans the election of Jesse Ventura as governor in 2000 seemed to indicate the close of the period of Nordic leadership in local politics. Yet then, at the end of the twentieth century, in the state capitol one Norwegian American, Republican Steve Sviggum, served as speaker of Minnesota's House of Representatives, and another, the Democratic-Farmer-Labor senator Roger Moe, was the majority leader in the state senate. Both men, highly conscious of their ethnic background, like many state legislators before them, came to the metropolitan area as elected officials from heavily Norwegian American rural areas of the state.

The electoral realities in the Twin Cities, on the other hand, had greatly changed from 1900, when the first two generations of Norwegian and Swedish Americans alone made up over 44 percent of the population of Minneapolis and more than 23 percent of the people living in St. Paul. In 2000, the two self-identifying Nordic ancestry groups had shrunk to 11 percent of Minneapolis and 8.4 percent of St. Paul. These much smaller groups nonetheless remained significant, given the history of the Twin Cities, even though the demographic situation had altered greatly.[4]

Early in these years, changes in who held and won state offices foreshadowed the coming of a new political era. In 2000, as noted, Norwegian Americans led both houses of the Minnesota legislature. When the Democrats regained control of the house in 2006, Sviggum's eight years as speaker ended. Meanwhile, Moe had kept his position longer than any legislator in the state's history. He left office not due to an election loss but because he resigned to run for governor in 2002. After he and running mate Julie Sabo, veteran representative Martin Sabo's daughter, lost that race on a 100 percent Norwegian American ticket, Moe left public life. These visible changes in leadership did not bring an immediate shift in officeholders' backgrounds. That depended on elections in Minneapolis–St. Paul, where large populations of recently naturalized Somali and Hmong Americans voted for compatriots, just as Norwegian Americans had decades before.[5]

In the politics of the metropolitan area, prominent Norwegian Americans left office and members of new immigrant communities replaced them. As Norwegian and other Scandinavian immigrants once won election to offices previously held by old-stock Americans, now people from recently settled groups from Asia and Africa replaced later-generation Norwegian Americans in public life. For example, representative to Congress Martin Sabo, who repeatedly won reelection between 1979 and 2007, retired, and the Democrat Keith Ellison, the first Muslim to serve in the House of Representatives and the first person of color to represent Minnesota in that chamber, took the seat.

Meanwhile African, especially Somali, immigration to the metropolitan area and the state's smaller cities rose sufficiently to provoke anti-Muslim feeling. In St. Cloud, for example, representatives of the tea party wing of the Republican Party called for an end to Muslims taking refuge in the city. In response, Ellison rallied public opinion against anti-Muslim prejudice through a full-page ad in the Minneapolis *Star Tribune* that proclaimed, "We must come together as a diverse and vibrant community. . . . We can't be tricked into betraying our values. It'd be so very un-Minnesotan of us." Many state Democrats, including the governor and its two US senators—as well as many business and educational leaders—signed the call in support of Muslim citizens.[6]

On the local level, children of immigrants from Africa or Asia also stepped into elected offices exited by later-generation members of long-resident ancestry groups. In 2014, the Minneapolis municipal elections provided an example of this development when its Sixth Ward voters gave Somali immigrant Abdi Warsame a landslide victory for the city council, making him the city's, state's, and nation's first Somali

American elected official. He replaced the council's first Native American, Robert Lilligren, of Swedish and Norwegian as well as Ojibwe descent. As David Lebedoff, veteran historian of the historically Scandinavian immigrant ward, summed up developments, "In Minnesota, the first were the WASPs, and then the Scandinavians and now the Somalis. . . . A group moves in and instead of remaining outside of the system and having no part of it, they take over the system," as he termed the effect of winning local government offices.[7]

Likewise, in St. Paul, Dai Thao won election as the city council's first Hmong member in Ward 1. Thus, the largest recent immigrant group in each city mobilized to gain a political voice in the urban district of its greatest concentration. Unique on its own terms, each nonetheless retraced the same path of political arrival through municipal elections that Norwegians followed in the 1870s and 1880s. The change in the ethnic background of local elected officials was not ephemeral. Those who ran for office, like earlier immigrant leaders, made careers in public service and acted as bridges between their community and other populations in the Twin Cities and beyond.[8]

Thao was reelected in 2015 to a four-year term. Warsame also won a second term and later headed the city's public housing authority. Ellison, the first Muslim member of the US House of Representatives, resigned to run successfully for election as Minnesota's attorney general in 2018. Elected to Ellison's seat, Somali immigrant Ilhan Omar became one of the first two Muslim women and the first former refugee to serve as a member of Congress. A year later, Nelsie Yang became the youngest person and first Hmong woman to serve on the St. Paul City Council. In her victory from the Sixth Ward she replaced the retiring Dan Bostrom, a long-serving east-side council member. And so, the pattern of representatives from newer population groups replacing local politicians from long-settled, later-generation Scandinavian American groups continued.[9]

Signs of a Resilient Community, 2000–2014

The first section of this chapter discusses signs that suggest the advent of a post-Scandinavian epoch in Minneapolis–St. Paul. Other events, however, indicate the continuing vitality of the ancestry group locally.

Arguably the most important of these is the successful development of Norway House in Minneapolis. The idea of a center where all local Norwegian American organizations could meet dates back to May 17, 1889, when the Normanna Society with great ceremony dedicated Normanna Hall, a four-story building on the southeast corner of Twentieth Avenue and Third Street, built expressly for that purpose. Many organizations moved in and the building bustled with life. By 1893, however, the society's board of directors could not pay expenses or the interest on the debt for putting up the building. Gradually, as the nucleus of Norwegian settlement moved farther south, community organizations set up elsewhere, and the building fell into other hands.[10]

More than a century later, in 2004, Norway's consul general, Thor Johansen, with an endorsement from King Harald V, launched the idea of establishing a national Norwegian American center in Minneapolis. Over five hundred donors contributed funds, a total of $15 million through 2015, when the Norway House business and culture center opened as the first phase of the National Norwegian Center in America. The prime movers of the project, according to the *Star Tribune*'s feature article for the occasion, were two Norwegian Americans—fourth-generation Julie Ingebretsen of the family-owned Scandinavian food and gift shop on East Lake Street established in 1921, and third-generation Jon Pederson, owner of Ruffridge-Johnson Equipment company, who "got a passion for this Norway project" when he donated money to it a decade earlier. Together, these leaders represent the central dynamic of the Norwegian American community's evolution since the mid-nineteenth century. Ingebretsen is part of the latest generation of a long-resident family exemplifying the early settlement and business activity of Norwegian immigrants in Minneapolis. Pederson's family joined in the 170 years of migration from the countryside that renewed the Norwegian community of the Cities and led to the many phases of its development. In 2015, Pederson proudly announced, "Five hundred donors so far," and further proclaimed, "We're going to get it done. It's amazing how many in Norway know about this project; Telemark County has even committed $200,000."[11]

Norway House operates in renovated space in a former credit union building at 913 East Franklin Avenue, on the other side of the block from the Norwegian Lutheran Memorial church (Mindekirken). In 2015 it contained an art and exhibition gallery, office space for Norwegian American and East African associations, such as East African Housing Services and Concordia Language Villages (including Skogfjorden for studying Norwegian), a lending library, Telemark County's trade office in the United States, and both Norwegian American and other ethnic businesses. The Ingebretsen family, for instance, has opened a coffee bar and gift shop in the center as a branch business of the well-known Lake Street store. As Julie Ingebretsen summed up her feelings about the project for the *Star Tribune*, "We look forward to contributing what we can to another street of immigrants. We love the Norway House building, and long-range vision. We look forward to using the basement space for classes that we don't have the space or equipment for, and collaborating with both Norway House and Mindekirken on creative, new ideas for classes and events."

On its internet site in 2020, Norway House announced its purpose to be "*Connecting the United States to contemporary Norway* through arts, business, and culture" (italics in the original). Another organization under its umbrella in 2015 was Lakselaget, a professional women's club founded in 2002 that is devoted to "contemporary Norwegian issues and all things Norwegian." The club's monthly meetings, guest speakers, and scholarships for exchanges between Norway and Minnesota are consistent with Norway House's goal of strengthening ties to and knowledge of contemporary conditions in the ancestral homeland.[12]

Phase two of the center, construction of which began in 2020, received financial support from Norway and Minnesota, local Norwegian American organizations, and families. As planned, Norway House will extend across a whole side of the block. The new building will house banquet and performance halls and provide research and library facilities for the *Bygdelagenes fellesråd*, the common council of Norwegian regional societies, to create a national genealogical facility for Norwegian Americans. The building will also include meeting rooms and a business center. The *fellesråd* and the Norwegian-American Chamber of Commerce (North Chapter) will move on campus.

Norway House honors young professionals and affiliate organizations through its Going Viking Awards, celebrating those "who embody the adventuresome and bold spirit of the Vikings by inspiring their communities to explore and discover new frontiers with courage

Opened in 2015, Minneapolis's Norway House has increasingly fulfilled its goal of becoming the National Norwegian Center in America as it gathers a growing array of the ancestry group's cultural, business, historical, and educational concerns and activities under its broad organizational umbrella. *Courtesy Norway House*

and determination." By 2020, Norway House had honored an array of essential Norwegian American institutions, such as Skogfjorden, the Norwegian-American Historical Association, the Memorial Church, Vesterheim Norwegian-American Museum, the consulate, and the common council of regional associations. During the same years, individual awards went to outstanding faculty members at Norwegian American colleges, leaders of Norwegian American organizations, and politicians from the ancestry group.[13]

For example, Norway House honored Janet Dolan and William Moore for their work with the Minnesota Peace Initiative, which they started in 2008 and have used to encourage public involvement in peacemaking efforts globally. Their initiative was connected with Augsburg College (now University), which for decades sponsored and provided the venue for the Nobel Peace Prize Forum, bringing together students with prominent local and international figures to discuss peace prize recipients in Norway and peacekeeping efforts generally. When the organizers in Oslo expanded their programs in 2016 to include a Nobel Peace Prize Forum there, Augsburg reconsidered its activities and began its Human Rights Forum, to "bring students, thoughtful leaders, global changemakers, and local activists together to explore innovative ways to take action in our ongoing pursuit of human rights globally and domestically."[14]

The Minnesota Peace Initiative has entertained figures such as Norway's former prime minister Kjell Magne Bondevik as president of the Oslo Center and J. Brian Atwood, dean of the Humphrey School of Public Affairs at the University of Minnesota. In addition, the initiative cooperates with a network that includes the Oslo Center, the Minnesota International Center, the Minnesota International NGO Network (MINN), the Humphrey School of Public Affairs, and the Sons of Norway. All of these programs fostering peace strengthen the involvement of local Norwegian Americans with Norway's foreign policy tradition of settling conflict through increased international understanding and peaceful negotiation. The Minnesota Peace Initiative does much to realize the intention of Norway House to be an institution with bonds to community and global issues.

Norway House is a testament to the vitality of Norwegian American community life today. Even as it recognizes and respects the work of the ancestry group's organizations that were founded in the past, it brings together efforts to record and share the group's historical experience with those of more recently launched projects. Norway House provides publicity and visibility to the whole ancestry group. And these later-generation Norwegian Americans also invite the organizations of their Somali neighbors to join them and reside in Norway House with them.

Scandinavian-Flavored Life in the Twin Cities in 2014

Choosing 2014 as the closing year of this history originally seemed appropriate to celebrate the changed status of local Norwegian Americans by the time of the bicentennial of Norway's constitution. That status as a dispersed, later-generation, metropolitan-area ancestry group was evident by 2000, however, and so became part of the previous chapter.

"On the Scandinavian Road," the concluding chapter in Swedish journalist Klas Bergman's history of Scandinavians in Minnesota politics, gives an overview of how distinctly Scandinavian flavored life in the Twin Cities remained in 2014. His order of precedence and examples offer a largely Swedish American view of the situation, but his catalog of the state's lasting Scandinavian characteristics are much the same as those noted in the final chapters of this study about life in the Twin Cities metropolitan area.

Both books stress Scandinavian surnames, business names, and place names; Lutheran Social Service and landmark charitable welfare and health institutions; as well as the distinctive foodways, favored sports, and patriotic celebrations of these ancestry groups. Religious institutions are central: Bergman remarks on finding a "Lutheran church on every corner in the Twin Cities" and attests that many Scandinavian Americans are still churchgoers. In an overview he featured events surrounding the bicentennial Seventeenth of May celebrations—including a gala banquet, a church service, and a parade from Mindekirken around Norway House and the now Somali-majority Franklin Avenue neighborhood. In addition, he notes the *Midsommar* festival and, in 2015, the first "Scandinavian Summer Fest," when, after over eighty years, Swedes joined forces with Norwegians. To many outside these Nordic groups, their members have long made up a generalized, regional European background group. Moreover, when local Scandinavians have needed resources or a large public presence, throughout their history in the Cities they have combined in common effort.[15]

In 1914, the centennial celebrations lavished acknowledgment on Norwegian immigrants. Jubilation paraded across the central districts of both cities and culminated in three days of sermons, speeches, and theatrical panoply at the state fairgrounds. A great cadre of Norwegian

In 2000, celebrations of Norway's Constitution Day, May 17, were held in and around the Norwegian Lutheran Memorial Church (Mindekirken) in Minneapolis. After a religious service, the congregation marched in a parade around the neighboring blocks and then enjoyed a picnic with local residents—mostly African immigrants—at a nearby park. After Norway House opened adjacent to the church, the parade circled both institutions and drew participants from both. *Courtesy of the author*

Americans returned to Oslo and their home districts, bringing with them their sense of success in America. One hundred years later, the bicentennial celebrations in Minneapolis were by comparison a modest affair. By then Norwegian Americans were a long-established, well-integrated European ancestry group that had no need of acknowledgment locally. Moreover, Norwegian Americans had for some years adjusted to being of less importance to Norway's foreign ministry.

Some larger historical questions arise from interviewing prominent state or metropolitan Nordic leaders about their ancestry groups' contribution to society and culture. Do politics in the Twin Cities still show a definable Scandinavian influence, for example? People within the groups often give their own members credit for the progressive politics and public policies of Minneapolis–St. Paul and Minnesota as a whole. Historian Odd Lovoll wrote in *The Promise Fulfilled* that to an extent such "perceived ethnic qualities and ideals . . . are simply idealized and cherished mainstream American attributes." This author and Bergman likewise discovered a similar transference of common ideals to a Norwegian or Nordic heritage. Many of the public figures interviewed shared a broad consensus that honesty, hard work, equity, and high civic engagement in communal betterment are a cultural inheritance from mass Scandinavian immigration to and integration in the Twin Cities and state. Of course, many other ancestry groups attribute the same virtues to their forebears. Nonetheless, political activist David Lebedoff in 2013 asserted that Scandinavians' "enduring contribution . . . is the civic participation to build a stronger society." According to many interviewed for this history, these public-minded attitudes led to a more developed social safety net as well as higher participation in elections than in other cities and states.[16]

A balanced view of developments between 2000 and 2020, therefore, reveals that the wider dispersion in the metropolitan counties of an increasingly later-generation ancestry group represents a later stage in Norwegian American community development. Hmong and Somali residents living close together on the east side of St. Paul and in the Cedar-Riverside–Franklin Avenue districts of Minneapolis were, in the classic pattern of ethnic succession, replacing Norwegian and Swedish politicians and negotiating their communities' place in the Twin Cities of the twenty-first century. Norwegian Americans welcomed them in elected office and also in Norway House. As a revitalizing umbrella organization, Norway House, with its resident, remote, and affiliate members, gave evidence of the vitality of the Norwegian American community as it responded to the concerns and interests of the ancestry group's families and enduring institutions.

When asked how important old-stock ethnicity was in the Twin Cities in 2000, the Minneapolis *Star Tribune* journalist Chuck Haga said, "It is important in one way—in how this residual established majority reacts to change." Between then and 2020, one of the most rapid changes old-stock white population groups in the Twin Cities needed to accommodate was the accelerating arrival of large numbers of immigrant and refugee groups from new places. The Minneapolis–St. Paul metropolitan area's largest foreign-born groups were no longer of European origin but Mexican, Hmong, Somali, Eritrean, Liberian, Sierra Leonean, or Tibetan. In the 1990s and early 2000s the growth in the percent of foreign-born residents in Minnesota was more than twice the national average; consisted mostly of Africans, Asians, and Hispanics (whose numbers roughly sextupled); and was centered in the Twin Cities, where the job market was largest and most varied. Katherine Fennelly of the Humphrey Institute of Public Affairs summed up the demographic situation as follows: "Sixty percent of the total state population lives in the Twin Cities Metro Area, and 75 percent of immigrants in the state reside there. The Twin Cities Metropolitan Area has always been the site of the largest concentrations of immigrants in the state, but in recent years the rate of increase has accelerated." Yet in 2014, Minnesota's population remained only 7 percent non-white, about half the 13.5 percent national average. The remarkable fact is that the state and the Twin Cities have a strong, long-term attractiveness for Mexicans, Hmong, Somalis, and others, in part because of nongovernmental Catholic and Lutheran organizations' largesse in resettlement support, as well as the state's progressive legislative record related to immigrants and refugees. The nation's largest Hmong community (almost 50,000 people) lives in St. Paul. The Somali community in Minneapolis (about 40,000 people) is one of the largest in the United States as well.[17]

Haga emphasized the social-psychological dimensions of the changing situation and the dangers it might hold for Norwegian Americans' self-image and their relations with new groups. The chief problem with such success, he said, was the sense of "entitlement" it gives, so that members of old-stock ethnic groups identify being Minnesotan with being Norwegian or Scandinavian American. As he concluded, "They think 'Minnesotan' when they see themselves.... Norwegians especially, but [also] other northern Europeans, have tended to act as though, as I said, they are Minnesota and that others are from elsewhere."

The Evolving Status of the Twin Cities' Norwegian Americans

Before 1890, during World War I, and through much of the 1920s, Nordic Americans in Minneapolis–St. Paul felt their cultural status was vulnerable. In response, they constructed versions of history that asserted their rights as first-class Americans—as the descendants of the discoverer of America and of ancient Vikings who practiced democracy. Until the decades after the Second World War, they strove to gain mainstream public acceptance for these ideas, locally and across the nation. This cultural uplift was an essential part of the burden of the 1914 and 1925 centennials and of the Leif Erikson Day and monument campaigns. The celebrations in 1975, on the other hand, showed the self-confidence and public assurance of a time when the ancestry group could laugh about "Norwegian jokes" from the secure position of social acceptance and integration that generations of forebears had earned for their descendants.

Remembering the struggles of the immigrant generation and living by the fundamental values of their cultural and religious heritage prompted Norwegian American churches and the group's civic leaders to reach out and assist not only their own but all who could benefit from support. Between 1945 and 1975, as part of the municipal establishment and local electorate, many Norwegian and Scandinavian Americans became deeply involved in negotiations to ensure the rights and improve the living conditions of minority groups in the Twin Cities. As the local Asian, African, and Latin American communities expanded in the 1970s and beyond, many in the Nordic ancestry groups again responded with generosity and acceptance. Not all did, however, and the repeated election of Charles Stenvik as mayor of Minneapolis showed the support local voters gave a law-and-order politician who promised to jail those who disturbed the peace with their protests. Some, no doubt, did not accept the recently arrived minorities as Minnesotans, forgetting that their ancestors, too, hailed from elsewhere. In these years, some Norwegian American organizations focused exclusively on relations between Norway and Norwegian America. Others devoted themselves to mutual support within a postwar group of first-generation Norwegian immigrants. These groups are not necessarily examples of "retreating" within one's ethnicity, because their members most often belonged to other institutions that were involved in the broader community.

In this last chapter of evolving Norwegian American community, between 2000 and 2020, new challenges and opportunities arose from maintaining the ancestry group's core institutions and sense of identity, fostering relations with the homeland, and reaching out to groups more recently settled in the metropolitan area. In each city, Norwegian Americans learned to acknowledge the loss of traditional institutions and businesses. They also learned, yet again, to adjust to new groups that now dominated the population of areas that once were their own historical first settlement districts. This time the groups were growing numbers of Mexicans—whose local community had long existed—and several less familiar, recently settled Asian and African communities. Vietnamese, Laotians, and Hmong from southeastern Asia settled in both cities, but the Hmong community in St. Paul not only grew dominant there but also became the nation's largest center of the group. In Minneapolis, Eritreans, Ethiopians, and Somalis became the largest groups in Cedar-Riverside and the Franklin Avenue district.

The Somali community in particular became well organized and civically active. Ethnic succession began to take place in local politics in Minneapolis, where Somali leaders won political offices previously held by Norwegian or other Nordic Americans. In St. Paul through a similar process, Hmong leaders likewise won offices earlier held by Nordic Americans. The majority in the Norwegian American ancestry group in these years resided in the suburbs of the multicounty metropolitan area. However, their most important and vital group institutions remained or, like Norway House, were founded near downtown in these years and included African and Asian immigrant associations in their plans and activities. Thus, through 171 years continued the saga of migration and urbanization and of meetings and cooperation with other peoples in a changing American urban framework.

Appendix

Twin Cities History Project (TCHP) Interviews

IN-DEPTH INTERVIEWS WITH COMMUNITY VETERANS AND THEIR FAMILIES WERE essential to the research for this history of Norwegian Americans in the Twin Cities. As much as possible, the aim was to tell a story based on the experience of the people who lived it, their relations with each other, and the perceptions they shared about their past. Moreover, the interviews provided a guide for knowing how to interpret and what to look for in public records and private written sources about the phases of the group's community life over a century and a half.

Everyone interviewed answered the same list of questions to make answers more easily comparable and to uncover common patterns of experience. An initial series of questions explored each person's personal sense of identity in familial, ethnic, economic, religious, and political terms. Interviewers looked for information and attitudes relevant to life in the Twin Cities in each dimension.

Then interviews researched family history back to the ancestral homeland three or more generations earlier, depending on how informed people were about their past. This line of questioning revealed migratory patterns and residential movement inside Minneapolis–St. Paul. When interview subjects could offer expertise or inside knowledge about aspects of the group's experience, additional questions or a separate interview explored these topics.

The author and two full-time assistants, Mette Løvås and Robert Mikkelsen, conducted most of the interviews from 1998 to 2000. A few interviews conducted by other oral historians at other times also provided vital information and perspectives. The author interviewed several more people in 2012.

The research team made concerted efforts to construct a balanced historical oral record from both cities, as well as a wide range of age groups, occupations, and socioeconomic status. The goal was to gain as broad a picture of community activities and involvement as possible. Norwegian Americans were also asked about their relations with other population groups, and when significant interactions became known, members of other groups, such as Jewish, Native, African, and Asian Americans, became the subject of interviews. In master's theses, students in Norway investigated inter-group contacts between Norwegian Americans and Jews in north Minneapolis and Norwegian immigrants and Native Americans in the 1860s and 1870s. Some of their interviews contributed to this study.

Considerable preparation preceded the interviews. The author built on previous oral history research in New York and conferenced with then NAHA editor Odd Lovoll and Minnesota Historical Society oral history officer James E. Fogerty, before training Løvås and Mikkelsen by interviewing with them. The Twin Cities History Project (TCHP) used adaptations of the Minnesota Historical Society's forms for permission to use material from interviews in this publication and for interview summaries. Insofar as TCHP funds allowed, transcriptions were made of what seemed the most fruitful interviews. All interview materials are in the author's possession and will be stored in the NAHA archives.

NAME	INTERVIEWER(S)	DATE OF INTERVIEW
Akslen, John	Mauk & Løvås	1999, January 18 and February 1
Almaas, Egil	Løvås	1999, November 5
Anker, Jens	Mauk	2000, February 2
Austensen, Mary-Jane & Alan	Mauk	1999, January 10
Baker, Eunice	Mauk	2000, June 12 and 24

NAME	INTERVIEWER(S)	DATE OF INTERVIEW
Bakke, Harald & Synnove	Mikkelsen	1998, November 4
Bakken, Elva M. & Lehman, Barbara G.	Mikkelsen	1998, October 5
Beal, Daniel E. & Gaelyn	Mauk	1999, December 3
Beckstrand, William A.	Mauk	1999, January 22
Bellecourt, Clyde	Mauk	2012, March 16
Bergaas, Samuel M.	Løvås	1999, April 20; 2000, January 8
Bergh, Kjell	Mauk	1999, September 3
Bloom, Sheldon	Mauk	1999, August 30
Boe, Marilyn Adelaide	Løvås	1998, October 8
Boe, Paul	Gjermund S. Thompson	1984, December 1
Brookins, Carl & Jean	Mauk	2000, April 17
Budd, Gladys	Mauk	2012, March 12
Campbell, Joan Elizabeth Mikkelson	Mikkelsen	1999, January 11 and 20
Chiat, Marilyn	Mauk	1998, November 10
Chrislock, Carl	Mauk	1999, May 16
Christiansen, Ulf	Mauk	1999, July 1
Cleven, Harry T.	Mauk	1999, October 20
Cogelow, Fred	Mauk	2000, February 25–26
Crane, Ruth Hanhold	Mauk	1998, October 8
Dahl, Liv	Mauk	1999, March 23
Daniels, Paul	Løvås	1998, September 21; 2000, May 3
Draxten, Nina	Mauk	2000, May 3
Draxten, Nina	Orlyn Kringstad	1987–98
Dyrstad, Joanell M.	Mikkelsen & Mauk	1998, October 27
Early, Ronald Patrick	Mikkelsen	1999, February 9
Eiden, Alphonse	Mikkelsen	1999, April 28
Elder, Lucille	Mauk	2012, March 12

NAME	INTERVIEWER(S)	DATE OF INTERVIEW
Eldevik, Bruce	Løvås	1998, October 2
Enstad, Dick & Nancy	Mauk	1999, January 15, March 13, and October 1; 2000, March 24 and August 4
Evenstad, Shirley & Earl	Mauk	1999, January 15, March 13, and October 1; 2000, March 24 and August 4
Faber, Kåre, Helen, Harald, & Karen	Mauk	1999, April 8
Ferdig, Ruth	Mauk	2012, March 12
Fevold, Eugene L.	Mauk	1999, November 30
Fewer, Sheldon	Mauk	2012, March 12
Flaten, Evelyn & Mary	Mauk	1998, December 17
Forde, Lois & Larry	Mauk	1998, September 12
Forde, Luther & Eileen	Mauk	1998, August 12
Freeman, Jane & Orville	Mikkelsen & Mauk	1999, June 1
Futcher, John S. & Jeanette	Mauk	1999, February 1, 10, 16, 17, 24 and March 17
Green, Bill	Mauk	2000, May 15
Green, Douglas E.	Mauk	2000, May 15
Green, William & Douglas	Mauk	2000, May 9
Greengard, Louis	Mauk	1998, November 10
Grimsby, Hoover	Mauk	1998, December 16
Grindal, Gracia	Løvås & Mauk	1999, April 10; 2000, April 16
Grindem, Bjarne & Else	Mauk	1999, May 25
Gronlie, Pete	Løvås	1998, October 3 and November 14
Haga, Charles "Chuck"	Mauk	2000, April 5
Hagen, Harald Leroy	Løvås & Mauk	1999, February 27
Hansen, Tor & Sunny	Mauk	1999, May 5
Harrisville, Roy Elgin	Løvås	1998, September 28

NAME	INTERVIEWER(S)	DATE OF INTERVIEW
Hatlevik, Magne	Mikkelsen	1998, September 28
Hauge, Lawrence Olav & Lois Cathryn	Mauk	1999, June 23
Heise, Marlin & Leroy	Mikkelsen	1998, December 14
Helgemo, Marlene Whiterabbit	Mauk	2012, March 12
Homstad, Torild	Mauk	2000, May 1
Hustvedt, Lloyd Norland	Mauk	1998, November 19
Ingebretsen, Bud & Julie	Mauk	1999, June 30
Johnson, Clarice	Mikkelsen	1999, January 12
Johnson, Krista Sande Ganderud	Mauk	1998, October 20; 1999, January 13
Johnson, Nellie Allan Stone	Mikkelsen	1999, January 22 and February 19
Johnson, Richard (& Krista)	Mikkelsen	1998, October 13 and 20
Julseth, Gudmund	Mikkelsen	1998, October 22
Kadden, Ione Narissa Brack	Mauk	1998, November 17
King, Dolores Celest Smaaladen	Mauk	1999, May 25
Kleber, Jo Ann Ruth Jordahl	Mauk	2000, May 31
Kringstad, Hilda Sophie Karlsgott	Mauk	1999, March 26; 2001, February 13
Kringstad, Marit Andol & Orlyn	Mauk	1999, February 22
Kringstad, Orlyn	Mauk	2000, May 21
Kristiansen, Gunnar Torfinn	Løvås	1999, January 27
Kucera, Barbara	Mauk	1998, November 10
Kvaal, Merlin Howard	Løvås	1999, July 1
Kvavik, Donald	Mauk	1999, November 4
Latimer, George Albert	Mikkelsen & Mauk	1999, April 21
Leman, Barbara & Bakken, Elva M.	Mikkelsen	1998, October 5
Lervik, Aase	Mauk	1999, June 8
Liabraaten, Kirk	Mikkelsen	1999, February 17

NAME	INTERVIEWER(S)	DATE OF INTERVIEW
Lindgren, Dallas R.	Mikkelsen	1998, December 15
Linneruth, Eleanor	Mikkelsen	1999, June 2
Markely, Tei-Tei (Marie L.) & Harry	Mauk	1998, October 3 and 21
Miller, Debbie Lynn	Mauk	1998, December 14
Moe, Donald M.	Mikkelsen & Mauk	1999, January 19
Moe, Roger Dean	Mikkelsen	1998, November 18; 1999, January 13
Mondale, Walter	Mauk	1999, August 2
Mosvik, Stan & Marion	Løvås	1998, November 30
Munger, William	Mikkelsen & Mauk	1999, February 10
Munther, Ardis	Mauk	1998, October 26
Muus, Hamm	Mauk	2012, March 14
Naftalin, Arthur	Mikkelsen	1999, June 25 and October 26
Nelson, Gordon Lee	Mikkelsen	1999, March 21 and June 5
Nelson, Kenneth	Løvås	1999, June 29
Nelson, Marion & Laila	Mauk	2000, March 4
Nelson, Terry, Gronlie, & Pete	Løvås	1998, November 14
Nestingen, Jim & Leslie (Sandvik)	Mauk	1999, September 1
Ofstie, Lorraine Charlotte	Mauk	2000, May 22, June 2, and July 27
Olsen, Mary Ann	Mauk	1999, May 11
Olson, Alice & Pieper, Ruth	Mauk	1998, December 15; 1999, February 19 and March 15
Olson, Ray	Løvås	1999, March 19
Olstad, Keith	Mauk	1999, March 16 and April 28
Orvick, George & Ruth	Mauk	1999, February 25
Ostby, Roger	Mikkelsen	1999, March 15

NAME	INTERVIEWER(S)	DATE OF INTERVIEW
Pastor Jane (Trinity Church)	Mauk	2012, March 12
Pederson, Helen Holmquist	Mauk	2000, May 12
Pederson, James	Mauk	1998, October 14 and November 5
Peterson, Jim	Mauk	1998, October 2
Qualey, Fred, Hans, Tonette, & Mert	Mauk	1999, January 15, March 13, and October 1; 2000, March 24 and August 4
Rand, Lois	Mauk	1998, September 23
Rand, Sidney	Mauk	1999, December 14
Ranheim, David and Judy	Mauk	2012, March 15 and 17
Rhude, Andreas Jordahl	Mauk	1999, November 16
Robinson, Martha	Løvås	1998, October 5
Roe, Bob	Mikkelsen	1998, October 20
Rudrud, Don	Mauk	2012, March 16
Rusten, Paul	Mauk	2000, March 22
Sabo, Larry	Mauk	1999, March 8
Sabo, Martin Olav	Mikkelsen & Mauk	1999, March 8; 1998, August 1
Sagness, John	Løvås	1999, February 13
Schueler, Phillip T.	Mikkelsen & Mauk	1998, September 2
Schultz, Mary	Løvås	1998, November 12
Selander, Lucy	Mauk	2012, March 12
Sersland, Carol	Mauk	2000, June 22
Sersland, Harold	Carol Sersland (daughter)	n.d.
Shaw, Joseph M.	Mauk	1999, November 11
Siverson, Lloyd	Løvås	1999, May 27
Skaff, Kristin	Løvås	1998, November 10
Skjerstad, Christopher	Mauk	1999, March 30
Skjervold, Christian	Løvås	1999, February 3 and March 31

NAME	INTERVIEWER(S)	DATE OF INTERVIEW
Slettemoen, Ingrid	Mauk	1999, May 3
Sorensen, Marilyn	Mauk	1999, March 24; 2012, March 12
Sorheim, Dennis	Mauk	1998, October 2
Sponheim, Eric	Løvås & Mauk	1998, September 5
Stene, Arthur Marlin	Mauk	1999, November 16
Stenvig, Charles	Ken Chuck, WWTC show	1977, July 21, 27, and 31
Stenvig, Todd C.	Mauk	2012, March 6 and 11
Stolpestad, James	Mauk	2012, March 10
Sundahl, Richard	Mikkelsen	1999, June 19
Svendahl, Mike	Mauk	1999, May 14
Svensby, Lloyd	Mauk	2012, March 12
Thompson, Alida	Løvås	1998, October 20
Thompson, Tom	Mauk	1998, November 3; 1999, August 19
Thorsheim, Mary Jo	Mauk	1998, October 2 and 8 and November 20
Tideman, Janet	Mauk	2012, March 12
Torberg, Virginia H. & Daniel J.	Mikkelsen	1998, September 23
Torgersen, Don	Løvås	1999, June 8
Torstenson, Joel	Mikkelsen & Mauk	1999, March 30 and April 6 and 27
Torvik, Lise	Mikkelsen	1999, May 26
Tunheim, John R. & Jackie	Mauk	1999, October 11
Tweet, Ella Valborg	Mauk	1999, April 1
Unstad, Odd	Mauk	1999, May 3
Voxland, Philip	Mikkelsen	1998, September 15
Wargelin, Marianne	Mauk	2000, May 16
Wasstrand, Ole & Bodil (Gundersen)	Mauk	1999, April 7

NAME	INTERVIEWER(S)	DATE OF INTERVIEW
Welchinger, Marianne	Løvås & Mauk	1998, September 6
Welchinger, Ruth & Vernon	Mauk	1999, December 4
Wolden, Jorunn	Mauk	1999, April 13 and 19
Woo, Carole Kwan	Mauk	1999, February 15
Woolworth, Alan R.	Mauk	1999, January 5
Zempel, Solveig	Mauk	2000, April 1

NOTES

Notes to Chapter One: An Introductory Overview

1. Schultz, *Ethnicity on Parade*, 132–33.

2. Jackson, *Scandinavians in Chicago*, 5–7.

3. For the Twin Cities History Project (hereafter, the TCHP), a team of researchers (Mette Løvås, Robert Mikkelsen, Lee Rokke, and the author) digitally systematized the information in Norway's police records of emigration, the emigrant protocols. The team collected information from all but one of the country's ports of embarkation (Oslo, Kristiansand, Bergen, Trondheim, and Tromsø) concerning Norwegians departing for St. Paul or Minneapolis between 1880, when the data from all these ports was the same and destinations were specific, through 1924. At the time of this work, the records from Stavanger were unavailable. (Since then, all of the protocols have become available online, but it seems unlikely that that city's data would significantly alter the overall pattern.) The team recorded the data about emigration status (excluding other nationalities, crew, and return immigrants), year, age, sex, and occupation, last place of residence in Norway, destination, and the commentary in the protocol. Dr. William Block of the North American Population Project (NAPP) of the University of Minnesota history department analytically systematized this data by category and made tables cross-referencing categories.

4. For some family histories documenting urbanization referred to in the text, see the following TCHP interviews conducted in the Twin Cities metropolitan area (here and below, see appendix for interview dates): Eunice Baker; Carl and Jean Brookins; Ruth Hanhold Crane; Paul Daniels; Evelyn and Mary Flaten; Luther and Eileen Forde; Pete Gronlie; Lloyd Hustvedt; Richard and Krista Johnson; Marion and Laila Nelson; Jim and Leslie Nestingen; Lorraine Ofstie.

5. The evidence from the 1880s first conclusively documented how important urbanization was in comparison with

arrivals directly from the homeland. The largest number of newcomers from Norway in one decade during the time span of the study (3,700) immigrated to the Twin Cities in the 1880s. Yet the number of foreign-born Norwegian Americans in the Cities grew by 12,830 people in those same years. The difference in the two figures indicates that the large majority (71 percent) of these arrivals came to the United States before 1880 and moved to the Cities during the decade. According to the data in the emigrant protocols up to 1880, they first settled in a host of rural places across Minnesota, Iowa, Wisconsin, and in a few cases, the eastern Dakotas. As the research into later periods continued through archival study, library work, and scores of interviews, the documented importance of urbanization for understanding the changing character of the Norwegian American community in the Twin Cities became ever more evident.

6. With the aid of NAPP personnel at the University of Minnesota, the TCHP team of Løvås, Mikkelsen, and Mauk analyzed the complete data set for Minneapolis–St. Paul from the federal census of 1880 that the Church of Jesus Christ of Latter-day Saints made available to the university. The team also took a 10 percent and a 20 percent sample of first- and second-generation Norwegian Americans from the manuscript censuses for Minneapolis–St. Paul in 1900 and 1920. The 10 percent sample provided a means of locating the districts of greatest Norwegian residence, while data collected from the 20 percent sample gave a close-up picture of those districts and their residents. The author used published federal census reports for 1860–2000 and Integrated Public Use Microdata Series (IPUMS) census microdata from the university to construct census samples for later periods.

7. Norlie, *History of the Norwegian People*, 312–13.

8. Herbert J. Gans, "Symbolic Ethnicity: The Future of Ethnic Groups and Cultures in America," in Gans, et al., eds., *On the Making of Americans*, 203–7. Another version of his treatment of the concept is "Symbolic Ethnicity: The Future of Ethnic Groups and Cultures in America," in *Ethnic and Racial Studies* 2, no. 1 (1979): 1–20. Gans discusses recent scholarly models for studying later-generation ethnic groups in *Making Sense of America: Sociological Analyses and Essays*; see especially Part III. Eric Kaufmann presents a theoretical approach to the concept of an ethnic core in "Ethnic or Civic Nation?: Theorizing the American Case," European Institute, London School of Economics and Political Science.

9. Oral sources for this and the next paragraph included TCHP interviews with Kjell Bergh; Liv Dahl; former consul general Bjarne and Else Grindem; Chuck Haga; Tei-Tei and Harry Markely; and Dennis Sorheim. The author learned the history of skilled arts, dance, and crafts practitioners in the Twin Cities and suburbs through TCHP interviews and social occasions with Gaelyn and Daniel Beal; Fred Cogelow; Dick and Nancy Enstad and the "Pie Group" (Shirley and Earl Evenstad; Fred, Hans, Tonette, and Mert Qualey); Hilda Kringstad; Laila and Marion Nelson; and Carole Sersland.

10. The last newspaper, *Minneapolis Posten* (1940–56), continued as *Minnesota Posten* to 1979. See Lovoll, *Norwegian Newspapers in America*, 337–38, 359–60.

Notes to Chapter Two: Foundations of Urban Life

1. Semmingsen, "Norwegian Emigration to America," 1–8; Lovoll, *The Promise Fulfilled*, 17.

2. Gjerde, *From Peasants to Farmers*, 61–63, 67, 74.

3. Lovoll, *The Promise of America*, 118–22; Holand, *De Norske Settlementers Historie*, 320–29, 344, 357–72, 379–417, 446–50, 483–97, 507–9, 532–43; Qualey, *Norwegian Settlement*, 97–129, 231–35. The latter pages in Qualey's book include detailed tables of the Norwegian-born and their children in Minnesota at early censuses from 1857 to 1900 from which the figures in the text are taken or derived. The figures from which the proportion of Norwegian Americans in Minneapolis up to 1960 was calculated were accessed in May 2014 via "Local Census Bin," Fisher Library, University of Virginia.

4. Larson, "The Norwegian Element." For Larson's background, see Blegen's "Preface," v, in *Minnesota*. The estimated percent of immigrant Norwegians and the boundaries of New Norway comes from Larson, page 71; the quotation is on page 72. Though Larson felt the personality accurately described Norwegian immigrants in the Upper Midwest, novelist Arne Garborg wrote about his neighbors in southern Norway.

5. Larson, "The Norwegian Element." The quotation from Garborg is found on page 21. For the best example of the historical literature citing the wish to maintain status in a rural peasant society as the cause of emigration from Norway, see Gjerde, *From Peasants to Farmers*.

6. Larson, "The Norwegian Element," 73.

7. Larson, "The Norwegian Element," 71–72, 72–73.

8. Qualey, *Norwegian Settlement*, 115, 118.

9. Holand, *De Norske Settlementers Historie*, 361–63, 370, 533–34, provides descriptions of a few of the many communities characteristic of the bygd phase of Norwegian pioneer settlement that are included in his study. Lovoll, *The Promise of America*, 52–55, 282–89; see also Lovoll's *A Folk Epic* and Gjerde's *From Peasants to Farmers* and *Minds of the West*, among other studies.

10. Holand, *De Norske Settlementers Historie*, 358; Lovoll, *The Promise of America*, 55; Qualey, *Norwegian Settlement*, 13–15.

11. Øverland's quoted words characterizing Janson's views are found on page 159 of *The Western Home*. Lovoll, *The Promise of America*, 137–39, describes the somewhat humorous overthrow of club law in Goodhue County. The original of the club law story is in Holand, *De Norske Settlementers Historie*, 375–78. See also Qualey, *Norwegian Settlement*, 98, on Norwegian settlers among squatters and the expectation of preemption rights that would legalize their claims and the American nature of their pioneer experience. Blegen, *Minnesota*, 178, makes a similar point about American squatters who founded Minneapolis and built a bridge across the Mississippi to their town in the same confident expectation of preemption rights—which was not disappointed. See the discussion of Minneapolis later in this chapter.

12. Holand, *De Norske Settlementers Historie*, 323–24, is the source of the translated quoted material. On the arrival of the news of territorial status for Minnesota, see Castle, *History of St. Paul and Vicinity*, 1:47,

85–86. On page 47, Castle unaccountably gives the *Highland Mary* the honor of being the first boat in his list of 1849's memorable events, while in accordance with other historians he later names the *Dr. Franklin, No. 2*, the first weekly steam packet of the year, as the bearer of the good news. See also Neill, *History of Minnesota*, 494.

13. The words in single quotation marks are in English in Holand's original Norwegian text. Blegen, *Minnesota*, 295–96.

14. Kane, *Falls of St. Anthony*, 99–100.

15. Kane and Ominsky, *Twin Cities*, 5, 11; Blegen, *Minnesota*, 88.

16. Gilman, "Territorial Imperative," 151–58.

17. Gilman, "Territorial Imperative," 160.

18. Williams, *History of the City of Saint Paul*, 42–43, 64–73; Shutter, *History of Minneapolis*, 79.

19. Williams, *History of the City of Saint Paul*, 99–113, 115–16, 118, 120–21.

20. Williams, *History of the City of Saint Paul*, 160, 162.

21. The quoted material is found in Williams, *History of the City of Saint Paul*, 149, 153, 207, 214, 274–75. For his comments on the Red River carts, see 304–8. Bremer, *Homes of the New World*, 2:34–38.

22. Gilman, "Territorial Imperative," 158; Williams, *History of the City of Saint Paul*, 207–8, 271. Gilman, "Territorial Imperative," 160–62, discusses the eagerness for land treaties with the Natives. See also Williams, *History of the City of Saint Paul*, 309–10, 326–27; Bremer, *Homes of the New World*, 2:25.

23. Williams, *History of the City of Saint Paul*, 170–71, 210–11, 241, 349, 357–59. On the effects of the Panic of 1857 in St. Paul, see Williams, *History of the City of Saint Paul*, 379–83, and Wingerd, "City Limits," 44–48.

24. Holand, *De Norske Settlementers Historie*, 324–25.

25. Holand, *De Norske Settlementers Historie*, 325, 424–26.

26. Holand, *De Norske Settlementers Historie*, 325; Hansen, *My Minneapolis*, 19.

27. Eighth US Census, Vol. 1, 261–62, Table 5: Nativities of the Population. Most of the chapters in Williams's *History of the City of Saint Paul* on the 1840s consist of capsule biographies of pioneer New Englanders in St. Paul; see pages 140–46, 198–201, 214–15, 266–71, 359, 379. The quoted phrases come from Bremer, *Homes of the New World*, 2:25–26.

28. Williams, *History of the City of Saint Paul*, 259–60, 357–58.

29. Williams, *History of the City of Saint Paul*, 228, 266; Eighth US Census, Vol. 1, 255–60.

30. Williams, *History of the City of Saint Paul*, 233–34; Bremer, *Homes of the New World*, 2:25–27, 29–41.

31. Bremer, *Homes of the New World*, 2:34–38, 58; Gjerde, *From Peasants to Farmers*, 192–99; Holand, *De Norske Settlementers Historie*, 325.

32. Andersen, *Salt of the Earth*, 51–53, 54–55. Andersen cites the quoted phrase from the Reverend Thomas M. Fullerton's letter to the Reverend Christian Willerup on page 54. Letter from the Reverend Thomas M. Fullerton to Benjamin F. Hoyt, March 22, 1859, in the Methodist Episcopal Church, Minnesota Annual Methodist Conference Papers, 1840–1909, box 1, Minnesota Historical Society, St. Paul (hereafter, MNHS).

33. Fullerton to Hoyt, March 22, 1859; Andersen, *Salt of the Earth*, 39–41; Erickson

and Erickson, "Scandinavian Methodist Episcopal Church," 172nn10–11.

34. Andersen, *Salt of the Earth*, 40, 54–55.

35. Fullerton to Hoyt, March 22, 1859; Andersen, *Salt of the Earth*, 54; Erickson and Erickson, "Scandinavian Methodist Episcopal Church," 173.

36. Andersen, *Salt of the Earth*, 55–56; *Kyrkobok*, 2–4. Some evidence of Swedish domestics in the congregation in the 1870s is found in Governor Ramsey's diary where he notes having taken his Swedish servants to the church: Alexander Ramsey, September 24, 1876, Diary, 1871–1903, MHHS; Blegen, *Norwegian Migration*, 118–23.

37. Andersen, *Salt of the Earth*, 45, 55. Charles William Wulff Borup, the congregation's Danish banker benefactor, died on July 6, 1859, in St. Paul; other members of his family were prominent businessmen in the city until the turn of the twentieth century: see "Minnesota Biographies," 65.

38. Andersen, *Salt of the Earth*, 46, 55–56; *Kyrkobok*, 2–4; Erickson and Erickson, "Scandinavian Methodist Episcopal Church," 164–67, 176n31, 188n54. Arlow W. Anderson, "Historical Statement," in *Home Coming Celebration, Methodist Aurora [Church], 1873–1926* (St. Paul: Aurora Methodist, 1926), n.p., and "The Midway Church Celebrates the Ninetieth Anniversary of Its Founding, May 14th and 15th, 1944," a two-page typescript, both in the archives of the Minnesota Annual Conference of the United Methodist Church, Minneapolis.

39. "100 Years with Christ," in *Our Second Century in Christ, 1868–1968* (centennial anniversary booklet) (St. Paul: Christ Church Lutheran congregation, 1968), 4–5.

40. The interpretation of events at St. Paul's Scandinavian Lutheran church here and below relies largely on an analysis of "100 Years with Christ." See also Larsen, *Laur. Larsen*, 69–72, for the broader context of the controversy and another account of the events.

41. The new institution's affiliation fit well because in 1858 the synod was both willing to accept such mixed groups and theologically orthodox in precisely the fashion that suited the new group's Norwegian majority. Larsen, *Laur. Larsen*, 69, 71; Campbell, *St. Paul City Directory for 1875*, 32.

42. *St. Paul City Directory, 1858–1859*, 22.

43. *St. Paul City Directory, 1858–1859*, 162–63. This directory mistakenly lists both a Scandinavian congregation on Tenth Street near Cooper and a Norwegian Methodist Church at Tenth and Temperance Streets (126, 162). The first address was the location of the Scandinavian Methodist congregation at the time, according to the church's records. The address near Cooper Street was the home of the Scandinavian congregation's assistant pastor, the former lay preacher John Tidlund. The second Nordic immigrant church, a Norwegian-dominated Scandinavian congregation, could easily have been inadvertently left out, especially since it did not organize until the time of the directory. But because other sources document the first Scandinavian Lutheran congregation's existence from 1854, it is more likely that a lack of familiarity with the city's Nordic populations and their languages may have contributed to the exclusion of their oldest institution from the directory. In time, the continuing influx of Germans—and Scandinavians—would add several Lutheran congregations to the list of churches in later directories. Polk and Danser, *St. Paul City Directory, 1884–1885*, 100, for example, lists nine Lutheran congregations—four German, two Norwegian,

two Swedish, and one without an indication of nationality background. No Norwegian congregations existing at the time are left out.

44. *St. Paul City Directory, 1858–1859,* 159–65.

45. An overview and list were tabulated from a cover-to-cover registration of Scandinavian-name entries in *St. Paul City Directory, 1858–1859*. See Lovoll, *The Promise of America*, 180.

46. *St. Paul City Directory, 1858–1859;* Andersen, "Historical Statement," in *Home Coming Celebration*, 5–6; "100 Years with Christ," historical sketch, 3.

47. Kane, *Falls of St. Anthony*, 15, 41.

48. Shutter, *History of Minneapolis*, 68, 72–73, 77–78; Kane, *Falls of St. Anthony*, 7.

49. This and the next several paragraphs build on Shutter, *History of Minneapolis*, 73–80, and Kane, *Falls of St. Anthony*, 7–14, but the basic facts of the story are also told elsewhere.

50. Shutter, *History of Minneapolis*, 80–84; the quoted phrases are on page 82.

51. This and the next paragraph build on Kane, *Falls of St. Anthony*, 12, 15–19, 26–29, 39, 44; Kane cites the appellation "New England of the West" on page 39. On the Winslow House in St. Anthony and its southern guests, including enslaved people such as Eliza Winston, see Kane and Ominsky, *Twin Cities*, 18, 27, and Gilman, *The Story of Minnesota's Past*, 107–10. Kane and Ominsky, *Twin Cities*, 6, summarizes the rise and fall of St. Anthony's fortunes.

52. The historian of the waterpower development at the falls, Lucile M. Kane, elucidates the factors that distinguished the growth of St. Anthony and Minneapolis: see *Falls of St. Anthony*, 30–61. See also, for example, Shutter, *History of Minneapolis*, 72–73, 88–100. The quotation concerning "sooners" is found in Kane, *Falls of St. Anthony*, 34; see also 203n14.

53. Kane, *Falls of St. Anthony*, 44–55; Wingerd, "City Limits," 42.

54. "St. Anthony and Minneapolis: Their Rise, Present Position, and Future Destiny," in Chamberlin, *St. Anthony and Minneapolis Directory, 1859–1860*, 15–21. The publisher ascribes the authorship of the piece to "one of the oldest and most respectable inhabitants of Minneapolis."

55. Chamberlin, *St. Anthony and Minneapolis Directory, 1859–1860*, 118.

56. Chamberlin, *St. Anthony and Minneapolis Directory, 1859–1860*, 158–62.

57. Qualey, *Norwegian Settlement*, 230–31, includes tables based on the author's registration and analysis of the relevant census data on Norwegian-born and Norwegian-stock individuals. Hansen, *My Minneapolis*, 14.

58. Histories based on contemporary accounts of the Indian war are replete with references to Euro Americans' surprise, no less in the river towns than in the frontier countryside. See, for example, Gilman, *The Story of Minnesota's Past*, 116, 118, and Andrews, "Narrative of the Third Regiment," 147.

59. For the inflated population figures, see page 10 of the St. Anthony and Minneapolis directory and page 20 of the St. Paul directory. The census population figures come from the Eighth US Census, *Population*, 1:255–60, and the Ninth US Census, *Population*, 1:178–79.

60. An overview and list from the St. Anthony and Minneapolis directory, parallel to that tabulated from a cover-to-cover registration of Scandinavian-name entries in the 1858–59 St. Paul city directory, are the basis of these estimations and the quoted phrases.

61. Lovoll, *The Promise of America*, 108.

62. Ager, *Oberst Heg og hans Gutter*, 289–320; Paulson, *Memoirs*, 72–75.

63. *Annual Report of the Adjutant General*, 20–22, 50–51, 92–93, 110–13; on Company D, 136–40.

64. Andrews, "Narrative of the Third Regiment," 147.

65. Calculated from the *Annual Report of the Adjutant General*, 136–40; Andrews, "Narrative of the Third Regiment," 149.

66. *Annual Report of the Adjutant General*, 139–40; Andrews, "Narrative of the Third Regiment," 151–55, 157–62.

67. Calculated from "Known Military and Civilian Dead during the Minnesota Sioux Indian Massacre in 1862," compiled by Clarence Stewart Peterson for the Minnesota Centennial Memorial, 1858–1958. Alan Woolworth, researcher emeritus at the Minnesota Historical Society, supplied a copy of this document and vouched for it as the most complete and accurate list of the whites slain during the Dakota War.

68. Anderson and Woolworth, "Introduction," in *Through Dakota Eyes*, 8–14; Curt Brown, "150 Years Later, War's Wounds Still Cut Deep," *Minneapolis Star Tribune*, January 29, 2012.

69. Guri Endreson Rosseland, letter from "Harrison P. O., Monongalia Co., Minnesota, December 2, 1866," translated and edited by Theodore C. Blegen, "Notes and Documents." See Lovoll, *The Promise of America*, 128–32, for a brief account of the events Guri Endreson wrote of which effectively places them in wider contexts. Blegen, "Notes and Documents," 425–26; the quotation from the letter is on page 428. Blegen, *Norwegian Migration*, 407–8, contains his repetition of the popular version of Endreson's heroism, despite his own discovery of her letter revealing how she viewed the attack and its aftermath.

70. Blegen, "Notes and Documents," 425–26; the quotation from the letter is on page 428.

71. Blegen, "Notes and Documents," 429.

Notes to Chapter Three: In the Aftermath

1. Lovoll, *The Promise of America*, 32–36, 118, 121–24.

2. This and the following paragraphs build on Hans Mattson to Governor W. R. Marshall, 1866–67, Marshall Papers, MNHS; *Annual Report of the Board of Immigration to the Legislature of Minnesota, 1867* (St. Paul: Minnesota State Printing Office, 1868); Shippee, "Effects of the Civil War," 404; Walker, *American City*, 13; Folwell, *History of Minnesota*, 2:1–2; Lovoll, *The Promise of America*, 29–30, 132–37; Blegen, *Minnesota*, 304–7; Qualey, *Norwegian Settlement*, 99–108; Mattson, *Reminiscences*, 97–103, 111, 117–18, 122–23.

3. Johannes B. Wist, "Pressen etter Borgerkrigen," in *Norsk-Amerikanernes Festskrift, 1914*, Johannes B. Wist, ed., 59–60, 64–65, 100. For examples of Hjelm-Hansen's newspaper articles concerning settlement in America and Minnesota in particular, see *Nordisk Folkeblad*, April 16, 1868, and September 22, 1869. See also Fagereng, "Norwegian Social and Cultural Life in America," 44–46.

4. The interpretation in this and the following paragraphs builds on information in Gilman, *The Story of Minnesota's Past*, 128–31; Folwell, *History of Minnesota*, 2:93–111; and Blegen, *Minnesota*, 52, 294–95, 306–7, 341–47, 390.

5. Neither the state enumeration in 1865 nor the federal censuses five years on

either side of it counted the foreign-born or their children in towns. But the only significant rural settlement of Norwegian immigrants in the same county as one of the river towns was a small group to the north of Minneapolis in today's Fridley, so it is relatively safe to assume that the increase of Norwegian-born residents in Ramsey County occurred mainly in St. Paul and that a large part of the phenomenal increase in Hennepin County took place in its two riverside communities.

6. Qualey, *Norwegian Settlement*, 231–35; US Census, *Population*, Vol. I, 1860, 1870, 1880.

7. The paragraphs on Civil War veterans draw on the following sources: Williams, *History of the City of Saint Paul*, 417–19; *Annual Report of the Adjutant General*, 22, 51, 93, 110–11, 138, 277, 279, 342, 410, 440–41, 488, 498, 638, 732–33, 862; Nelson, ed., *History of the Scandinavians*, 1:365–66, 405–6, 480–81, 502–3; Hansen, *My Minneapolis*, 32–33; "Deltagelsen in Statspolitiken og Lokalpolitiken i 70-Aarene," in "Tvillingbyernes norske saga, XIII," *Skandinaven*, June 28, 1935; Lovoll, *The Promise of America*, 107–9; Atwater, *History of Minneapolis*, 2:811–15, 840–50.

8. Minnesota Third Regiment first lieutenant Lars K. Aaker frequented St. Paul as a state senator. One veteran of the Norwegian Wisconsin's Fifteenth Regiment, Mons Grinager, lived in St. Paul for two years and ran a business in Decorah, Iowa, before the war, then entered politics and was nominated as Minnesota's secretary of state before ending his career in Minneapolis. Like Albert Rice and Lars Aaker—and many another early Norwegian American politician—Grinager's home base was in a small town or rural area of the state, but opportunity in the Twin Cities beckoned both early and late in his career.

9. See for example, Nelson, ed., *History of the Scandinavians*, 365–66, 369–74, 376–84, 394–95, 400, 402–6, 408–9, 411–13, 416, 437, 438, 464, 466–67, 469–70, 472, 479, 480, 487–88, 489–90, 494, 498, 502–3, 512–13, 517–18, and Hansen, *My Minneapolis*, 16–22, 27–28, 31–36, 39, 48–52. See also Julius B. Baumann, "Fra Gamle Dage" and "Gamle Minder," *Minneapolis Tidende*, March 1, 7, and 14, 1917; and Carl G. O. Hansen, "Tvillingbyernes norske saga, VI, VIII and XIII," *Skandinaven*, May 17 and 24 and June 28, 1935.

10. See Gilman, *The Story of Minnesota's Past*, 128–31.

11. Watts, "The Technology that Launched a City," 86–97; Adams and VanDrasek, *Minneapolis–St. Paul*, 32–37; Atwater, *History of Minneapolis*, 2:611–12, 631–32.

12. Kane, *Falls of St. Anthony*, 57–59; Adams and VanDrasek, *Minneapolis–St. Paul*, 32–35.

13. "Fracas," *St. Paul Daily Press*, June 28, 1863; "The Progress of Industrial Development," *St. Paul Daily Press*, August 1, 1864; "Dead and Live, the Remarkable Experience of Jonas Nilson, a Lumberman," *St. Paul and Minneapolis Pioneer Press*, March 16, 1877.

14. Hansen, *My Minneapolis*, 12, 19–20; undated interview between Nina Draxten and Orlyn Kringstad, "Immigrant Star Search Program," Sons of Norway (ca. 1987 or 1988, according to Kringstad); TCHP interviews with Nina Draxten and John S. Futcher. The description of the rural, semirural, and central districts that are now in the city of Minneapolis

depends largely on Pedersen, *Selbygbogen*, 356–65.

15. The narrative of the early career of Andreas Ueland depends on his autobiography, *Recollections of an Immigrant*, 3–36. It is a curious coincidence that the English textbook he used has the same title as the one Johannes Wist has his greenhorn Norwegian buy in his *Nykomerbilleder*, 30.

16. *Second Annual Directory of the City of St. Paul for 1871* (St. Paul: Rice and Company, 1871), 32, 34–37.

17. The information on Vice-Consul Sahlgaard, which is evident in the papers from the vice-consulate (in late 2001 still in the Dokumentarkiv of the Norwegian Foreign Ministry in Oslo), is also summarized in Carl G. O. Hansen, "Tvilingbyernes norske Saga, En Avstikker til Pionertiden i St. Paul–En bank Mand den første Bankier i Minnesota–Nordmænd i St. Paul i 60-Aarene, VIII," *Skandinaven*, May 24, 1935.

18. Adams and VanDrasek, *Minneapolis–St. Paul*, 77. Interviews with latter-day residents confirm Scandinavian rather than purely Swedish settlement in Phalen Creek ravine in the earliest period.

19. Andersen, *Salt of the Earth*, 62–65, 73, 75–78. The quotation, cited and translated by Andersen, is found on pages 64–65n2. Haagensen, *Den Norsk-Danske Methodismes Historie*, 36–40, quotation page 39, author's translation. See also Andersen, "Historical Statement," in *Home Coming Celebration*, n.p.

20. Anonymous, *Serving Christ in Our Second Century: Christ Lutheran Church on Capitol Hill* (St. Paul: the church, 1968); interview and tour of "Norwegian St. Paul" with Eunice Baker.

21. This and the succeeding paragraphs interpret information from *Eighty-fifth Anniversary* (St. Paul: Christ Lutheran Church on Capitol Hill, 1953); *Serving Christ in Our Second Century*; conferences during 1999–2000 with Eunice and Luci Baker, members of Christ Church; and Eunice Baker, interview and tour.

22. A tabulation of names in the 1871–72 city directory revealed 486 residents of the towns at the falls of the Mississippi who were likely of Scandinavian origin; see Qualey, *Norwegian Settlement*, 231–35.

23. The figures were 85 percent in St. Anthony compared with 88 percent in St. Paul.

24. "Minneapolis and St. Anthony Briefly Epitomized," vi; US Census, *Population* (Washington, DC: Government Printing Office, 1872), 1:178, 180.

25. Hansen, *My Minneapolis*, 23, and Carl G. O. Hansen, "De norske Kirker i Minneapolis. Det grunnlæggende Arbeide paa det Kirkelige Omraade," *Minneapolis Tidende*, January 24, 1912; Our Saviour's Lutheran Church, "A Half Century's History, 1869–1919," in *Sixtieth Anniversary*, 4, and "The Annals of a Church," in *Diamond Anniversary*, 4; David A. Lanegran, "Swedish Neighborhoods of the Twin Cities: From Swede Hollow to Arlington Hills, from Snoose Boulevard to Minnehaha Parkway," in Anderson and Blanck, eds., *Swedes in the Twin Cities*, 39–56. In spite of a continued Scandinavian presence in the northeast section of Minneapolis, the area developed a lasting citywide reputation as the home of southern and eastern European immigrants by 1900.

26. This and the following paragraphs build on Minneapolis city directories from the 1870s; advertisements in *Nordisk*

Folkelad and *Budstikken* during the decade; Adams and VanDrasek, *Minneapolis–St. Paul,* 77, 80–81; Kane and Ominsky, *Twin Cities,* 45–79; and Hansen, *My Minneapolis,* 19–21, 32–34, 38–40, 132–33.

27. Carl G. O. Hansen, "Tvillingbyernes norske saga, XII," *Skandinaven,* June 21, 1935; Hjelm-Hansen, *Business Directory,* 66–75.

28. Rosheim, *The Other Minneapolis,* 11, 18–27; see also the sources in note 31, below.

29. Contemporary newspaper advertisements and local histories, checked against the falls cities directory, confirm the locations of Scandinavian stores and workshops.

30. Paulson, *Memoirs,* 114–15.

31. Carl G. O. Hansen, "Minneapolis' historie—Kapitlet om den norske koloni," *Minneapolis Daglig Tidende,* January 24, 1912; "Tvillingbyernes norske saga, IV," *Skandinaven,* May 17, 1935; and "Tvillingbyernes norske saga, XII," *Skandinaven,* June 21, 1935; Hansen, *My Minneapolis,* 16–17. The correspondence of H. Sahlgaard, the second man to serve as Swedish Norwegian vice-consul, notes repeatedly that W. T. Rambusch was the first man to hold the position and that the vice-consulate was moved from Minneapolis to St. Paul when Rambusch resigned from its duties in 1871. Wist, ed., *Norsk-Amerikanernes Festskrift,* 57, 60, provided the information about W. T. Rambusch. Söderström, *Minneapolis Minnen,* 39, describes the regular meetings of local bachelors in Edsten's backyard.

32. Carl G. O. Hansen, "Tvillingbyernes norske saga, IX," *Skandinaven,* June 7, 1935; Hansen, *My Minneapolis,* 26–27.

33. Carl G. O. Hansen relates the anecdote about Bull's private comments at the Syttende mai banquet in Wisconsin in *My Minneapolis,* 26–27.

34. This and the following paragraphs concerning the early history of Trinity congregation synthesize information in *Trefoldighets Menighet,* 6–9; Hamre, *From Immigrant Parish to Inner City Ministry,* 9–10; Hansen, "De norske kirker i Minneapolis." At the falls, Lutherans rather than Methodists founded the first Scandinavian congregation. Methodist activities among the Scandinavians of St. Anthony and Minneapolis resulted in the organization of First Dano-Norwegian M. E. Church (also known as Asbury Methodist congregation of Minneapolis) eight years after the Evangelical Lutheran Augustana Congregation was established in 1866. Like the earlier Lutheran church, Asbury Methodist originated largely as a result of migration to Minneapolis from rural Scandinavian immigrant communities in the region—in its case from Lake Elizabeth and Newburg, Minnesota—and to begin with, it also depended on clerics from rural settlements to conduct services when they visited. Anderson, *Salt of the Earth,* 75–76.

35. *Tribune's Directory for Minneapolis and St. Anthony, 1871–72,* 214–16. The lists of churches in the directory show much the same mix of religious denominations but no Scandinavian American congregations.

36. Paulson, *Memoirs,* 115–17; *Trefoldighets Menighet,* 11, 17. Hamre, *From Immigrant Parish to Inner City Ministry,* 12–14, also indicates rapid growth in membership for similar reasons but finds different figures based on Trinity's Communion Book from the period.

37. The Norwegian-Danish Evangelical Lutheran Trinity Congregation of Minneapolis, congregational minutes, 1868–69, especially October 1869, 27–31; Nelson and

Fevold, *The Lutheran Church Among Norwegian-Americans*, 1:222.

38. Nelson and Fevold, *The Lutheran Church Among Norwegian-Americans*, 198–210, quotation page 210. Church historian Todd Nichol believes the founders of Trinity and other Norwegian immigrant congregations may have learned important elements of church organization and polity before leaving Norway through the local involvement of laymen in such matters there. According to Nelson and Fevold, *The Lutheran Church Among Norwegian-Americans*, 1:210–12, the other Norwegian American religious body that formed on the dissolution of the Augustana Synod, the Norwegian Augustana Synod, showed a contrasting combination of preserving elements of the religious heritage (in its case as lay preachers and a non-liturgical worship style inspired by the Haugean awakening in Norway) and accommodating conditions in the United States (evident in its cultivation of connections with American religious bodies and early emphasis on the use of English). See Nichol's "Introduction" in Preus, *Vivacious Daughter*, 20–23, for a concise summary of the circumstances leading to the conference's formation. Lovoll, *The Promise of America*, 147, offers a brief, clear analysis of the conference's middle position in Norwegian American Lutheranism and rapid growth.

39. Chrislock, *Fjord to Freeway*, 6–7, 18–20; Paulson, *Memoirs*, 119–23; Hamre, *From Immigrant Parish to Inner City Ministry*, 16–18. "Minnesota Biographies" includes a brief description of Judge Vanderburgh's career.

40. Chrislock, *Fjord to Freeway*, 7–8; Paulson, *Memoirs*, 122. Helland, *Augsburg Seminar*, 80–81, cites Paulson's reference to local businessmen's preoccupation with preserving the falls in his 1872 report to the conference. Kane, *Falls of St. Anthony*, 71–79, documents that the controversy over how to pay for preventing the collapse of the falls raged locally just as Augsburg's supporters were soliciting financial support. See the *Tribune's Directory for Minneapolis and St. Anthony, 1871–72*, 96, 223.

41. *Minneapolis Daily Tribune*, November 1, 1872, 4.

42. Haanes, "*Hvad skal da dette blive for prester?*," 200–203, 208; Helland, *Augsburg Seminar*, 119; Chrislock, *Fjord to Freeway*, 11.

43. Chrislock, *Fjord to Freeway*, 6, 15, 20; Haanes, "*Hvad skal da dette blive for prester?*," 200, 210–16; for a fuller view of the Augsburg professors' similarities and differences with the reformer Gisle Johnson, see 129–30, 160–63, 171, 201, and Nelson and Fevold, *The Lutheran Church Among Norwegian-Americans*, 1:226–29. Johnson, for example, favored democratizing the church's voluntary and official work but not organizing as loosely associated "free" congregations. See Augsburg faculty, *Program for Augsburg Seminary*, for the author's quoted translations of passages on page 6 in "Græskafdeling" and page 8 in "Augsburg Seminariums teologiske cursus."

44. Chrislock, *Fjord to Freeway*, 3–6, 10–12, 15–17, 26; Hamre, *Georg Sverdrup*, 47–48, 49, 122, 161, 173, 199–202, 217–20; Augsburg faculty, *Program for Augsburg Seminary*, 2–3, quotation page 8, author's translation; Jacob Sverdrup, "Augsburg seminarium bedømt i Norge," in *Kvartalsskrift* (1875): 81–90.

45. Haanes, "*Hvad skal da dette blive for prester?*," 208–31; Helland, *Augsburg Seminar*, 96–105; Chrislock, *Fjord to Freeway*,

10–12; Nelson and Fevold, *The Lutheran Church Among Norwegian-Americans,* 1:224–30; *Trefoldighets Menighet,* 7–9, 15–17; Hamre, *From Immigrant Parish to Inner City Ministry,* 18–20, quotation page 18. In the late 1990s, interviews with former students and faculty members at Augsburg (Joel Torstenson, Jim Petersen, Larry Sabo, and Carl Chrislock, among others) revealed an enduring loyalty to a cultural tradition that they identified with both Trinity and Augsburg and felt to be distinct from other Norwegian American institutional networks. The values they praised and saw as rooted in the views of Augsburg's first faculty members were an adamant commitment to academic freedom in the search for truth, however unpopular the truths found were, and the sense that the conference and later the Free Church was a religious body that expected laymen to question pastoral pronouncements and sermons until they thoroughly understood and could live by them.

46. Hansen, "De norske Kirker i Minneapolis"; Haanes, "*Hvad skal da dette blive for prester?,*" 208–18; Our Saviour's Lutheran Church, "A Half Century's History, 1869–1919," in *Sixtieth Anniversary,* 1–4, and "The Annals of a Church," in *Diamond Anniversary,* 1–4; Nichol, "Introduction," in Preus, *Vivacious Daughter,* 22–23.

47. See note 52, below, and Nichol, "Introduction," in Preus, *Vivacious Daughter,* 23; Malmin, Norlie, and Tingelstad, trans. and eds., *Who's Who Among Pastors,* 562–64, 648–52; Lovoll, *The Promise of America,* 55–58, 85.

48. Nichol, "Introduction," in Preus, *Vivacious Daughter,* 13–20, quotation page 19; see also Haanes, "*Hvad skal da dette blive for prester?,*" 131–33, 136–42, 148–56, 208–13, quotation page 154, author's translation.

49. See Lovoll, *The Promise of America,* 161–65, on the ties between religious and educational institutions during this period. Lovoll, *The Promise Fulfilled,* 79–80, provides an informed statement of the wider influence of Norwegian American churches and conventional historical estimate that the majority of nineteenth-century Norwegian Americans were not formally enrolled members of Lutheran congregations.

50. Hansen, *My Minneapolis,* 16, 23–24; Minnesota State Census, 1875. For exact figures for Norwegian-, Swedish-, and Danish-born in Minneapolis in that year, see John R. Jenswold, "The Rise and Fall of Pan-Scandinavianism in Urban America," 168n4, in Lovoll, ed., *Scandinavians and Other Immigrants,* 159–70. Norlie, *Norsk Lutherske Menigheter i Amerika,* 541, 563. Harold E. Jensen, "Sixty Years of Trinity Lutheran Congregation," in *Sixtieth Anniversary, 1870–1930, Trinity Lutheran Congregation, St. Paul* (St. Paul: the church, 1930); Immanuel Lutheran Church, St. Paul, "History" (St. Paul: the church, 1946), and "Immanuel Lutheran Church, Dedication Program" (St. Paul: the church, 1961)—all in NAHA Congregations Collection, P 537, Norwegian-American Historical Association Archives, St. Olaf College, Northfield, MN (hereafter, NAHA).

51. Hansen, *My Minneapolis,* 29; Söderström, *Minneapolis Minnen,* 34–37. See Jenswold, "The Rise and Fall of Pan-Scandinavianism," for a good brief analysis of cooperation among Scandinavians in the later 1800s.

52. Söderström, *Minneapolis Minnen,* 262; Carl G. O. Hansen, "Foreningslivet," 4, in *Minneapolis, En Række Artikler fra Minneapolis Tidende i December 1922* (Minneapolis, a Series of Articles from *Minneapolis Tidende* in December 1922).

53. Hansen, *My Minneapolis*, 27–31; Söderström, *Minneapolis Minnen*, 262–63.

54. Chrislock, *Fjord to Freeway*, 28–32; Helland, *Augsburg Seminar*, 129–48.

55. Nelson and Fevold, *The Lutheran Church Among Norwegian-Americans*, 1:230–32; Helland, *Augsburg Seminar*, 146; Chrislock, *Fjord to Freeway*, 32–33. The quoted phrases are taken from Chrislock's translation of what he asserts is Oftedal's account of the conference's annual meeting in 1877 as it is reported in *Beretning om det . . . aarlige Konferentsemøde . . . 1877*.

56. Haanes, *Hvad skal da dette blive for prester?*, 217–18; Nelson and Fevold, *The Lutheran Church Among Norwegian Americans*, 1:228.

57. *Minneapolis Tribune*, August 13, 1869, reports on the convention of the state's Scandinavian Republicans in the city. The lobbying for Scandinavian policemen was reported again much later in *Minneapolis Tribune*, January 27, 1935, where the prophecy of the city's Scandinavian future quoted in the text is also noted. All this information is cited in Rosheim, *The Other Minneapolis*, 20. Söderström, *Minneapolis Minnen*, 132–33, lists the Scandinavian policemen in Minneapolis. Best, "Keeping the Peace in St. Paul," 240–48, includes evidence of political lobbying for ethnic representation on the local police force, and the portrait gallery of police constables in the city in 1874 on page 241 includes one officer with a Norwegian name and another with a Swedish name. The names listed on the board of aldermen in the St. Paul City Directory between 1885 and 1913 include Norwegian Americans Hans P. Jensen in 1892 and Hans P. Jansen in 1893 in the Ninth Ward; Swedish Americans John Blom in the First Ward in 1888 and John Lindahl in the First Ward in 1894 and 1896; and Norwegian American John Larsen in the Ninth Ward in 1888, 1896, and 1897. The *St. Paul Daily Globe* names these Scandinavian American delegates to the Ramsey County Republican Convention and as aldermen elected to the above-named wards in the 1890s: see the *Globe*, April 8, 1888, April 22, 1892, April 11, 1896, and September 23, 1898, for examples of announcements of candidates chosen at conventions and local elections.

58. Qualey, *Norwegian Settlement*, 112–19, 129; Soike, *Norwegian Americans and the Politics of Dissent*, 44–45, 211; Andersen, *The Immigrant Takes His Stand*, 58–83.

59. For the information in this and the next paragraph, see *Nordisk Folkeblad*, April 21, June 30, and August 18, 1869; *Minneapolis Tribune*, August 13, 1869; Andersen, *The Immigrant Takes His Stand*, 136, 143–46; Wist, "Pressen efter borgerkrigen," in *Norsk-Amerikanernes Festskrift*, 57.

60. Wist, "Pressen efter borgerkrigen," 58; Hansen, *My Minneapolis*, 33.

61. Hansen, *My Minneapolis*, 16–17, 38–40, 133–34, and "Tvillingbyernes norske Saga, XIII," *Skandinaven*, June 28, 1935; Söderström, *Minneapolis Minnen*, 213–14. For Hansen's assertion that most early Scandinavians in Minneapolis came through secondary migration, see "Vor Pionertid," 1, in *Minneapolis, En Række Artikler*. Dr. J. S. Johnson makes the same assertion in "Norsemen Come to Minnesota," *Ungdmmens Ven*, 1915, a clipping in the Carl Gustav Otto Hansen Papers, P 543, NAHA.

62. Söderström, *Minneapolis Minnen*, 214–15; Norlie, *History of the Norwegian People*, 183–84, 490; Nelson, ed., *History of the Scandinavians*, 365–66, 441–44, 480–81.

63. Lovoll, *Norwegian Newspapers in America*, 102–8, 240, 250, 273, 358–60; Hansen, *My Minneapolis*, 28, 120; Wist, "Pressen efter borgerkrigen," 58–63;

Andersen, *The Immigrant Takes His Stand*, 10–11, 143–47, 150–51.

64. Hansen, *My Minneapolis*, 122–23; Söderström, *Minneapolis Minnen*, 213–15, quotation page 213, author's translation.

Notes to Chapter Four: Expansion's Golden Age

1. US Census, *Population 1890, Part I*, List of the Fifty Principal Cities in 1880 [and 1890] in the Order of their Rank, lxvii. For the change in the rank of St. Paul and Minneapolis among the fifty largest cities in the United States, see US Bureau of the Census, Table 19: Nativity of the Population for the 50 Largest Urban Places: 1870–1990, in "Tech Paper 29," 21–24, https://www.census.gov/library/working-papers/1999/demo/POP-twps0029.html.

2. US Census, *Population 1890, Part I*, clxii, gives the percentages of foreign parentage in the Cities. The federal censuses of 1870 and 1880 give data on the foreign-born but not the second generation. The percentage of foreign-born in St. Paul was 43.4 percent in 1870, 36.3 percent in 1880, and 39.9 percent in 1890. The foreign-born in Minneapolis accounted for 34.1 percent of the population in 1870, 32.0 percent in 1880, and 36.8 percent in 1890. See Table 19: Nativity of the Population for the 50 Largest Urban Places: 1870–1990 in "Tech Paper 29," 24, and US Census, *Statistics of the Population*, 1880, 451.

3. US Census, *Statistics of the Population*, 1880, 538–41, and *Population 1890, Part I*, 198, 203, 670–73, 710, 716, 722, 726, provided the data for calculating the size of foreign-born populations and their percentage of the general population in the Cities. Frank Renkiewicz, "The Poles," 364–66, and Hyman Berman, "The Jews," 489–93, in Holmquist, *They Chose Minnesota*.

4. The figures in this and the next paragraph were found in or derived from US Census, *Statistics of the Population*, 1880, 538–41, and *Population 1890, Part I*, 198, 203, 670–73, 710, 716, 722, 726. On the religious composition of the Cities' German American and Canadian American communities, see Hildegard Binder Johnson, "The Germans," 169–72, Berman, "The Jews," 489–93, Sarah P. Rubinstein, "The French Canadians," 45–48, and Sarah P. Rubinstein, "The British," 112–13, 123–26, in Holmquist, *They Chose Minnesota*.

5. Rudolph J. Vecoli, "The Italians," Theodore Salutos, "The Greeks," and Berman, "The Jews," in Holmquist, *They Chose Minnesota*, 450, 474, and 489–93. US Census, *Population*, 1880, 538–41, and *Population 1890, Part I*, 198, 203, 670–73, 710, 716, 722, 726.

6. Wingerd, *Claiming the City*, 3–4, 6, 39–41, 47, 68–84.

7. Wingerd, *Claiming the City*, 19–28, 35–36; the percentages of foreign-born Irish and German residents in St. Paul are found on 35–36.

8. Wingerd, *Claiming the City*, 28, 36, 39–41, 43–47, 77–79; US Census, *Statistics of the Population*, 1880, 538–41.

9. J. F. Williams, "St. Paul, Ramsey County, Minnesota: Historical Sketch," in US Census of 1880, Volume 19, *Report on the Social Statistics of Cities, Part II, Southern and Western States*, 697–98; the quoted material is on page 698. Figures for the occupation of first- and second-generation Norwegian American men in the city are derived from the Manuscript Census Schedules for St. Paul, 1880 US Census of Population, digitalized by the Church of Jesus Christ of Latter-day Saints and deposited with the history department of the University of Minnesota in 2000. Analysis of this data

shows that Norwegian-born immigrants were as often skilled as unskilled workers. On the other hand, very small percentages of Norwegian-born men in 1880 were employed as small-businessmen, as professionals, or in semiskilled and low white-collar jobs. The second generation of workmen in the Norwegian immigrant community, moreover, was very small at the start of the decade, consisting of only sixteen men, but of these only three were unskilled and the largest number were in low white-collar work. These figures about the Norwegian-born and their children, though they rely on a small number in the case of the second generation, illustrate the rapid mobility possible for children of immigrants in St. Paul at the time, the incompleteness of Williams's commentary on immigrants' employment, and the essential correctness of his vivid sense of the rising numbers of Scandinavian newcomers in the capital city's job market.

10. Wingerd, *Claiming the City*, 29–31; for a statement of the unusual exclusivity of the Minneapolis Yankee elite compared to the elite in St. Paul, see especially 36–38.

11. "Minneapolis, Hennepin County, Minnesota," in *Report on the Social Statistics of Cities, Part II, Southern and Western States*, US Census of 1880, Vol. 19, 687–89; the quoted passage is on page 688.

12. Wingerd, *Claiming the City*, 47–48; *Minneapolis Daily Tribune*, November 1, 1872, 4; Hansen, *My Minneapolis*, 26–27, 62–63, 142–44. The mayor and Minnesota's governor, neither of them Scandinavian Americans, joined the list of notables on the Norwegian Constitution Day program in 1889, for example, when the Norwegian American community dedicated its own central meeting place, Normanna Hall. Bourgeois civic groups such as the Knights of Pythias early founded German and Scandinavian lodges, and Catholic immigrants established local divisions of the Ancient Order of Hibernians and the Knights of Columbus in the city: Shutter, *History of Minneapolis*, 1:625–31, 644–48, 650–51, 676–77; Söderström, *Minneapolis Minnen*, 213–14.

13. The quoted phrases come from Steffens, "The Shame of Minneapolis," in *The Shame of the Cities*, 43. On Black and Scandinavian Republicans in St. Paul, see Wingerd, *Claiming the City*, 77–79.

14. This and the next paragraphs build largely on Kane and Ominsky, *Twin Cities*, 45–46, 81–82, and Wingerd, *Claiming the City*, 43–47.

15. For the main sources for the analysis of job opportunities provided by the industrial growth of Minneapolis in the 1880s, see Schmid, *Social Saga of Two Cities*, 12–19; Kane and Ominsky, *Twin Cities*, 45–46, 81–82; Kane, *Falls of St. Anthony*, 99–100, 103–8, 115–17.

16. Cronon, *Nature's Metropolis*, 283–84, 446–54.

17. Cronon, *Nature's Metropolis*, 276–77.

18. For examples of local journalism and the comments of participants in the rivalry that reported and inflamed the intercity competition, see the quoted articles in Kane and Ominsky, *Twin Cities*, 83, and the contemporary comments cited in Wingerd, *Claiming the City*, 13–16. The two urban centers bickered over a permanent location for the state fair, at the time the preeminent occasion for displaying the state's progress. Minneapolis leaders proposed a fair site at the district surrounding the famous tourist attraction of Minnehaha Falls on their side of the river in Hennepin County. When St. Paul's chamber of commerce won the prize

in 1885 by secretly cooperating with Ramsey County officials to offer a site for the fair free of charge in the Midway, Minneapolitans cried foul. Within a year, its civic leaders offered the competing Minneapolis Industrial Exposition exactly at state fair time. The capital's *Pioneer Press* called the exposition the "product of a jealous brain," and St. Paul leaders lit up their downtown and provided a fireworks display every night of the fair in response. By winter they had mounted a competing municipal festival, the St. Paul "Winter Festival." In the following years St. Paul's civic leaders supported Civil War reenactments at "Camp Ramsey" and Farmers' Day at the fairgrounds to strengthen its magnetism for the public. Speer and Frost, *Minnesota State Fair*, 15–19; Kane and Ominsky, *Twin Cities*, 83.

19. The words of the Minneapolis booster are cited in Wingerd, *Claiming the City*, 14. Hansen, *My Minneapolis*, 92; Söderström, *Minneapolis Minnen*, 266; Mary Swanley Townson, "Pictures from a New Home: Minnesota's Swedish American Artists," in Anderson and Blanck, *Swedes in the Twin Cities*, 137–48; see especially pages 137–38 and 146n2.

20. Wingerd, *Claiming the City*, 13–18; Kane and Ominsky, *Twin Cities*, 83.

21. Schmid, *Social Saga of Two Cities*, 41–52, 56–65, 70–73, 387–88.

22. Schmid, *Social Saga of Two Cities*, 70–77, 153–64; Ann Regan, "The Irish," 131, 134, 140–42, Johnson, "The Germans," 169–72, and John G. Rice, "The Swedes," 255, 262–64—all in Holmquist, ed., *They Chose Minnesota*; Hansen, *My Minneapolis*, 52–54, 92–94, 145–52; Wingerd, *Claiming the City*, 68–75.

23. David Vassar Taylor, "The Blacks," 75–78, and Berman, "The Jews," 493–95, in Holmquist, ed., *They Chose Minnesota*.

24. Kane and Ominsky, *Twin Cities*, 98, 104–5; Wingerd, *Claiming the City*, 79–82. For Norwegian-name residents with Bohemian Flats and Swede Hollow addresses, see Polk and Dancer, *St. Paul City Directory, 1884–85*, and Davidson, *Davidson's Minneapolis City Directory, 1885–86*. See also Thaddeus Radzilowski, "Introduction to the Reprint Edition," Works Progress Administration writers, *The Bohemian Flats*, xvi–xxiii.

25. US Census of Population, totals for St. Paul and Minneapolis in 1880 (538–41) and 1890 (670–73) indicate an increase of 12,850 Norwegian-born during the decade. In the same ten years, 3,014 Norwegians departing from Oslo gave their destination as one of the Twin Cities and small numbers of Norwegians leaving the country's other major emigration depots announced the same goal. See discussion of the data from the Norwegian emigrant protocols, page 387, notes 3 and 5. Andres Svalestuen, "Nordisk Emigrasjon—en komparativ oversikt," in Hvidt, ed., *Emigrationen fra Norden*, 42, 44, includes the data indicating that the gender balance and age profile of the Cities' Norwegian-born population was also what one might expect in a Norwegian immigrant population that had arrived in the years from the Civil War to 1880.

26. Mauk, *The Colony that Rose from the Sea*, 47–50, 119–21; Lovoll, *A Century of Urban Life*, 151–52, 157.

27. The comparisons are based on the published census figures for the population of Norwegian-born and their children in each city for 1880 and 1890: US Census of Population, 1880, 538–41, and 1890, 670–73. The North Atlantic Population Project (NAPP) and Minnesota Population Center, complete population data file for Minneapolis and St. Paul, in "1880 United States Census: Complete Count Microdata,"

Preliminary Version NAPP-US-0.1 [computer files], Minneapolis: Minnesota Population Center [distributor], 2001, http://www.pop.umn.edu/napp (hereafter designated as NAPP-TC 1880). William Block, the center's information technology core director, extracted the data for the Twin Cities and analyzed it according to the author's requests. Manually registering and tabulating the Norwegian-born and their children in the Cities from the manuscript responses to the 1857, 1860, 1870, and 1875 censuses was outside the design of this project, which instead relies on the analysis of city directories for the earliest periods, when the origins of Norwegian immigration to the Cities are best portrayed as part of a small Scandinavian influx. Dr. Block and the IPUMS staff of the University of Minnesota history department helped the author and his research assistants create a series of systematic population samples from other federal censuses for later periods in this history. Through computer analysis of local residents' responses to census enumerators for the 1880 census, the snapshot of the enclaves' residents at the start of the decade could include all the Norwegians in the Cities, separate them from other nationalities, and compare the characteristics of Norwegian-born and Norwegian American residents with those of the rest of the urban population. Used in combination with other records from the decade, this large, relatively neutral source of information also made possible a uniquely complete delineation of the immigrant subculture that evolved as it incorporated the mass of newcomers who joined it during the decade.

28. US Census of Population, 1880, 538–41, and 1890, 670–73. *Children* here means people under fifteen years of age. Information about age groups and comparisons between the age of the general population in the Cities and their Norwegian-born and second-generation Norwegian American residents are derived from Block's analyses of data in NAPP-TC 1880. The younger age groups among the Cities' Norwegian-born were 0–15 years (7.2 percent), 20–29 years (40.3 percent), 30–39 years (26.8 percent), and 40–49 years (9.0 percent). In the rest of the population, the same age groups represented the following percentages: 0–15 (28.4 percent), 20–29 (26.8 percent), 30–39 (16.6 percent), and 40–49 (9.6 percent).

29. Haugen, "The Struggle over Norwegian," 2.

30. The author's interpretation of intermarriage in this and the following paragraph depends on analyses of household and family data in NAPP-TC 1880 by Marit Dale Mauk.

31. Abundant evidence of residential and occupational mixing of the Norwegian-born and other population groups in the 1880s is available in the composition of households recorded in the census manuscripts.

32. NAPP-TC 1880 and statistical analyses by William Block and the author. See the discussion of occupations later in the chapter for commentary on the greater importance of domestic service in St. Paul for Norwegian American women. Norwegian American men made up only a very small group among servants in the Cities. The preliminary version of the NAPP-TC data for 1880 does not include addresses, but city directories and other records reveal the location of these groups in the Cities. What we learn about domestics and lodgers at the decade's start provides a basis for comparison later with similar information from 1890. The city directories analyzed in earlier chapters showed much higher

percentages of domestic servants than the 1880 census did, but that is likely because these women or their well-to-do employers decided to record their occupations in the directories, while women who saw no advantage in advertising their occupations did not; consequently, domestics became a larger portion of the women included in the directories. Only the ninety women in St. Paul whose work is described as "keeps house" composed a larger female contingent, and they were likely housewives who received no wages. The next-largest category of women workers in Minneapolis, occupations in the needle trades, employed just a little under 5 percent of Norwegian American women. There were sixty-four Norwegian American servants in the capital, ten of them in the second generation. Their average age was twenty-six, but the median age among them was eighteen. Six women described their domestic employment in more specific terms, such as housekeeper or "ironing." In Minneapolis, 147 women and thirteen men worked as domestics. Their average age was twenty-three, and their median age twenty. About the same small number of additional women worked in specified kinds of domestic work, such as housekeeping.

33. This and next two paragraphs derive from an analysis of Bratager, *Over Hav og Land*, 20–27.

34. The discussion of ethnic mixing in the households where Norwegian American domestics worked derives from analyses of the household patterns revealed in NAPP-TC 1880 for both cities.

35. In other family stories, a female domestic worker sometimes initiated a generations-long history of moving to the city. During an interview, for example, Luther Forde told how the earliest member of his extended family to take up life in the Cities was an aunt who did housework in town. She was followed by another aunt, and over succeeding generations men and women of assorted occupations for various periods of time followed those first urban pioneers.

36. Interview and guided tour of "Norwegian" St. Paul with Eunice R. Baker; email messages and Larsen family genealogical documents from her daughter, Luci J. Baker, October-November 1999. Interviews with Lorraine Ofstie; conversation with Audrey Simmons (Lorraine Ofstie's niece) on April 28, 2000; Carl G. O. Hansen notes John E. Ofstie's participation in the attempt of some immigrants to form an exclusive social circle in the city's south-side Norwegian community in *My Minneapolis*, 92, 114.

37. Goeken, "Unmarried Adults and Residential Autonomy," 39, 41–45. The figures on the marital status and median age of Norwegian American boarders were derived by the author from William Block's compilation and analysis of data in NAPP-TC 1880.

38. Ueland, *Recollections of an Immigrant*, 33, 38–39, 59. The NAPP-TC 1880 data for the Norwegian-born and their children in Minneapolis includes the information on the family with whom Andreas Ueland and his doctor friend were boarders.

39. The few Norwegian American boarders in the NAPP-TC 1880 material who were married included several young women on their own with small children, as well as couples with a small child and a handful of widowers and widows. Twenty-six second-generation Norwegian American adults appear among the boarders, all of them single people who had been born in Iowa, Wisconsin, or

elsewhere in Minnesota. Over 70 percent of these were young women working as servants. See Davidson, *Davidson's Minneapolis City Directory, 1885–86*, and Polk and Danser, *St. Paul City Directory 1884–85*, from which data on occupation and living addresses were analyzed for 113 Scandinavian names, which resulted in the registration of information concerning 2,242 men and 700 women, including scores of people with identical surnames who lived together as roomers or lodgers, often had the same occupation, and frequently were employed at the same place of work.

40. The quoted phrases, translated from the Norwegian by the author, are found on pages 25–27 of Bratager, *Over Hav og Land*.

41. This and the following paragraphs interpret Hansen, *My Minneapolis*, 49–54, 92–94; Sanborn Fire Insurance Maps, July 3, 1885, Minneapolis, Minnesota, Vol. 1, 54; Jenswold, "The Hidden Settlement," 46–47; and US Census, *Population 1890*, 1:939–40.

42. Byron J. Nordstrom, "Ethnicity and Community in the Sixth Ward of Minneapolis in 1919," in Lovoll, ed., *Scandinavians and Other Immigrants*, 35; David Markle, "Dania Hall: At the Center of a Scandinavian-American Community," in Anderson and Blanck, *Swedes in the Twin Cities*, 174.

43. Kristian Prestgard, "Veien jeg gikk," in *Fra Heidal til Decorah*, 122–23.

44. Markle, "Dania Hall," 175; Hansen, *My Minneapolis*, 52, 57, 149–51.

45. Hansen, *My Minneapolis*, 52–54, 145–52; TCHP data for Minneapolis from 1900 for the 20 percent sample.

46. Hansen, *My Minneapolis*, 93–94; Norlie, *Norsk Lutherske Menigheter i Amerika*, 542–45.

47. Markle, "Dania Hall," 179–82.

48. Söderström, *Minneapolis Minnen*, 132–35.

49. Nordstrom, "Ethnicity and Community in the Sixth Ward," 43, 48.

50. Hansen, *My Minneapolis*, 17–18, 52–53, 145–50.

51. The discussion of changes in Norwegian and Scandinavian American political behavior here and later in the chapter owes much to Soike, *Norwegian-Americans and the Politics of Dissent*, 53–68, 75–83; Barone, "The Social Basis of Urban Politics: Minneapolis and St. Paul, 1890–1905," 2–5, 7–9, 21–22; Gieske and Keillor, *Norwegian Yankee*, 147–53; Söderström, "Skandinavernas Insats i Politiken," in *Minneapolis Minnen*, 213–15, 140–47; and Wingerd, *Claiming the City*, 47, 51.

52. TCHP interviews with Eunice Baker, Lorraine Ofstie, Mary Ann Olsen, Christian Skjervold, and Jorunn Wolden.

Notes to Chapter Five: Social Issues in Expansion's Golden Age

1. Lovoll, *The Promise of America*, 155; Draxten, *Kristofer Janson in America*, especially 3–8, 21–26, 31–34, 38–41, 248–58, 338–46; Øverland, *The Western Home*, 157–69.

2. This and the following paragraph are based on Øverland, *The Western Home*, 165; Hansen, *My Minneapolis*, 101–4; Lovoll, *Norwegian Newspapers in America*, 229–31. See also Thorsen, "Tinsel and Dust."

3. Hansen, *My Minneapolis*, 105–9; "Knut Hamsun," *Norsk Biografisk leksikon* online: https://nbl.snl.no/Knut_Hamsun.

4. Olson, *Vikings across the Atlantic*, 62–65; Lovoll, *The Promise of America*, 156–57; Hansen, *My Minneapolis*, 41–47.

5. Bakken, "Our Country Gives Us

the Vote," 130–32; Stuhler, *Gentle Warriors*, 42–44, 47–50, 55–56, 79–87.

6. Peterson, "Adding a Little Suffrage Spice to the Melting Pot," 289–90.

7. The information and analysis in the following paragraphs come largely from Peterson, "Adding a Little Suffrage Spice to the Melting Pot," and Bakken, "Our Country Gives Us the Vote."

8. Chrislock, *The Progressive Era in Minnesota*, 32–35; Nydahl, *Afholdssagens historie*, 261–74.

9. Nydahl, *Afholdssagens historie*, 212–13, 219, 250.

10. The 1880 Classified Business Directory and Guide Book of St. Paul and Minneapolis (St. Paul: n.p., 1881), 24, 29, 66, 88, 121; Scandinavian Temperance Calendar 1896, 55, manuscript collection P594, NAHA; Hansen, *My Minneapolis*, 228; Lande, *Afholdsfolkets festskrift, 1914*, 23.

11. *Minneapolis Journal*, November 26, 1903, 1–2; *St. Paul and Minneapolis Directory*, 1880–81 (St. Paul: Davidson Co., 1881), 143, 147, 207–8; Carl H. Chrislock, "Profile of a Ward Boss: The Political Career of Lars M. Rand," in Lovoll, ed., *Scandinavians and Other Immigrants*, 93–110.

12. The quotation is found in Nydahl, *Afholdssagens historie*, 261–62.

13. Söderström, *Minneapolis Minnen*, 390–91. This and the next two paragraphs are based on Nydahl, *Afholdssagens historie*, 262–72; Hansen, *My Minneapolis*, 84–85; Lovoll, *The Promise of America*, 154–55.

14. Davidson, *Davidson's Minneapolis Directory, 1885–86*, 80, 84; Lovoll, *The Promise of America*, 155; *Minneapolis Journal*, May 1, 1902, 9.

15. Chrislock, "Profile of a Ward Boss," 95–100; Hansen, *My Minneapolis*, 133–36.

16. Davidson, *Davidson's Minneapolis City Directory, 1885–86*, 84.

17. Nydahl, *Afholdssagens historie*, 154–57; Hansen, *My Minneapolis*, 227–29; Stovby, "Scandinavian Temperance-Kalender," 23–25, 76–77; Lande, *Afholdsfolkets Festskrift, 1914*, 2.

18. Associated Charities of Minneapolis, *A Quarter Century of Work among the Poor*. The Andersen Library's Social Welfare History Archives of the University of Minnesota contains the Associated Charities records of the Twin Cities. *The Charities Association of Minneapolis, Annual Reports for 1901, 1904, 1907, 1909, 1910, 1912*, 5–10, Summarized Statistics, 1889–1916; St. Paul Associated Charities, "Constitution and Summary of Annual Reports, 1893–1908"; individual annual reports for 1901, 1902, 1903, 1904, 1906, 1909, 1911; Klaassen, "The Deserving Poor"; Stadum, "Family Casework with the Minneapolis Poor," 43–54, especially 43–45.

19. Hamre, *From Immigrant Parish to Inner City Ministry*, 24–28.

20. The discussion of the depression of the mid-1890s and the founding of mutual benefit organizations builds on material in Folwell, *A History of Minnesota*, 3:198; Blegen, *Minnesota*, 367–68; Hansen, *My Minneapolis*, 48, 84, 153–58.

21. Norborg, *An American Saga*, 33–35, 41–43, 49–86; Blomvik, "Heritage, Sisterhood and Self-Reliance," 58–64.

22. The sources for this and the next paragraph are *Minneapolis Tidende*, January 20, 1905; Hansen, *My Minneapolis*, 159–68; and Olson, *Vikings across the Atlantic*, 83.

23. The chief sources for this and the following paragraphs are Hamre, *Trinity Lutheran Congregation*, 18–19, 23–27; Hansen, *My Minneapolis*, 95, 111, 254–59; and Associated Charities of Minneapolis, *A Quarter Century of Work among the Poor*, 6–9.

24. Rønning and Lien, *They Followed Him*, 37–42, 51–57; Sponland, *My Reasonable Service*, 35–45, 49–53; Hansen, *My Minneapolis*, 94–97, 111; Associated Charities of Minneapolis, Annual Report for 1890, 29, Social Welfare History Archives, Andersen Library, University of Minnesota.

25. The sources for this and the following paragraphs concerning the St. Paul Hospital are Nichol, "Introduction" to Preus, *Vivacious Daughter*, 22–25; *Decorah-Posten*, February 7 and 14, 1902; annual report of the Norwegian Hospital Society and the Training School for Nurses for 1916, manuscript file P625, "Benevolent Institutions," NAHA; and Hansen, *My Minneapolis*, 111, 255–56.

26. The sources for information about Fairview Hospital are: Fairview Hospital Minneapolis Papers, P620, NAHA; "Bethlehem Lutheran Church, Minneapolis, Minnesota, 1894/1969 75th Anniversary," 33–36; and "Bethel Evangelical Lutheran Church 100 Years," both American Lutheran Church (ALC) Archives, Luther Seminary, St. Paul; Hansen, *My Minneapolis*, 94–98, 255.

27. Sources for the paragraphs on Progressive Era welfare institutions and Associated Charities in the Twin Cities are the following: "Lyngblomsten, 1906–1996: 90 Years of Service and Commitment to Seniors" (St. Paul: Lyngblomsten, 1996); "Dedication Day Issue, Ebeneezer Home Society," *Ebeneezer* 27, no. 2 (May 1960); "History of the Walker Methodist Residence and Nursing Home," in *Walker Methodist Residence and Health Care Center, 25th Anniversary, 1945–1970*, 3; Lutheran Social Service of Minnesota, "Orphanage Reunions to Be Held," May 12, 1982; "Lutheran Girls' Home: A Refuge from the Storms of Life" (Minneapolis, 1931–32); "Tenth Anniversary of the Wartburg Home for Young Men" (Minneapolis: Wartburg, 1936)—all ALC Archives, Luther Seminary. Klaassen, "The Deserving Poor"; Kane and Ominsky, *Twin Cities*, 176; Deborah Miller, research file of clippings and pictures from the Scandinavian Relief Home for the Aged and the Ebeneezer Home; "The 1919 War Chest: 60 Funds in One," Minneapolis and Hennepin County, December 2–9, 1918 (St. Paul: Minnesota Historical Society), 4–13, 18–21; Hansen *My Minneapolis*, 254–59.

28. See Stadum, "Family Casework with the Minneapolis Poor," 43–54, especially 50–53, and Lutheran Social Service of Minnesota, "Orphanage Reunions to Be Held."

29. St. Paul Associated Charities, Annual Reports 1–17, 1894–1909; see especially the reports for 1892–94, 10–11, and for 1895, 8–9; Annual Report, 1895, 15; Annual Report, 1896, 12–13—all in Social Welfare History Archives, Andersen Library, University of Minnesota.

30. Associated Charities of Minneapolis, *A Quarter Century of Work among the Poor*, 33.

31. The chief sources concerning the causes of poverty and the nationalities of the people receiving charitable assistance in this and the next paragraphs are the annual reports of the associated charities organization in each of the Twin Cities. See in particular Associated Charities of Minneapolis, "Financial Report 1889," 6–7; Annual Report, 1891, 8; *A Quarter Century of Work among the Poor*, 8–9. St. Paul Associated Charities, Annual Reports for 1894–1896, 5; "The St. Paul Provident Fund," in Fifth Annual Report, 1897, 24; Annual Report, 1889, 13. Stadum, "Family Casework with the Minneapolis Poor," 43–46, 48, 52–53.

32. Associated Charities of Minneapolis, *A Quarter Century of Work among the Poor*, 14.

33. St. Paul Associated Charities, Annual Report, 1909, 43–45.

34. For the estimate of Norwegian Americans' participation in ethnic organizations and events, see Chrislock, *Ethnicity Challenged*, 15–18.

35. Concerning Knut Hamsun in Dania Hall, see Markle, "Dania Hall," 173–97, especially 181–82, and Hansen, *My Minneapolis*, 57–66, 70–71, 74–86, 95. This and the next paragraphs build on information in the following sources: Hansen, *My Minneapolis*, 31–33, 57–59; Hamre, *Georg Sverdrup*, 20–21; Lovoll, "1905 og norsk-amerikanerne," 46; "Ole Gabriel Ueland," *Norsk Biografisk leksikon* online: https://snl.no/Ole_Gabriel_Ueland.

36. Lovoll, *Norwegian Newspapers in America*, especially 206–10, 245, 253–54.

37. Olson, *Vikings across the Atlantic*, 78–80; Hansen, *My Minneapolis*, 193–94; *Minneapolis Tidende*, June 8, 9, and 11, 1905, 1; November 26, 1905, 1; and June 24, 1906, 1; Lovoll, *Norwegian Newspapers in America*, 206–10; Chrislock, *Ethnicity Challenged*, 4.

38. Eleventh through Thirteenth US Censuses of Population, Reports by States, Illinois, Minnesota, and New York. US Census of 1920, Table 15 "Distribution of Foreign-born Population . . . for Cities Having, in 1920, 100,000 Inhabitants or More: 1920, 1910 and 1900," 744–47.

39. Lovoll, *A Folk Epic*, 64–80.

40. For more information about Lutheran church fusions, see Lovoll, *Det løfterike landet*, 130–35; Hamre, *From Immigrant Parish to Inner-City Ministry*, 35–40; Hamre, *Georg Sverdrup*, 131–44; Haanes, "*Hvad skal dette blive for prester?*," 213–18; Nichol, "Introduction" to Preus, *Vivacious Daughter*, 21, 24; Hansen, *My Minneapolis*, 94–97, 178–81; Sverdrup, *Samlede skrifter i Udvalg*, 2:144–46, 3:256–93. For a detailed exposition of the controversy between Augsburg and the United Church, see Nelson and Fevold, *The Lutheran Church among Norwegian-Americans*, 2:38–81.

41. Lovoll, *Det løfterike landet*, 159–70.

42. For this and the next paragraph, Lovoll, *Det løfterike landet*, 133–35; Norlie, *History of the Norwegian People*, 311–13; Haugen, "The Struggle over Norwegian," 1–35, census figures page 34; US Census of 1920, Table 15, 744–47.

43. The analysis based on census figures derives from systematic 10 and 20 percent samples of first- and second-generation Norwegian American households in Minneapolis–St. Paul. The 10 percent sample provided a way of locating the city precincts with the most concentrated Norwegian American population, while the 20 percent sample provided the subject population for the figures and proportions cited in the text.

44. Lovoll, *A Folk Epic*, 1–5.

45. "Appendix, The Bygdelag and Their Officers," in Lovoll, *A Folk Epic*, 8–17, 241–73; see also pages 22–23, 117–23, 126–28, 164–70, 241; Haugen "The Struggle over Norwegian," 20–21; Lovoll, *Det løfterike landet*, 212–16.

46. Regarding the Norwegian Society in America, see Haugen, "The Struggle over Norwegian," 21–23. Hansen, *My Minneapolis*, 250–53; Olson, *Vikings across the Atlantic*, 81–82, 85, 102, 152; Lovoll, *Celebrating a Century*, 44–46; Lovoll, *Det Løfterike landet*, 221. See a somewhat later statement of these ideas in Rølvaag, *Omkring fædrearven*, 53–54, 88–94.

47. The paragraphs on Nordmanns-Forbundet derive largely from Olson,

Vikings across the Atlantic, 92–93; Lovoll, *Det løfterike landet*, 210–11; and Lovoll, *Celebrating a Century*, 8–14, 16–17, 21–22, 28–29, 32–33.

48. Olson, *Vikings across the Atlantic*, 94–96; Lovoll, *Celebrating a Century*, 28, 39–40, 47.

49. Lovoll, *Celebrating a Century*, 37–42; Hansen, *My Minneapolis*, 259–61, quotation page 259.

50. Lovoll, *A Folk Epic*, 96–114; "*Universitets-Mindegaven*," Archives of the Royal Norwegian Foreign Ministry for the Consulate in St. Paul, box 42, National Archives of Norway, Oslo; Lovoll, *Celebrating a Century*, 48–49.

51. Øverland, *Immigrant Minds, American Identities*, 146–50; Olson, *Vikings across the Atlantic*, 24–25, 48–50, 74–76, 81–82, 101.

52. Olson, *Vikings across the Atlantic*, 95; Lovoll, *Det løfterike landet*, 183; Hansen, *My Minneapolis*, 262–63.

53. Schultz, *Ethnicity on Parade*, 50.

54. Olson, *Vikings across the Atlantic*, 109–10.

55. "Central Lutheran Church, Palm Sunday, April 13, 1919," bulletin for services, church archives, Minneapolis; Seth Ernst Gordon, "The New Central Lutheran Church: The Story of Central" (Minneapolis: Central Lutheran Church, 1924), 1–21; "Anniversary Service in Honor of [the] Twenty-fifth Anniversary of the Ministry of Jacob Aall Ottesen Stub, D.D., 1901–1926," Central Lutheran Church bulletin, September 19, 1926, church archives, Minneapolis.

56. The sources for the paragraphs on the Norwegian Lutheran Memorial Church are as follows: The translated phrases come from Den Norske Lutherske Mindekirke, "25-års Jubileum, 1922–1947" (Minneapolis: Memorial Church, 1947), 6–11, in Luther Seminary Archives. "Mindekirken: The Norwegian Lutheran Memorial Church," 2, contains the other quotation; see also pages 3–5 in that historical narrative.

57. The main sources of the paragraphs about the erection of public monuments to Norwegian cultural icons in the Twin Cities are Hansen, *My Minneapolis*, 159–65, and Mauk, "Syttende mai Vignettes from Minneapolis–St. Paul," 33–53. See also Olson, *Vikings across the Atlantic*.

58. For sources of material on Norwegian Americans and World War I, see Holbrook and Appel, *Minnesota in the War with Germany*, 1:2–15, 24–27, 35–42; Chrislock, *Ethnicity Challenged*, 12–31, 34, 44, 53–55, 59–61, 66, 75–76, 83–87, 90, 99, 101–3; Hansen, *My Minneapolis*, 267–69; and Haugen, "The Struggle over Norwegian," 28–31. See also Holbrook, *St. Paul and Ramsey County in the War of 1917–1918*, 1:61.

59. Peterson, "Adding a Little Suffrage Spice to the Melting Pot," 295–96.

60. On restrictionist legislation and postwar changes in the local community, see Olson, *Vikings across the Atlantic*, 11, 118–19; Lovoll, *The Promise of America*, 28–29, 115–19; and Chrislock, *Ethnicity Challenged*, 128–33. Blegen, *Norwegian Migration to America*, 1:18.

61. Haugen, "The Struggle over Norwegian," 31–35; Lovoll, *A Folk Epic*, 164.

62. *Norse-American Centennial, 1825–1925*, 1–96; Gutterson and Christensen, eds., "Souvenir: Norse-American Women, 1825–1925"; Hansen, *My Minneapolis*, 281; Lovoll, *A Folk Epic*, 165, 172.

63. The sources of the text concerning the 1925 centennial and the concluding paragraph are Hansen, *My Minneapolis*, 275–83; Lovoll, *A Folk Epic*, 164–71; Lovoll, *The Promise of America*, 10, 195–96; and Olson, *Vikings across the Atlantic*, 116, 133–42.

64. Schultz, *Ethnicity on Parade*, 126–28; Olson, *Vikings across the Atlantic*, 116.

Notes to Chapter Six: Community Transformations

1. Gordon, "The New Central Lutheran Church," 6, 9–10, 17–18, 21, quotation page 9.

2. Gordon, "The New Central Lutheran Church," 6, 11, 15.

3. Gordon, "The New Central Lutheran Church," quotation page 2; see also 9.

4. Blegen, *Minnesota*, 481–82; Kane and Ominsky, *Twin Cities*, 119, 185, 193–94; Nathanson, *Minneapolis in the Twentieth Century*, 58–60; Paul Maccabee, "Alias Kid Cann," *Mpls.St.Paul Magazine* 19, no. 11 (November 1991): 88–91, 160–63; TCHP interviews with Lorraine Ofstie.

5. Paragraphs on the Depression in the Twin Cities derive from Kane, *Falls of St. Anthony*, 167, 172–73; Kane and Ominsky, *Twin Cities*, 121–22, 157–59, 167–68, 172–73, 188, 191–200; and Blegen, *Minnesota*, 521–24, 530.

6. Jacob Stefferud, "Memories: Jacob Stefferud, Some Experiences, During My 44 Years of Service with the Norwegian America Line and 7 Months Previous Work in Barron, Wisconsin" (manuscript memoir shared by Stefferud's daughters; in author's possession), 9. See Lovoll, *Norwegian Newspapers in America*, 309–10, for Norwegian and American census figures documenting changes in national immigration patterns in this period.

7. Elizabeth Faue, *Community of Suffering and Struggle*, 24–27; Lovoll, *The Promise of America*, 38. Lovoll notes that thirty-two thousand Norwegian Americans returned to Norway during the 1930s.

8. See section on poverty in the Twin Cities, pages 197–211.

9. Hilda Kringstad, interview by Nina Angelsen, February 13, 2001. The main sources for this and other paragraphs regarding general ways of coping among Norwegian Americans during the Depression are TCHP interviews with Egil Almaas; Eunice Baker; Elva M. Bakken and Barbara Lehman; Ione Kadden; Dolores King; Ardis Munther; Mary Ann Olsen; and Jorunn Wolden.

10. The quotations in this and the next paragraph come from the TCHP interview with Ione Kadden.

11. The source of this and other paragraphs referring to or quoting comments by Joel Torstenson is the TCHP interview with Torstenson.

12. The chief published sources for the discussion of labor relations in the Twin Cities and the 1934 teamsters strike are Millikan, *A Union Against Unions*, 264–88, especially 5–6, 8, 9, 11–15, 264–66; Nathanson, *Minneapolis in the Twentieth Century*, 66–91; and Faue, *Community of Suffering and Struggle*, 28–32, 41–46, 58–68, 72–83, 97–99.

13. TCHP interviews with James Pederson.

14. TCHP interview with Carl Chrislock; see also https://www.augsburg.edu/sociology/torstenson.

15. The information concerning Trinity Lutheran in Minneapolis comes from Hamre, *From Immigrant Parish to Inner City Ministry*, 70–73. In St. Paul, the other congregation bearing the name of Trinity also faced financial difficulties in the 1930s. Its pastor, custodian, and organist "generously assisted" the church's financial problems by accepting salary reductions. See P. H. Friseth, "A Short Historical Sketch of Trinity Lutheran Church, ALC," typescript, 1963, 6, P537, NAHA.

16. Blegen, *Minnesota*, 530–31; Chrislock, *Fjord to Freeway*, 171–73, 177–80;

TCHP interviews with Carl Chrislock, Bill Green, and Joel Torstenson.

17. Lovoll, *Norwegian Newspapers in America*, 278–79, quotation page 313.

18. Hansen, *My Minneapolis*, 303–7; Blegen, *Minnesota*, 530–31; TCHP interviews with Jens Anker, Ella Valborg Tweet, and Solveig Zempel.

19. The sources of this and the next paragraph are *Minneapolis Sundag Tidende*, January 24, 1932; Hansen, *My Minneapolis*, 310–14, quotation page 313; Maren Michlet, *First Year Norse*, 6th rev. ed. (Minneapolis: Lutheran Free Church Publishing Company, 1924); and copies of the Norwegian club newspapers (1931–34), *Saga* (North High School) and *Fram* (South High), in the schools' collections at MNHS. O. L. Kirkeby published *Lærebog for Børn* (Textbook for Children) through the Augsburg Publishing House for use in the schools in 1910.

20. Until her death in 1932, Maren Michelet taught high school and college Norwegian; her textbook, *First Year Norse*, appeared in several editions in the 1920s and 1930s. In 1932, Michelet wrote that a record 394 students at four high schools took Norwegian. She taught the electives in the subject at South High and advised its Edda club. At that point, North High had a Viking club for pupils, and Pauline Farseth had succeeded Dikka Reque as instructor and club advisor. A. C. Erdahl taught the subject and supervised the Scandinavian Club at Central High, while Ben R. Eggan had the same duties with the Norse club and four parallel classes of the elective at Roosevelt High. The clubs and their instructors took active part in the Ibsen, Amundsen, and Erikson festivals. The club newspapers *Saga* and *Fram* from North and South High Schools, respectively, printed brief news stories from the classes; Norwegian, American, and local news in the column "Fra Fjern og Nær" ("From Near and Far"); sports news; short quotations from the works of Norwegian writers; announcements of films and other activities in Norwegian outside school; jokes in Norwegian in "Det Muntre Hjørne" ("The Cheerful Corner"); reports of May 17 and other holiday activities; and accounts of trips to Norway.

21. Hansen, *My Minneapolis*, 288–91; Olson, *Vikings across the Atlantic*, 175–76.

22. The sources for the passage about the founding of the Norwegian National League and its activities in 1927 are "Henrik Ibsen, 100-Aarsfestunder Auspicier av Det Norske Nationalforbund i Minneapolis, Lyceum Teater, 20de og 21de Marts 1928" (program for the opening evening of the festival in Norwegian and English) (Minneapolis: Norwegian National League, 1928), n.p.; Det Norske Nationalforbund i Minneapolis, "Aarsberetning for 1927–1928" (Minneapolis: Norwegian National League, 1928), 2–6; Hansen, *My Minneapolis*, 182–83, 287–88.

23. Olson, *Vikings across the Atlantic*, 152–55, quotation page 153.

24. Hansen, *My Minneapolis*, 237–39; "Beretning for 1928, Ibsen-jubileet," *Aarsberetning 1927–1928* (Minneapolis: Norwegian National League, 1928), 7–16; Chrislock, *Ethnicity Challenged*, 60–62, 86, 122, 131–35, 140.

25. "Ibsen-Festen. Bedste Ibsen-festdik Skrevet av P. O. Bugge. Nils Collett Bogts Prolog tiladt brukt ved Festen," *Minneapolis Tidende*, February 26, 1928.

26. *Nationalforbundet*, "Annual Report, 1928," 9; Hansen, *My Minneapolis*, 237–38, 322; "Roald Amundsen, Født 1872–Death 1928, Mindefest arrangert av Det Norske Nationalforbund i Minneapolis, Fjortende December 1928, Central Lutheran Church"

(program by the Norwegian National League, 1928), n.p. See also Olson, *Vikings across the Atlantic*, 74–75.

27. Rølvaag, *Concerning Our Heritage*, 41–51, quotation page 49–50.

28. The sources for interpretation of celebratory events in 1930 are *Minneapolis Tidende*, July 30, 1930; *Nordisk Tidende*, August 7, 1930; Lovoll, *A Folk Epic*, 184–85.

29. "Den norske Storfest 1930, Minneapolis Auditorium, Den 10de og 11th Juni" (program for the event), n.p.; "29de juli—29de juli 1930—'Fram, kristmenn, krossmenn, kongsmenn,' St. Olafsfest, Olsokkvelden" (program for the high mass); Hansen, *My Minneapolis*, 284, 299; Chrislock, *Ethnicity Challenged*, 140; Olson, *Vikings across the Atlantic*, 169–70.

30. Olson, *Vikings across the Atlantic*, 173–76; Hansen, *My Minneapolis*, 288–91, 318–19, 326–33.

31. Hansen, *My Minneapolis*, 327–28; "Fellesreisen til America 1935" (Oslo: Den norske Amerikalinje, 1935), 4–19.

32. Sources for the discussion of the royal visit in 1939 are *Nordmanns-Forbundets Tidsskrift* (Oslo: Norsemen's Federation, 1939), 239–43; Hansen, *My Minneapolis*, 326–45; Olson, *Vikings across the Atlantic*, 179, 184–85; Lovoll, *A Folk Epic*, 194. See also Schultz, *Ethnicity on Parade*, 52.

33. Hansen, *My Minneapolis*, 341–42.

34. The quotations come from the author's TCHP interview with Hilda Kringstad and Mary Ann Olsen. See also TCHP interviews with John Akslen; Jane and Orville Freeman; Bjarne and Else Grindem; and Chuck Haga.

35. TCHP interviews with Eunice Baker; Elva M. Bakken and Barbara Lehman; Evelyn and Mary Flaten; Ione Kadden; Dolores King; Ardis Munther; Mary Ann Olsen; Jorunn Wolden. Carl L. Manfred, "Central Lutheran Church: '75 Years of Spirit—A Vision Still Unfolding'" (Minneapolis: Central Lutheran Church, 1994), n.p.; Strand, *The Story of Lutheran Brotherhood*, 62–64; Hansen, *History of Sons of Norway*, 108–12, 226–88; Kirsti Alette Blomvik, "Heritage, Sisterhood, and Self-Reliance: The Evolution and Significance of the Daughters of Norway, 1897–1950," master's thesis, Norwegian University of Science and Technology, Trondheim, 2002, 108–12.

36. Blegen, *Minnesota*, 526–27, 538–49; Even Lange, *Samling mot felles mål, 1935–1970*, vol. 11, *Aschehoug's Norges Historie* (Oslo: H. Aschehoug and Company [W. Nygaard], 1998), 62–66, 68–70, 77.

37. Sources for this and the next paragraph are Hansen, *My Minneapolis*, 345–57, quotation page 345–46; Lovoll, *Norwegian Newspapers in America*, 321, 325, 328, 331; Rygg, *American Relief for Norway*, 208–18; Vanberg, *From So Many . . . for So Few*, 34–36.

38. See, for example, the documentation in Haidet, *Twin Cities Ordnance Plant*.

39. The information in this and the following paragraph stems from Olson, *Vikings across the Atlantic*, 192–93; *Minneapolis Star Journal*, April 30, 1942; Hansen, *My Minneapolis*, 350–53. On Jacob Stefferud's and his daughters' engagement in ARFN activities, see TCHP interview with Alice Olson and Ruth Pieper, and Jacob Stefferud's autobiographical sketches mailed to the author by his daughters.

40. Lovoll, *Norwegian Newspapers in America*, 325; *Minneapolis Posten*, January 24–December 12, 1941; October 9 and 16, November 6 and 13, 1942; February 4–December 24, 1943; June 2–December 2, 1944; January 5–November 30, 1945.

41. "Mindekirken, The Norwegian Lutheran Memorial Church," 5. Sources from the Norwegian Foreign Ministry's files for 1941–47 include "Foredrag til statsråd," October 23, 1941, 1–2; Per Askim to Theodor Broch, July 16, 1942; Cooperative for American Remittances to Europe (CARE), correspondence and information flyers, 1946–47; correspondence from the consulate to the Norwegian Embassy in Washington, DC, dated August 19, 1946. The author translated the quoted material from the Norwegian. Olson, *Vikings across the Atlantic*, ch. 5, "A Shared Homeland," especially 188–93.

42. Hansen, *My Minneapolis*, 348–57.

Notes to Chapter Seven: A Later-Generation Ethnic Group

1. Parts of the text in this chapter derive from earlier versions of the author's interpretation of the Norwegian American community's development during these twenty-five years.

Interview with Paul A. Boe by Gjermund S. Thompson, Northfield, MN, December 1, 1984, 30–33, ELCA Oral History Collection of the American Lutheran Church, Association of Evangelical Lutheran Churches and Lutheran Church in America, filed in the ELCA Headquarters Archives, Chicago, IL; Paul A. Boe, "Biographical Record," Code No. B-3888, ELCA Archives, Chicago. Cover letter by Gjermund S. Thompson with the transcript of his interview with Boe, in the ELCA Archives, Chicago. The son of an NLCA minister in Wisconsin, Boe was born and bred in Norwegian Lutheran circles. The course of his life developed in that sphere, even as he increasingly lived for periods in big cities farther afield to further his education and inclination toward social work. After attending St. Olaf College, Boe completed graduate study at the University of Chicago before studying at Luther Seminary in St. Paul and being ordained as a Lutheran minister. He served as a pastor in Wisconsin and Iowa for six years and then worked as director of the Lutheran Welfare Society of Iowa in Des Moines between 1952 and 1958. After earning a master's degree in social work in Seattle in 1960, he moved to the ALC headquarters in Minneapolis, where he headed its Division of Charities and remained in that executive position when the ALC renamed it the Division of Social Service. Between 1961 and 1974, he became deeply involved with the ALC's and the Twin Cities' services to the poor and minorities. He commuted from his home in St. Louis Park, a suburb west of the city, to church offices in the Cedar-Riverside district. Interviewer Thompson says in the letter accompanying the transcript of their conversation that Boe speaks "as a pastor, but more particularly as a social worker."

2. See Table 1.1 (pages 16–17) for the census statistics here and in the following paragraphs.

3. Lovoll, *A Folk Epic*, 195, and Lovoll, *Celebrating a Century*, 87, 91–98; Olson, *Vikings across the Atlantic*, 191–206.

4. On the size of the third generation, see, for example, Norlie, *History of the Norwegian People*, 312–13. The quotation comes from Odd S. Lovoll, "From Norway to America: A Tradition of Immigration Fades," in Cuddy, *Contemporary American Immigration*, 100–101.

5. For popular views of the Scandinavian American presence in the Twin Cities and the quoted phrases, see Brink, *The Twin Cities*, 70–71, and Steffens, *The Shame of the Cities*, 43. See also Thomas J.

Abercrombie, "A Tale of Twin Cities: Minneapolis and St. Paul," *National Geographic* (November 1980): 665–91.

6. Lovoll, "A Tradition Fades," 89–96. TCHP interviews with Egil Almaas; Harald and Synnove Bakke; Kjell Bergh; Kåre and Helen Faber; Tor and Sunny Hansen; Donald Kvavik; Ingrid Slettemoen; Odd Unstad; Ruth and Vern Welchinger. Observations and conversations with members of the Norwegian-American Technical Society, December 10, 1999, and May 17, 2000; with members of Kontakt Ungdomsklubb, January 8, 2000.

7. This and the following paragraphs about the associational life of the Twin Cities' Norwegian American community rely on Hansen, *My Minneapolis*, 228; the TCHP interviews cited in the previous note; notes taken at the annual NATS picnic on August 1, 1998; NATS records copied for the author by its board; and note cards written in 1973 about Norwegian American associations in the Twin Cities for the MNHS Ethnic History of Minnesota files of the *They Chose Minnesota* project. See Peg Meier, "After Almost 40 Years, Concordia's Language Villages Still Growing," *Minneapolis Star-Tribune*, July 19, 1998, E7; TCHP interview with Liv Dahl; and telephone conversations with village director of Skogfjorden Tove Dahl in September 2000.

8. For examples of the repression and retreat of an open German American ethnicity in Minnesota due to the world wars, see Chrislock, *The Progressive Era in Minnesota*, 139–44, and essays in Glasrud, ed., *A Heritage Deferred.*

9. *The Ambassador, Summer Book, The University Oslo American Summer School, 1947–1954* (Oslo: G. Lindkvist—Boktrykkeri, A. W. Brøggers bøktrykkeri, 1947–54); Reidar Dittman, "Oslo Summer School for American Students (1947–1958)," in *Fifty Years of Achievement and International Good Will*, ed. Einar Vannebo (Oslo: International Summer School, University of Oslo, 1996), 14–35. TCHP interview with Torild Homstad.

10. Gans, *Making Sense of America*, especially ch. 9, "Symbolic Ethnicity: The Future of Ethnic Groups and Cultures in America," 167–201.

11. The quoted passages come from the TCHP interview with Krista Sande Johnson. Reverend Keith Olstad, senior pastor at University Lutheran Church of Hope, discussed how common views about Native Americans were spread among the white community in both rural areas and the Twin Cities in his TCHP interview on April 28, 1999.

12. A Minnesota Public Radio interview with Alan R. Woolworth, a curator for the Minnesota Historical Society (September 26, 2002), presents both sides of the Dakota-white conflict with unusual insight and balance. See also Anderson, *Kinsmen of Another Kind*, 261–71; Peterson, comp., *Known Military and Civilian Dead*; Elin Fagnastøl, "The Dakota War and Changing Norwegian-American Attitudes toward Native Americans," unpublished master's thesis, Norwegian University of Science and Technology, 2003; Øverland, *Immigrant Minds, American Identities*, especially ch. 3 and 150, 159, 169–173.

13. For statistics on intermarriage frequencies between Norwegian immigrants and other immigrant groups, see David C. Mauk, "Finding Their Way in the City: Norwegian Immigrant Women and Their Daughters in Urban Areas, 1880s–1920s," in Bergland and Lahlum, eds., *Norwegian American Women*, 147. On Norwegian

American relations with the Jewish community in north Minneapolis, see Nina Sandstrøm Angelsen, "Relations between Norwegian Americans and Jewish Americans in North Minneapolis from the 1920s to the 1950s," unpublished master's thesis, Norwegian University of Science and Technology, 2005. TCHP interviews with Mary-Jane and Alan Austensen; Eunice Baker; Sheldon Bloom; Marilyn Chiat; Carl Chrislock; Evelyn and Mary Flaten; John and Jeanette Futcher; Rev. Hoover Grimsby; Nellie Allan Stone Johnson; Ione Kadden; Dolores King; Hilda Kringstad; Arthur Naftalin; Lorraine Ofstie; Mary Ann Olsen; Roger Ostby; Paul Rusten; Christian Skjervold; Marilyn Sorensen; James Stolpestad; Mike Svendahl; Don Torgersen; Joel Torstenson; Marianne Wargelin; Carole Woo.

14. David Vassar Taylor, "The Blacks," in Holmquist, ed., *They Chose Minnesota*, 73–80; *Annual Report of the Adjutant General, of the State of Minnesota for the Year Ending December 1, 1866, and of the Military Forces of the State from 1861 to 1866* (St. Paul: Pioneer Printing Company, 1866), 136–40, 224, 277, 279, 284, 334, 342, 409–12, 440, 470–71, 487–88, 615, 639.

15. Taylor, "The Blacks," 73–91. For a brief, insightful overview of the succession of immigrant groups arriving in Minneapolis–St. Paul, see Rudolph J. Vecoli, "Immigrants and the Twin Cities: Melting Pot or Mosaic," in Anderson and Blanck, eds., *Swedes in the Twin Cities*, 17–27. See also David C. Mauk, "*Norskdommens Høydepunkt*: 1880–1914, the Golden Age of Norwegian Immigrant Community in Minneapolis–St. Paul," in Øverland, ed., *Norwegian-American Essays 2004*, 185–20, and TCHP interviews with Joel Torstenson and Ella Valborg Tweet.

16. Kane and Ominsky, *Twin Cities*, 232–34, 237, 244, 254–55, 262; Joseph W. Zalusky, ". . . Bridge Square *Going . . . Going . . . Gone*," *Hennepin County History* (Summer 1961): 3–7; TCHP interviews with Elva M. Bakken and Barbara G. Lehman; Ruth Hanhold Crane; Luther and Eileen Forde; Rev. Hoover Grimsby; Joel Torstenson.

17. TCHP interviews with Mary-Jane and Alan Austensen; John S. Futcher; Bjarne and Else Grindem; Tor and Sunny Hansen; Lawrence and Lois Hauge; Hilda Kringstad; Ardis Munther; Lorraine Ofstie; Mary Ann Olsen; Dennis Sorheim.

18. Herbert J. Gans, "Symbolic Ethnicity: The Future of Ethnic Groups and Cultures in America," *Ethnic and Racial Studies* 2, no. 1 (January 1979): 1–20. See also C. A. Valentine, "Voluntary Ethnicity and Social Change: Classism, Racism, Marginality, Mobility, and Revolution with Special Reference to Afro-Americans and Other Third World Peoples," *Journal of Ethnic Studies* 3, no. 1 (Spring 1975): 1–27; and TCHP interviews with Carl Chrislock; Rev. Hoover Grimsby; Chuck Haga; Krista Johnson; Mary Ann Olsen; Jim Peterson; Martin Sabo; Marilyn Sorensen; James Stolpestad.

19. TCHP interviews with Eunice Baker, Marilyn Sorensen, James Stolpestad, and Tom Thompson.

20. Nils William Olsson and Lawrence G. Hammerstrom, "Swan Johan Turnblad and the Founding of the American Swedish Institute," in Anderson and Blanck, eds., *Swedes in the Twin Cities*, 104–23, especially 121–23.

21. Chrislock, *Fjord to Freeway*, 228, 233–36; Norberg, *An American Saga*, 169, 178–79, 203–4; Nichol, "Introduction" to *Vivacious Daughter*, 25–29.

22. TCHP interviews with Paul Daniels; Eugene L. Fevold; Rev. Hoover Grimsby; Keith Olstad.

23. This and the previous paragraph build on TCHP interviews with Rev. Eugene L. Fevold; William Green; Gracia Grindal; Rev. Keith Olstad; Carol Sersland; Mary Jo Thorsheim; Joel Torstenson. For a theoretical approach to the concept of an ethnic core, see Eric Kaufmann, "Ethnic or Civic Nation?: Theorizing the American Case," European Institute, London School of Economics and Political Science.

24. Hansen, *My Minneapolis*, 360; Rygg, *American Relief for Norway*, 13–20, 38, 65–70, 90; TCHP interviews with Bjarne and Else Grindem; Alice Olson and Ruth Pieper.

25. TCHP interviews provided much of the information about "adopting" DPs in this and the next paragraph: Eunice Baker; Harald and Synnove Bakke; Paul Daniels; Rev. Eugene Fevold; Rev. Hoover Grimsby; Harald Hagen; Lawrence and Lois Hauge; Ione Kadden; Dolores King; Helen Pederson. These paragraphs also derive in important ways from the correspondence and reports of the National Lutheran Council's Resettlement Service for 1948 at the ELCA Archives, Chicago; Solberg, *As Between Brothers*, 150–54; and Timo Riippa, "The Baltic Peoples: Estonians, Latvians, and Lithuanians," 329–31; Frank Renkiewicz, "The Poles," 376; Keith P. Dyrud, "East Slavs, Rusins, Ukrainians, Russians, and Belorussians," 416–17—all in Holmquist, ed., *They Chose Minnesota*.

26. TCHP interviews with Eugene Fevold; Ione Kadden; Rev. Keith Olstad.

27. This and the following paragraph build on Taylor, "The Blacks," especially 74, 80–81, 84–85, and Risa Palm, "Plymouth Avenue in Transition, 1965–1965," *Minnesota Geographer* 22, no. 1 (January 1970): 1–2.

28. "Minneapolis Community Self-Survey of Human Relations, Reports and Recommendations of the Committees," Vol. 1 (Civic Organizations, Education and Training, Health and Hospitals) and Vol. 3 (Real Estate and Housing, Recreation and Group Work, Religious Faiths and Denominations, Welfare Services), Minneapolis, 1947; Kane and Ominsky, *Twin Cities*, 267; Joseph W. Zalusky, "The Mayors of St. Anthony and Minneapolis; Installment IV—Conclusion," *Hennepin County History* (Summer 1962): 8; Minnesota Election Trends, http://www.electiontrendsproject.org/; "Arthur Naftalin, 87, Professor and Former Minneapolis Mayor, Dies," *New York Times*, May 19, 2005; TCHP interviews with Carl Chrislock; Jane and Orville Freeman; Bill Green; Walter Mondale; Arthur Naftalin; Jim Peterson; Martin Sabo; Chrislock, *Fjord to Freeway*, 233.

29. Zalusky, "Mayors of St. Anthony and Minneapolis," 8; TCHP interviews with Carl Chrislock; Arthur Naftalin; Jim Peterson; Martin Sabo; "Arthur Naftalin . . . Dies," *New York Times*.

30. The primary sources for this and the following paragraphs concerning antisemitism, the demographic profile of Minneapolis in 1946, and Mayor Humphrey's massive effort to document and improve intergroup relations in the city are Carey McWilliams, "Minneapolis: The Curious Twin," *Common Ground* (1946): 61–65; John Hope II, specialist on industrial relations, Race Relations Department, American Missionary Association,

Fisk University, "Industrial Minorities in the Minneapolis Labor Market," Charles S. Johnson, director, Herman H. Long, associate director, typescript report, 1947, reproduced from the Jewish Community Relations Council of Minnesota Papers, Collection P445, MNHS, quotation page 2; Social Science Institute, Race Relations Department, Fisk University, "Minneapolis Community Self-Survey on Human Relations," ten reports of separate committees and reports of the Mayor's Council on Human Relations, boxes 10–19, Hubert Humphrey Papers, MNHS; Solberg, *Hubert Humphrey*, 72, 78, 91–93, 102, 105–6, 117–18.

31. Hope, "Industrial Minorities in the Minneapolis Labor Market," 5.

32. This and the following two paragraphs build on Willard A. Hutt, "Smoke on Plymouth Avenue: Celebrating the 25th Anniversary of Pilot City Services," *Minnesota History* 51, no. 3 (1993): 25–29; Chrislock, *Fjord to Freeway*, 228; Jeffrey T. Manuel and Andrew Urban, "'You Can't Legislate the Heart': Minneapolis Mayor Charles Stenvig and the Politics of Law and Order," *American Studies* 49 (Fall/Winter 2008): 195–219; TCHP interviews with Mary-Jane Austensen; John and Jeanette Futcher.

33. Nicholas Swardson, "Plymouth Avenue: A Taste of Violence," 15, and Gerald Vizenor, "1966: 'Plymouth Avenue Is Going to Burn,'" 20–21—both *Twin Citian*, October 1966.

34. "Fires, Fights Continue on North Side" and "Police Aide Says '66 Race Strife Was Different," *Minneapolis Tribune*, July 21, 1967, 1, 12, 13; "The Minneapolis Riot That Wasn't," *Minneapolis Tribune*, July 21, 1967, 6; "Wednesday Night's Arrests Are Listed," *Minneapolis Tribune*, July 21, 1967, 13. For the larger context of the riots in the summer of 1967, see the numerous articles and editorials about urban race riots in the same newspaper from July 16 to July 28. This pattern of local news articles surrounds the riots in Minneapolis in 1966 and 1968 as well.

35. Comments about the deterioration of neighborhoods were made in interviews with Sheldon Bloom; Marilyn Chiat; John S. Futcher; and Christian Skjervold. The quoted remarks come from the interview with John Futcher. Hutt, "Smoke on Plymouth Avenue," 25–29; Manuel and Urban, "You Can't Legislate the Heart"; TCHP interviews with Alan and Mary-Jane Austensen; Sheldon Bloom; Marilyn Chiat; Carl Chrislock; John and Jeanette Futcher; Rev. Keith Olstad; Rev. Donald Rudrud.

36. US Department of the Interior, Bureau of Indian Affairs, "Employment Assistance Program," Washington, DC, 1956, 1–4; Minneapolis Area Office, US Department of the Interior, Bureau of Indian Affairs, "Suggestions for Ways of Maximizing Opportunities for Indian People," Minneapolis, 1966, 1–2—both in the International Institutes Collection, box 13, FF244, Bureau of Indian Affairs Publications, Immigration History Research Center, Andersen Library, University of Minnesota, Minneapolis. Pauline Brunette, "The Minneapolis Urban Indian Community," *Hennepin County History* (Winter 1989–90): 4–15, especially 5 and 8; Mitchell E. Rubinstein and Alan R. Woolworth, "The Dakota and Ojibway," in Holmquist, ed., *They Chose Minnesota*, 28–30 (census statistics page 29). For Minneapolis, the increase in population was from 5,828

to 8,932; for St. Paul it grew from 1,906 to 2,538.

37. Nee-Gon-Nway-Wee-Dung, "Thunder before the Storm," aka Clyde Howard Bellecourt, "Curriculum Vitae," 1968–98, and telephone interview, March 16, 2012; Rubinstein and Woolworth, "The Dakota and Ojibway," 29; TCHP interviews with the Revs. Hamm Muus; Keith Olstad; Donald Rudrud.

38. Clyde Howard Bellecourt, telephone interview, March 16, 2012; interview with Paul A. Boe by Gjermund S. Thompson, December 1, 1984, 32–41.

39. Boe File Number 1, "Biographical Record," B-3888, ELCA Archives, Chicago. The most informative of many newspaper articles explaining Paul Boe's relationship to AIM and the events at Wounded Knee are Bob Lundegaard, "Lutheran Clergyman Faces Jail over Wounded Knee," *Minneapolis Times*, December 24, 1973, 1A, 8A, and *Lutheran Standard* interview with Boe, January 15, 1974, 25–26—both in the Paul A. Boe Collection, #30369 3/16, Newspapers—December 1973, Center for Western Studies, Augustana College, Sioux Falls, SD. The Boe Collection contains the correspondence he received in response to his reports to the ALC leadership and congregations about his actions at Wounded Knee, as well as articles about the beginning of the trial of Banks and Means in St. Paul. See also Sayer, *Ghost Dancing the Law*, especially 71–73, and "Banks, Dennis J.," encyclopedia.com, http://www.encyclopedia.com/topic/Dennis_J._Banks.aspx.

40. East Franklin Avenue in south Minneapolis is known as the American Indian Cultural Corridor because several institutions (the American Indian Center, a Native health clinic, a Native church, the Little Earth public housing complex, and Native art galleries) are all located there. This stretch of blocks is adjacent to Norway House and the Norwegian Memorial Church. See Krithika Varagur, "Patrolling Minneapolis's Native American History," *New York Review of Books*, July 31, 2020, nybooks.com/daily/2020/07/31/patrolling-minneapolis-native-american-history/.

41. The analysis of Mayor Stenvig's campaigns and views in this and the following paragraphs depend primarily on the TCHP interview with his son, Todd C. Stenvig, and CD/DVD copies of recordings from the mayor's career. Those used here are Stenvig History—Family—School—Military (Police Federation) Start and Fight Benefits; U of M Riot; Feeling on Race & Country, Communism & Indian Meeting, Indians & Parker Office; and Former Mayor Charles Stenvig Interview, 1977. The best analytic study of Mayor Stenvig's political career is Manuel and Urban, "You Can't Legislate the Heart."

42. See note 38 for this chapter. Kane and Ominsky, *Twin Cities*, 266; Chrislock, *Fjord to Freeway*, 233; TCHP interviews with Carl Chrislock; John and Jeanette Futcher; Arthur Naftalin; Rev. Keith Olstad; Rev. Donald Rudrud.

43. Manuel and Urban, "You Can't Legislate the Heart"; TCHP interviews with Mary-Jane Austensen; John and Jeanette Futcher; Donald Rudrud.

44. TCHP interviews with Eunice Baker; Carl Chrislock; Joanell Dyrstad; Jane and Orville Freeman; John and Jeanette Futcher; Chuck Haga; Nellie

Stone Johnson; Walter Mondale; William Munger; James Pederson; Judy and David Ranheim; Todd C. Stenvig; Joel Torstenson.

Notes to Chapter Eight: The Norwegian American Ancestry Group

1. Parts of the text in this chapter derive from earlier versions of the author's interpretation of the Norwegian American community's development during these twenty-five years. The comments attributed to journalist Chuck Haga in this and the following paragraph come from the author's TCHP interview with Chuck Haga.

2. Jeppesen, *Scandinavian Descendants,* 88–89. Census data informing the interpretation of metropolitan-area Norwegian American life in 1990 and 2000 was calculated on March 8, 2013, by Brandon Trampe of IPUMS-USA (with guidance and statistical research by Steven Ruggles, J. Trent Alexander, Katie Genadek, Ronald Goeken, Matthew B. Schroeder, and Matthew Sobek). Integrated Public Use Microdata Series (IPUMS): Version 5.0 [machine-readable database]. Herbert J. Gans, "Symbolic Ethnicity: The Future of Ethnic Groups and Cultures in America," in Gans, et al., eds., *On the Making of Americans,* 203–7. Another version of his treatment of the concept appears in *Ethnic and Racial Studies* 2, no. 1 (1979). For Gans's most recent expression of these views concerning later-generation "old" ethnic groups, see "The Coming Darkness of Late-Generation European American Ethnicity," 757–61. TCHP interviews with president Dick Johnson in Minneapolis, January 12, 1999 (Building Trades Council, visit and conversations, September, 30, 1998), and with president Louis Greengard in St. Paul, November 10, 1998; telephone conversations with *Union Advocate* newspaper editor Barb Kucera, October-November 1998; TCHP interview with Barb Kucera and Bob Roe.

3. Lovoll, *The Promise Fulfilled,* 51; TCHP interviews with the following substantiated these migration patterns in the metropolitan area: Joanell Dyrstad; Kåre and Helen Faber and family; Eileen and Luther Forde; Lawrence and Lois Hauge; Lloyd Hustvedt; Jim Pederson; Christian Skjervold; Tom Thompson. See US Census, *Ancestry of the Population, 1990, Minnesota* (Washington, DC: Economics and Statistics Administration, 1993), 205, 207, 211, for the Norwegian ancestry population of the metropolitan region in 1990.

4. The author completed much of the basic research for this history in 1998–2000, while Lovoll's study was complete in time for publication in 1998.

5. Gans discusses recent scholarly models for studying later-generation ethnic groups in *Making Sense of America*; see especially Part 3. Lieberson and Waters, *From Many Strands,* is a fine example of views expressed in studies of later-generation, "old" ethnic groups. On effects of urban life, see Lovoll, *The Promise of America,* 247, 249–53, 271, and *The Promise Fulfilled,* 16, 98–102, 139–41, 154–56.

6. See the previous note for scholars who have focused on trends among later-generation white ethnics. Another insightful work on the topic is Alba, *Ethnic Identity*; see especially 1–36. See also Jeppesen, *Scandinavian Descendants,* 78–79.

TCHP interviews with less or little ethnically involved people include those with Mary-Jane and Alan Austensen and sons; Kåre and Helen Faber and family; Marlin

Heise; Keith Olstad; Roger Ostby; Philip T. Schueler.

7. Gans, *Making Sense of America*, 173–86; Alba, *Ethnic Identity*, 1–36; Datel and Dingemans, "Urban Multiethnicity," 458–77; TCHP interviews with Consul General Ulf Christiansen; Liv Dahl; Chuck Haga; Dennis Sorheim.

8. TCHP interviews with Samuel Bergaas; Kjell Bergh; Kåre and Helen Faber; Norwegian-American Technical Society, bylaws, meeting, and interviews, October 23, 1998; Odd Unstad. See also David C. Mauk, "Scandinavians," in Barkan, ed., *A Nation of Peoples*, 464–81, especially 472–80.

9. Lovoll, *The Promise Fulfilled*, 37–41. This study emphasizes the two elements of the ethnic core, not least because they were the majority of the people identified and interviewed. David C. Mauk, "Norwegian 17th of May Celebrations and Princely Visits in the Diverse Ethnographic Landscapes of Minneapolis," a forty-six-page report with thirty illustrations concerning the 5th Congressional District of Minnesota, in *Local Legacies* (Washington, DC: Library of Congress, 2000). Mauk, "Scandinavians," especially 472–80. For introductory information about Lakselaget, Torskeklubben, and Den Norske Torskeklubben, see http://www.lakselaget.org/, www.torskeklubben.org/info.php, http://www.norske-torske-klubben.com/. See also Svendsen, "Codfish and Assimilation," 14–16. TCHP interviews with Sam Bergaas, *Kontakt ungdomsklubb*, observer at a club dinner (January 8, 2000); Kjell Bergh; Consul General Ulf Christiansen; former consul general Bjarne and Else Grindem; Lois and Sidney Rand; Dennis Sorheim.

10. On the use of "LGE" for later generation white ethnics, see Gans, "The Coming Darkness of Late-Generation European American Ethnicity," 757–65; see also Øverland, *Immigrant Minds, American Identities*, especially 144–73.

11. TCHP interviews with Harry T. Cleven; Orlyn and Marit Kringstad; Jim and Leslie Nestingen; Keith Olstad; Jim Pederson; Ingrid Slettemoen; Odd Unstad.

12. This and the next paragraph build on the author's experience in Dinkytown, Minneapolis, on August 1, 1998. See Lovoll on ethnic humor in *The Promise Fulfilled*, 223–28.

13. TCHP interviews with Daniel and Gaeyln Beal; Carl Chrislock; Liv Dahl; Bill Green; Doug Green; Orlyn and Marit Kringstad; Roger Moe; Walter Mondale; Jim and Leslie Nestingen; Jim Pederson; Larry Sabo.

14. TCHP interviews with Paul Daniels; Rev. Hoover Grimsby; Gracia Grindal; Debbie Miller; Keith Olstad.

15. TCHP interviews with Daniel and Gaeyln Beal; Torild Homstad; Lloyd Hustvedt; Jim and Leslie Nestingen; Tom Thompson; Ella Tweet; Solveig Zempel.

16. Primary sources for the interpretation of the events in 1975 are programs for the "Norwegian American 1975 Sesquicentennial Concert" and the "Salute to Heritage" evening; Norwegian American 1975 Sesquicentennial Association, "Sesqui—Log, 1825–1975," no. 2 (January 1975) and no. 3 (April 1975); flyers, "Lutheran Brotherhood Presented All Lutheran Youth Choir Concert" and "Norwegian Sesquicentennial Folk Concert, Birgitte Grimstad, Soprano Ballad Singer"; "Mindekirken: The Norwegian Lutheran Memorial Church," 7. See also the list of newspapers

articles by Chuck Haga cited in the next note.

17. A selection of Chuck Haga's articles in the *Star Tribune* is as follows: "Olav's Journey Follows an American Dream," November 29, 1987, 1B; "1,300 Salute Olav; King Returns Favor," November 28, 1987; "What Today Means to Norwegians," May 17, 1994, 1A; "King Harald and Queen Sonja of Norway Wrapped up their Two-day Visit . . . ," October 21, 1995, 1B; "As Norwegian Americans Mark Syttende Mai—the 17th of May—a Historian Questions Their Ideas about Their Homeland," May, 17, 1996, 1A; "Norwegians Keep Storybook Tradition; Today on Syttende Mai Minnesotans with Norwegian Roots Celebrate . . .," May 17, 1998, 1B; "Norway's Future King Forms New Ties," June 8, 1999. TCHP interviews with Harry T. Cleven; Dick and Nancy Enstad and Shirley Evenstad; Lois and Larry Forde; former consul general Bjarne and Else Grindem; Chuck Haga; Lawrence and Lois Hauge; Tei-Tei and Harry Markley.

18. TCHP interviews with Ruth Hanhold Crane; Lloyd Hustvedt; Debbie Miller; Lovoll, *The Promise Fulfilled*, 262.

19. TCHP interviews with Kjell Bergh; Liv Dahl; former consul general Bjarne and Else Grindem; Tei-Tei and Harry Markley; Norwegian-American Technical Society Christmas dinner, January 16, 1999.

20. Grigoleit, "Coming Home? The Integration of Hmong Refugees."

21. "Good Question: Why Did Somalis Locate Here?" WCCO-TV CBS Minnesota, January 19, 2011.

22. On migration to suburbs in the immigrant clusters that had earlier emigrated from Norway, see TCHP interviews with Lois and Larry Forde; Mary Ann Olsen; Christopher Skjerstad; and Jorunn Wolden. On commuting from the exurbs to the Twin Cities, see for example the interviews with Tom Thompson about being in a carpool from Red Wing and Jim Pederson about commuting from Stillwater and Eau Claire.

23. TCHP interviews: John Akslen; Egil Almaas; Sam Bergaas; *Kontakt ungdomsklubb* New Year's Party, pamphlets, and interviews, January 8, 2000; Norwegian-American Technical Society, bylaws, meeting, and interviews, October 23, 1998, and Christmas dinner, January 16, 1999.

24. This and the following paragraph are based on TCHP interviews with Daniel and Gaeyln Beal; Hilda Kringstad; and Carol Sersland, which illuminated folk dance networks and generations in the Twin Cities. TCHP interviews with Fred Cogelow; Dick and Nancy Enstad and Shirley Evenstad; Marion and Laila Nelson, focused on material culture and crafts. See also Cogelow, *Sculptor in Wood*; Marion Nelson, "Foreword," vii–x, and Fred Cogelow, "Introduction," 1–7, in Nelson, ed., *Material Culture and People's Art*, especially 3–72. TCHP interview with Carol Sersland; Carol Sersland's interview with her father, Harold Sersland.

25. Conversations and TCHP interviews with Liv Dahl; Lakeville Sons of Norway lodge, March 13, 1999; Mindekirken, March 14, 1999; Norsemen's Federation, February 14, 1999; at Torskeklubben, May 1, 1999; at Den Norske Torskeklubben, March 27, 1999.

26. TCHP interview with Kåre and Helen Faber and family.

Notes to Chapter Nine: A Glance Forward and Concluding Remarks

1. The last newspaper, *Minneapolis Posten* (1940–56), continued as *Minnesota Posten* to 1979: see Lovoll, *Norwegian Newspapers in America*, 337–38, 359–60.

2. "Obituary: Arley Bjella Dies; He Led Lutheran Brotherhood," *Minneapolis Star Tribune*, May 23, 2001; Strand, *The Story of Lutheran Brotherhood*, 11, 13–17, 133, 135–38, 181–90; Lovoll, *The Promise Fulfilled*, 193–97.

3. TCHP interviews with Consul General Ulf Christiansen; Consul General Bjarne and Else Grindem; Consular Secretary Tei-Tei Markley.

4. For the sources of this and the following paragraphs, see Dane Smith, "Steve Sviggum and Roger Moe . . . Not Such Polar Opposites," *Star Tribune*, June 21, 2001, BA1, 13; Table 1.1 in chapter 1 (pages 16–17); Lovoll, *Norwegian Newspapers in America*, 337–38; TCHP interviews with Consul General Ulf Christiansen; Consul General Bjarne and Else Grindem; Tei-Tei Markley; former vice president Walter Mondale. Regarding the change to an honorary consulate, see Ministry of Foreign Affairs, "Gary Gandrud Appointed Honorary Consul General in Minneapolis," press release, January 20, 2010, https://www.regjeringen.no/en/aktuelt/minneapolis_gc/id591596/.

5. Michael Khoo, "Profile: Roger Moe," Minnesota Public Radio, September 16, 2002; Bergman, *Scandinavians in the State House*, 71–74, 175, 226, 246–47.

6. Bergman, *Scandinavians in the State House*, 244–45; TCHP interview with Martin Olav Sabo.

7. "Abdi Warsame," Wikipedia, https://en.wikipedia.org/wiki/Abdi_Warsame; Bergman, *Scandinavians in the State House*, 195–98.

8. For example, on January 24, 2019, *MinnPost* reported, "While last November's election marked a historic milestone for Hmong-Minnesotans as four were newly elected to the Minnesota Legislature, the group is already focused on something bigger—its representation of the larger Asian Pacific community." The Hmong American officeholders announced they had formed an Asian Pacific caucus in the legislature to achieve that goal.

9. *Minneapolis Star Tribune*, November 6, 2019; "Abdi Warsame," Wikipedia; Yaron Steinbuch, "Minnesota AG Keith Ellison to Take Lead in George Floyd Case," *New York Post*, June 1, 2020; "5th District 1 of Many Key Minnesota Primary Races," WCCO News, August 14, 2018; Ilhan Omar, House of Representatives webpage, https://omar.house.gov.

10. Hansen, *My Minneapolis*, 142–45.

11. Neal St. Anthony, "$15 Million Remake of South Minneapolis Block Has Roots in Norway," *Minneapolis Star Tribune*, July 16, 2015; Haugo Genealogical Archives + Library, Norway House, The National Norwegian Center in America, https://norwayhouse.org/expansion/genealogy.

12. Lakselaget website, https://www.lakselaget.org.

13. Going Viking Honorees, Norway House, The National Norwegian Center in America, https://www.norwayhouse.org/gala/going-viking.

14. Human Rights Forum, Augsburg University, www.augsburg.edu/humanrightsforum; for further information about the Minnesota Peace Initiative, see Norway House's Minnesota Peace Initiative, https://www.norwayhouse.org/mpi.

15. Bergman, *Scandinavians in the State House*, 225.

16. Bergman, *Scandinavians in the State House*, 210–11, 238–43; Lovoll, *The Promise Fulfilled*, 6, 214.

17. TCHP interview with Chuck Haga for his comments in this and the following paragraphs; Katherine Fennelly, "Latinos, Africans, and Asians in the North Star State: Immigrant Communities in Minnesota," in *Beyond the Gateway*, 1–15; "Report—November 2003—Minneapolis/St. Paul in Focus: A Profile from Census 2000," Brookings, November 1, 2003, http://www.brookings.edu/research/reports/2003/11/livingcities-minneapolis-stpaul.

BIBLIOGRAPHY

Primary Sources

Manuscript Collections

Central Lutheran Church Archives, Minneapolis.
Evangelical Lutheran Church of America Archives, Chicago.
Luther Seminary Archives, St. Paul.
  American Lutheran Church Archives.
Minnesota Annual Conference of the United Methodist Church, Minneapolis.
Minnesota Historical Society, St. Paul.
  Hubert H. Humphrey Papers, [1883?]–1982.
  Jewish Community Relations Council of Minnesota Papers, Council Records, 1922–1974.
  William Rainey Marshall Papers, 1849–1921.
  Methodist Episcopal Church, Minnesota Annual Methodist Conference Papers, 1840–1909.
  Minnesota Ethnic History Project Records, 1969–1982.
National Archives of Norway, Oslo.
  Archives of the Royal Norwegian Foreign Ministry for the Consulate in St. Paul.
Norway House, The National Norwegian Center in America, Haugo Genealogical Archives and Library, Minneapolis.
Norwegian-American Historical Association, Northfield, MN.
  Congregations Records.

Fairview Hospital and Thomas Hospital Papers, 1910–1942.
Carl Gustav Otto Hansen Papers, 1862–1958.
Simon Johnson Papers, 1907–1925.
O. M. Norlie Collection.
Norwegian Hospital Society, St. Paul, Papers, circa 1901.
Temperance Movement Papers, 1841–1962.
University of Minnesota, Anderson Library, Minneapolis.
Social Welfare History Archives, Minneapolis Family and Social Service Records, 1895–1945.

Newspapers

Budstikken
Decorah-Posten
Folkebladet
Folkets Røst
Gaa Paa
Minneapolis Posten
Minneapolis Star Tribune
Minneapolis Tidende
Minnesota Posten
New York Times
Saamanden
St. Paul Pioneer Press

Interviews: *See Appendix.*

Secondary Sources

Adams, John S., and Barbara J. VanDrasek. *Minneapolis–St. Paul: People, Place, and Public Life*. Minneapolis: University of Minnesota Press, 1993.

Ager, Waldemar. *Oberst Heg og hans Gutter* (Colonel Heg and His Boys). Eau Claire, WI: Fremad Publishing, 1916.

Alba, Richard. *Ethnic Identity: The Transformation of White America*. New Haven, CT: Yale University Press, 1990.

Andersen, Arlow W. *The Immigrant Takes His Stand: The Norwegian-*

American Press and Public Affairs, 1847–1872. Northfield, MN: Norwegian-American Historical Association, 1953.

———. *The Salt of the Earth: A History of Norwegian-Danish Methodism in America*. Nashville, TN: Norwegian-Danish Methodist Historical Society, 1962.

Anderson, Gary C. *Kinsmen of Another Kind: Dakota-White Relations in the Upper Mississippi Valley, 1650–1862*. St. Paul: Minnesota Historical Society Press, 1997.

Anderson, Gary Clayton, and Alan R. Woolworth. *Through Dakota Eyes: Narrative Accounts of the Minnesota Indian War of 1862*. St. Paul: Minnesota Historical Society Press, 1988.

Anderson, Philip J., and Dag Blanck, eds. *Swedes in the Twin Cities: Immigrant Life and Minnesota's Urban Frontier*. St. Paul: Minnesota Historical Society Press, 2001.

Andrews, Gen. C. C. "Narrative of the Third Regiment." In *Minnesota in the Civil and Indian Wars, 1861–1865*, Board of Commissioners for the Legislature of Minnesota. St. Paul: n.p., 1891.

Annual Report of the Adjutant General of the State of Minnesota for the Year Ending December 1, 1866, and of the Military Forces of the State from 1861 to 1866. St. Paul: n.p., 1866.

Arnjot (Johannes B. Wist). *Scenes from the Life of a Newcomer: Jonas Olsen's First Years in America*. Trans. and ed. Orm Øverland. 1920; Minneapolis: University of Minnesota Press and the Norwegian-American Historical Association, 2006.

Associated Charities of Minneapolis. *A Quarter Century of Work among the Poor, 1884–1909*. Minneapolis: Associated Charities of Minneapolis, 1909.

Atwater, Isaac. *History of the City of Minneapolis, Minnesota*. New York: Munsell and Company, 1893.

Augsburg Faculty. *Program for Augsburg Seminary and Its College Departments with Interpretative Statement*. Minneapolis: Konferentsens forlagstrykkeri, 1874.

Bakken, Anja. "'Our Country Gives Us the Vote—America Refuses It': Norwegian-American Suffrage Workers in Brooklyn and Minneapolis, 1880–1920 and Their Gendered Sense of Ethnicity." MA thesis, Norwegian University of Science and Technology, 1998.

Barkan, Elliott Robert, ed. *A Nation of Peoples: A Sourcebook on America's Multicultural Heritage*. Westport, CT: Greenwood Press, 1999.

Barone, Michael. "The Social Basis of Urban Politics: Minneapolis and St. Paul, 1890–1905." Graduate essay in American politics, Harvard University, 1977.

Bergland, Betty A., and Lori Ann Lahlum. *Norwegian American Women: Migration, Communities, and Identities.* St. Paul: Minnesota Historical Society Press, 2011.

Bergman, Klas. *Scandinavians in the State House: How Nordic Immigrants Shaped Minnesota Politics.* St. Paul: Minnesota Historical Society Press, 2017.

Best, Joel. "Keeping the Peace in St. Paul: Crime, Vice, and Police Work, 1869–74." *Minnesota History* 47, no. 6 (Summer 1981): 240–48.

Bjork, Kenneth. *Saga in Steel and Concrete: Norwegian Engineers in America.* Northfield, MN: Norwegian-American Historical Association, 1947.

Blegen, Theodore C. *Minnesota: A History of the State.* Minneapolis: University of Minnesota Press, 1963.

———. *Norwegian Migration to America: The American Transition.* Northfield, MN: Norwegian-American Historical Association, 1940.

———. "Notes and Documents: Guri Endreson, Frontier Heroine." *Minnesota History* 10, no. 4 (1929): 425–30.

Blomvik, Kirsti Alette. "Heritage, Sisterhood and Self-Reliance: The Evolution and Significance of the Daughters of Norway, 1897–1950." MA thesis, Norwegian University of Science and Technology, 2002.

Board of Commissioners for the Legislature of Minnesota. *Minnesota in the Civil and Indian Wars, 1861–1865.* St. Paul: n.p., 1891.

Bratager, Laura Ringdal. *Over Hav og Land: Lyngblomstens Historie, Pionerliv i Minneapolis med flere skildringer.* Minneapolis: The author, 1925.

Bremer, Fredrika. *The Homes of the New World: Impressions of America.* Vol. 2. Trans. Mary Howitt. New York: Harper and Brothers, 1868.

Brink, Carol. *The Twin Cities.* New York: Macmillan Company, 1961.

Campbell, W. M. *St. Paul City Directory for 1875.* St. Paul: n.p., 1876.

Castle, Henry A. *History of St. Paul and Vicinity.* Vol. 1. Chicago: Lewis Publishing Company, 1912.

Chamberlin, H. E. *St. Anthony and Minneapolis Directory, 1859–1860.* Minneapolis: n.p., 1861.

Chrislock, Carl H. *Ethnicity Challenged: The Upper Midwest Norwegian-American Experience in World War I*. Northfield, MN: Norwegian-American Historical Association Topical Studies 3, 1981.

———. *From Fjord to Freeway: 100 Years—Augsburg College*. Minneapolis: Augsburg College, 1969.

———. "Profile of a Ward Boss: The Political Career of Lars M. Rand." In *Scandinavians and Other Immigrants in Urban America: The Proceedings of a Research Conference, October 26–27, 1984*, edited by Odd S. Lovoll. Northfield, MN: St. Olaf College Press, 1984.

———. *The Progressive Era in Minnesota, 1899–1918*. St. Paul: Minnesota Historical Society, 1971.

Cogelow, Fred. *Sculptor in Wood: The Collected Woodcarvings of Fred Cogelow with Comments by the Artist*. Whitewater, WI: Heart Prairie Press, 1991.

Cronon, William. *Nature's Metropolis: Chicago and the Great West*. New York: W. W. Norton, 1991.

Cuddy, Dennis L. *Contemporary American Immigration: Interpretative Essays*. Boston: Twayne Publishers, 1982.

Datel, Robin, and Dennis Dingemans. "Urban Multiethnicity." *Geographical Review*, 85, no. 4, Thematic Issue: American Urban Geography (October 1995): 458–77.

Davidson, C. Wright. *Davidson's Minneapolis City Directory, 1885–86*. Minneapolis: n.p., 1886.

Draxten, Nina. *Kristofer Janson in America*. Northfield, MN: Norwegian-American Historical Association, 1976.

Edgar, William C. *The Medal of Gold: A Story of Industrial Achievement*. Minneapolis: Bellman Company, 1925.

Erickson, James E., and Laura J. Erickson. "Scandinavian Methodist Episcopal Church, St. Paul, MN Members, 1853–1860." *Swedish-American Genealogist* 14, no. 4 (December 1994): 64–67, 176n31, 188n54.

Fagereng, John A. "Norwegian Social and Cultural Life in America, 1861–1891: An Analysis of Typical Norwegian Newspapers." MA thesis, University of Minnesota, 1932.

Faue, Elizabeth. *Community of Suffering and Struggle: Women, Men, and the Labor Movement in Minneapolis, 1915–1945*. Chapel Hill: University of North Carolina Press, 1991.

Folwell, William Watts. *A History of Minnesota*. 1921; St. Paul: Minnesota Historical Society Press, 2006.

Gans, Herbert J. "The Coming Darkness of Late-Generation European American Ethnicity." *Ethnic and Racial Studies* 37, no. 5 (2014): 757–61.

———. *Making Sense of America: Sociological Analyses and Essays*. Lanham, MD: Rowman and Littlefield, 1999.

———. "Symbolic Ethnicity: The Future of Ethnic Groups and Cultures in America." *Ethnic and Racial Studies* 2, no. 1 (1979): 1–20.

Gans, Herbert J., Nathan Glazer, Joseph R. Gusfield, and Christopher Jencks, eds. *On the Making of Americans: Essays in Honor of David Reisman*. Philadelphia: University of Pennsylvania Press, 1979.

Gieske, Millard L., and Steven J. Keillor. *Norwegian Yankee: Knute Nelson and the Failure of American Politics, 1860–1923*. Northfield, MN: Norwegian-American Historical Association, 1995.

Gilman, Rhoda R. *The Story of Minnesota's Past*. St. Paul: Minnesota Historical Society, 1991.

———. "A Territorial Imperative: How Minnesota Became the 32nd State." In *Making Minnesota Territory, 1849–1858*, a special issue of *Minnesota History* 56, no. 4 (Winter 1998–99): 154–71.

Gjerde, Jon. *From Peasants to Farmers: The Migration from Balestrand, Norway to the Upper Midwest*. Cambridge: Cambridge University Press, 1985.

———. *The Minds of the West: Ethnocultural Evolution in the Rural Middle West, 1830–1917*. Chapel Hill: University of North Carolina Press, 2002.

Glasrud, Clarence A., ed. *A Heritage Deferred: The German-Americans in Minnesota*. Moorhead, MN: Concordia College, 1981.

Goeken, Ronald Allen. "Unmarried Adults and Residential Autonomy: Living Arrangements in the United States, 1880–1990." PhD diss., University of Minnesota, 1999.

Gordon, Seth Ernst. "The New Central Lutheran Church: The Story of Central." Minneapolis: Central Lutheran Church, 1924. Norwegian-American Historical Association Archives, O. M. Norlie Collection.

Gozdziak, Elzbieta M., and Susan F. Martin, eds. *Beyond the Gateway: Immigrants in a Changing America*. Migration and Refugee Studies. Lanham, MD: Lexington Books, 2005.

Grigoleit, Grit. "Coming Home? The Integration of Hmong Refugees from Wat Tham Krabok, Thailand, into American Society." *Hmong Studies Journal* 7 (2006): 1–22.

Gutterson, Alma A., and Regina Hilleboe Christensen, eds. "Souvenir: Norse-American Women, 1825–1925." Minneapolis: Lutheran Free Church Publishing Company, 1926.

Haagensen, Andrew. *Den Norsk-Danske Methodismes Historie: På Begge Sider Havet*. Chicago: Norwegian-Danish Bookstore, 1894.

Haanes, Vidar L. *"Hvad skal da dette blive for prester?": Presteutdannelsen i spenningsfeltet mellom universitet og kirke, med veskt på modernitetens gjennombrudd i Norge*. Trondheim: Tapir Forlag, 1998.

Haidet, Mark. *The Twin Cities Ordnance Plant During World War II*. St. Paul: Ramsey County Historical Society, 2019.

Hamre, James S. *From Immigrant Parish to Inner City Ministry: Trinity Lutheran Congregation, 1868–1998*. Minneapolis: The author, 1998.

———. *Georg Sverdrup: Educator, Theologian, Churchman*. Northfield, MN: Norwegian-American Historical Association, 1986.

Hansen, Carl G. O. *History of Sons of Norway: An American Fraternal Organization of Men and Women of Norwegian Birth or Extraction*. Minneapolis: Sons of Norway Supreme Lodge, 1944.

———. *My Minneapolis: A Chronicle of What Has Been Learned and Observed about the Norwegians in Minneapolis through One Hundred Years*. Minneapolis: The author, 1956.

Haugen, Einar. "The Struggle over Norwegian." *Norwegian-American Studies and Records* 17 (1952): 1–35.

Helland, Andreas. *Augsburg Seminar gjennem femti Aar, 1869–1919*. Minneapolis: Folkebladet Publishing Company, 1920.

Hjelm-Hansen, Paul. *Business Directory of Scandinavians in Minnesota*. Minneapolis: Budstikken Print, 1878.

Holand, Hjalmar Rued. *De Norske Settlementers Historie*. Ephraim, WI: Forfatteren, 1908.

Holbrook, Franklin F. *St. Paul and Ramsey County in the War of 1917–1918*. St. Paul: Ramsey County War Records Commission, 1929.

Holbrook, Franklin F., and Livia Appel. *Minnesota in the War with Germany*. 2 vols. St. Paul: Minnesota Historical Society, 1928.

Holmquist, June Drenning, ed. *They Chose Minnesota: A Survey of the*

State's Ethnic Groups. St. Paul: Minnesota Historical Society Press, 1981.

Hvidt, Kristian, ed. *Emigrationen fra Norden indtil 1. Verdenskrig: Rapporter til det Nordiske Historikermøde i København 1971, 9–12 August*. Copenhagen: n.p., 1971.

Jackson, Erika K. *Scandinavians in Chicago: The Origins of White Privilege in Modern America*. Urbana: University of Illinois Press, 2019.

Jenswold, John. "'The Hidden Settlement': Norwegian Americans Encounter the City, 1880–1930." PhD diss., University of Connecticut, 1991.

Jeppesen, Torben G. *Scandinavian Descendants in the United States: Ethnic Groups or Core Americans?* Odense: Odense City Museums and the author, 2011.

Kane, Lucile M. *The Falls of St. Anthony: The Waterfall that Built Minneapolis*. St. Paul: Minnesota Historical Society Press, 1987.

Kane, Lucile M., and Alan Ominsky. *Twin Cities: A Pictorial History of Saint Paul and Minneapolis*. St. Paul: Minnesota Historical Society Press, 1983.

Kaufmann, Eric. "Ethnic or Civic Nation?: Theorizing the American Case." European Institute, London School of Economics and Political Science, 2014. http://www.sneps.net/OO/images/Theo_American_Case.pdf.

Klaassen, David J. "'The Deserving Poor': Beginnings of Organized Charity in Minneapolis." *Hennepin County History* 47, no. 2 (Spring 1988): 15–25.

Kyrkobok fór Skandinaviska Metodisk Episkopaliska Forsamlingen uti St. Paul, Minnesota år 1854.

Lande, Otto Sr. *Afholdsfolkets festskrift, 1914*. Minneapolis: The Association's Secretary, 1914. Norwegian-American Historical Association Archives, Simon Johnson Papers.

Larsen, Karen. *Laur. Larsen: Pioneer College President*. Northfield, MN: Norwegian-American Historical Association, 1936.

Larson, Laurence M. "The Norwegian Element in the Northwest." In *The Changing West and Other Essays*, edited by Laurence M. Larson. Northfield, MN: Norwegian-American Historical Association, 1937.

Lieberson, Stanley, and Mary C. Waters. *From Many Strands: Ethnic and Racial Groups in Contemporary America.* New York: Russell Sage Foundation, 1988.

Lovoll, Odd S. *Celebrating a Century: Nordmanns-Forbundet and Norwegians in the World Community, 1907–2007.* Oslo: Nordmannsforbundet, 2009.

———. *A Century of Urban Life: The Norwegians in Chicago before 1930.* Northfield, MN: Norwegian-American Historical Association, 1988.

———. *Det løfterike landet: En Norskamerikanisk historie.* Oslo: Universitetsforlaget, 1997.

———. *A Folk Epic: The Bygdelag in America.* Northfield, MN: Norwegian-American Historical Association, 1975.

———. *Norwegian Newspapers in America: Connecting Norway and the New Land.* St. Paul: Minnesota Historical Society Press, 2010.

———. *The Promise Fulfilled: A Portrait of Norwegian Americans Today.* Minneapolis: University of Minnesota Press, 1998.

———. *The Promise of America: A History of the Norwegian-American People*, rev. ed. Minneapolis: University of Minnesota Press, 1999.

Lovoll, Odd S., ed., *Scandinavians and Other Immigrants in Urban America: The Proceedings of a Research Conference, October 26–27, 1984.* Northfield, MN: St. Olaf College Press, 1985.

Malmin, Rasmus, O. M. Norlie, and O. A. Tingelstad, trans. and eds. *Who's Who Among Pastors in All the Norwegian Lutheran Synods of America, 1843–1927: Third Edition of Norsk Lutherske Prester i America.* Minneapolis: Augsburg Publishing House, 1928.

Mann, Arthur, ed. *The Progressive Era: Liberal Renaissance or Liberal Failure?* New York: Holt, Rinehart and Winston, 1963.

Markle, David. "Dania Hall: At the Center of a Scandinavian American Community." In *Swedes in the Twin Cities: Immigrant Life and Minnesota's Urban Frontier*, edited by Philip J. Anderson and Dag Blanck, 173–97. St. Paul: Minnesota Historical Society Press, 2001.

Mattson, Hans. *Reminiscences: The Story of an Immigrant.* St. Paul: D. D. Merrill Company, 1891.

Mauk, David C. *The Colony that Rose from the Sea: Norwegian Maritime Migration and Community in Brooklyn, 1850–1910.* Northfield, MN: Norwegian-American Historical Association, 1997.

——. "Finding Their Way in the City: Norwegian Immigrant Women and Their Daughters in Urban Areas, 1880s–1920s." In *Norwegian American Women: Migration, Communities, and Identities*, edited by Betty A. Bergland and Lori Ann Lahlum, 119–54. St. Paul: Minnesota Historical Society Press, 2011.

——. "Syttende Mai Vignettes from Minneapolis–St. Paul: The Changing Meaning of Norway's Constitution Day in the Capital of Norwegian America, 1869–1914." *American Studies in Scandinavia* 34, no. 2, Immigration and Ethnicity Issue (Autumn 2002): 32–53.

Mead, Frank J., and Alix J. Muller. *History of the Police and Fire Departments of the Twin Cities: Their Origin in Early Village Days and Progress to 1900*. Minneapolis–St. Paul, MN: American Land and Title Register Association, 1899.

Millikan, William. *A Union Against Unions: The Minneapolis Citizens Alliance and Its Fight against Organized Labor, 1903–1947*. St. Paul: Minnesota Historical Society Press, 2001.

Mindekirken: The Norwegian Lutheran Memorial Church, 1922–1982. Minneapolis: Den Norske Lutherske Mindekirken, 1982.

"Minnesota Biographies, 1655–1912." *Collections of the Minnesota Historical Society* 14 (1912).

Mowry, George E. "The Urban Gentry on the Defensive." In *The Progressive Era: Liberal Renaissance or Liberal Failure?*, edited by Arthur Mann, 28–39. New York: Holt, Rinehart and Winston, 1963.

Nathanson, Iric. *Minneapolis in the Twentieth Century: The Growth of an American City*. St. Paul: Minnesota Historical Society Press, 2010.

Neill, Rev. Edward Duffield. *The History of Minnesota from the Earliest French Explorations to the Present Time*. Minneapolis: Minnesota Historical Company, 1883.

Nelson, E. Clifford, and Eugene I. Fevold. *The Lutheran Church Among Norwegian-Americans: A History of the Evangelical Lutheran Church*. Minneapolis: Augsburg Publishing House, 1960.

Nelson, Marion, ed. *Material Culture and People's Art among the Norwegians in America*. Northfield, MN: Norwegian-American Historical Association, 1994.

Nelson, O. N., ed. *History of the Scandinavians and Successful Scandinavians in the United States*. Minneapolis: The author, 1900.

Nichol, Todd. "Introduction" to Herman Amberg Preus, *Vivacious Daughter: Seven Lectures on the Religious Situation Among Norwegians in America*, edited and translated by Todd Nichol. Northfield, MN: Norwegian-American Historical Association, 1990.

Norborg, C. Sverre. *An American Saga*. Minneapolis: Sons of Norway, 1970.

Norlie, Olaf Morgan. *History of the Norwegian People in America*. Minneapolis: Augsburg Publishing House, 1925.

———. *Norsk Lutherske Menigheter i Amerika, 1843–1916*. Minneapolis: Augsburg Publishing House, 1918.

Norse-American Centennial, 1825–1925, souvenir ed. Minneapolis: Augsburg Publishing House, 1925.

Nydahl, J. L. *Afholdssagens historie*. Minneapolis: The author, 1896.

Olson, Daron W. *Vikings across the Atlantic: Emigration and the Building of a Greater Norway, 1860–1945*. Minneapolis: University of Minnesota Press, 2013.

Our Saviour's Lutheran Church. *1869–1944: Diamond Anniversary—75 Years to the Glory of God, Our Saviour's Lutheran Church in Minneapolis*. Minneapolis: The church, 1944.

———. *Sixtieth Anniversary: Our Saviour's Lutheran Church, 1869–1929*. Minneapolis: The church, 1929.

Øverland, Orm. *Immigrant Minds, American Identities: Making the United States Home, 1870–1930*. Urbana: University of Illinois Press, 2000.

———. *The Western Home: A Literary History of Norwegian America*. Northfield, MN: Norwegian-American Historical Association, 1996.

Øverland, Orm, ed. *Norwegian-American Essays 2004*. Oslo: Norwegian-American Historical Association–Norway and Norwegian Emigrant Museum, 2005.

Parrington, Vernon L. "The Progressive Era: A Liberal Renaissance." In *The Progressive Era: Liberal Renaissance or Liberal Failure?*, edited by Arthur Mann, 6–12. New York: Holt, Rinehart and Winston, 1963.

Paulson, Rev. Ole. *Memoirs: Reminiscences of a Pioneer Pastor in America, 1850–1885*. Ed. Sven Oftedal; English trans. Torstein O. Kvamme, Lois Paulson Kvamme, and Carl O. Paulson. Stoughton, WI: L. & T. O. Kvamme, 1981.

Pedersen, J. U. *Selbygbogen: Meddelelser om Selbyggernes Slægt i Amerika og deres Virke*. Minneapolis: Selbulaget's Press, 1921.

Peterson, Anna Marie. "'Adding a Little Suffrage Spice to the Melting Pot': Minnesota's Scandinavian Woman Suffrage Association." *Minnesota History* 62, no. 8 (Winter 2011–12): 288–97.

Peterson, Clarence S., comp. *Known Military and Civilian Dead during the Minnesota Sioux Indian Massacre in 1862*. St. Paul: Minnesota Centennial Memorial, 1958.

Polk, R. L., and A. C. Danser. *St. Paul City Directory, 1884–1885*. St. Paul: R. L. Polk and Company, 1885.

Prestgard, Kristian. *Fra Heidal til Decorah*. Otta, Norway: Norwegian-American Historical Association—Norge and Snøhetta Forlag, A/S, 1996.

Preus, Herman Amberg. *Vivacious Daughter: Seven Lectures on the Religious Situation among Norwegians in America*. Ed. and trans. Todd Nichol. Northfield, MN: Norwegian-American Historical Association, 1990.

Qualey, Carlton C. *Norwegian Settlement in the United States*. Northfield, MN: Norwegian-American Historical Association, 1938.

Rølvaag, O. E. *Omkring fædrearven*. 1922; Northfield, MN: Norwegian-American Historical Association, 1998.

Rølvaag, Ole Edvart. *Concerning our Heritage*. Trans. Solveig Zempel. 1922; Northfield, MN: Norwegian-American Historical Association, 1998.

Rønning, N. N., and W. H. Lien. *They Followed Him: The Lutheran Deaconess Home and Hospital, Fiftieth Anniversary, 1889–1939*. Minneapolis: Lutheran Deaconess Home and Hospital, 1939.

Rosheim, David L. *The Other Minneapolis; or, The Rise and Fall of the Gateway, the Old Minneapolis Skid Row*. Maquoketa, IA: Andromeda Press, 1978.

Rygg, A. N. *American Relief for Norway: En oversikt over Amerikas hjelpearbeid for Norge under og etter den annen verdenskrig*. Chicago and New York: Arnesen Press, 1947.

St. Paul City Directory, 1858–1859. St. Paul: Newson and Barton, 1859.

Sanborn Fire Insurance Maps. Minnesota. New York: Sanborn Map Publishing Company.

Sayer, John William. *Ghost Dancing the Law: The Wounded Knee Trials*. Cambridge, MA: Harvard University Press, 1997.

Schmid, Calvin F. *Social Saga of Two Cities. An Ecological and Statistical Study of Social Trends in Minneapolis and St. Paul.* Minneapolis: Minneapolis Bureau of Social Research and Minneapolis Council of Social Agencies, 1937.

Schultz, April R. *Ethnicity on Parade: Inventing the Norwegian American through Celebration.* Amherst: University of Massachusetts Press, 1994.

Semmingsen, Ingrid. "Norwegian Emigration to America during the Nineteenth Century." *Norwegian-American Studies and Records* 11 (1940): 66–81.

Shippee, Lester B. "Social and Economic Effects of the Civil War with Special Reference to Minnesota." *Minnesota History* 2, no. 6 (1918): 389–412.

Shutter, Rev. Marion Daniel. *History of Minneapolis, Gateway to the Northwest.* Vol. 1. Chicago: Clarke, 1923.

Söderström, Alfred. *Minneapolis Minnen: Kulturhistorisk Axplockning från Qvarnstaden vid Mississippi.* 1899; Nabu Public Domain Reprints, 2011.

Soike, Lowell J. *Norwegian Americans and the Politics of Dissent, 1880–1924.* Northfield, MN: Norwegian-American Historical Association, 1991.

Solberg, Carl. *Hubert Humphrey: A Biography.* New York: W. W. Norton and Company, 1984.

Solberg, Richard W. *As Between Brothers: The Story of Lutheran Response to World Need.* Minneapolis: Augsburg Publishing House, 1957.

Speer, Ray P., and Harry J. Frost. *Minnesota State Fair: The History and Heritage of 100 Years.* N.p.: Argus Publishing Company, 1964.

Sponland, Ingeborg. *My Reasonable Service.* Minneapolis: Augsburg Publishing House, 1938.

Stadum, Beverly A. "'Says There's Nothing Like Home': Family Casework with the Minneapolis Poor, 1900–30." *Minnesota History* 51, no. 2 (Summer 1988): 42–54.

Steffens, Lincoln. *The Shame of the Cities.* 1904; New York: Hill and Wang, 1957.

Stovby, N. S. "Scandinavian Temperance-Kalender." Brooklyn, NY: Temperance Society Press, 1896. Norwegian-American Historical Association Archives, Simon Johnson Papers.

Strand, Philip K. *A Common Bond: The Story of Lutheran Brotherhood.* Minneapolis: Hakala Associates, 1989.

Stuhler, Barbara. *Gentle Warriors: Clara Ueland and the Minnesota Struggle for Woman Suffrage*. St. Paul: Minnesota Historical Society, 1995.

Svendsen, Gustav Rolf. "Codfish and Assimilation." *Hennepin County History* 31, no. 3 (Summer 1972).

Sverdrup, Georg. *Samlede skrifter i Udvalg, I–VI*. Ed. A. Helland. Minneapolis: Frikirkens Boghandel, 1909–12.

Thorsen, Gerald. "Tinsel and Dust: Disenchantment in Two Novels from the 1880s." *Minnesota History* 45, no. 6 (Summer 1977): 210–22.

Trefoldighets Menighet Minneapolis, Minnesota, 1868–1918. Minneapolis: Folkebladets trykkeri, 1918.

Ueland, Andreas. *Recollections of an Immigrant*. New York: Minton, Balch and Company, 1929.

Vanberg, Bent. *From So Many . . . for So Few: The Norwegian–North American Aid to Norway during World War II*. Minneapolis: Sons of Norway Heritage Productions, n.d.

Walker, Charles Rumford. *American City: A Rank and File History of Minneapolis*. New York: Farrar and Rinehart, Inc., 1937.

Watts, Alison. "The Technology that Launched a City: Scientific and Technological Innovations in Flour Milling during the 1870s in Minneapolis." *Minnesota History* 57, no. 2 (Summer 2000): 86–97.

Williams, J. Fletcher. *A History of the City of Saint Paul and of the County of Ramsey, Minnesota*. St. Paul: Minnesota Historical Society, 1876.

Wingerd, Mary Lethert. "City Limits: Politics, Faith, and the Power of Place in Urban America, St. Paul, Minnesota, 1838–1934." PhD diss., Duke University, 1998.

———. *Claiming the City: Politics, Faith, and the Power of Place in St. Paul*. Ithaca, NY: Cornell University Press, 2003.

Wist, Johannes B. *Nykomerbilleder*. Decorah, IA: Anunsen Publishing Company, 1920.

Wist, Johannes B., ed. *Norsk-Amerikanernes Festskrift, 1914*. Decorah, IA: Symra Company, 1914.

Works Progress Administration writers. *The Bohemian Flats*. St. Paul: Minnesota Historical Society Press, 1986.

INDEX

The Heart of the Heartland
was designed and set in type by
Judy Gilats in St. Paul, Minnesota.
The text face is Ten Oldstyle
and the display face is Priori Sans.